THE CAMBRIDGE CO1
TO AMERICAN LITERATURE

C000067894

The human body has been depicted in a var..., .. ...,
cultural and historical locations. It has been described, variously, as a
biological entity, clothing for the soul, a site of cultural production, a
psychosexual construct, and a material encumbrance. Each of these different
approaches brings with it a range of anthropological, political, theological, and
psychological discourses that explore and construct identities and subject
positions. This *Companion* examines connections between American literature
and bodies from the eighteenth century through the present. It reveals the
singular way that literature can help us understand the body's entanglement
within social and biological influences, and it traces the body's existence within
histories of race, gender, and ability. This volume details the genres, critical
fields, and interpretive practices that best facilitate the analysis of bodies in the
full span of American literary imaginings.

Travis M. Foster is an associate professor of American literature at Villanova
University, where he is also the academic director of Gender and Women's
Studies. He is the author of *Genre and White Supremacy in the
Postemancipation United States* (Oxford University Press, 2019).

*A complete list of books in the series is at the back of the book.*

# THE CAMBRIDGE
# COMPANION TO
# AMERICAN
# LITERATURE AND
# THE BODY

EDITED BY
## TRAVIS M. FOSTER
*Villanova University*

CAMBRIDGE
UNIVERSITY PRESS

# CAMBRIDGE
### UNIVERSITY PRESS

University Printing House, Cambridge CB2 8BS, United Kingdom

One Liberty Plaza, 20th Floor, New York, NY 10006, USA

477 Williamstown Road, Port Melbourne, VIC 3207, Australia

314–321, 3rd Floor, Plot 3, Splendor Forum, Jasola District Centre, New Delhi – 110025, India

103 Penang Road, #05–06/07, Visioncrest Commercial, Singapore 238467

Cambridge University Press is part of the University of Cambridge.

It furthers the University's mission by disseminating knowledge in the pursuit of education, learning, and research at the highest international levels of excellence.

www.cambridge.org
Information on this title: www.cambridge.org/9781108841924
DOI: 10.1017/9781108895170

© Cambridge University Press 2022

This publication is in copyright. Subject to statutory exception and to the provisions of relevant collective licensing agreements, no reproduction of any part may take place without the written permission of Cambridge University Press.

First published 2022

*A catalogue record for this publication is available from the British Library.*

*Library of Congress Cataloging-in-Publication Data*
NAMES: Foster, Travis M., editor.
TITLE: The Cambridge companion to American literature and the body / edited by Travis M. Foster.
DESCRIPTION: Cambridge ; New York, NY : Cambridge University Press, 2022. | Includes bibliographical references and index.
IDENTIFIERS: LCCN 2021053926 (print) | LCCN 2021053927 (ebook) | ISBN 9781108841924 (hardback) | ISBN 9781108815291 (paperback) | ISBN 9781108895170 (epub)
SUBJECTS: LCSH: American literature–History and criticism. | Human body in literature.
CLASSIFICATION: LCC PS169.H86 C36 2022 (print) | LCC PS169.H86 (ebook) | DDC 810.9/3561–dc23/eng/20220307
LC record available at https://lccn.loc.gov/2021053926
LC ebook record available at https://lccn.loc.gov/2021053927

ISBN 978-1-108-84192-4 Hardback
ISBN 978-1-108-81529-1 Paperback

Cambridge University Press has no responsibility for the persistence or accuracy of URLs for external or third-party internet websites referred to in this publication and does not guarantee that any content on such websites is, or will remain, accurate or appropriate.

# CONTENTS

# CONTRIBUTORS

COLLEEN GLENNEY BOGGS
Dartmouth College

SONY CORÁÑEZ BOLTON
Amherst College

DELIA BYRNES
Allegheny College

STEPHANIE CLARE
University of Washington

THOMAS CONSTANTINESCO
Sorbonne University

ERICA FRETWELL
University at Albany, SUNY

LINDSEY GRUBBS
California State University, East Bay

ANNA HINTON
Rutgers University

MARVIN MCALLISTER
Winthrop University

AGNIESZKA SOLTYSIK MONNET
University of Lausanne

CHRISTINE OKOTH
King's College London

CLAUDIA STOKES
Trinity University

SEAN TEUTON
University of Arkansas

FRANCES TRAN
Florida State University

MAURICE WALLACE
Rutgers University, New Brunswick

XINE YAO
University College London

| | |
|---|---|
| 1619 | The first enslaved Africans arrive at Jamestown, marking the start of chattel slavery in North America. |
| 1692 | Several young girls claim to be possessed by the devil, accusing local women of witchcraft and igniting the hysteria of the Salem Witch Trials. |
| 1767 | Andrew Barton, *The Disappointment, or the Force of Credibility*. |
| 1775 | The American Revolutionary War begins. |
| 1777 | The American drama, *The Downfall of Justice*, is published anonymously. |
| 1783 | The American Revolutionary War ends, marking the official beginnings of the United States of America. |
| 1787 | Royall Tyler's play *The Contrast* debuts; delegates at the Constitutional Convention decide that enslaved people will count as three-fifths of an individual person for determining political power. |
| 1794 | Susanna Haswell Rowson, *Slaves in Algiers*; Anne Julia Kemble Hatton, *The Songs of Tammany, or the Indian Chief*. |
| 1797 | Hannah Webster Foster, *The Coquette; or the History of Eliza Wharton*. |
| 1799 | Charles Brockden Brown, *Arthur Mervyn*. |
| 1817 | The American School for the Deaf is founded in Hartford, Connecticut. |
| 1829 | John Augustus Stone, *Metamora, Last of the Wampanoag*. |
| 1830–1850 | During this time, the US government forcibly relocates approximately 60,000 Natives, in what is now referred to as the Trail of Tears. |
| 1836 | Ralph Waldo Emerson, *Nature* |
| 1844 | Dr. James Marion Sims, the "father of modern gynecology," begins painful gynecological experimentation on enslaved Black women in Alabama. |

| | |
|---|---|
| 1845 | Fredrick Douglass, *Narrative of the Life of Frederick Douglass.* |
| 1850 | Nathaniel Hawthorne, *The Scarlet Letter* |
| 1851 | Herman Melville, *Moby-Dick; or, The Whale.* |
| 1853 | Solomon Northup, *Twelve Years a Slave.* |
| 1854 | Henry David Thoreau, *Walden; or, Life in the Woods.* |
| 1855 | First publication of Walt Whitman's *Leaves of Grass.* |
| 1860 | The Bureau of Indian Affairs establishes the first Indian boarding school on the Yakima Reservation in Washington. |
| 1861 | The American Civil War begins; Harriet Jacobs, *Incidents in the Life of a Slave Girl.* |
| 1864 | George Perkins Marsh, *Man and Nature*; the Columbia Institution for the Instruction of the Deaf and Dumb and Blind becomes the first college specifically for those with disabilities. |
| 1865 | The American Civil War ends; Congress passes the Thirteenth Amendment to the US Constitution, formally abolishing chattel slavery; the Ku Klux Klan is founded. |
| 1866 | Henry Bergh founds the American Society for the Prevention of Cruelty to Animals (ASPCA), the first animal rights and welfare organization in the United States; S. Weir Mitchell publishes "The Case of George Dedlow" in *The Atlantic.* |
| 1867–1974 | Various US cities adopt and uphold unsightly beggar ordinances, colloquially known as "ugly laws." |
| 1869 | Louisa May Alcott, *Little Women.* |
| 1879 | Col. Richard Henry Pratt establishes the first off-reservation Indian boarding school, under the motto "kill the Indian, save the man." |
| 1882 | US federal government passes the Chinese Exclusion Act, prohibiting all immigration of Chinese laborers. |
| 1883 | Sir Francis Galton coins the term "eugenics" in *Inquiries into Human Faculty and Its Development.* His writing is widely read in the United States, leading to the creation of the American eugenics movement. |
| 1892 | Frances Ellen Watkins Harper, *Iola Leroy.* |
| 1903 | W. E. B Du Bois, *The Souls of Black Folk.* |
| 1903–1906 | The American Breeders' Association creates the first committee on eugenics in America. |
| 1906 | Upton Sinclair, *The Jungle.* |
| 1911 | The Eugenics Record Office is founded in New York by biologist Charles B. Davenport; the Triangle Shirtwaist Factory fire in New York City causes the deaths of 146 garment workers; James Oppenheim, "Bread and Roses." |

| | |
|---|---|
| 1916 | Margaret Sanger opens one of the first American birth control clinics in Brooklyn, New York. |
| 1917 | The United States declares war on Germany, officially entering World War I. |
| 1918 | The H1N1 influenza virus begins to spread worldwide, first hitting the United States in the spring. |
| 1927 | The US Supreme Court rules in *Carrie Buck* v. *John Hendren Bell*, deciding that compulsory sterilization of the intellectually disabled does not violate any Constitutional rights. |
| 1929 | The American stock market crashes, marking the start of the Great Depression. |
| 1930s | The Southern Plains region of the United States is hit with drought and dust storms, killing crops and livestock, and leaving many people to die. |
| 1930s–1970s | Approximately one-third of the child-bearing female population of Puerto Rico is forcibly or unknowingly sterilized. |
| 1932–1972 | The Public Health Service and the Tuskegee Institute begin the "Tuskegee Study of Untreated Syphilis in the Negro Male," infecting unknowing Black men with syphilis. |
| 1939 | John Steinbeck, *The Grapes of Wrath*. |
| 1940 | President Franklin D. Roosevelt signs the Selective Training and Service Act into law, requiring all men between ages 21 and 45 to register for the draft. |
| 1941 | Japan attacks US naval base Pearl Harbor. Months later, President Franklin D. Roosevelt declares war on Japan, officially entering the United States into World War II. |
| 1942–1945 | Executive Order 9066 is signed into law by President Franklin D. Roosevelt, forcing roughly 117,000 people of Japanese descent into isolated internment camps. |
| 1945 | The first successful test of an American atomic bomb is conducted at the Trinity test site in Alamogordo, New Mexico; American pilots drop the world's first atomic bomb on the Japanese city of Hiroshima. Three days later, another bomb is dropped on Nagasaki. |
| 1949 | Aldo Leopold, *A Sand County Almanac: And Sketches Here and There*. |
| 1951 | After Henrietta Lacks passes away from cancer, her cells are harvested and used for research without consent from her family. |

1952 The American Psychiatric Association publishes the first edition of their *Diagnostic and Statistical Manual of Mental Disorders* (DSM).

1955 Fourteen-year-old Emmett Till is tortured and murdered by whites for allegedly whistling at a white woman; Gregory Pinchus begins testing the birth control hormone progesterone on Puerto Rican women, withholding from them the dangers of this experimental clinical trial.

1956 James Baldwin, *Giovanni's Room*.

1958 The first federal animal welfare legislation, the Humane Slaughter Act, is passed. This act is designed to decrease suffering of livestock during slaughter, ruling that an animal must be completely sedated in order to be killed.

1959 California court case *Jesse James, Jr.* v. *Screen Gems Inc.* is ruled in favor of Screen Gems Inc., establishing that the right to privacy does not extend to deceased people.

1960 Enovid is approved as the first contraceptive pill in America.

1962 Rachel Carson, *Silent Spring*.

1963 Betty Friedan, *The Feminine Mystique*.

1964 The Civil Rights Act is passed by President Lyndon Johnson, prohibiting discrimination on the basis of race, color, religion, sex, or national origin; Leo Marx, *The Machine in the Garden: Technology and the Pastoral Ideal in America*.

1965 The Supreme Court rules in favor of *Griswold* v. *Connecticut*, allowing married couples to buy and use contraceptives without government restriction.

1965–1970 Filipino-American grape workers link with Cesar Chavez and the National Farm Workers Association to fight against exploitation of farm workers.

1965 Malcom X is assassinated in New York City.

1966 The Animal Welfare Act is signed into law as a means of regulating the treatment of animals used in research and exhibition.

1968 Martin Luther King, Jr., is assassinated in Memphis, Tennessee; the Uniform Anatomical Gift Act is passed in order to set regulations regarding the donation of organs, tissues, and other body parts.

1969 President Richard Nixon signs the National Environmental Policy Act (NEPA) into law. NEPA will later be consolidated into the larger body of the Environmental Protection Agency (EPA) in 1970; targe protests break out in response to a police raid of the Stonewall Inn, a gay bar in New York

|  | City; American physician Robert N. Butler coins the term "Ageism" in order to describe the discrimination faced by individuals based on their age. |
|---|---|
| 1970 | About 25 percent of Native women of childbearing age are sterilized following the passing of the Family Planning Services and Population Research Act. |
| 1973 | The Supreme Court rules in favor of *Roe* v. *Wade*, affirming every woman's right to an abortion; the American Psychiatric Association (APA) removes homosexuality from the second edition of the DSM; Military conscription ends, and the all-volunteer force is established; Toni Morrison, *Sula*. |
| 1977 | The Supreme Court rules in favor of *Carey* v. *Population Services International*, affirming the right to contraceptives for any person at least sixteen years of age. |
| 1978 | Harvey Milk is assassinated in San Francisco; Ten Latina women accuse Dr. James Quilligan of forced or coerced sterilization in *Madrigal* v. *Quilligan*. The judge rules in favor of the doctor; the Indian Child Welfare Act (ICWA) is passed, governing the removal and placement of Indigenous children. |
| 1980 | People for the Ethical Treatment of Animals (PETA) is founded by Ingrid Newkirk and Alex Pacheco. |
| 1980–1981 | The HIV virus begins spreading rapidly in the United States. |
| 1981 | Cherríe Moraga and Gloria E. Anzaldúa publish *This Bridge Called My Back*. |
| 1985 | Donna Haraway, *A Cyborg Manifesto*. |
| 1987 | Toni Morrison, *Beloved*. |
| 1990 | Judith Butler, *Gender Trouble: Feminism and the Subversion of Identity*; the Americans with Disabilities Act (ADA) is signed into law. |
| 1991 | Leslie Marmon Silko, *Almanac of the Dead*; Rodney King is brutally beaten by four Los Angeles Police Department officers, leading to the Rodney King protests. |
| 1992 | Toni Morrison, *Playing in the Dark: Whiteness and the Literary Imagination*. |
| 1993 | Leslie Feinberg, *Stone Butch Blues*; Tony Kushner's two-part play, *Angels in America: A Gay Fantasia on National Themes*, debuts on Broadway. |
| 1999 | Eli Claire, *Exile and Pride: Disability, Queerness, and Liberation*. |

2003    The US Supreme Court rules in *Lawrence* v. *Texas*, overturning laws that prohibited private homosexual activity
between consenting adults.

2005    The San Francisco Human Rights Commission report investigates "normalizing" surgeries performed on intersex
infants, finding them to be unethical.

2006    Robert McRuer, *Crip Theory: Cultural Signs of Queerness
and Disability*; a revised version of the Uniform Anatomical
Gift Act makes clear that it neither allows nor disallows the
usage of donated embryos for research.

2007    The Nonhuman Rights Project is founded with the goal of
changing the legal status of some animals from that of
property to that of person.

2013    Alicia Garza, Patrisse Cullors, and Opal Tometi cofound the
Black Lives Matter movement after the murder of Trayvon
Martin and the subsequent acquittal of his murderer.

2014    Claudia Rankine, *Citizen: An American Lyric*.

2015    The US Supreme Court rules in *Obergefell* v. *Hodges*, federally legalizing same-sex marriage for all Americans; Ta-
Nehisi Coates, *Between the World and Me*.

2016    The US Department of Health officially extends legal protec-
tions against discrimination to intersex people; Kai Cheng
Thom, *Fierce Femmes and Notorious Liars: A Dangerous
Trans Girl's Confabulous Memoir*.

2017    Virginia Grise, *Your Healing Is Killing Me*; Andrea Lawlor,
*Paul Takes the Form of a Mortal Girl*.

2018    The Pet and Women Safety Act (PAWS) is signed into law,
amending the federal criminal code in order to broaden the
definition of stalking to include any conduct which causes a
person to experience a reasonable fear of death or injury to
their pet.

2019    The Preventing Animal Cruelty and Torture Act (PACT) is
signed into law, federally outlawing acts of purposeful violence against animals.

2020    The COVID-19 virus begins spreading rapidly, and the
World Health Organization will classify it as a pandemic
by March; the murders of George Floyd and Breonna Taylor
at the hands of police officers spark mass protests all over
America, demanding justice for Black lives lost to white
supremacy and police brutality.

# ACKNOWLEDGMENTS

Many thanks go to Madeline Davids, who put tremendous thought and care into the Chronology and Further Reading sections; to Devon Thomas, for such a thorough index; and to the Villanova University Subvention Program.

TRAVIS M. FOSTER

# Introduction

This volume provides students of American literature with models and methods for approaching the question of embodiment. It underscores the body as at once dynamic – shaping our experience of the world through complex interplay between social and biological influences – and intersectional – resisting attempts for discrete analysis at every turn. By highlighting these two qualities, *The Cambridge Companion to American Literature and the Body* foregrounds the body's enmeshed interspersal throughout core concerns of American literary studies, including those focused on race, gender, sexuality, history, and ecology.

Despite this range, insights from one particular field – disability studies – comprise the volume's most prominent conceptual resource, providing a thread linking essays on topics as seemingly varied as sentimental fiction, slave narratives, the history of reading, and ecocriticism. The significance of disability studies to discussions of embodiment in American literature shouldn't be surprising. Disability, illness, and chronic pain were among the first topics within Americanist criticism to veer away from a Cartesian mind/body split that otherwise frequently manifested in starker and more binary terms than even Descartes envisioned. To take just one example, William Joseph Long's 1913 *American Literature: A Study of the Men and the Books that in the Earlier and Later Times Reflect the American Spirit* almost exclusively speaks of authors as disembodied creators. The notable exception occurs when Long turns to those writers experiencing sickness and chronic pain, such as Puritan Michael Wigglesworth, whose experience as a "lifelong sufferer from disease" finds itself reflected in the "powerful but morbid imagination" of his poetry.[1] Despite the limitations of his ableist worldview, the disabled bodies of his subjects force Long into a nascent understanding of how bodies and creative imaginations collaborate to produce visions of the world that influence readers' perceptions and understandings. More recently, feminist literary critic Christina Crosby's memoir *A Body, Undone: Living on After Great Pain* (2016) addresses how bodily suffering forced her to reckon with the many different links rendering mind and body different yet inseparable. "There are," she notes, "108 single-word prepositions in the English language, and none is adequate to representing the relation of mind to body. Body and mind are simultaneously one and the same and clearly distinct. Thinking my body, I am thinking in my body, as my body, through my body, of my body, about my body, and I'm oriented around my body. I'm beside myself."[2] As the chapters in this volume attest, American literature has long born witness to what we might call the all-at-onceness of this incredible multiplicity, seeking to fill in the details of these prepositional relationships binding and separating our minds and our bodies, filling out representations of the self that cannot neatly divide into material and immaterial components. Simultaneously, American literature and Americanist criticism have provided accounts for how unequal distributions of access and power shape even this most intimate of relationships between being and embodying.

No critical work has been more influential for thinking about these hierarchies than cultural theorist Hortense J. Spillers's "Mama's Baby, Papa's Maybe: An American Grammar Book" (1987), an essay that comes up repeatedly in the contributions to this volume. In a tour de force of conceptual analysis, Spillers tracks how racial, economic, and gendered configurations animate our bodies, tactically rooting theory within the lived realities of Black women's captive bodies under plantation economies and Atlantic world slavery. Distinguishing between the body and the flesh, Spillers describes a system of "total objectification" that "sear[s]" Black flesh from Black bodies.[3] If the body is discrete – affording relations between a distinct "human personality and its anatomical features, between one human personality and another" – the flesh, Spillers suggests, names an undifferentiated "captive community."[4] By rendering Black beings as flesh, depriving captives of differentiation and placing them outside the symbolic grammar of the family, the Atlantic slave trade and its legacies in "a post-emancipation neo-enslavement" leave Black people "ungendered."[5] For whites, on the other hand, Spillers's theorization tracks how embodiment proffers access to the validated, recognized, and proper subject positions of family life, as well as the economic organizations designed to benefit these gendered subjects: "the vertical transfer of a bloodline, of a patronymic, of titles and entitlements, of real estate and the prerogatives of 'cold cash,'" which, together, become "the mythically revered privilege of a free and freed community."[6] Yet for Spillers, the denial of access to these positions might itself offer promising and even queer potential for an "altered reading of gender" and the opportunity to embody, through the "problematizing of gender," a "different social subject."[7] The lesson here is thus not to understand Black women's bodies solely through the lens of marginalization and subjection, which, as Jennifer Nash argues, would "ultimately romanticize and idealize positions of social subordination and reinstall conceptions that black women's bodies are sites of 'strength' and 'transcendence' rather than complex spaces of multiple meanings."[8] The point, especially for a volume like this, is instead that the teaching, theorizing, and thinking that come out of Black Study, as Spillers notes in a 2006 interview revisiting the essay, occupy a central position for the study of American literature and the body more broadly. The conceptual resources of Black Study and Black feminisms provide "a discourse, or a vocabulary" for Americanist work, one that makes it necessary "that black women be in the conversation."[9]

Spillers's subtitle, "An American Grammar Book," indicates an argument that parallels her distinction between the body and the flesh: namely, that the process of embodiment occurs within systems of language and meaning, and that bodies and their gestures enter as signifiers back into those same systems. Hence, in Spillers's critical vocabulary, structures shaping the childhoods of Frederick Douglass and Malcolm El Shabazz comprise an "amazing thematic synonymity"; the intergenerational inheritance of trauma and displacement occurs through "symbolic substitutions"; "the body" serves as "a resource for metaphor"; and so on.[10] Using the vocabulary of literary criticism to describe systems of embodiment and disembodiment (or enfleshment), Spillers shows how the key terms of this volume – "American literature" and "the body" – denote an interdependency.

Queer theorists have similarly charted this relationship, exploring the distinctly literary factors that produce bodies, embodiments, and bodily acts as intelligible and knowable. When Christopher Looby describes sexuality as "essentially a literary phenomenon," for example, he indicates how literature brings into existence the very terms and categories through which we understand bodies and their desires, those of others as well as our own: "Sexual identities (or labels or categories or scripts) need to be articulated, promulgated, circulated, and encountered in order to be received and adopted and performed, and this requires a literary public sphere."[11] The chapters in this volume provide careful, patient accounts of precisely these relationships. Yet they take an additional step as well, finding in literary representation a resource that helps us follow theorist E. Patrick Johnson's insistence that we identify concepts for describing not only how the body "is brought into being, but what it does once it is constituted and the relationship between it and the other bodies around it."[12] In so doing, these chapters heed literature's interest in embodiment as a source for considering bodies in relation to one another. Simultaneously, they track American literature's interest in alternative modes of knowledge creation and how such incipient knowledge often emerges through the proximity between bodies and the concrete embeddedness of bodies in their social settings.

Resisting the tendency diagnosed by Michel Foucault, among many others, to place non-normative subjects and bodies under analysis while neglecting study of normative subjects and bodies, this book's chapters highlight white bodies as well as those racialized nonwhite, nondisabled bodies as well as disabled, cisgender embodiment as well as transgender, bodies going about their everyday activities as well as bodies in states of exception. Moreover, the book resists any tendency to treat race and gender as discrete categories. Instead, as the summaries below detail, the contributors to this volume provide us with multiple different models, concepts, and analytical frameworks for viewing the bodies we encounter in literature precisely through their intersectional relationship with multiple different aspects of embodied experience ranging from war trauma to reading to illness.[13]

The volume groups its chapters into two sections, which lay out formal and methodological parameters for analyzing bodies in American literature. Part I, "Genres," explores how eight key American literary genres – early Atlantic world theater, the sentimental novel, slave narratives, the Gothic, multiethnic fiction, science fiction, and the contemporary transgender novel – record particular relationships between history and corporeal existence. A chapter on slave narratives, for instance, traces how that genre meticulously itemizes, first, slavery's impact on all aspects of enslaved people's somatic existence – from illness to sensory capacity – and, second, slavery's impact on the corporeality of the women and men who did the enslaving. Or, to highlight a more recent example, a chapter on the contemporary transgender novel interrogates how the genre focuses on realignments of the nexus between subjectivity and bodily presentation even as it points to the limits of "wrong body" narratives for understanding transgender identity. As the breadth of these two examples shows, the representation of bodies in American literature is an inexhaustible topic. These critical readings of key American genres therefore won't provide anything like a comprehensive treatment, but they will provide readers with a rigorous and accessible overview of archives and historical contexts for thinking carefully about bodies in literature.

Opening the volume with his chapter on the genre of early US-Atlantic theater (Chapter 1), Marvin McAllister explores how physical bodies of the early American stage enabled playwrights, actors, and theater goers to link their individual bodies with the social body and the body politic. Doing so permitted people to reimagine relationships between individual variation and larger gendered, racial, and imperial collectivities. Focusing on three types commonly found on the Atlantic world stage – the American girl, the

Yankee, and the racialized stage Indian – McAllister shows myriad ways that Old World dramatic characters found themselves refashioned into "a New World repertoire." In the process, he reveals the stage as a privileged literary-performative medium for presenting "the thinking subject as a corporeal or bodied being."

Turning her attention to a longstanding emphasis on literature as an aesthetic mode that produces feeling, Claudia Stokes links the susceptibility of the reading body to corporeal vulnerability. In Chapter 2, which considers a range of works – from the correspondence of Nathaniel Hawthorne, to Susanna Rowson's *Charlotte Temple* (1791), to Harriet Beecher Stowe's novels *Uncle Tom's Cabin* (1852) and *Dred* (1856) – Stokes makes a powerful argument that sentimental fiction conceives of disability as a universal rather than an exceptional category. If sentimentalism began with narratives depicting the dangers of seduction to vulnerable young women, it simultaneously presented sympathy as a source of bodily danger. Hence in texts like Stowe's *Dred*, characters' sympathetic assistance to those in need frequently results in infection and even death. Yet such debility, Stokes finds, did not couple bodily impairment with depravity, as do so many American literary depictions of disabled characters. Rather, in texts such as Maria Susanna Cummins's *The Lamplighter* (1854), sentimentalism often upholds the disabled, atypical body as the corporeal expression of Christian piety.

Continuing this focus on how nineteenth-century prose genres theorized disability, in Chapter 3 Maurice Wallace examines the slave narrative as a genre that reveals how slavery's physical violence against Black captives acted to write white power onto Black bodies as an everyday display of white domination. Considering the banality of Black bodily injury and disability in Harriet Jacobs's *Incidents in the Life of a Slave Girl* (1861) and Josiah Henson's *The Life of Josiah Henson, Formerly a Slave, Now an Inhabitant of Canada as Narrated by Himself* (1849), Wallace tracks both slavery's production of Black disability and the historical panic over white bodily depletion. In so doing, the chapter conceptualizes what Wallace terms a Black body/white body complex, a parasitic struggle in which whites aimed to recover waning vigor by exerting brute power over the Black bodies they held captive.

Such a tension, Agnieszka Soltysik Monnet (Chapter 4) argues, frequently plays out against fault lines within and against the category of the human that are so frequently the topic of American gothic fiction across white and Black, undead and dead, male and female, normative and monstrous, sane and insane, straight and queer. The chapter first situates the origins of the American Gothic at the meeting ground between the British gothic novel in the late eighteenth century and three sociocultural forces within early

American history – settler colonialism, Puritan distrust of the body, and the Atlantic slave trade. The chapter then examines how, as the genre shifted through the nineteenth and twentieth centuries, it began to reorient the axis between the normal and the monstrous toward divisions within ableness, health, race, gender, and sexuality.

In Chapter 5, Colleen Glenney Boggs covers tremendous historical ground to explain a key means by which American literature grapples with representations of the body at war. By shifting from the battlefield violence we might expect in such a chapter to white women's bodily suffering as an affirmation of national innocence, Boggs argues that American war literature finds its greatest strength in the refusal of its topic, obscuring genocidal violence waged against Black Americans and Natives. With readings of texts by authors including Louisa May Alcott, William Apess, James Fenimore Cooper, Stephen Crane, Frederick Douglass, Frances E. W. Harper, Ernest Hemingway, Julia Ward Howe, Phil Klay, Herman Melville, Toni Morrison, and Harriet Beecher Stowe, Boggs broadens our consideration of the impact war literature has on racializing bodies and on influencing which lives matter.

Similarly attentive to the legacies of settler colonialism and white supremacy, in Chapter 6 Sony Coráñez Bolton highlights a set of novels written by Asian American and Latinx writers, revealing how multicultural fiction situates bodies within the historical legacies of hybridity and racial mixture. By analyzing historical flashpoints in the meanings of race – including the conquest, the transatlantic slave trade, transpacific imperialism, the civil rights movement, and contemporary debates on US American multiculturalism – Bolton identifies the seemingly incommensurate ways that multiethnic bodies have been shaped through representation. In the process, the chapter uses readings of texts such as Bryan Ascalon Roley's *American Son* (2001), Jessica Hagedorn's *Dogeaters* (1991), Junot Díaz's *The Brief and Wondrous Life of Oscar Wao* (2007), and Martin Luther King, Jr.'s "Beyond Vietnam" (1967) to show how the racialization of bodies within the United States always occurs within a larger framework of the Americas and US imperialism.

In Chapter 7, Frances Tran examines the possibilities the genre of science fiction offers for exploring alternative embodiments, from technological enhancement and genetic modification to mutation and multispecies assemblages. Tran analyzes common science fictional tropes and representations of humanoid bodies with attention to how they are embedded in long histories of coloniality, enslavement, and racialization. By engaging the work of authors such as Octavia Butler, W. E. B. Du Bois, N. K. Jemisin, Sabrina Vourvoulias, and Charles Yu, Tran illuminates how minoritized subjects have to grapple with what she terms the *stickiness* of their corporeality, even in speculative landscapes. Above all, the chapter accentuates how visionary science fiction can be as it presents the body as a site of contestation and revolution necessary for realizing more equitable, livable, and joyful worlds.

The final chapter of the "Genres" section, Chapter 8, examines a recent wave of transgender literature that situates itself beyond the realism and memoir to which trans* narratives have too frequently been consigned. Looking at North American transgender fictional texts, like Kai Cheng Thom's *Fierce Femmes and Notorious Liars* (2016), which defy any pressure to perform authenticity and realness in the service of truthful embodiment, Stephanie Clare identifies a trans* fantastic that uses fantasy to practice freedom and create community. In so doing, Clare argues, recent transgender writers have focused less on a sense of genuine selfhood than on the social contexts that shape embodied experiences.

Part II, "Critical Approaches," provides a series of critical fields, concepts, methods, and genealogies for analyzing bodies in literature. By delineating the role embodiment plays in seven influential fields within American literary studies – feminist theory, the history of reading and the book, disability studies, health humanities, Native studies, Black studies, and ecocriticism – this section provides readers new ways to think about bodies in research, teaching, and study Deliberately, this section features not only critical approaches with obvious relationships to the body (e.g., disability studies and the health humanities) but also those with a perhaps less-than-clear relationship to the body (e.g., the history of reading). Doing so underscores the importance of featuring bodies as objects of analysis across multiple different inquiries and fields, foregrounding the potential for interdisciplinary approaches to the study of American literary texts. As a whole, then, the chapters in Part II highlight how thinking critically about the body in literature interacts with other theoretical and critical categories that situate the aesthetics of literature within politics and histories of lived, embodied experience in America.

Taking Barbara Christian's "The Race for Theory" (1988) and *This Bridge Called My Back* (1983) as points of departure, Chapter 9, which focuses on feminist theory, interrogates not only the changing definitions of "sex" and "gender" but also the preoccupation with these terms as abstract universals. In it, Xine Yao looks at Black, Indigenous, and other feminist of color theorists, who have critiqued how "sex" and "gender" are articulated through racial and other biopolitical differences in order to govern and produce bodies and populations. The chapter then surveys illustrative feminist tactics – such as those navigated via queer theory and trans studies – that undermine this hegemonic dichotomization. Approaching American literature through feminist theory, Yao ultimately finds, means reckoning with the national, historical, and ongoing policing of bodies as well as American cultural imperialism on a global scale.

In Chapter 10, focusing on the history of reading and the reading body, Thomas Constantinesco uses examples from colonial America to contemporary US literature to ask what we might learn from paying attention to the body as the site where reading takes place. In contrast to a longstanding critical tradition that conceives of reading exclusively as an act of the mind, the chapter first emphasizes how the long history of tactile reading facilitates alternative timelines, shifting literary historians' focus to readerly communities largely occluded from more canonical histories of literature and reading. It then redescribes reading as a sensory practice. Finally, the chapter accents how somatics of reading foregrounds the materiality of the literary text and valorizes hapticality as the meeting ground of writerly practice and readerly hermeneutics.

Given the centrality of disability studies within scholarship and teaching on American literature and the body, the volume includes two chapters that introduce readers to that field: one focusing on how disability studies helps us to read and understand literary texts published before the twentieth century; and one that highlights crip-of-color critique, focusing on more recent literature. In the former (Chapter 11), Erica Fretwell tracks the development of disability studies, while suggesting how we might read disabled bodies not merely as symbolic representations but also as a way to pressure the very status of the normate body. To do so, she takes as a case study the literary history of the phantom limb: that invisible disability that both materializes the production of human difference at the level of perception and confounds facile distinctions between reality and representation. By tracing a cultural and literary history that includes writers from S. Weir Mitchell, to Charles Chesnutt, to Frances E. W. Harper, the chapter demonstrates that reading disabled bodies entails critical attunement to the affective attachments directed toward and around the idea of the unitary body and the ways that disability itself operates as a narrative structure.

In a companion chapter, Anna Hinton (Chapter 12) provides an overview of crip studies and crip-of-color critique as a method of approaching disability in contemporary American literature, particularly that by women of color. The chapter makes a case that we benefit from considering the texts of writers like Toni Morrison, Leslie Marmon Silko, and Virginia Grise as crip literature. At its conclusion, Hinton then moves into the burgeoning field of feminist crip technoscience to position crip literature's representation of spirituality as a crip technoscience of the spirit. Indeed, Hinton ultimately argues, it is within crip techno spaces that spiritual practices, particularly magic, unmake and remake worlds as well as the bodies that inhabit them.

Shifting from disability studies to the sometimes overlapping field of the health humanities, Lindsey Grubbs begins Chapter 13 by providing an overview of methodological approaches to medicine. She then offers case studies spanning the eighteenth through twenty-first centuries to ask how health humanities can offer new ways to read the body in American literature. From analyses of texts from Charles Brockden Brown's *Arthur Mervyn* (1799) to Charlotte Perkins Gilman's "The Yellow Wall-Paper" (1892), the chapter examines the framing of disease within hierarchies of race and gender. Closing with recent poetry by Bettina Judd and Kwoya Fagen Maples, Grubbs turns to how the health humanities can help us better understand structural racism in healthcare, ultimately demonstrating how narratives of illness are not just discursive but also have real impacts on bodies and minds.

Sean Teuton's chapter on Native studies (Chapter 14) works to recast racist imaginings about Native bodily inferiority – a damaging colonial legacy that continues stubbornly to function in American literature – by asking readers either to revere a romanticized and pristine precontact Indigenous body or to pity or fear a broken, tainted, even monstrous Native body. Yet as colonialism pervades the permeable border between settler and Indigenous states, so does dominant thinking also affect the Native world, in which Indigenous people at times internalize and reproduce distorted perceptions of the ideal Indigenous body. The chapter therefore argues that critique of this ideology of Indigenous corporeal perfection engenders the potential to imagine a "new" Native body – one perhaps better connected to traditional models of wellness, but also one more realistically and honestly placed within inclusive literary and lived realities. With that new Indigenous body and a politics of identity and sovereign nationhood to serve it, Teuton argues, scholars in both Indigenous and American literary studies may better theoretically justify their work for justice.

Chapter 15 turns to Black and critical race studies to delineate the often-vexed boundary between the discursive construct of the Black body and the bodies of Black people, tracing the critical trajectory of an originary displacement through the writings of Black thinkers including Frantz Fanon, Kimberly Juanita Brown, and Tavia Nyong'o. In so doing, Christine Okoth challenges the recent scholarly tendency to use "bodies" as metonyms for all aspects of racialized existence, foregrounding instead the continuous interplay between racialization, corporeality, aesthetics, and embodied theorizing. Through a thematic focus on reading and being read, the chapter also identifies literary texts and participants in racializing displacements, showing how Black writers and artists have engaged with and subverted demands for legibility.

Finally, in Chapter 16, Delia Byrnes provides an overview of how key concepts in twenty-first century US ecocriticism relate to human embodiment, focusing particularly on embodied differences of race, gender, and disability within the broader articulation of environmental thought. With readings of writers including Jesmyn Ward, Leslie Marmon Silko, and Don DeLillo, the chapter looks at how American literature negotiates the interconnection of the human and the nonhuman. In particular, it focuses on the materialist turn in ecocriticism, analyses of "ecological otherness" as a mode of disability studies, and biopolitical theories of toxicity within the unequal distribution of environmental hazards. The chapter provides a fitting conclusion to the volume as a whole, reminding us, as it does so well, of all the ways our human bodies are embedded within ecologies that collect us to life writ large.

## NOTES

1 William J. Long, *American Literature: A Study of the Men and the Books that in Earlier and Later Times Reflect the American Spirit* (Boston: Ginn and Company, 1913), 50–51.
2 Christina Crosby, *A Body, Undone: Living on after Great Pain* (New York: New York University Press, 2016), 198.
3 Hortense Spillers, "Mama's Baby, Papa's Maybe: An American Grammar Book," *diacritics* 17, no. 2 (1987): 68, 67.
4 Ibid., 68.
5 Ibid., 76, 68.
6 Ibid., 74. Emphasis in original.
7 Ibid., 77, 80.
8 Jennifer C. Nash, "Rethinking Intersectionality," *Feminist Review* 89 (2008): 8.
9 Hortense Spillers, Saidiya Hartman, and Farrah Jasmine Griffin, "'Whatcha Gonna Do?' – Revisiting 'Mama's Baby, Papa's Maybe: An American Grammar Book,'" *Women's Studies Quarterly* 35, no. 1/2 (2007): 300.
10 Spillers, "Mama's Baby," 76, 67, 66.
11 Christopher Looby, "The Literariness of Sexuality: Or, How to Do the (Literary) History of (American) Sexuality," *American Literary History* 25, no. 4 (2013): 841, 843.
12 E. Patrick Johnson, "'Quare' Studies, or (Almost) Everything I Know about Queer Studies I Learned from my Grandmother," *Text and Performance Quarterly* 21, no. 1 (2001): 10.
13 Many of the chapter summaries that follow draw extensively from abstracts authored by the contributors.

# PART I

# Genres

# I

## MARVIN MCALLISTER

# Bodies in Early US-Atlantic Theater

In a 1703 discourse on the nature of comedy, Anglo-Irish dramatist George Farquhar declared "an English play is intended for the use and instruction of an English audience." He further identified this audience as a "mixture of many nations" and as "a people not only separated from the rest of the world by situation, but different also from other nations as well in the complexion and temperament of the natural body as in the constitution of our body politick."[1] By "body politick," Farquhar imagined an imperial nation defined by its variegation and collectivity. Theater scholars Jeffrey Richards and Elizabeth Maddock Dillon have adapted and applied Farquhar's prescription for a national drama to the New World. Richards characterizes the American audience as "a changeable cluster of identities that individuals or groups might recognize as pertaining to them," specifically a cluster of Irish, Black, female, and working-class identities that are not fixed or predetermined. Richards also defines early American theater as "a cultural space that was transatlantic and without fixed national borders, even though the content may have appeared nationalistic and local." Dillon names this transatlantic cultural space a "performative commons" in which North American theatrical artists interact with cultural material drawn from a broad "Atlantic geography."[2] Inspired by both Richards and Dillon, I have adopted the term US-Atlantic to signal how the young republic was shaped by a "mixture of many nations" – some European, some Native American, and some African.

This chapter draws on various critical and cultural fields to reverse engineer the "body politick" produced by US-Atlantic theaters during the colonial, revolutionary, and early national periods.[3] Anthropologist Margaret Lock and Nancy Scheper-Hughes provide important theorizing on three kinds of body: the individual body, the social body, and the body politic. The individual body "is understood in the phenomenological sense of the lived experience of the body-self."[4] The social body names "the representational uses of the body as a natural symbol with which to think about nature, society, and culture." Finally, the body politic is a nationalizing, border-defining body, which manifests through "the regulation, surveillance, and control of bodies (individual and collective)."[5] For Locke and Hughes, the body politic has the power to discipline individual bodies and regulate social bodies like theaters; the body politic is "the most dynamic in suggesting why and how certain kinds of bodies are socially produced."[6]

To help us understand this national social production, historian David Waldestreicher explains how citizens often process the relationships between individual bodies and the state by anthropomorphizing the nation as a "body" with a "psychology" or a reputation.[7] Yet, Waldestreicher asserts that, more than narratives defining nations, a "nationalist ideology" refers to "a script or course of action." His use of "script" anticipates later work by theater scholar Robin Bernstein. Building upon a range of material culture from novels to baby dolls, Bernstein defines a "script" as a loose perform-ance plan with an in-built invitation, or series of invitations, to resist and reinterpret a text in ways that the original author may never have intended.[8] Bernstein argues "scriptive things," like early US-Atlantic plays, come with what performance scholar Diana Taylor calls a repertoire, "embodied memory" or "ephemeral, non-producible knowledge," and when we experi-ence and interpret these scripts we divulge that repertoire.[9]

I am interested in excavating the dominant narratives, scripts, and actions of the US-Atlantic body politic by examining how – through theater – writers, actors, and spectators lifted individual bodies from the page onto the stages of unruly, triple-tiered social bodies. Throughout this nationaliz-ing process, newly minted Americans reimagined Old World dramatic char-acters into a New World repertoire that included several recurrent character types: American Girls who resisted objectification to reimagine the relation-ships between mind and body, male and female; Yankees who set the tone for class dynamics, patriotism, and racism; and, finally, stage Africans and Indians who were erased, absorbed, and repurposed in service to white identities in a white republic.

## The American Girl: Mind/Body ... Male/Female

In theater, philosophy, literature, and cognitive sciences, the individual body has, for centuries, been understood within a Cartesian dualism of soul versus body, or mind versus body. Anthropologist Andrew Strathern highlights how, dating back to Saint Augustine, the mind has been associated with the "male sphere of reason and culture" while the body has been deemed the "female sphere of emotions and nature," with the former viewed as superior to the latter.[10] In subsequent sociological and representational discourses, the individual body and mind were saddled with this gendered opposition. Yet, building on the work of neuroscientist Antonio Damasio and phenomenologist Maurice Merleau-Ponty, performance scholar Elizabeth Hart reimagines the familiar binaries of mind versus body or male versus female. Hart recasts the individual body in a more fluid relationship with brain and mind, as part of a "complex system of integration" where consciousness, which is the basis of all thought, is embodied in "response to the lived-in body within a lived-in world."[11] Similarly, feminist theorist Elizabeth Grosz argues for relocating the body "to the center of analysis" where we can recognize and fully embrace the thinking subject as a corporeal or bodied being.[12]

These dualisms and countervailing theories carry important implications for how we read the subjectivity and agency of female bodies in US-Atlantic theaters. Writing about women actors in early national performance, Faye Dudden identifies acting as an embodied art associated with femaleness, unlike writing or print culture, which was linked to maleness. She writes, "to act you must be present in the body, available to be seen. The woman who acts is thus inherently liable, whatever her own intent, to become the object of male sexual fantasy and voyeuristic pleasure." For both female and male actors, the body on display risks becoming "a sexual object against one's will."[13] Within the representational field of live theater – a space for putting on, performing, and perhaps reshaping specific bodies – Dudden articulates "two divergent possibilities for female bodies: transformation and objectification." In more detail, the options are to "enable women to rehearse the most radical projects of self-creation" or "reduce them to bodies and present them as objects."[14] Dudden uses the term "acting female" to describe a woman who carries the potential to threaten "the prevailing definition of womanhood" and to "undermine assumptions about the fixity of identity."[15]

One early national theatrical stock character that fully embodied Dudden's "acting female" was the "American Girl." This character was a "witty, coquettish and enthusiastically tomboyish heroine," who often defied familial expectations and gender norms to pursue her truest self.[16] This US-Atlantic figure emerged partly from the European dramatic tradition of women passing as men or taking on "masculine" traits of leadership to "soldier up" or fight back and partly from breeches roles, which originated during the Restoration period to objectify female actors and arouse spectators with the titillating sight of women in tights. One especially assertive and radical American Girl is Rebecca from Susanna Rowson's *Slaves in Algiers* (1794). Through her rhetoric and her active insurrectionary leadership, Rebecca works to dissolve mind/body, male/female dualisms and place women in full control of their bodies and minds. Rowson's comic opera chronicles a serious episode of "white slavery" in Algiers where the local Dey, Muley Moloc, and other Algerians have captured and enslaved a group of white Americans and Brits. To the rescue comes the "radical" heroine Rebecca, who functions as "a virtual missionary of republicanism to the North Africans" and whose "teachings on liberty extend to the matters of gender."[17]

In Act I we are introduced to Rebecca's teachings through Fetnah, a member of the Dey's harem:

FETNAH: ... But some few months since, my father, (who sends out many corsairs,) brought home a female captive, to whom I became greatly attached; it was she, who nourished in my mind the love of liberty, and taught me, woman was never formed to be the abject slave of man. Nature made us equal with them, and gave us the power to render ourselves superior.

SELIMA: Of what nation was she?

FETNAH: She came from that land, where virtue in either sex is the only mark of superiority. – She was an American.[18]

For clarification, this harem is a cloistered space for wives and concubines in the Muslim world, and Fetnah's father is Ben Hassan, a British-born Jewish man who converted to Islam and amassed some wealth as a slave dealer. Ben Hassan had previously captured Rebecca and brought her into his home, but little did he know that this American Girl had begun politicizing his daughter, and now Fetnah is preaching American values on gender and equality to Selima, a servant in the Dey's harem. During this dialogue, Fetnah proclaims, "Nature made us equal with them and gave us the power to render ourselves superior," which perfectly articulates the self-creating potential of the "acting female." As now dangerous role models, both Fetnah and Rebecca become catalysts for social change who reject the bondage, abjection, and objectification of women.

Rowson illustrates how female bodies do not have to masquerade as male bodies to perform in leading roles and how their discourse can inspire acts of radical self-creation or re-creation. After planting seeds of freedom and equality in Fetnah, this American Girl, or more accurately "American Woman," foments a successful mutiny of women, men, captives, slaves, harem members, Brits, Americans, and Algerians against the despotic ruler Muley Moloc. When Rebecca assumes this leadership role, perhaps as an intentional statement about female agency in late eighteenth-century performance, Rowson refuses to cross-dress and potentially objectify her main character. Interestingly, other Rowson characters do engage in gender bending. Inspired by Rebecca, Fetnah dresses as a boy to escape the Dey's harem, and Fetnah's father Ben Hassan dons a woman's veil to avoid detection and punishment from Moloc. Through Rebecca, a performative commons fusion of European convention and American exceptionalism, Rowson gave audiences a woman in full self-creating control of her gendered body, a woman who inspires others to do the same.

### Stage Yankees: Shaping and Taming the Social Body

Individual bodies like Rowson's Rebecca played an important role in the construction of cultural and social meaning in US-Atlantic theaters. Such theatrical embodiment makes the immaterial – values and beliefs – material. For anthropologist Andrew Strathern, these disembodied values are always social: "What is embodied is always some set of meanings, values, tendencies, orientations that derive from the sociocultural realm."[19] In a nation conditioned by lingering revolutionary rhetoric and the continued presence of slavery, Rowson's Rebecca helped associate values like bravery and freedom with white female bodies, and she did so in a unique transatlantic social space: the playhouse.

As part of her New World performative commons, Elizabeth Dillon characterizes the transatlantic playhouse as "a space at which large numbers of common (and elite) people gathered with regularity, and thus a space at which the body of the people was, literally, materialized."[20] Sociologist Richard Butsch explains how "in the early republic the audience in the theater was sometimes referred to as 'the town' since all (politically significant) sectors of the community were present, and despite the fact that some groups were not represented or were present but had no voice."[21] Consistent with a revolutionary rhetoric rooted in egalitarianism, these social bodies viewed attendees as theoretically equal citizens gathered to deliberate on, perform, and perhaps expand their rights. However, early Americanist Peter Reed highlights how "class" was very much present but understood "as a discursive construct," meaning these theatrical spaces hosted "ongoing rehearsal, repetitions, and improvisations" around what signified as high or low culture.[22] During these improvised deliberations around class, rights, and belonging, Butsch notes "a tenuous balance between debate and order on the one hand and crowd action and disorder on the other," and he finds "ultimately, inclusion of the lower classes created such heterogeneity that debate produced dissension rather than decision."[23]

The lower or artisan classes did not fully embrace the "bourgeois concept" of polite debate and often forcefully exerted themselves, even to the point of inhouse disturbances that obliterated middle-class notions of decorum. Butsch further argues that in Boston and Philadelphia theaters, communal debate and dissension were "part of the battle between Federalists and Republicans that flowed through the press, the streets, and all the rest of the society."[24] Theater was no longer considered an extraneous indulgence; rather it "was conceived as an arena for political expression in this intense national debate over the form of the government. Artisan Republicans, who previously would have attacked the entire institution, accepted it."[25] Equally important, "Elite Federalists" conceded theater could serve as a legitimate forum for "the national confrontation between classes and their political values."

Playwrights, actors, and audiences were well aware of the improvisational and barely containable nature of these social spaces that came to be known as "the town," a three-tiered, class-based urban theater structured around a pit, dress boxes, and a gallery. From Restoration theaters to Boston playhouses, Butsch identifies a "knowingness" shared between artists and "the town" wherein writers expected, encouraged, and even played upon public participation. In early US-Atlantic theaters, these audience dynamics and unavoidable class tensions were best represented by the stage Yankee, a fiercely honest, plainspoken, and native-born American antidote to European pretension. Throughout the early national period, two iterations of the stage Yankee emerged: one that represented the more patrician Federalist audience member and one that embodied the proletarian Republican spectator. Both stage Yankees feature prominently in Royall Tyler's comedy *The Contrast* (1787), which debuted in New York at the John Street Theatre.

Working specifically within the social hierarchies of "the town," Tyler's *The Contrast* crafts two very different Yankee bodies to materialize distinctive American values. Tyler begins by "contrasting" his aristocratic yet patriotic Yankee, Colonel Henry Manly, against his well-connected and social-climbing sister Charlotte Manly. In the first scene of Act II, we realize the highly divergent agendas of brother and sister during a conversation over federal bank notes:

> MANLY: ... Their full amount is justly due to me, but as embarrassments, the natural consequences of a long war, disable my country from supporting its credit, I shall wait with patience until it is rich enough to discharge them. If that is not in my day, they shall be transmitted as an honourable certificate to posterity, that I have humbly imitated our illustrious Washington, in having exposed my health and life in the service of my country, without reaping any other reward than the glory of conquering in so arduous a contest.
>
> CHARLOTTE: Well said heroics. Why, my dear Henry, you have such a lofty way of saying things, that I protest I almost tremble at the thought of introducing you to the polite circles in the city.[26]

Manly is responding to Charlotte's suggestion that he cash in his notes to finance his romantic intrigues, but, ever the loyal Federalist, Manly places the needs of the struggling nation above his own. Through these hyper-virtuous thoughts and actions, Tyler works to distance his principled stage Yankee from the "polite circles" who frequented New York's culture-defining "towns." However, according to Jason Shafer, Manly embodied a "learned stoicism and self-identification with the public good in the service of the republic," values many early national Americans, even cultural elites, wished to emulate.[27]

Tyler next places Colonel Manly in opposition to another cultural elite, the condescending British visitor Billy Dimple. Their contrast directly involves the social traffic of "the town":

CHARLOTTE: Pray, Mr. Dimple, was it a tragedy or a comedy?

DIMPLE: Faith, madam, I cannot tell; for I sat with my back to the stage all the time, admiring a much better actress than any there – a lady who played the fine woman to perfection; though, by the laugh of the horrid creatures round me, I suppose it was comedy. Yet, on second thoughts, it might be some hero in a tragedy, dying so comically as to set the whole house in an uproar. – Colonel, I presume you have been in Europe?

MANLY: Indeed, sir, I was never ten leagues from the continent.

DIMPLE: Believe me, Colonel, you have an immense pleasure to come; and when you shall have seen the brilliant exhibitions of Europe, you will learn to despise the amusements of this country as much as I do.

MANLY: Therefore I do not wish to see them; for I can never esteem that knowledge valuable which tends to give me a distaste for my native country.

(478–479)

Dimple quickly establishes his social or class position in "the town"; he sat in the dress boxes where "a much better actress," or a socially ambitious young woman, monopolized his amorous attention. As for the activity onstage, Dimple was hardly interested and attempts to entice Manly to visit Europe and learn the truth about the inadequate amusements in this second-rate country. Of course, Manly rejects any knowledge that would drive a wedge between a true patriot and his beloved United States of America.

Tyler's other stage Yankee, the more plebeian and comedic Jonathan, is well-known for singing his signature melody "Yankee Doodle" in Act III and for proudly proclaiming his identity as a masterless man. When Dimple's servant Jessamy mistakes Jonathan for a fellow servant, Jonathan erupts: "Servant! Sir, do you take me for a neger, – I am Colonel Manly's waiter" (457). Racism aside, Jonathan is a self-described "true blue son of liberty" who refuses to see himself as subservient; rather he perceives himself as just as free, just as privileged as his boss Colonel Manly. An aspirational Jonathan wants to see the world beyond his family farm, and he sees his employment through Manly as the perfect vehicle.

We learn about Jonathan's relationship to "the town" when he recounts his first visit to a raucous New York playhouse:

> As I was going about here and there, to and again, to find it, I saw a great crowd of folks going into a long entry that had lanterns over the door; so I asked a man whether that was not the place where they played hocus-pocus? He was a very civil, kind man, though he did speak like the Hessians; he lifted up his eyes and said, "They play hocus-pocus tricks enough there, Got knows, mine friend"... So I went right in, and they shewed me away, clean up to the garret, just like meeting-house gallery. And so I saw a power of topping folks, all sitting round in little cabins, "just like father's corn-cribs;" and then there was such a squeaking with the fiddles, and such a tarnal blaze with the lights, my head was near turned. At last the people that sat near me set up such a hissing – hiss – like so many mad cats; and then they went thump, thump, thump, just like our Peleg threshing wheat and stampt away, just like the nation; and called out for one Mr. Langolee, – I suppose he helps act[s] the tricks ... Gor, I – I liked the fun, and so I thumpt away, and hiss'd as lustily as the best of 'em. (466–467)

Unlike Dimple, Jonathan was led to the cheapest seats in the playhouse, to a gallery far from the boxes filled with "topping folks" or superior aristocrats. From the "heavens," Jonathan could look down and see the dress boxes divided into stalls, resembling the "corn-cribs" on Jonathan's family farm. But, focused on his gallery mates, Jonathan admits he enjoys the hissing, thumping, and stamping; he "liked the fun" and even compares the unruly atmosphere to his country's recent revolutionary action: "stampt away, just like the nation." As a "true son of liberty," Jonathan feels at home as he dissents, roars, and revolts with the best of the rowdies fighting to be heard from this uppermost "garret."

In a deeper reading of these two Yankee bodies in relation to the broader social body of "the town," Sarah Chinn identifies how white masculinity served not simply as "a model of selfless dedication to the new nation, but as a precursor to the market-driven individualism that took hold among nineteenth-century theatrical audiences."[28] Jason Shaffer adds, "the staged performance of these self-consciously colonial (or American) and lower-class 'Yankee' personae offers their audience a similar means of political participation in the development of a post-British nationality."[29] Although he might appear self-sacrificing, Colonel Manly knows the value of the bonds he owns, and, with the market in mind, he opts to defer cashing them in until his recently postcolonial, post-British nation is more financially secure. Similarly, the waiter Jonathan knows his intrinsic value as a proud farmer, never a servant, and seeks to enhance his prospects by seeing more of the world.

"The town's" collective, class-driven rehearsals of pasts, presents, and possible futures did not end at the stage front or in the laps of audiences in the boxes or galleries. These individual fictive bodies accrued social and market values not only on US-Atlantic stages but within the young republic's painfully real cultural hierarchies. Within this emerging body politic, stage Yankees like Jonathan and Colonel Manly, as well as Euro-constructed stage Indians and stage Africans, would contribute to an exclusionary conversation on national identities and scripts.

## Stage Indians: The Body Politic, Onstage and Beyond

One explicit national script, fully supported by the repertoire of early US-Atlantic theaters, was the absorption or erasure of Africans and Native Americans from the body politic. As Daphne Brooks writes, the Black "transatlantic body in performance is repeatedly called on to forge some kind of national consciousness, at the very moments in which its figure exposes and affirms the tenuousness of nationalism and its fiction."[30] Marginalized bodies are often used to create, sustain, or explain national identity, but, like any outsiders, these Black subjects ultimately reveal how any conception of "American" is not as unified as it presumes to be. Conditioned by racial hierarchies operating beyond the playhouse, the social body participated in a politics of attaching relative values to whiteness, blackness, and redness.

The New World's racial and cultural hierarchies are rooted in a western Christian tendency to overrepresent "European" as synonymous with "human." As cultural theorist Sylvia Wynter argues, European colonials came "to invent, label, and institutionalize the indigenous peoples of the Americas as well as the transported enslaved Black Africans as the physical referent of the projected irrational/sub-rational Human Other to its civic-humanist, rational self-conception."[31] Saidiya Hartman, in her work on self-making in nineteenth-century America, further explains how essential Black abjection was to whiteness and white pleasure. She claims, "blacks were envisioned fundamentally as vehicles for white enjoyment, in all its sundry and unspeakable expressions; this was as much the consequence of the chattel status of the captive as it was of the excess enjoyment imputed to the other."[32] Euro-Americans associated "others" with the corporeal and the irrational, but, due to the totalizing debasement of slavery, whites expressly viewed enslaved Black bodies as vehicles for their enjoyment. Although fully embodied Black characters were rare on early American stages, blackness was still integral to constructions of whiteness onstage and beyond.[33] Drawing on Toni Morrison's important work *Playing in the Dark*, Jeffrey Richards argues Euro-Americans understood themselves through an "Africanism" or a Black "other" that helped them define whiteness.[34] For example, Jonathan's vicious "neger" slur was designed to disassociate his masterless yet vulnerable whiteness from a blackness degraded by servitude or enslavement. Within the social body of the theater, the fiction of a unified, fully participatory nation is exposed, as Jonathan – a most American stage Yankee – reveals the nation's true hierarchical views on Black bodies.

Unlike stage Africans, Euro-constructed stage Indians appeared frequently on the streets and stages of the young republic. American drama historian Walter Meserve identifies Native Americans as a people naturally drawn to theatricality, especially in their treaty ceremonies, and he highlights how "the general procedure of the treaty ceremony had become established by the Six Nations of the Iroquois Nation and accepted by the white man."[35] As models for future US-Atlantic theatrical and extra-theatrical production, Iroquois-defined treaty performances incorporated the visual spectacle of danced mimetic action along with dramatic action rooted in specific real-world disagreements.

However, to serve a nationalizing script of native absorption and erasure, these real Iroquois-led ceremonies had to be converted to performed Indian-ness. Perhaps the most famous example of "playing Indian" was the Boston Tea Party of 1773 when the Sons of Liberty dressed up as Mohawk Indians to attack British ships filled with tea. Yet cultural historian Philip Deloria locates the first fully committed acts of "playing Indian" in fraternal organizations like the Tammany Society of New York, which was founded in 1789 and named in honor of Chief Tamanend. Tammany Members dressed and paraded in feathers and war paint, created a powerful Democratic political machine known as Tammany Hall, and enthusiastically supported ballad operas like Anne Julia Kemble Hatton's *The Songs of Tammany, or the Indian Chief* (1794). However, as enthusiastic or "authentic" as the Tammany Society might have been, Deloria warns this multimodal "playing Indian" did not represent a "wilderness marriage" of white and Indian cultural bloodlines.[36] Stage Indians, in the streets or onstage, operated not as a merged identity but as a doubled or contrarian identity with a constant tension between whiteness and redness.

While unpacking this dual or dueling national identity, Elizabeth Dillon argues that by "playing Indian" Euro-Americans were angling to claim "a popular sovereignty that evicts Indians from their land."[37] New World whiteness depended not only on establishing commonality with Indian bodies onstage but also on the vanishing of native populations. This script is embodied in John Augustus Stone's *Metamora, Last of the Wampanoag* (1829). This tragedy is based on the real native chief Metacomet, who fought to the death against Plymouth, Massachusetts Puritans when they seized his ancestral lands. Metacomet was such a popular New World figure that he appeared in at least eight different American dramas from 1822 to 1894. In an effort to promote national culture, the fiercely patriotic actor Edwin Forrest sponsored a playwriting contest to find and produce the best "native" or American-authored tragedy. One newspaper, *The New York Mirror*, praised Forrest for how he "single-handedly initiated American drama."[38] The double meaning of "native" was not lost on literary scholar Theresa Gaul, who highlights how what qualified Stone's *Metamora* as "native" or truly "American" was its very reliance on the cultural history, myths, and customs of aboriginal peoples.[39]

In 1824, well before he launched his contest to find the best "native" tragedy and define America's emerging body politic, Edwin Forrest disappeared for a couple of months and lived among the Choctaw nation near New Orleans. He learned their customs, wore their clothes, performed their ritual dances, sang their songs, and absorbed their gestural and verbal forms of communication.[40] Theresa Gaul argues that "Forrest's painstaking observations of Choctaw culture and life position him as an anthropologist proffering his performance as an ethnographic text to the audience before him."[41] Yet, in performance, Forrest's complete transformation into Metamora marked his transition from "anthropologist to native." While onstage, his relationship to Metamora changed, as he was no longer the careful observer bringing a dispassionate ethnographic account to his audience. Instead, Forrest became the "genuine Indian" and allowed his audiences to "become the direct observers of the native, imaginatively inhabiting the role of anthropologists themselves."[42]

As for the real-world politics behind *Metamora*, where did Forrest and Stone's "native" drama stand on the heated debate over physically relocating first Americans? Was Forrest in favor of displacing native nations under Andrew Jackson's Indian Removal act of 1830? In his memoir, *The Stage, or Recollections of Actors and Acting* (1880), James Murdoch recalls a famous 1831 performance of *Metamora* in Augusta, Georgia, where the locals accused Forrest of siding with the Indians and against whites. They took particular exception to sentiments expressed in Metamora's final, dying speech in Act V scene five:

> My curses on you, white men! May the Great Spirit curse you when he speaks in his war voice from the clouds! Murderers! The last of the Wampanoags' curse be on you! May your graves and the graves of your children be in the path the red man shall trace! And may the wolf and the panther howl o'er your fleshless bones, fit banquet for the destroyers! Spirits of the grave, I come! But the curse of Metamora stays with the white man! I die! My wife! My Queen! My Nahmeokee![43]

With these scorching last words, Metamora not only curses murderous whites but calls on greater natural forces to curse future generations of white settlers long after he is dead and gone. According to Murdoch's memoir, after hearing this speech, one prominent Augusta Lawyer was convinced where Forrest stood: "Why, his eyes shot fire and his breath was hot with the hissing of his ferocious declamation. I insist upon it, Forrest believes in that d————d Indian speech, and it is an insult to the whole community."[44] Augustans took the issue of Indian removal personally and openly charged Mr. Forrest "with insulting the people of Augusta by appearing in a character which condemned the course of their State in dealing with the land-claims of the Cherokee Indians."[45]

Interestingly, the Augustans failed to fully appreciate the complicated body politic Forrest and Stone were scripting. Scott Martin argues Stone's *Metamora* is not predicated on a conflict between natives and Anglo-American colonists, but rather on an English–Indian rivalry. For Martin, Metamora "symbolizes a distinctively American character, a product of the unsullied natural environment of the New World, superior physically and morally to the arrogant and treacherous English."[46] The irate lawyer and his fellow Augustans were still seeing themselves as the descendants of Old World England and therefore intruders. According to Bruce McConachie, John Augustus Stone dissuaded white audiences from identifying as "colonizers" and instead encouraged them to embrace their role as inheritors. Stone departs from the common association of English settlers with the founding fathers, and he never attempts to connect the villainous Puritans and English aristocrats with contemporary American citizens. The Anglo-Saxon bodies Stone stages are "driven by their nature to enforce their oppressive social discriminations in the New World," and serve as the literal enemies of both Native Americans and early national Euro-Americans.[47]

Stone and Forrest's work on this historical Wampanoag tragedy effectively avoided the removal debate while building a bridge to a new "America." Historian Douglas Harvey concludes that Metamora and other stage Indians constituted a "passing of the torch to white, male Americans as the possessors of the continent."[48] A few beats before the chief's fiery speech, Stone initiates this process of torch passing. Metamora's wife Nahmeokee poses the question, "Metamora, is our nation dead," and Metamora's response is "we are destroyed – not vanquished; we are no more, yet we are forever" (226). With his cryptic response, Metamora declares the Wampanoag both extinct and eternal; how is that possible?

The epilogue for *Metamora*, first spoken at the Park Theatre in New York City in December 1829, solves the riddle. The orator first clarifies that the forever "we" refers to the "native bard" Stone and the "native actor" Forrest, who created a "native picture" for all to enjoy. As the epilogue progresses the "native" torch is officially passed to the white republic:

> Inspired by genius and by judgment led,
> Again the Wampanoag fought and bled;
> Rich plants are both of our own fruitful land,
> Your smiles the sun that made their leaves expand. (226)

Stone's epilogue asks his audience to contemplate the vanishing Wampanoag, as they witness these fading individual bodies representative of a deeper conversation or script on exclusion and inclusion. More than a conversation, this social gathering reflected and reinforced the relative market values of new and old Americans, as well as the racial and cultural hierarchies that ordered whiteness, blackness, and redness beyond the stage. Forrest and Stone's "native picture" closes with a fading indigenous nation embodied by two bleeding stage Indians, and the "rich plants" refer to the two white theatrical artists who have cultivated their gifts thanks in part to the smiling approbation of the Park Theatre public.

The close of Forrest and Stone's "native" drama encapsulates the primary focus of this essay: how individual, social, and political bodies were crafted and put to work in early American theatrical and cultural production. The process begins with individual bodies like Susanna Rowson's Rebecca, an "American Girl" who confronts and conquers the ubiquitous mind-body split – with its associations of maleness and femaleness – to broadcast an iconic image of US-Atlantic leadership. Within the raucous social body of "the town," Royall Tyler attempted to resolve political and class tensions between Federalists and Republicans by carving room for two stage Yankees: one patrician, one proletarian. Unfortunately, in social spaces like the Park Theatre, Tyler's communal vision of civic belonging was effectuated on the debasement and exclusion of Black citizens from the body politic, onstage and offstage. In addition, this developing national script was rooted in the personal, political, and anthropological transformation of real Indians, leaders like Tamanend or Metacomet, into disposable stage Indian ciphers. Forrest and Stone's *Metamora* announces the arrival of this new white republic, "our own fruitful land" of genius-inspired next Americans nurtured by the support of "the town" and the sacrifice of indigenous blood.

## NOTES

1  George Farquhar, "A Discourse Upon Comedy in Reference to the English Stage in a Letter to a Friend," in *Dramatic Essays of the Neoclassic Age*, ed. Henry Hitch Adams and Baxter Hathaway (New York: Columbia University Press, 1950), 225.
2  Jeffrey H. Richards, *Drama, Theatre, and Identity in the American New Republic* (Cambridge: Cambridge University Press, 2005), 4 and 19; Elizabeth Maddock Dillon, *New World Drama: Performative Commons in the Atlantic World* (Durham, NC: Duke University Press, 2014), 14.
3  By "colonial," I refer to the early 1600s arrival of British settlers in North America; by "revolutionary," I refer to the period of national struggle from the early 1770s to the ratification of a US Constitution in 1788; and, by "early national," I refer to the period from 1789 to 1837, bracketed by the presidencies of George Washington and Andrew Jackson.
4  Margaret Locke and Nancy Scheper-Huges, "The Mindful Body," *Medical Anthropology Quarterly* 1, no. 1 (1987): 7–8.
5  Ibid.
6  Ibid., 8.
7  For the next series of quotes, see David Waldestreicher, *In the Midst of Perpetual Fetes: The Making of American Nationalism, 1776–1820* (Chapel Hill: University of North Carolina Press, 1997), 141–142.
8  See the "Introduction" of Robin Bernstein to *Racial Innocence: Performing American Childhood from Slavery to Civil Rights* (New York: New York University Press, 2011).
9  Diana Taylor, *The Archive and the Repertoire: Performing Cultural Memory in the Americas* (Durham, NC: Duke University Press, 2003), 20.
10  Andrew J. Strathern, *Body Thoughts* (Ann Arbor: University of Michigan Press, 1996), 4.
11  Elizabeth Hart, "Performance, Phenomenology, and the Cognitive Turn," in *Performance and Cognition: Theatre Studies and the Cognitive Turn*, ed. Bruce McConachie and F. Elizabeth Hart (New York: Routledge, 2006), 13 and 29.
12  Elizabeth Grosz, *Volatile Bodies: Toward a Corporeal Feminism* (Bloomington: Indiana University Press, 1994), ix.
13  Faye E. Dudden, *Women in the American Theatre: Actresses and Audiences, 1790–1870* (New Haven, CT: Yale University Press, 1994), 2–3.
14  Ibid., 2.
15  Ibid.
16  Ibid., 20.
17  Ibid., 9.

18 Susannah Rowson, *Slaves in Algiers; or, A Struggle For Freedom: A Play, Interspersed with Songs, in Three Acts* (Philadelphia: Susanna Rowson, Wrigley and Berriman, 1794; Ann Arbor: Text Creation Partnership, 2011), 9, http://name.umdl.umich.edu/N21056.0001.001.

19 Strathern, *Body Thoughts*, 197.

20 Dillon, *New World Drama*, 4.

21 Richard Butsch, *The Making of American Audiences: From Stage to Television, 1750–1990* (New York: Cambridge University Press, 2000), 14.

22 Peter P. Reed, *Rogue Performances: Staging the Underclass in Early American Theatre Culture* (New York: Palgrave Macmillan, 2009), 22.

23 Butsch, *The Making of American Audiences*, 30–31.

24 Ibid., 41

25 Ibid.

26 Royall Tyler, *The Contrast in Representative Plays by American Dramatists: Vol. 1, 1765–1819*, ed. Montrose J. Moses (New York: Benjamin Blom, 1964), 453–454. Subsequent citations in the essay refer to this text.

27 Jason Shaffer, *Performing Patriotism: National Identity in the Colonial and Revolutionary American Theater* (Philadelphia: University of Pennsylvania Press, 2007), 172.

28 Sarah E. Chinn, *Spectacular Men: Race, Gender, and Nation on the Early American Stage* (New York: Oxford University Press, 2017), 103.

29 Shaffer, *Performing Patriotism*, 143.

30 Daphne A. Brooks, *Bodies in Dissent: Spectacular Performances of Race and Freedom, 1850–1910* (Durham, NC: Duke University Press, 2006), 29.

31 Sylvia Wynter, "Unsettling the Coloniality of Being/Power/Truth/Freedom: Towards the Human, after Man, Its Overrepresentation – An Argument," *The New Centennial Review* 3, no. 3 (Fall 2003): 281–282.

32 Saidiya V. Hartman, *Scenes of Subjection: Terror, Slavery, and Self-Making in Nineteenth-Century America* (New York: Oxford University Press, 1997), 22–23.

33 Chinn makes the case for the scarcity of stage Africans in early American theatre; see *Spectacular Men*, 19.

34 Richards, *Drama, Theatre, and Identity*, 214 and 218.

35 Walter Meserve, *An Emerging Entertainment: The Drama of the American People to 1828* (Bloomington: Indiana University Press, 1977), 5.

36 Philip Deloria, *Playing Indian* (New Haven, CT: Yale University Press, 1998), 34.

37 Dillon, *New World Drama*, 237.

38 Eugene H. Jones, *Native Americans as Shown on the Stage 1753–1916* (Metuchen, NJ: The Scarecrow Press, 1988), 66.

39 Theresa Strouth Gaul, "'The Genuine Indian Who Was Brought Upon the Stage': Edwin Forrest's Metamora and White Audiences," *Arizona Quarterly: A Journal of American Literature, Culture, and Theory* 56, no. 1 (Spring 2000): 3.

40 Joseph Roach, "The Emergence of the American Actor," in *The Cambridge History of American Theatre: Volume 1, Beginnings to 1870*, ed. Don B. Wilmeth and Christopher Bigsby (Cambridge: Cambridge University Press, 1998), 354. Roach relies heavily on William Rounseville Alger's biography, *Life of Edwin Forrest: The American Tragedian* (1877).

41 Gaul, "The Genuine Indian Who Was Brought Upon the Stage," 8.

42 Ibid., 10.

43 John Augustus Stone, Metamora, or The Last of the Wampanoags, in *Dramas from the American Theatre, 1762–1909*, ed. Richard Moody (Boston: Houghton Mifflin, 1969), 226. All subsequent quotes come from this text and are cited in the essay.

44 Murdoch quoted in Gaul, "The Genuine Indian Who Was Brought Upon the Stage," 14.

45 Quoted in Jones, *Native Americans as Shown on the Stage*, 67–68.

46 Scott Martin, "Interpreting 'Metamora': Nationalism, Theater, and Jacksonian Indian Policy," *Journal of the Early Republic* 19, no. 1 (Spring 1999): 98.

47 Bruce McConachie, "Metamora's Revenge," in *Native American Performance and Representation*, ed. S. E. Wilmer (Tucson: University of Arizona Press, 2009), 201.

48 Douglass Harvey, *The Theatre of Empire: Frontier Performances in America, 1750–1860* (London: Pickering & Chatto, 2010), 146.

# 2

## CLAUDIA STOKES

# Sentimentalism and the Feeling Body

Sentimental literature of the nineteenth century depicts the struggles of errant young women as they attempt to achieve self-control and comply with normative ideals of feminine conduct. Religious piety often figures centrally in these efforts, as sentimental heroines learn to imitate Christ in their pursuit of self-mastery and acquire moral instruction through the study of scripture. Sentimentalism's preoccupation with spiritual matters, however, did not preclude an interest in corporeal matters, and sentimental writers afford particular attention to the body. Focused principally on depicting female development – and sustained by women writers and readers alike – sentimentalism attended to the female body in particular and warned of the special dangers that it posed, whether through its susceptibility to seduction or through its capacity to instill vanity in worldly young women. Sentimentalism characterized the female body as an especial hazard in need of protection, and, through the repeated depiction of the perils that may befall the defenseless female body, sentimental texts often assumed a public pedagogic role in teaching female readers to exercise caution and avoid unnecessary danger. While prudence and restraint may enable young women to evade temptation and grievous bodily harm, sentimentalism also recognized that some forms of bodily affliction may prove unavoidable because of accident or illness. As a result, sentimentalism taught readers to regard debility with sympathy and pious resignation. Young women should not submit to sexual exploitation, but bodily malady may provide a vital opportunity to submit to the divine will. In this respect, sentimentalism regarded the body not only as a source of vulnerability but also as a potential site of religious enlightenment: The body in sentimentalism may cause either ruin or salvation, and the heroine's decisions alone may lead her to either of these two moral outcomes

In its portrayal of the vulnerable female body, sentimentalism often diverges from conventional scholarly understandings of nineteenth-century bodily attitudes. Elaine Scarry asserted decades ago that bodily suffering "is not *of* or *for* anything ... [and] it takes no object," but sentimental texts offered an alternate view of pain as a purposeful and even providential opportunity to acquire religious wisdom and salvation.[1] As a result, sentimental texts also depict disability in a manner that markedly deviates from the standard literary template discerned by scholars. Rosemarie Garland-Thompson influentially argues that disabled bodies in American literature are typically "perceived as out of control. Not only do they violate physical norms, but by looking and acting unpredictable they threaten to disrupt the ritualized behavior upon which social relations turn."[2] Sentimentalism often registers a countervailing view of the disabled, upholding them as paragons of religious piety who have learned to renounce worldly desires and minister to the needs of others. In this respect, they often serve as role models whom both sentimental heroines and readers themselves are implicitly encouraged to emulate.

## The Reading Body

Sentimental novels emerged in the late eighteenth century alongside the United States itself, and the first novel by a native North American published in the United States, William Hill Brown's *The Power of Sympathy* (1789), is generally recognized as the earliest work of sentimental fiction. As with such novels as Susanna Rowson's *Charlotte Temple* (1791) and Hannah Webster Foster's *The Coquette* (1797), early sentimental novels typically recount the seduction and consequent ruin of a young woman who falls prey to a rake and dies in childbirth. In the nineteenth century, sentimental novels adopted a different narrative template and more typically depict the development of isolated orphan girls – who are often the product of the ill-advised unions portrayed in eighteenth-century sentimental novels – as they find community and loving guidance from an assemblage of voluntary caregivers.[3] Sentimental novels in this vein had been in circulation for decades, as with Catharine Maria Sedgwick's *A New-England Tale* (1822), but they became a sudden popular sensation with the publication of Susan Warner's *The Wide, Wide World* (1850), which achieved unexpected success. Warner's novel was quickly followed by Harriet Beecher Stowe's blockbuster, *Uncle Tom's Cabin* (1851–1852), and Maria Susanna Cummins's *The Lamplighter* (1854), the popularity of which prompted Nathaniel Hawthorne's famed complaint about "that damned mob of scribbling women" who had come to dominate the literary market.[4] Sentimental fiction remained popular through the century, as with Martha Finley's Elsie Dinsmore series (1867–1905) and L. M. Montgomery's *Anne of Green*

*Gables* (1908), and Lauren Berlant contends that sentimentalism continues to influence American popular culture.[5]

Sentimentalism's preoccupation with the body became evident from the very outset, with novels that narrated the fatal dangers of sex for unmarried young women. Scholars have argued that these eighteenth-century seduction novels conveyed anxieties about the vulnerability of the new nation, with the body of the novel's heroine standing in for the United States itself.[6] The young woman's impregnation and death in childbirth thus dramatized concerns that the United States was vulnerable to malign forces and might prove unviable. But these early seduction novels also convey a developing preoccupation with the particular impact of reading on the female body. This concern found dramatic expression in Rowson's *Charlotte Temple*, in which the titular heroine falls prey to seduction primarily through the act of reading. Charlotte unwisely accepts a love letter from the licentious Montraville, and, though she resolves to assert the "impropriety of [their] continuing to see or correspond with each other," she nonetheless allows herself to read his letter repeatedly. This reading proves disastrous, for "each time she read it, the contents sunk deeper in her heart," and in consequence Charlotte loses her resolve and allows herself to succumb to Montraville's designs.[7] Within this scenario, unrestrained reading allows Montraville's seductive words to reverberate in Charlotte's consciousness, where they meet no resistance or opposition and where, as a result, they take root and grow in persuasiveness and influence.[8]

Rowson's description, in which Montraville's letter sinks ever "deeper in [Charlotte's] heart," characterizes the act of reading as a form of bodily intercourse, for rereading causes his words to achieve access to a vulnerable and intimate part of her body. Rowson suggests that Montraville's letter effectively primes Charlotte for the sexual penetration that will effect her ruin, and indeed this textual exchange metonymically prefigures his later illicit access to her body. At the same time, this scene also comports with a late eighteenth-century phenomenon recently observed by Sari Altschuler, who notes that Americans in this period believed that exposure to an unwanted text – such as narratives about the yellow fever – could result in infection and illness, with the circulating text functioning as a contagion that causes disease.[9] A similar occurrence underlies this episode in *Charlotte Temple*, for reading allows Montraville's words to breach her body – as they burrow deeply into "her heart" – and cause a weakening of her judgement as well as her bodily defenses. Reading does not cause infection per se, but it enables the corporeal access that will allow a growing foreign entity – her unborn child – to occupy her body and cause her premature death. In keeping with eighteenth-century belief in the entanglement of textual circulation with viral contagion, mere exposure to an inappropriate, ill-advised text directly causes Charlotte's bodily compromise and eventual death in disgrace.

Apprehension about the gullible susceptibility of the female reader is as old as the novel itself, and these concerns animated such texts as Charlotte Lennox's *The Female Quixote* (1752) and Jane Austen's *Northanger Abbey* (1817). These worries, however, redounded to the early sentimental novel itself, which was widely characterized as a menace to the impressionable female reader and which, as a result, was often likened to the dangerous libertine whose seductions it depicted. Critics contended that young female readers were particularly passive and compliant, and, like Charlotte Temple, lacked the inner resources to rigorously scrutinize alluring texts. As a result, young women were presumed to follow the directives of their reading, often by imitating or dramatizing the characters and plots of novels. Critics warned that the reading of seduction novels might result in the asexual reproduction of countless Charlotte Temples and Eliza Whartons, who, in their unthinking imitation of these heroines, would become similarly vulnerable to seduction and ruin. This line of reasoning underlay Lydia Maria Child's warning that such novels could irrevocably corrupt young readers: She asserted that the young female reader of "shameless stories ... has in fact prostituted her mind by familiarity with vice."[10] Child suggests that novels of this kind cause the depravity of impressionable female readers: In allowing salacious stories access to her mind and imagination, the female reader has effectively allowed herself to be penetrated by corrupt influences and has become intellectually, if not bodily, ruined.

In the nineteenth century, sentimentalism shifted its focus from bodily seduction to narratives about the maturation and socialization of isolated young women. In narratives about female development, sentimental novels sought to leverage the presumed imitativeness and susceptibility of young women, using wholesome narratives to encourage imitative readers to embark on similar campaigns of self-improvement. Sentimental literature markedly changed its contents in this period, but it nonetheless retained a linkage with the reading female body. Observers noted that nineteenth-century sentimental texts frequently elicited bodily responses in receptive readers, though these responses tended to be sighs and tears rather than seduction and impregnation. One early critic commented on "the 'hand-kerchiefy' feeling" of sentimentalism, which seemed designed to elicit such a bodily response in readers.[11] In producing a visible corporeal response, sentimental texts ran the risk of exposing the female reader, making her private textual responses visible before an observing public. Sentimental texts occasionally acknowledge this effect on the reader: In Warner's *The*

*Wide, Wide World*, for instance, a physician interprets the flushed face of Mrs. Montgomery, the heroine's ailing mother, as bodily confirmation that she has been furtively reading a novel.[12] The embodied reading of sentimental literature became most closely associated with Stowe's *Uncle Tom's Cabin*, which was engineered to provoke sympathetic tears in the reader and which famously concluded by urging the reader to "feel right," thereby designating sensation, both bodily and affective, as the ideal outcome of reading and the seat of social change.

However, the association of embodied reading with the sentimental female reader would lead to the scholarly denunciation of this reading practice as mawkish and uncritical. As Jane Thrailkill notes, embodied reading fell out of favor at the urging of the New Critics, who contended that reading ought to be cerebral and unemotional and who reserved special contempt for such "physiological effect … as … the flowing of tears, visceral or laryngeal sensations," and the putatively lowbrow reading practices favored by "women's clubs."[13] In the decades following New Criticism, sentimental embodied reading received mockery even from some of the field's most influential critics.[14]

In producing bodily reactions, sentimentalism rendered the female reader legible to observers, and this phenomenon comports with the common sentimental perception of the human body as an intelligible, accurate record of character and disposition. In keeping with mainstream nineteenth-century view, sentimental texts contain countless examples attesting to a belief in the decipherability of the body. For instance, in Louisa May Alcott's *Little Women* (1868), Mr. March observes the visible changes that have occurred in his daughters' bodies during his absence in the Civil War, taking these changes as evidence of corresponding alterations in their character: He interprets the coarsening of his daughter Meg's hands as proof of her declining vanity and her hard work. Similarly, Fanny Fern's autobiographical novel *Ruth Hall* (1854) includes a lengthy phrenological reading of the heroine's skull, in which her bodily features provide a thorough inventory of her abilities and temperament. Likewise, the face of Gabriella Lynn, the heroine of Caroline Lee Hentz's *Ernest Linwood* (1856), perfectly reflects her precocity, as with the "peculiar depth of expression" in her "wise" eyes.[15] In *Uncle Tom's Cabin*, Stowe mocked the misinterpretation of bodily signifiers in the slave trader Haley's comments about Tom's forehead: "'Look at his head; them high forrads allays shows calculatin niggers, that'll do any kind o' thing.'"[16] With his willing submission to authority, Tom altogether lacks the disposition to treachery that Haley attributes to him, and Stowe suggests not only that Haley is a bad reader of the body but also that Tom's high forehead instead denotes his noble character. Stowe mocks

Haley's ignorance, but her novel elsewhere registers a similar inclination to interpret the enslaved body and discern markers of ability and intelligence in bodily traces of racial heritage. She notes, for instance, that the biracial slave George Harris inherited from "one of the proudest families in Kentucky . . . a set of fine European features, and a high, indomitable spirit," suggesting that both his handsomeness and manly refusal to submit to slavery are bequests from his white father (182). By extension, she also suggests that compliance with enslavement was an inherited biological trait that rendered Africans naturally docile.

## The Vulnerable Body

Eighteenth-century sentimental novels dramatized the sexual vulnerability of the young female body, and later nineteenth-century works retained this concern, though they seldom articulate this worry outright. Instead, these anxieties often go unspoken and implicitly underlie the advice given by concerned caregivers, who attempt to institute restraints on girls' conduct and self-presentation. For instance, in *The Hidden Hand* (1859), E. D. E. N. Southworth's somewhat parodic treatment of the sentimental novel, Major Warfield forbids Capitola, his unruly ward from solitary horse riding, the reasoning for this directive becoming evident when she disobeys him and encounters the menacing Craven Le Noir, who tries to force her off her horse for evidently nefarious purposes. The motherless girl, unsupervised and untaught, is presumed to be particularly vulnerable to malevolent influence, and, in teaching young female readers to follow prudent advice and cultural convention, sentimental texts implicitly offered protection from predation. For instance, Child insisted that girls must never be allowed to present themselves in disarray: She wrote, "Buttons off, muslins wrinkled, the petticoat below the edge of the gown, shoe strings broken, and hair loose and straggling, should never pass unnoticed" (138). Child never explains why she finds untidiness intolerable, but, in urging mothers to enlist their husbands in offering "[s]erious advice," she reveals that her prohibition derives from concern about the male response to such an appearance. Child's description of untidiness evokes not only undress but also the aftermath of sexual violence, with clothing items torn and the hair disheveled. An untidy, careless appearance, she suggests, may convey a lack of concern for the care of the body, and it may thus invite the attentions of men with improper designs who discern vulnerability in the bedraggled young woman. Child thus characterizes untidiness as both a cause and an effect of sexual assault. In instructing young readers to comport with normative standards of conduct and appearance, sentimental texts thus work not only to socialize readers in mainstream convention but also to protect them from sexual predators on the lookout for possible targets. In so doing, they place the onus of sexual assault prevention on young women and even implicitly blame them for attracting the notice of predators.

Sentimental novels dramatized these dangers with the occasional character who preys on vulnerable young women, such as Mr. Saunders, the cruel salesman in Warner's *The Wide, Wide World*, and Arthur in *Elsie Dinsmore*, who delights in inflicting pain on the hapless Elsie. However, it is primarily in writings about slavery that sentimental literature most overtly addressed sexual predation and vulnerability. Stowe's *Uncle Tom's Cabin* offered the most expansive treatment of this topic, with innumerable enslaved women whose beauty attracts the attentions of men intent on making them their sex slaves. The novel begins with the slave trader Haley taking notice of Eliza's comely body and asking to purchase her, thereby seeking to dash her wholesome life as a doting mother and consign her to a wretched life of sexual exploitation. Later in the novel, the enslaved woman Susan watches in terror as a slaver appraises her daughter Emmeline's body, knowing full well the fate that awaits her daughter if she is "sold to a life of shame" (472). Stowe dramatizes the fate of such women in the embittered figure of Cassy, who has survived years of sex trafficking and admits to killing her infant daughter to prevent her from enduring a similar fate. With these characters, Stowe revealed how slavery commodified the intrinsic sexual vulnerability of isolated young women and reduced them to mere sexualized bodies in thrall to rapacious male desire.

*Uncle Tom's Cabin* was followed by innumerable publications that sought to capitalize on its popularity and offer rejoinders to Stowe's claims. Numerous sentimental texts – among them Hentz's *The Planter's Northern Bride* (1852), Mary Henderson Eastman's *Aunt Phillis's Cabin* (1852), and Augusta Jane Evans's *Macaria* (1864) – sought to justify slavery and present it as preferable to the labor conditions and racism of the north. Advocates for other women's causes tried to enlist sentimentality to publicize comparable dangers to the female body. Critics of Mormon polygamy, for instance, claimed that it operated as a form of white slavery that similarly preyed on vulnerable young women and led to sexual exploitation, and advocates sought to mobilize sentimentalism's reformist authority by recruiting Stowe to their cause, an effort that resulted in Stowe's preface to Fanny Stenhouse's memoir of polygamy, *Tell It All* (1872).[17] Harriet Jacobs similarly tried to enlist Stowe's help for her memoir, *Incidents in the Life of a Slave Girl* (1861), which depicts her struggles to evade sexual predation and her decision to become the mistress of another prominent white man. Stowe objected to the commodification of the enslaved woman's body, but she was not above conscripting these women's sufferings for her own purposes: Stowe failed to respond to Jacobs's request and instead appropriated her story for *A Key to Uncle Tom's Cabin* (1853), which provided factual corroboration for Stowe's novel.

Following Stowe's disappointing response, Child instead sponsored Jacobs's account, and in her preface Child used the language of bodily undress to explain her support for Jacobs's narrative. She wrote, "This peculiar phase of Slavery has generally been kept veiled; but the public ought to be made acquainted with its monstrous features, and I willingly take the responsibility of presenting them with the veil withdrawn."[18] With her metaphor of unveiling, Child intimates that customs of propriety have long shielded sexual slavery from public view and thereby enabled its continuation, and she suggests that some forms of scandalous narrative exposure are necessary to effect social change. Thirty years earlier, Child insisted that young female readers avoid sexually scandalous narratives, but she here suggests that concerns about the bodily dangers posed by reading are partially culpable for the continuing atrocities of slavery, which are "so foul, that our ears are too delicate to listen to them" (748). White women have been insulated from these facts because of the enduring belief that their bodies are too fragile to receive such information without sustaining damage, and she suggests that the protection of the white reader's body has come at the expense of the enslaved woman's safety, providing a discursive shield for her continuing sexual abuse. Overturning both her own prior claims as well as a century of prohibition, Child suggests that the reading of Jacobs's sexually explicit narrative may help protect the bodies of enslaved women and correct major social ills.

Child's comments on the bodily delicacy of middle-class white women accord with the conventional sentimental portrayal of feminine virtue, for sentimental texts often depict devout, righteous women as particularly prone to illness and bodily affliction. Sentimental novels commonly include the untimely death of a beloved female figure – such as Alice Humphreys in Warner's *The Wide, Wide World* and Eva St. Clare of *Uncle Tom's Cabin* – whose tutelage and example help socialize the wayward orphan girl. Even the most stalwart female authority figure may be vanquished by the inherent vulnerability of the female body. However, this standard convention of the sentimental novel – the premature death of the virtuous young woman – also conveys some important information about the limits and even dangers of sympathy, the emotional disposition that scholars have long recognized as the affective cornerstone of sentimental literature. As with the suggestive title of Brown's foundational sentimental novel *The Power of Sympathy*, sentimental texts commonly depict the transformative powers of fellow feeling, both in their narration of the heroines' developing sympathies for the needs of others and in their efforts to provoke the reader's own sympathetic identification with the characters' sufferings. Shared sentiment is a fundamental good in sentimental literature, and scholars have shown how sympathy underlies such varied entities as nationalism, campaigns of social reform, abolition, and even consumerism.[19] However, the persistent susceptibility of sympathetic young women to illness and premature death suggests that sympathy may also pose a significant bodily hazard. Sympathy denotes the possession of a shared feeling, but this affect evidently entailed both emotions as well as bodily sensations, for medical discourse throughout the nineteenth century commonly used the term "sympathy" to denote shared bodily conditions. To be sure, sentimental texts often depict illness as an incitement to sympathy, as with Hentz's novel *Ernest Linwood*, in which illness draws an isolated family out of its seclusion and leads them to rely on their neighbors in their hour of need: The novel's narrator comments, "We felt the drawings of that golden chain of sympathy which binds together the great family of mankind."[20] At the same time, however, sentimental texts often characterize sympathy as a potential biohazard that enables exposure to contagion, for the possession of mutual sentiment often leads to shared bodily ailment. Priscilla Wald reminds us that the word "contagion" etymologically means "to touch together," and it thus suggestively invokes the shared bodily sensation that often underlies sympathy. Even while encouraging sympathy, especially for the sick, sentimental texts warn that openness to the feelings of others might also lead to infection and even death.[21]

The bodily perils of sympathy underlie Stowe's *Dred* (1856), which depicts a slave uprising modeled on the Nat Turner rebellion. When the novel begins, the orphaned heroine, Nina Gordon, has allowed herself to become engaged to three different men, and as a result she is repeatedly described as a "coquette": This description invokes Hannah Webster Foster's famed early sentimental novel *The Coquette*, and it suggests that Nina carelessly toys with others' feelings and, like Foster's Eliza Wharton, runs the risk of seduction and infamy.[22] However, Nina's life takes a different turn when she witnesses the dead body of a young mother who, like herself, also hailed from an elite family but who, in keeping with the narrative template of the seduction novel, made a disastrous marital choice and died in neglect and ruin. Nina recognizes her similarity to Mrs. Cripps and remarks, "To think that that poor woman was just such a girl as I am, and used to be just so full of life, and never thought any more than I do that she should lie there all cold and dead!"[23] Nina's act of sympathetic identification causes her to abandon her coquettish ways, acquire religious piety, and become sympathetic to the sufferings of others. Nina's sentimental transformation becomes complete when her household is overrun with cholera and she unselfishly cares for others, putting her own health at risk. As a result of these unselfish attentions, Nina dies unexpectedly halfway through the novel: Sympathetic identification with another woman's bodily mortality causes Nina's maturation and moral awakening, but it also leads to her own premature death. In this respect, *Dred* somewhat revises the longstanding belief that exposure to scandalous narrative could cause young women to imitate and reproduce these events in their own lives. Hearing Mrs. Cripps's sad story and seeing her body impel Nina to make changes in her own life, and, like this tragic figure, she too dies prematurely and tragically. However, Nina does so not because she has allowed herself to be seduced but because her new capacity for sympathy has exposed her to contagion. Justine Murison has shown that the body in the nineteenth century was understood to be "open" and "susceptible," and sentimental fiction, in both the seduction novel and in its later nineteenth-century iteration, suggests that this was particularly the case with the female body, which was endangered not just by contagious illness but by other people's feelings.[24] Whether through the submission to seduction or through sympathy, the sentimental heroine typically remains fundamentally permeable and capable of allowing other people's sensations – whether emotional or corporeal – to puncture her defenses and overtake her body. Feelings in sentimentalism may be contagious, and this exposure may, at best, render the young woman more pious and sympathetic, but, at worst, it may also render her seduced, impregnated, or fatally infected. The powers of sympathy, sentimentalism reminds us, carry with them the power of life and death.

## The Disabled Body

Bodily malady did not always conclude in death; it instead often resulted in impairment. For instance, Beth March in Alcott's *Little Women* contracts scarlet fever after caring for an immigrant family's dying infant, and, though she survives, she spends the rest of her life in delicate health. As a result, the vulnerability of the body in sentimental literature also manifested in widespread disability, as innumerable characters manage such long-term conditions as impaired mobility, blindness, and degenerative disease. Scholars have noted that the disabled often reside only at the margins of the literary text, in "secondary or even minor parts," where they function primarily to induce pity in fellow characters and readers alike.[25] This is frequently the case in sentimentalism, in which the disabled provide a site for the practice of sympathetic caregiving, as with, for instance, Warner's *Wide, Wide World*, in which Ellen Montgomery attends to her impaired and housebound grand-mother in concert with her growing piety.[26] In this respect, the impaired often occupy narratively instrumental roles in which they merely provide testcases for the heroine's developing sentimental maturation, as she learns to subordinate her own desires and provide attentive care for those in need. Perhaps because the disabled are so often objects of care, sentimental litera-ture also included innumerable malingerers – such as Marie St. Clare in *Uncle Tom's Cabin* and Mrs. Dean in Alcott's "Psyche's Art" (1868) – who falsely claim bodily infirmity in order to attract the attentions and sympathy that accompany impairment. Where the genuinely impaired are pitiable and sympathetic, these malingerers instead become the subjects of mockery and disdain.

Sentimental literature coincided with the mid-century development of enduring medical systems of classification, which devised new diagnostic standards of bodily normality and which deemed the atypical body abnor-mal and thus in need of clinical treatment; bodily diversity, that is, became pathologized in the mid-century.[27] Amid this change, numerous mid-century writers portrayed the atypical body as corporeal confirmation of the intrinsic monstrosity of the disabled, as with, for instance, the hunchbacked Roger Chillingworth in Nathaniel Hawthorne's *The Scarlet Letter* (1850) and Captain Ahab in Herman Melville's *Moby-Dick* (1851). In medical dis-course and in such literary depictions, disability and bodily difference often appear unwholesome and unnatural, and these depictions contributed to a growing clinical opinion that disabled persons should be consigned to insti-tutions where they might remain out of public view and avoid posing an undue burden on others.

Sentimental texts often treat the impaired as mere narrative props, but they did not sanction this emerging view. On the contrary, sentimentalism more commonly consecrates the disabled, elevating them as saintly models of patient suffering who have endured terrible travails and learned vital religious lessons that other characters strain to acquire. Furthermore, senti-mentalism typically upholds caregiving as the apex of "true womanhood," to use Barbara Welter's famous phrase.[28] Within sentimental literature, the adult woman's portfolio of responsibilities includes caring not only for children and households but also for the elderly, the ill, and the dependent. As one skeptical critic notes, the sentimental woman's proper "place was in the sick chamber and in the squalid abodes of poverty and suffering," where she seeks to alleviate suffering and administer care.[29] Sentimental texts depict the home as the appropriate site of caregiving, though scholars have noted that sentimental nurturance would eventually contribute to a national supervisory ethos that sought to intervene in the lives of the poor and minorities, and in this respect sentimentality ultimately underlay the institutional management of bodily difference emerging in this era.[30]

In this way, sentimentalism sharply deviates from the emerging medical rhetoric of bodily abnormality, and it instead characterizes impairment as a normal and even inevitable consequence of bodily vulnerability. In sentimental literature, anyone may become sick or impaired at any time, though, to be sure, the particularly virtuous seem especially likely to contract fatal illness. In Cummins's *The Lamplighter*, for instance, illness and accident seem to lie in wait behind every corner, with virtually every character enduring a devastating sickness or disability: The main character, Gertrude Flint, survives several serious bouts of illness, and both of her surrogate parents, Trueman Flint and Emily Graham, are impaired due to catastrophic accident. The body in *The Lamplighter* is fundamentally fragile, and everyone – men and women, adults and children, the rich and the poor – is equally at risk of impairment and dependence.[31]

Where other mid-century novels portrayed the disabled body as a marker of wickedness, *The Lamplighter* suggests that bodily affliction may provide a conduit to religious salvation. In describing the accident that caused her blindness, Emily Graham admits that in her early life she had pursued only worldly pleasures, but her impairment led her to renounce her attachment to material matters and devote herself to the invisible, unseen world of the spiritual. In this respect, blindness only enhanced Emily's spiritual development, for it required her to detach from worldly pleasures and find meaning and value in the unseen. In addition, Emily intimates that, within the Christian worldview, affliction, impairment, and dependence are the fundamental state of all human beings. Happiness amid life's suffering may be available, she asserts, "only [to those] who have learned submission; those who, in the severest afflictions, see the hand of a loving Father, and, obedient to his will, kiss the chastening rod."[32] Citing the Protestant doctrine of affliction, she depicts suffering as a providential, purposeful gift from a loving god and an opportunity to learn submission to the divine will. For Emily, suffering is inevitable for everyone, and it entails the acceptance of limitations and dependence, both of which are common conditions of disability: As she describes it, the life of the devout Christian is uncannily similar to that of the impaired. In this respect, the disabled have a decided religious advantage over their body-typical peers, for their bodily afflictions compel them to submit to the divine will and accept their limitations while the body-typical characters in the novel instead struggle to achieve this acquiescence. In confirmation of the particular advantage of the impaired in this religious difficulty, Gertrude feels a flicker of envy while hearing Emily recount the impact of blindness on her religious piety, as she longs for a similar "endurance of trial": It is "through suffering only that we are made perfect," Gertrude comes to realize.[33] An imperfect body may lead to the perfection of character and piety, a view that markedly distinguishes sentimentalism from that of much contemporary fiction.

Ultimately, however, sentimental literature repeatedly suggests that this religious perfection entails the renunciation of the body altogether.[34] Countless sentimental texts describe the illness and final decline of the righteous as a process of sloughing off bodily matters and achieving a spirituality that concludes in union with the divine. This common trope in sentimentalism is often referred to as "the angel in the house," a moniker taken from the title of Coventry Patmore's 1856 poem, and it denotes the idealized sentimental figure whose body deteriorates in tandem with advancing spiritual growth. In *Little Women*, for instance, Beth March's "soul grew strong" as "the wreck of her frail body" weakens.[35] Stowe similarly enlists this trope in her depiction of saintly Eva St. Clare's death, but she also adapted it for the death of Tom, in which he asserts that Simon Legree's power is confined only to the body while his heart and piety remain untouched by his abuse: Tom tells Legree, "'after ye've killed the body, there an't no more ye can do. And O, there's all ETERNITY to come, after that!'" (539). Amid all of sentimentalism's advice and concern for the management of the female body, sentimentalism repeatedly suggests that the ideal condition is characterized by pious disembodiment and liberation from bodily demands.

## NOTES

1 Elaine Scarry, *The Body in Pain: The Making and Unmaking of the World* (New York: Oxford University Press, 1985), 5, original emphasis.

2 Rosemarie Garland-Thomson, *Extraordinary Bodies: Figuring Disability in American Culture and Literature* (New York: Columbia University Press, 1997), 37.

3 For a discussion of adoption in sentimental literature, see Cindy Weinstein, *Family, Kinship, and Sympathy in Nineteenth-Century American Literature* (Cambridge: Cambridge University Press, 2004).

4 Nathaniel Hawthorne to William D. Ticknor, January 19, 1855, in *Letters, 1853–1856*, ed. Thomas Woodson et al., vol. 17, *The Centenary Edition of the Works of Nathaniel Hawthorne* (Columbus: Ohio State University Press, 1962), 304.

5 See, for instance, Lauren Berlant, *The Female Complaint: The Unfinished Business of Sentimentality in America Culture* (Durham, NC: Duke University Press, 2008).

6 Elizabeth Barnes, *States of Sympathy: Seduction and Democracy in the American Novel* (New York: Columbia University Press, 1997), 8; Bruce Burgett,

*Sentimental Bodies: Sex, Gender, and Citizenship in the Early Republic* (Princeton, NJ: Princeton University Press, 1998), 3–4; Shirley Samuels, *Romances of the Republic: Women, the Family, and Violence in the Literature of the Early American Nation* (New York: Oxford University Press, 1996), 5ff.

7 Susanna Rowson, *Charlotte Temple*, ed. Patti Cowell (Boston: Bedford, 2011), 61.

8 Barnes, *States of Sympathy*, 8.

9 Sari Altschuler, *The Medical Imagination: Literature and Health in the Early United States* (Philadelphia: University of Pennsylvania Press, 2018), 54–55.

10 Lydia Maria Child, *The Mother's Book* (1831, reprint; New York: Arno, 1972), 152.

11 Herbert Ross Brown, *The Sentimental Novel in America 1789–1860* (Durham, NC: Duke University Press, 1940), vii.

12 Gillian Silverman, *Bodies and Books: Reading and the Fantasy of Communion in Nineteenth-Century America* (Philadelphia: University of Pennsylvania Press, 2012), 139.

13 Jane F. Thrailkill, *Affecting Fictions: Mind, Body, and Emotion in American Literary Realism* (Cambridge: Harvard University Press, 2007), 4; John Crowe Ransom, "Criticism, Inc," *The Norton Anthology of Theory and Criticism*, ed. Vincent B. Leitch et al. (New York: W. W. Norton, 2001), 1115, 1116.

14 See, for instance, Ann Douglas, *The Feminization of American Culture* (1977; New York: Doubleday, 1988), 4.

15 Caroline Lee Hentz, *Ernest Linwood; A Novel* (Boston: John P. Jewett, 1856), 23.

16 Harriet Beecher Stowe, *Uncle Tom's Cabin or, Life among the Lowly*, ed. Ann Douglas (New York: Penguin, 1981), 182.

17 For further discussion, see Claudia Stokes, *The Altar at Home: Sentimental Literature and Nineteenth-Century American Religion* (Philadelphia: University of Pennsylvania Press, 2014), 142–159.

18 Lydia Maria Child, Introduction to "Incidents in the Life of a Slave Girl" by Harriet Jacobs, *Slave Narratives* (New York: Library of America, 2000), 748.

19 Marianne Noble has recently offered a thorough reappraisal of the dynamics of sympathy in nineteenth-century American literature. See Marianne Noble, *Rethinking Sympathy and Human Contact in Nineteenth-Century American Literature: Hawthorne, Douglass, Stowe, Dickinson* (Cambridge: Cambridge University Press, 2019).

20 Hentz, *Ernest Linwood*, 46.

21 Priscilla Wald, *Contagious: Cultures, Carriers, and the Outbreak Narrative* (Durham, NC: Duke University Press, 2008), 12.

22 Harriet Beecher Stowe, *Dred; A Tale of the Great Dismal Swamp*, vol. 1 of 2 (1856, reprint; Grosse Point: Scholarly Press, 1968), 36.

23 Ibid., 136.

24 Justine S. Murison, *The Politics of Anxiety in Nineteenth-Century American Literature* (Cambridge: Cambridge University Press, 2011), 3.

25 Garland-Thomson, *Extraordinary Bodies*, 82.

26 Mary Klages, *Woeful Afflictions: Disability and Sentimentality in Victorian America* (Philadelphia: University of Pennsylvania Press, 1999), 4; Thomson, *Extraordinary Bodies*, 81.

27 Douglas C. Baynton, "Disability and the Justification of Inequality in American History," in *The New Disability History: American Perspectives*, ed. Paul K. Longmore and Lauri Umansky (New York: New York University Press, 2001), 35–36; Lennard J. Davis, *Enforcing Normalcy: Disability, Deafness, and the Body* (London: Verso, 1995), 23–49; Ellen Samuels, *Fantasies of Identification: Disability, Gender, Race* (New York: New York University Press, 2014), 2.

28 Barbara Welter, "The Cult of True Womanhood, 1820–1860," *American Quarterly* 18 (Summer 1966): 151–174.

29 Brown, *Sentimental Novel*, 113.

30 See, for instance, Laura Wexler, "Tender Violence: Literary Eavesdropping, Domestic Fiction, and Educational Reform," in *The Cultures of Sentiment: Gender, Race, and Sentimentality in Nineteenth-Century America*, ed. Shirley Samuels (New York: Oxford University Press, 1992), 9–38.

31 I discuss *The Lamplighter's* attitudes toward disability more fully in my essay "'Sinful Creature, Full of Weakness: The Theology of Disability in Cummins's *The Lamplighter*," *Studies in American Fiction* 43 (Fall 2016): 139–159.

32 Maria Susanna Cummins, *The Lamplighter* (New Brunswick, NJ: Rutgers University Press, 1988), 104.

33 Ibid., 321, 322.

34 For a fuller discussion of this phenomenon, see Nina Baym, Introduction to *Woman Fiction: A Guide to Novels by and about Women in America 1820–1870*, 2nd ed. (Urbana: University of Illinois, 1993); Nancy F. Cott, "Passionlessness: An Interpretation of Victorian Sexual Ideology, 1790–1850," *Signs*, 4, no. 2 (Winter 1978): 219–236; Marianne Noble, *The Masochistic Pleasures of Sentimental Literature* (Princeton: Princeton University Press, 2000), 22–37.

35 Louisa M. Alcott, *Little Women or Meg, Jo, Beth and Amy*, ed. Anne K. Phillips (New York: W. W. Norton, 2004), 325.

# 3

## MAURICE WALLACE

# Slavery, Disability, and the Black Body/White Body Complex in the American Slave Narrative

> In the very effort to recognize the slave as person, Blackness was reinscribed as pained and punitive embodiment and Black humanity was constituted as a state of injury and punishment.
> —Saidiya V. Hartman, *Scenes of Subjection: Terror, Slavery, and Self-Making in Nineteenth Century America*

The sufferings of the enslaved in the Americas and Europe in the eighteenth and nineteenth centuries were myriad and complex. They were general and particular – which is to say, on the one hand, elemental to the slave condition, and, on the other, differential according to age, sex, and (though often understated) geography. The regular allusions to the formerly enslaved narrators' "life and sufferings" in the titles and subtitles of their published testimonies – Briton Hammon's *A Narrative of the Uncommon Sufferings, and Surprizing Deliverance of Briton Hammon, a Negro Man* (1760), for instance, or *The Life, History, and Unparalleled Sufferings of John Jea, the African Preacher* (1811) by John Jea – foreshadowed chroniclings of unspeakable abuses to the captives' bodies and minds. While these violations of the physical and psychological personhood of the enslaved were so severe as to be mostly indivisible categories of Black captive injury, it is undeniable that they were borne on and by the body. Even as the most significant reflections on the body in antebellum American culture – Hortense Spillers, Walter Johnson, Thavolia Glymph, and Saidiya Hartman included – devote invaluable attention to the bodies of Black women and men in bondage, Toni Morrison also made clear in *Playing in the Dark: Whiteness and the Literary Imagination* (1992) that Black captivity had deep consequences for enactments of white embodiment too. Thus, in this chapter, I show how "the routinized violence of slavery," as Hartman put it, acted not only to write white power onto Black skins as an everyday display and reassurance of white domination over the antebellum social imaginary but also to demonstrate white racial supremacy as ensured and preserved by physical assertions of white disciplinary power over the material and social worlds of the nineteenth century.

Perhaps there is no more important propaedeutic to this abiding complex of white and Black bodily spites and sufferings in the nineteenth century than *Playing in the Dark*. Distilled from a series of public lectures delivered at Harvard in 1992, Morrison reflects on the imaginative possibilities created by the tropic devotion of so many nineteenth-century American writers to that "dark, abiding, signing Africanist presence,"[1] which has tended to haunt the self-regard of so much (white) American literature. Even though Morrison depicts this racial hauntology in American literature metaphorically as a "disabling virus within literary discourse,"[2] the virologic analogy extends from a bodily one that is rather more implied than asserted. If the force of Blackness on the conscious and unconscious antebellum imagination was such that it passed through to the very lifeblood of American identity, as Morrison argues, then it was the white racial body through which it passed. This "disabled" the fiction of white identity as a corporeal superiority, even as Black racial bodies, which incited white bodily angst, were made to answer the panic as imagined prostheses for the fear, fact, or feeling of white debility.

Such an instigation routinized violence inflicted on captive Black bodies, a pattern that obtains across canonical works in Morrison's lectures: from Edgar Allen Poe's *Narrative of Arthur Gordan Pym* (1838) and Mark Twain's *Huckleberry Finn* (1884) to William Faulkner's *Absalom! Absalom!* (1936) and Ernest Hemingway's *To Have and Have Not* (1937). None exemplifies Morrison's formulation of American Africanism at the level of the body, however, more vividly than Willa Cather's 1940 *Sapphira and the Slave Girl*. Although written in the first half of the twentieth century, Cather's last novel "has the shape and feel of a tale written or experienced much earlier."[3] Inasmuch as it is set in the Southland of Back Creek, Virginia, in 1856, *Sapphira and the Slave Girl* represents a kind of looking back, and thus constitutes a study in itself of the white body/Black body complex to which the antebellum ex-slave narrative had given prior testimony. I take Cather, then, to be an aid to, but not a replacement for, our understanding of the interracial dynamics of corporeal power and punishment in the slave regime, and especially the bodily effects of the madness of white supremacy on white racial bodies in the antebellum period.

Morrison lamented that critics have mostly dismissed Cather's novel as a late-career letdown. "I suspect that the 'problem' of *Sapphira and the Slave Girl*," she wrote, "is not that it has a weaker vision or is the work of a weaker mind. The problem is in trying to come to terms critically and artistically with the novel's concerns: the power and license of a white slave mistress over her female slave."[4] This power Cather seems to have approached with a certain baldness impervious to any other meaning but what is portrayed. "How can that content be subsumed by some other meaning?" Morrison wanted to know. "How can the story of a white mistress be severed from a consideration of race and violence,"[5] as traditional literary scholarship has been wont to do? *Playing in the Dark* does not so much recover *Sapphira and the Slave Girl* as take it on its own terms, terms over which Cather herself may or may not have maintained control. It is as if in *Playing in the Dark* Cather's late work finally received the hearing critics refused it a half century earlier, being unwilling or unable to treat its "content" as a critical matter.

The plot of *Sapphira and the Slave Girl* centers on the obsessive envy and spiteful machinations of Sapphira Colbert, an embittered white woman slaveholder confined to a wheelchair by a disabling case of edema, to ruin the nubile slave-girl, Nancy, whom she has established, purely by invention, is her husband's young odalisque. Sapphira is (mostly) wrong about the imagined affair between Nancy and her husband, Henry, but her paranoia is unchecked. Thusly convinced of Nancy and Henry's involvement, she conspires to welcome her randy nephew to town, expecting that the young lecher will have his own way (violently if necessary) with the young girl Nancy, punishing her and spoiling her desirability to Henry. Eventually, Nancy takes Sapphira's adult daughter into her confidence when she cannot endure any more of the nephew's harassment. With Rachel Colbert Blake's help, Nancy flees her lascivious pursuer and the Colbert estate on the Underground Railroad to Canada.

Although it is Sapphira Colbert's nephew, Martin, who is the active threat to Nancy's physical safety, Morrison sees the central conflict of the novel as that between Nancy and "the reckless, unabated power of [Sapphira] gathering identity unto herself from the wholly available and serviceable lives of Africanist others."[6] Given the Mistress's disability, Morrison might just as easily have substituted "bodies" for "lives" and not altered her reading of the white body/Black body complex in *Sapphira and the Slave Girl*. Sapphira's jealousy, after all, lies in Henry's prizing the girl's nimbleness and youthful agility ("Nancy is quiet and quick," he'd boast to his wife[7]). Sapphira, by contrast, is, in Morrison's words, "confined to the prison of her defeated flesh,"[8] an ironic reversal of the physical fortunes of the novel's free white woman and her captive parlor maid not the least bit lost on Sapphira. Unlike her feeble mistress anchored in her place at the dining table or upon her bed, Nancy is regularly described as "runnin' down" (814) to look after Henry's mill room, "scurr[ying] down the long hall and out of the kitchen" (838) of the house, and "run[ning] through ... the yard" (897) to Mrs. Blake, "spring[ing] from her chair" (898) to express exasperation at the nephew's lewd, unremitting hounding – all motor acts defying the fact of her enslavement to Sapphira. Fleet-footed, Nancy is a practiced fugitive well before she absconds north. Her flight initiates a second, ever more acute, crisis for Sapphira. Nancy having now cut and run, Sapphira's body is twice lost to her – once by physical impairment and again by Nancy's stolen serviceability as Sapphira's companionate. Although the mistress surmises early in the novel that she might rid herself of the slave girl's perceived threat to the Colberts' marriage by selling Nancy to an interested neighbor, the proposal, rejected outright by Henry, only underlines the claim she has on Nancy's body as hers to direct or dispose of at will. "It is after all hers, this slave woman's body, in a way that her own invalid flesh is not,"[9] Morrison would stress.

But the projection of her physical-become-sexual disability onto Nancy – Henry keeps a separate bed in the mill room away from the main house, which is Nancy's task to arrange daily – is not the novel's most damning charge against the white will to power over captive Blacks. If, in the judg-ment of Cather's coevals, *Sapphira and the Slave Girl* is a failed novel, it is not hard to imagine that the fault lies, first, in its representation of an unbounded exercise of power physically exacted upon the captive bodies of the enslaved and, second, in its demonstration of how this power weakened whiteness itself into an invalid identity. It seems scarcely an accident that Sapphira's final dialogue in the novel should be followed closely by an epilogue, set twenty-five years on, that paints a local picture of the Civil War's consequence on the land and society of Back Creek. For Sapphira's disability – which worsens on Nancy's escape north – is the accrued handicap of Southern slavers gone to war to preserve the very institution whose captive Blacks would greatly expand its strength in battle but which they distrust, for obvious reasons, to call into service for itself.[10]

Although *Sapphira and the Slave Girl* is a fiction and falls well outside the immediacy of antebellum authorship, it is an historically inflected explor-ation of the psychic and somatic serviceabilities of Black flesh to the physical assertions of white power in the antebellum era. It is a novel of historical recovery, one might say, intent upon a reconstruction of slavery's white body/Black body complex. And yet, despite Cather's illumination of the bodily effects of unrestrained white power on its wielder – exceptional as it is in American letters – *Sapphira and the Slave Girl* perhaps takes too much (or too little) for granted where it concerns the effects of violent subjection on the captive body. Nancy escapes her tormenter terrorized but physically unscathed, a happy outcome indeed but one inconsistent with the record of Black testimony to the physical strains of targeted Black womanhood under slavery. Implicitly, Harriet Jacobs's *Incidents in the Life of a Slave Girl* (1861) testifies to Cather's sentimentalization of the bodily hazards of the slave's condition. As a Black woman's first-person account of the everyday psychological and physical duress experienced by enslaved women, thematically *Incidents in the Life of a Slave Girl* anticipates *Sapphira and the Slave Girl* (and might well have been a source for Cather), especially insofar as it testifies to the slave girl's sexual insecurity in the slaveholding environment.[11] What *Incidents* discloses, though – wholly obscured in *Sapphira and the Slave Girl* – is the extent of the Black body's susceptibility to the injurious threats of white disciplinary power in flight and "freedom" as well as in captivity.

Importantly, Jacobs's *Incidents* does not neglect the enervating effects of profligate white power violently exercised on captive Black bodies. Escaped to New York, Linda Brent, the author's alias, encounters an old acquaintance, a fugitive named Luke she remembers from the vicinity of her old plantation home. Luke had been enslaved to a wealthy young master who fell "prey to the vices growing out of the 'patriarchal institution.'"[12] Rendered bedridden by the effects of his indulgences, the young sybarite – lame and without the full strength of his upper limbs – nevertheless "kept a cowhide beside him, and, for the most trivial occurrence, he would order his attendant to bare his back, and kneel beside the couch, while he whipped him till his strength was exhausted" (158). With each lashing Luke bore on his back the writing of white dreams of unbounded authority over the Other, scenes of subjection stirred to sadistic affect by desperate, existential fears of racial revenge and the vanishing of whiteness itself as an identity and inheritance. At a still deeper level, however, Luke's offenses were so many projections of the corporal disobedience of his master's own infirm body against his own motive will. His master's whippings then could only be as self-flagellatory as they were maniacal and cruel. In Jacobs's memory of Luke in chains – "some days … not allowed to wear anything but his shirt, in order to be in readiness to be flogged" (158) – sadistic instincts merge with masochistic impulses as he whose "despotic habits were greatly increased by exasperation at his own helplessness" (158) – some "too filthy to be repeated" (159) – madly struggled to command corporal obedience again of Self and Other. And yet, try as he might, "the arm of [the] tyrant grew weaker, and was finally palsied" (159). The notion among nineteenth-century Anglo-Saxonists, especially, that "better bodies" were necessary "to perpetuate our institutions, insure a higher development of the individual, and advance the conditions of the race" could not have found a more staggering picture of the degenerative threat to white racial embodiment than this.[13] That a contemporaneous physical culture movement should enter the American scene intent upon counteracting a growing sense of the imagined hardiness of the white body going soft, then, is hardly any surprise.

Though rarely said aloud, it seems no small part of the physical vigor previously ascribed to white men, in particular, was withering on account of the prosthetic availability of the country's captive Blacks. If examples like the one Jacobs recalled on encountering Luke in New York did not in fact inspire the convergence of the physical culture movement with pseudo-scientific ideas about white racial dominance, then they were poised to embarrass even so much as a casual countenancing of the physical and biological superiority of whites as truthful. In chaining his bondsman to his bedside, Luke's debauched master repeated his own bodily imprisonment and disability of which Luke's fit body, even as he moved according to his master's self-serving orders, was an intolerable mockery.

But whereas the madness associated with the presumption and exercise of unbounded power by the master visited on the slave renders Luke's master finally disabled, Luke on the other hand escapes more debilitated than disabled. This differentiation of injuries follows from Jasbir K. Puar's recent study of the biopolitics of the modern liberal state, *The Right to Maim: Debility, Capacity, Disability* (2017). As I understand Puar, debility is vestibular to disability. "Debilitation" foregrounds the material and political conditions within which "disablement" is produced in "certain bodies and populations" having "greater risk to become disabled than others."[14] Put another way, debilitation differs from disability inasmuch as disability "hinges on a narrative of before and after for individuals who will eventually be identified as disabled," while debility refers to "the slow wearing down of populations" and is foreclosed from "the social, cultural, and political translation to disability" through which, today, modern liberal discourse promises inclusion, empowerment, and pride.[15] "Debility," Puar writes, "addresses injury and bodily exclusion that are endemic rather than epidemic or exceptional"; in other words, debility leaves certain bodies and populations in perpetual precarity "precisely through making them available for [visible and invisible] maiming."[16] Thus, even if Jacobs makes no note of Luke, the fugitive, showing any manifest signs of the unspeakable cruelties Massa Henry inflicted on his flesh, it is not possible that the "much-abused" (160) bondsman could not have gone uninjured when chained to Henry's bedside and repeatedly whipped. Moreover, his appearance in *Incidents* in the chapter titled "The Fugitive Slave Law" reflects the precarious condition of "freedom" in New York and the illegibility of Black disablement there as nothing other than the body's betrayal of the runaway from bondage, its injuries and impairments the certain proof of its captive history. One wonders, then, if the seeming health of Luke's "much-abused" body was not, rather, a performance of ableism and corporeal conformity to the leisured gait of free men so convincing as to be, finally, unremarkable.

"Poor Luke" may well have concealed the disablements of his body passing through New York's back streets since he has had to be especially artful, we learn, to steal away from the speculator into whose possession he fell upon his master's death. But the debilitation of that body, its inescapable proneness to bodily hurts, harms, and danger, would seem unmitigated by Luke's flight to the North. It is no surprise, then, that from New York, "a city of kidnappers" (159), Luke "went to Canada forthwith" (160).

As Luke's example in *Incidents* demonstrates, debility needn't be accompanied by obvious disability since the enslaved or fugitive body, to echo Puar, "might not be hailed as disabled" in the sense of the free white subject whose state is taken to be exceptional, aberrant, accidental – in a word, unlucky – but it hardly enjoys the range of corporeal and motor affordances of the able- or so-called better-bodied. Still, *Incidents in the Life of a Slave Girl* does not preclude debility's coextensiveness with Black disablement. For Jacobs herself is nothing if not the antebellum exemplar of the overlapping realization of debility and disability in the self-same body. In fact, if Sami Schalk is correct that disability, specifically, "can take on both concrete and metaphoric meanings in a text" – if it can "symbolize something other than disability while still being about disability"[17] – then Jacobs's struggle with "walk[ing] much" (140) after seven years' voluntary imprisonment in the narrow garret above the shed of her grandmother's house – a handicap of the legs and feet that "continued to trouble me with swelling" (140) long after escaping to New York – is both concretely "about" the fugitive's poor orthopedic health and, abstractly, a symbol of the permanence of Black debility. This critical double-valence – which, as Schalk argues, inheres in disability metaphors to distinguish them from ableist metaphors that exploit disability – is easily discernible in chapter XXIX. The chapter opens thusly:

> I hardly expect that the reader will credit me, when I affirm that I lived in that little dismal hole, almost deprived of light and air, and with no space to move my limbs, for nearly seven years. But it is a fact; and to me a sad one, even now; for my body still suffers the effects of that long imprisonment. (124)

More than once, Jacobs and her friends worried that she would "become a cripple" (107), secreted away so long in her grandmother's garret. By the time she is ready to quit her hiding place and flee the Flint plantation forever, their worry, it seems, has been slowly realized, even if Jacobs doesn't explicitly and finally take on the identity of the "cripple" she feared she'd become. Perhaps the "pains and aches in my cramped and stiffened limbs" (125), which Jacobs bemoans (again) only several sentences later, were not legible to antebellum disability discourse in a pained Black body because the figure of the invalid presumed an injured or infirmed body, a white body, safeguarded from social death by the compensatory aid of others. Following Ellen Samuels, "if we understand the [nineteenth-century] invalid as 'one who is served,'"[18] then there is no logic by which the injured or infirmed body of the Black slave may arrive at the condition or character of the sympathetic cripple in early disability thought. Oddly, her impairments issue not from an imagined accident of racial fate, as with white subjects of the period, but from the inexorable hazards of enslavement as racial destiny.

Except for the greater worries of representation associated with portraying Black subjects as unfit for freedom, Jacobs and not a few additional Black antebellum formerly enslaved narrators – including Frederick Douglass, Harriet Wilson, William and Ellen Craft, and Josiah Henson – might have contested the racist machinations of antebellum body politics more explicitly. This is not to say that these fugitive writers did not critique the whiteness of sentimental disablement. Schalk's case for disability metaphors as having both material and metaphorical capacity argues for a closer consideration of the possibility of a nineteenth-century tradition of Black disabilities thought and critique than either ableist Black or white literary criticism – or even white disabilities studies for that matter – has allowed. Somewhat muted by metaphor, Black disability is everywhere in antebellum African American writing. Even when it is scarcely legible as such, the conditions of Black debility are almost always indexed by a pained Black body, which, instead of eliciting sympathy, is heroically represented, tenacious, physically resilient but not unmarked by the disciplinary obsessiveness of white supremacy upon (the hint of) volitional Black bodies. In a way, the antebellum period in the United States – arguably, the long nineteenth century itself – has this self-same white body/Black body complex as one of its definitive historical features. Perhaps none makes this point so persuasively as historian Stefanie Hunt-Kennedy.

Although Hunt-Kennedy's *Between Fitness and Death: Disability and Slavery in the Caribbean* (2020) set itself the task of demonstrating, for one thing, "how disability functioned within the law to disable the enslaved, [and] to limit their mobility, freedom, and political autonomy"[19] in the eighteenth- and nineteenth-century British West Indies, neither her illumination of how physical and discursive production of Black disability in the British Caribbean was bound up with English imperial expansionism nor her preferred methodologies of archival recovery and disabilities analysis is unavailable or unsuited in the general sense to reflections on slavery in the United States. Indeed, many historians of US slavery have already devoted significant attention to the runaway slave advertisement in the United States, the Jamaican and Barbadian counterpart of which Hunt-Kennedy derived so much vital information from about material, psychological, and legal representation of the disabilities of enslaved Blacks in the Caribbean.[20] To extend a disabilities analysis to these primary and critical sources, especially under pressure of the overlapping discursivity of Blackness and disability as advanced by Black disabilities scholars like Schalk and Therí Pickens, seems a logical move for disabilities history and for an ever clearer picture of the violent everyday of racial slavery in the New World, as Hunt-Kennedy shows "how the conditions of enslavement produced disabled bodies and racialized ideas about disability."[21] Although I maintain that the figure of the invalid in early disabilities discourse in the United States was inextricable from a certain notion of leisure sufficient to the expectation of compensatory support or aid by others, it is incontestable that American and Caribbean slavery alike "undermined Africans' abilities"[22] in obvious and invisible ways.

In the antebellum ex-slave narrative in the United States, Josiah Henson's *The Life of Josiah Henson, Formerly a Slave, Now an Inhabitant of Canada as Narrated by Himself* (1849) and its expanded revisiting in *Truth Stranger Than Fiction: Father Henson's Story of His Own Life* (1858) illustrate the obvious harm done to captive Black bodies – including how such harm reflects the panic of white bodily depletion and invalidity stoked by the seeming indefatigability of Black muscular service to the white bodily ego. Henson's autobiographies draw a lurid picture of slavery's production of Black corporal disability. Although both narratives accord with scores of other formerly enslaved persons' testimonies in their common representation of the disabling and disfiguring sufferings of the enslaved, Henson shows the extent to which bondage physically "undermined Africans' abilities," from superior fitness to permanent motor defect, as few other formerly enslaved narrators have. In *The Life of Josiah Henson*, Henson boasts of having grown up from his youth "to be an uncommonly vigorous and healthy boy and man."[23] Notwithstanding the mean, uncaring conditions of the slaves' lot in the South, he proudly declares,

> I grew to be a robust and vigorous lad, and at fifteen years of age, there were few who could compete with me in work, or in sport – for not even the condition of a slave can altogether repress the animal spirits of the young negro. I was competent to all the work that was done upon the farm, and could run faster and farther, wrestle longer, and jump higher, than anybody about me. My master and my fellow slaves used to look upon me, and speak of me, as a wonderfully smart fellow, and prophecy the great things I should do when I became a man. (LJH, 7)

By the time he was nineteen or twenty, Henson would crow, "I was young, remarkably athletic and self-relying" (LJH, 14). And in a scene which can only recall Frederick Douglass's unforgettable fight with the overseer Covey, Henson too recalled staving off the overseer's lash by the combinatory force of will and "my physical power" (LJH, 16). Unlike young Douglass' thorough trouncing of Covey, however, Henson's successful parrying of Mr. Litton's bare-knuckled blows and wild-eyed cuffs was short-lived:

> [T]he cowardly overseer was availing himself of every opportunity to hit me over the head with his stick, which was not heavy enough to knock me down, though it drew blood freely. At length, tired of the length of the affray, he seized a stake, six or seven feetlong, from the fence, and struck at me with his whole strength. In attempting to ward off the blow, my right arm was broken, and I was brought to the ground; where repeated blows broke both my shoulder blades, and made the blood gush from my mouth copiously. The two Blacks begged him not to murder me, and he just left me as I was, telling me to learn what it was to strike a white man ... [I]t was not long before assistance arrived to convey me home. It may be supposed it was not done without some suffering on my part; as, besides my broken arm and the wounds on my head, I could feel and hear the pieces of my shoulder-blades grate against each other with every breath. No physician or surgeon was called to dress my wounds, and I never knew one to be called to a slave upon R.'s estate, on any occasion whatever, and have no knowledge of such a thing being done on any estate in the neighborhood. I was attended, if it may be called attendance, by my master's sister, who had some reputation in such affairs; and she splintered my arm, and bound up my back as well as she knew how, and nature did the rest. It was five months before I could work at all, and the first time I tried to plough, a hard knock of the colter against a stone, shattered my shoulder-blades again, and gave me even greater agony than at first. I have been unable to raise my hands to my head from that day to this.   (LJH, 17)

Whereas *The Life of Josiah Henson* is undivided, in the later *Truth Stranger Than Fiction*, Henson's memory of the assault by "Mr. L." (LJH, 16) is the central concern of the narrative's fifth chapter, "Maimed for Life." Very nearly repeating the original violence of the text – his father's public punishment by one hundred lashes and the severing of an ear for striking a white man – *The Life of Josiah Henson* relates not only two of the most brutal scenes of slavery's production of Black physical and mental disability – Henson reports his father "became utterly changed. Sullen, morose, and dogged"[24] – but, worse, the conditions of plantation debilitation ("I never knew [a physician or surgeon] to be called to a slave upon R.'s estate"), which normalizes such injuries and impairments, and renders them "endemic rather than epidemic or exceptional"[25] to the corporeal experience of Southern slavery. Henson's shattered shoulder blades, reinjured "the first time I tried to plough" after five months' convalescence, underlines the

53

debilitating non-accident of the bodily traumas visited on him. They are but nodal experiences in what Puar has termed "the biopolitics of debility"[26] subtending slavery. Here, the "right to maim" belongs to the slaveowner and overseer who, in league, require the bondsman's continuous labor and subjection for their common racial profit as hoe and lash "are mobilized to make [white] power visible on the body."[27] Forever "unable to raise [his] hands," Henson's disability stamped his eventual flight to freedom in Canada with a memory so awful and ineradicable that it would make Black freedom dreams no more possible than quitting one's own body and perpetual fugitivity, therefore, the only real hope of the whip-scarred runaway, Josiah Henson chief among them.

If Jacobs's *Incidents* strategically dissimulates the bodily disablements and debilitations of bondage on the Black captives of the "peculiar institution," then *The Life of Josiah Henson* and *Stranger Than Fiction* refuse the choice between the ableist imperative to represent the ex-slave as a muscular nondependent, and the truth (stranger than fiction) of slavery's ongoing panic-stricken mutilations of Black flesh. When British abolitionist and missionary to Barbados Rev. Henry Bleby spied Henson, "a person of the middle size, firm and well knit; his skin ... of the true African jet,"[28] seated among the white divines at a Methodist preacher's meeting in Boston in 1858, it was clear Henson was a figure for embodied self-sufficiency and Black debility alike – his arms, Bleby observed, still crippled "so that he could by no means use them freely,"[29] the appearance of fitness ("middle size, firm and well knit") notwithstanding. Still, it bears noting that while the assaultive consequences of white disciplinary power over captive Black bodies are obviously portrayed in Henson, the psychosocial cause and bodily effects of the violent compulsions of said power, like those seen in Massa Henry in Jacobs's *Incidents*, are not. Rather they appear behind a screen.

In *The Life of Josiah Henson* and its much enlarged reissue as *Stranger Than Fiction* ("with an introduction by Mrs. H. B. Stowe," who had famously appropriated Henson's true story for her own blockbuster novel), the traditional invisibility of white bodiliness and its discernible antagonist materiality in canonical literary expression is betrayed in episodes of white profligacy vis-à-vis orthotic Blackness as practical aid and surrogate self. In Henson's narrative(s), it is the inebriate, both slave owner and overseer, who puts the materiality of white bodiliness in sharpest relief.

In his *Spirits of America: Intoxication in Nineteenth-Century American Literature* (1997), Nicolas Warner attends closely to antebellum American literature's portrayal of intoxicant use (alcohol, mainly, and drugs). Among the key themes in this history of literary concern for intoxication, Warner identifies a transcendent, mystical order of intoxication that elevates the mind to a higher level of consciousness, and "a lower, physical intoxication," he writes, "that debilitates and coarsens."[30] It is the lower order which prevails in Henson. That he should suffer a critical injury by the hand of a slighted overseer whose drunken condition Henson exploits is not wholly unexpected since, such drunkenness, "such as [was] common enough among the dissipated planters of the neighborhood" (LJH, 14), aptly metaphorizes the worrisomely unruly habits and racially degenerative potentiality of the lawlessness of white racial domination. Henson's vigor and "pride of conscious superiority" (LJH, 15) over other men were an affront to the overseer besotted with whiskey. Having gotten into a row with Henson's master, also sloshed, at a popular in-town tavern, Litton "got a severe fall" (TSTF 34) when the devoted young body-servant intervened to extract his master from the conflict and carry him home. Too roughly shoved by young Henson, Litton, "falling upon the floor" (LJH, 15), suffered the embarrassment meanly. His fall dramatizing the future failure of a formulation of racial whiteness enfeebled by its ironic dependencies on Black bodily subjection, the humiliated overseer sets his mind to physical vengeance against Henson's obviously stronger hand. A few days on, he spies his opportunity. With three enslaved men ordered to his aid, Litton springs with determined, if ungainly, abandon upon Henson traveling alone on a backroad. Seizing a heavy fence-rail "six or seven feet long" (LJH, 17) and striking Henson at last "with his whole strength" (LJH, 15), Litton recovers his bodily ego from that racial fall/failure-of-body he was to charge to the brash, overconfident bondsman with one fell body blow. Henson's arm broken, Litton reverses Covey's fate, overwhelms the intrepid slave, and sends him bloodied and aching to the ground, which his own body must fearfully remember as a racial crucible. What else but the memory of that fall and a burning racial animus intense enough to kill but content to maim (not allowing death, in a sense) must fuel Litton's continuing battery upon Henson's cut-down form, already roundly crushed? What else but the sober assurance of "his whole strength" must incite him to inflict a drunken pummeling so severe (if not also so calculating) as to disfigure young Henson irreversibly and call the reasonability of white disciplinary force into public question? Little else illuminates the white body/Black body complex under slavery quite so much as the terms of these queries.

In very different but complementary ways, then, *The Life of Josiah Henson* and *Incidents in the Life of a Slave Girl* are exemplary of the obvious and invisible ways nineteenth-century Black writers contemplated the politics of corporeality in racialized contexts of power and subjection. Not only Henson and Jacobs but publications from formerly enslaved narrators as various as Frederick Douglass, Harriet Wilson, Ellen and

William Craft, Henry Bibb, and Solomon Northrup offer keen additional reflections on the endemic conditions of Black debility in the nineteenth century and its active and passive productions of bodily disability, even as invalidity was scarcely imaginable as a social or economic condition pertinent to enslaved people. Where most nineteenth-century writers obscured Black disability and the pained body into narratives of physical endurance and heroic escapes to freedom and self-sufficiency, not a few twentieth-century writers who distantly reimagined the slave past – Toni Morrison, Shirley Anne Williams, Edward P. Jones, Octavia Butler, and Alex Haley among them – surfaced the muted musings of their antebellum antecedents on slavery's central role in the historical disabling of Black bodies and corollary production of (the racial politics of) white ableist embodiment.

Put in balder terms, the Black body/white body complex outlined in this essay is at once an everyday and spectacular affair, as banal as it is monstrous in the parasitic struggle of racial whiteness in the antebellum era to survive its lived precarity by disciplinary power and the structural reproduction of Black injury. To allay the racist fear and envy of Black corporeality threatening liberty in manifestly specific and speculative ways everywhere on the South's antebellum landscape, the slave power – straining to maintain its lordship over its captive Black population and persuade itself of the dream of its racial supremacy – arrogates to itself a punitive prerogative, inscribing its record of racial terrorism and acts of anti-Black aggression repressively onto pained Black flesh. As an historical figure, the Black body is thus a palimpsest of the madness of whiteness as a category of power.

## NOTES

1 Toni Morrison, *Playing in the Dark: Whiteness and the Literary Imagination* (Cambridge: Harvard University Press, 1992), 5.
2 Ibid., 7.
3 Ibid., 20.
4 Ibid., 18. Emphasis Morrison's.
5 Ibid.
6 Ibid., 25.
7 Willa Cather, *Sapphira and the Slave Girl* (1940), in *Willa Cather: Later Novels*, ed. Sharon O'Brien (New York: Library of America, 1990), 775–939, 813. Subsequent references are to this edition with pages appearing in parentheses above.
8 Morrison, *Playing in the Dark*, 25.
9 Ibid., 23.
10 I am not unaware of the challenges posed by disability studies to the metaphorization of disability as an ableist formulation of lamentable lack or a dangerous deformation that has nothing to do with the lived experience of persons with

disabilities. To the extent that my reading of *Sapphira and the Slave Girl* perceives Sapphira's condition as a figure for, and possibly a warning against, the enervation of white power as a muscular ideology, I suggest this ableist metaphorization belongs first to Cather. As I shall show, however, some representations of disability by nondisabled writers are not ableist metaphors. As Sami Schalk has argued, "disability can take on both concrete and metaphoric meaning in a text. This approach to disability metaphors seeks to understand how these representations can symbolize something other than disability while still being about disability." This is especially true in African American writing, Schalk maintains, because of "the parallel and overlapping forms of discrimination that have occurred for both Black and disabled people." See Sami Schalk, "Interpreting Disability Metaphor and Race in Octavia Butler's 'The Evening and the Morning and the Night,'" *African American Review* 5, no. 2, Special Issue: Blackness & Disability (Summer 2017): 139–151, 141. On whiteness as nineteenth-century muscular ideology (as early as 1855), see, too, Jürgan Martschukat, "'The Necessity for Better Bodies to Perpetuate Our Institutions, Insure a Higher Development of the Individual, and Advance the Condition of the Race.' Physical Culture and the Formation of the Self in the Late Nineteenth and Early Twentieth Century USA," *Journal of Historical Sociology* 24, no. 4 (December 2011): 472–493.

11 This formal influence has been proposed by Sarah Clere in her article, "Cather's Editorial Shaping of *Sapphira and the Slave Girl*," *Studies in the Novel* 45, no. 3 (2013): 442–459.

12 Harriet Jacobs, *Incidents in the Life of a Slave Girl*, 2nd ed. (New York: W. W. Norton, 2019), 158. Subsequent references are to this edition with pages appearing in parentheses.

13 See Martschukat, "'The Necessity for Better Bodies to Perpetuate Our Institutions, Insure a Higher Development of the Individual, and Advance the Condition of the Race,'" 478.

14 Jasbir K. Puar, *The Right to Maim: Debility, Capacity, Disability* (Durham, NC: Duke University Press, 2017), xix.

15 Ibid., xvi.

16 Ibid., xvii.

17 Schalk, "Interpreting Disability Metaphor and Race in Octavia Butler's," 141.

18 Ellen Samuels, "'A Complication of Complaints': Untangling Disability, Race, and Gender in William and Ellen Craft's *Running a Thousand Miles for Freedom*," *MELUS* 31, no. 3 (Fall 2006): 15–47, 37.

19 Stefanie Hunt-Kennedy, *Between Fitness and Death: Disability and Slavery in the Caribbean* (Urbana: University of Illinois Press, 2020), 4.

20 In the context of US slavery, one thinks, for instance, of Lathan Windley's four-volume *Runaway Slave Advertisements: A Documentary History from the 1730s to 1790* (Westport, CT: Greenwood, 1983); see, also, Daniel Meadors *Advertisements of Runaway Slaves in Virginia, 1801–1820* (New York: Routledge, 2014); Graham R. Hodges and Alan Brown, *"Pretends to Be Free": Runaway Slave Advertisements from Colonial and Revolutionary New York and New Jersey* (New York: Fordham University Press, 2019); John Hope Franklin and Loren Schweninger, *Runaway Slaves: Rebels on the Plantation* (New York: Oxford University Press, 2000); and Erica Armstrong Dunbar, *Never Caught:*

    *The Washingtons' Relentless Pursuit of Their Runaway Slave, Ona Judge* (New York: Simon and Schuster, 2017).

21 Hunt-Kennedy, *Between Fitness and Death*, 5.

22 Ibid., 6.

23 Josiah Henson, *The Life of Josiah Henson, Formerly a Slave, Now an Inhabitant of Canada as Narrated by Himself* (Boston: Arthur D. Phelps, 1849), 5, https://lccn.loc.gov/11021827. All subsequent references to this work, indicated parenthetically in the text of this essay, are to this edition.

24 Josiah Henson, *Truth Stranger Than Fiction: Father Henson's Story of His Own Life* (Boston: John P. Jewett and Company, 1858), 7, https://docsouth.unc.edu/neh/henson58/henson58.html.

25 Puar, *The Right to Maim*, xvii.

26 Ibid.

27 Ibid., x.

28 Henry Bleby, *Josiah: The Maimed Fugitive, A True Tale* (London: William Nichols, 1873), 7, https://docsouth.unc.edu/neh/bleby/bleby.html.

29 Ibid., 8.

30 Nicolas Warner, *Spirits of America: Intoxication in Nineteenth-Century American Literature* (Norman: University of Oklahoma Press, 1997), 217.

# 4

AGNIESZKA SOLTYSIK MONNET

# Monstrous Bodies of the American Gothic

Disordered bodies preoccupied early British gothic novels: bodies unable to control their appetites or their fear; bodies in pain; bodies undone by emotions, violence and invasive institutions. Similarly, in the United States the first gothic author, Charles Brockden Brown, wrote fitfully plotted novels full of strange and unruly bodies, such as the odd-looking victim-villain Carwin in *Wieland* (1798), the diabolical 'Indian' in *Edgar Huntley* (1799), and the pestilent bodies gripped by yellow fever in *Arthur Mervyn* (1799). Brown wrote for a young nation, rehearsing political ideas in literary fictions so convoluted that their implications could never be determined with any certainty, even as they clarified the main axes of a national preoccupation with racial hierarchy and other forms of somatic classification.

The American Gothic is full of monstrous bodies, terrifying and dangerous and frequently marked by some sort of deformity or injury. The range of monsters in these texts includes 'savages' (as Native Americans were often called), sadistic villains, cunning tyrants, sexual predators, and various kinds of unusual or 'unnatural' bodies, but the gothic genre has also posed difficult questions about monstrosity and its possible meanings. Operating within and against the binary fault lines of normative somatic categorisations in the United States – healthy and sick, white and Black, civilized and primitive, male and female, and, with the emergence of modern sexual categorisation, straight and queer – the American Gothic is a genre that both informs and often critiques our ideas of racial subjectivity and biopolitical hierarchy.

Starting from these observations, this chapter will make two sets of claims. First, it will show how American gothic fiction has always oscillated between more subversive and more conservative forms, producing in the nineteenth and twentieth century instances of gothic literature that stabilize cultural hierarchies as well as instances that trouble or refuse them. Second, it will show how the emergence of Black, Native, Latinx, and Asian American recuperations of the Gothic during the latter half of the twentieth century turned the genre's penchant for representing bodily permeability and variability into a sign of hopeful instability, pointing to what Juana Maria Rodriguez terms 'a way to conjure and inhabit an alternative world in which other forms of identification and social relations become imaginable'.[1] By surveying the trope of corporeal instability across nineteenth- and twentieth-century gothic narratives, this chapter will situate both progressive and imperial gothic embodiment at the fulcrum of American understandings of race and white supremacy.

First, however, a brief overview of the origins of the American Gothic, as it arose from three broad sources that intermingled with the British gothic novel form in the late eighteenth century: hostile encounters between settler colonialists and Native Americans; Puritan repressions and distrust of the body; and the horror of the enslaved African's plight in American history.[2] All of these cultural roots of the American Gothic are predicated upon rigid and deterministic discourses of the body, especially the racially marked or gendered body.

In order to justify their morally and often legally unjustifiable actions, white settler colonists told themselves that Native Americans were savage, bestial, and possibly cannibalistic. The animalistic Indian is a trope that figures among the very first American gothic novels, such as *Edgar Huntley* by Charles Brockden Brown, which also features the related gothic device of the non-native narrator's 'need' to become like the Indian (i.e., savage, bestial) in order to survive in the wilderness he finds himself in. After the narrator of that novel discovers that a friend of his has been murdered by a Leni-Lenape Indian, he himself then murders five members of this tribe, collapsing the moral difference between them and him. In this way, *Edgar Huntley* is an early instance of how savagery, guilt, and confusion between self and 'other' are themes that haunt American gothic fiction whenever a Native American character appears.

A second important cultural source of American gothic writing is the history of the Puritans and especially the witchcraft trials they conducted in Salem. At the heart of Puritan horror is the strict control they attempted to impose over their bodies, turning repression and contempt for the physical world and bodily existence into a way of life. The gothic themes emanating from this material include religious madness and fanaticism, the persecution of unmarried or independent women, the use of torture to extract signs of guilt or innocence from accused (male or female) witches, and notoriously sadistic forms of punishment: live burnings, slow crushing by heavy stones, and public hangings. Such paranoid surveillance of the body for signs of forbidden desires or identities recurs in American culture and gothic writing throughout the nineteenth and twentieth centuries.

Finally, the history of the enslaved African on North American soil is a tale of physical dispossession, control, and exploitation that required constant maintenance through ideological sleight-of-hand and physical torture. In reaction to a rising abolition movement in the nineteenth century, this ideological work increasingly relied on pseudo-scientific discourse to justify treating people as less-than-human. This discourse seized upon the darkness of African-descended people's skins but did not make exceptions for enslaved people who were able to pass as 'white'. The irrationality of race-based ideology and discourse, according to Karen and Barbara Fields, operates much like the Puritan concept of witchcraft, producing a belief that 'presents itself to the mind as a vivid truth' even if it is invisible and indeed non-existent.[3]

The American Gothic thus concerns (usually) human bodies and the injuries and constraints they bear, as well as the fears they can incite. Because the body is central also to the categories and hierarchies of American society under a capitalist economy and settler colonialism, the Gothic has inevitably been closely concerned with these issues as well. From the late eighteenth century to the present, monstrous bodies in gothic literature have allowed authors to explore the complexities of identity, power, privilege, safety, and freedom in the United States. Itself very much a baggy monster, the Gothic has not produced any simple patterns or formulas about the cultural work of monstrosity or bodily signification. Roughly speaking the Gothic has always worked both sides of the political divide, offering conservative authors ready-made forms for conflating difference with danger and progressive authors a means for questioning and unsettling normative categories and cultural certainties. Nevertheless, a cautious generalisation can be made in asserting that the twentieth century saw a significant expansion in the contributions of Black, Native American, Latinx, and Asian American authors. These authors brought a rich revitalisation and hybridity to the gothic genre, as well as a new sense of the genre's disruptive, anti-racist, and decolonial political possibility.

Given the importance of the body to the Gothic as a genre, it is not surprising that scholarship on the subject is growing. Jack Halberstam's *Skin Shows* (1995) focused on the cultural logic and construction of monstrosity, a project that has been developed more recently by Jeffrey Cohen in *Monster Theory* (1996) and *Monster Culture* (2007). Jack Morgan's *The Biology of Horror* (2002) also focused on physicality and embodiment in gothic literature and horror cinema, and Marie Mulvey's *Dangerous Bodies: Historicizing the Gothic Corporeal* (2015) is the most thorough recent examination of the body in gothic fiction, exploring themes of medical

Gothic, menstrual Gothic, and war Gothic, each of which has substantial scholarship around it as well. Yet there has been relatively little critical attention paid to the specific topic of the body in the American Gothic as such. The following sections will address this topic by focusing on three main themes: the sick or injured body, the racially marked body, and the gendered body.

## The Sick or Injured Body

This sick, leaky, injured, or infirm body occupies a broad swath of the American Gothic. This section will focus on the contagious body and the literary sub-genre of plague fiction. Illness and injury are less 'classical' gothic tropes than other forms of monstrosity and violence but represent an important, perhaps the most important, human fear: that of death. The body gripped by disease is an object of intense anxiety in Anglo-European and North American culture, possibly because it represents the breakdown of an entire chain of values that white American liberalism holds dear: autonomy, individualism, self-mastery, and freedom of mobility. Sick people are quarantined, shunned, dependent upon others for food and care, and often untreatable and dying. For these reasons, perhaps, the contagious body and contagion itself lend themselves well to sometimes subtle and sometimes shrill political allegory.

One of the earliest American Gothic treatments of contagious disease is Charles Brockden Brown's *Arthur Mervyn*, the first-person narrative of an ambiguous victim-villain who tells his self-justifying tale against the backdrop of the 1793 yellow fever epidemic in Philadelphia, which killed roughly 10 percent of the city's population. Mervyn himself is ill as he begins his story, which involves much human greed, trickery, and predation even before the epidemic hits the narrative, in keeping with Brown's preoccupation with individualism and its potential ill-suitability for democracy. A radical in his youth, Brown ended his days as a staunch conservative, and the pessimism about a human propensity to act in self-interest that led him from one extreme to the other is perceptible in his anxious plots about ambiguous narrators dealing with even more dishonest and untrustworthy characters. The passages in the novel that describe a city undone by yellow fever are meant to simply exaggerate and distil the anti-social tendencies present at all times:

> Terror had exterminated all the sentiments of nature. Wives were deserted by husbands, and children by parents. Some had shut themselves in their houses, and debarred themselves from all communication with the rest of mankind ...

The chambers of disease were deserted, and the sick left to die of negligence. None could be found to remove the lifeless bodies. Their remains, suffered to decay by piecemeal, filled the air with deadly exhalations, and added tenfold to the devastation.[4]

We see here not just diseased bodies but a diseased body politic. The social bonds and 'sentiments of nature' that hold up society itself, as conceived by European political thought – namely, those of the family – are dissolved as 'wives were deserted by husbands, and children by parents'. The ill and the poor are shunned and allowed to die in the streets, their bodies left to rot. The healthy of means isolate themselves and cut off 'all communication' with their neighbours and fellow countrymen. In short, civil society completely breaks down as an extreme individualism seems to guide people's actions. Brown presents altruism, cooperation, care, and even love as flimsy social fictions adorning brute egotism and self-interest. The 'deadly exhalations' devastating the city are not only decaying human remains but the nauseating funk of human nature, as conceived by Brown, exposed by the plague.

Edgar Allan Poe's 'The Masque of the Red Death' (1842) revisits the theme of the sudden plague and the social breakdown it occasions. In this enigmatic and seemingly allegorical tale, a disease that causes 'profuse bleeding at the pores' ravages an unnamed country led by a prince with the ironic name of 'Prospero'. The narrator is unreliable, a faithful subject of the useless prince, and unable to recognize the abdication of responsibility and leadership apparent in the prince's decision to isolate himself and a small elite in a castle, making merry while the disease destroys his people. While the unrealistic style of the story invites allegorical readings, no clear allegory emerges besides the obvious fact that the silent guest who appears at the masked ball at the end dressed as a corpse is actually Death.

The story is elusive but raises a number of crucial themes that shape pandemic fiction to this day. First of all, the illness appears as a visible mark on the skin and therefore resonates with the issue of race and other skin-based identity markers as signs of the disease create social exclusion: 'The scarlet stains upon the body and especially upon the face of the victim, were the pest ban which shut him out from the aid and from the sympathy of his fellow-men.'[5] The racial connotations of the disease are further reinforced by the emphasis on 'blood', which, in American racial discourse, has played a ghoulishly prominent role (one need only think of the 'one-drop' rule established in 1896 by the Supreme Court). Finally, the story can be read as a morality tale about the denial of death, as the prince distracts himself with feasts and entertainments while his subjects perish, but the mortality that he tries to keep out through wealth and distraction catches up with him in the end.

Since the Spanish flu devastated the world at the tail end of the First World War, plague fiction has been a minor but steady presence in the American Gothic. As in the nineteenth century, disease often reverberates in these stories in socially significant and even allegorical ways. For this last example, we return to the yellow fever of 1793, but retold by John Edgar Wideman in his short story 'Fever' (1989). Narrated by what Fritz Gysin calls a 'collage of communal voices and visions',[6] the story begins with an epigraph from Robert Morris, a wealthy merchant and signer of the Declaration of Independence, who describes the central place of Philadelphia to the new nation: 'Consider Philadelphia ... to be to the United States what the heart is to the human body in circulating the blood.'[7] One of the main focalizers of the story is Richard Allen, a historical figure, co-founder of the African Methodist Episcopal Church, who describes the advance of the epidemic on the city with a particular attention to the fate of African Americans. While there are descriptions of bodily fluids and other typical features of plague fiction, it is clear that Philadelphia is afflicted by more than just a disease. It is also sickened by racism and hypocrisy, as first the illness is blamed on African Americans and called 'Barbados Fever', and then later, when most doctors and nurses have fled, the pernicious myth that Black bodies are immune to the disease is propagated in order to justify pressing African Americans into service as caregivers to the sick and dying. Richard Allen denounces this twisting of truth by way of a return to the heart metaphor of the epigraph: 'How the knife was plunged in our hearts, then cruelly twisted ... We were proclaimed carriers of the fever and treated as pariahs, but when it became expedient to command our services to nurse the sick and bury the dead, the previous allegations were no longer mentioned' (281). In short, the yellow fever epidemic revealed the metaphorical 'heart' of the sickness gripping the young republic: the ruthless exploitation of Black bodies according to shifting fictions of race, an ailment that continues to afflict the United States to this day, and which brings me to the next section.

## The Racially Marked Body

Race occupies a central place in the American Gothic, and the racialized body constitutes a recurrent theme. As Eugenie de la Motte argues in *The Gothic Other: Racial and Social Constructions in the Literary Imagination*, the gothic genre arose at exactly the same historical moment that the fiction of race as a 'biological division' emerged.[8] While the biological myth of race has been scientifically discredited, it continues to haunt American society, as does the unresolved violence and collective trauma of slavery. As mentioned earlier, Fields and Fields attribute the enduring belief in race despite its biological non-existence and its frequent phenotypical invisibility to a set of ideological practices that they call 'racecraft'. This term refers to the entangled cycle of imagining and acting upon the fiction of race, which creates its effects and testifies to the ongoing presence of racism.[9] Christina Sharpe has similarly argued that the post-slavery subject has been created by an ongoing process of subjectification that is 'readable and locatable still through the horrors enacted on the black body after slavery'.[10]

The racially marked bodies of the American Gothic can be approached in a number of ways. One is the overtly racist use of African (or other) race as a signifier of monstrosity, often linked to what Johan Höglund calls the Imperial Gothic, a reactionary strand of gothic fiction that uses gothic tropes to characterize the racially marked Others that threaten the white protagonists. Although H. P. Lovecraft is not usually considered a writer of empire, he definitely uses race in this manner in his fiction. For example, in 'Call of Cthulhu', the ancient monsters that the narrator discovers have become the object of a primitive cult observed by local non-white worshippers in a forest outside New Orleans. The description of these people – presumably African Americans and possibly Native Americans – during a ceremony (described by the narrator as a 'voodoo orgy') is a racist diatribe that equates the ceremony's participants with devils and wild beasts: 'Animal fury and orgiastic license here whipped themselves to dæmoniac heights by howls and squawking ecstasies that tore and reverberated through those nighted woods like pestilential tempests from the gulfs of hell.'[11] The rhetorical potpourri here combines bestiality, sexual promiscuity, devilishness, and disease ('pestilential') into a monstrosity described as all the more horrific for its racial mix: The 'indescribable horde of human abnormality' is a 'hybrid spawn' of 'mongrel celebrants' (179). The Imperial Gothic's fear of native and dark-skinned others is surpassed only by its fear of miscegenation and the confusion of racial groups, though here the hybridity seems almost to be between human and animal rather than between races: 'There are vocal qualities peculiar to men, and vocal qualities peculiar to beasts; and it is terrible to hear the one when the source should yield the other' (179). In any case, monstrosity is clearly linked to racial otherness, with the narrator noting that the forest area where the ritual takes place is 'substantially unknown and untraversed by white men' (179). This first strain of the race-inflected American Gothic is thus defined by an overt demonisation of the non-white body as monstrous.

A second kind of American Gothic concerned with race has focused on the violence inflicted upon the Black bodies of enslaved Africans and African Americans and their descendants. A common feature of abolitionist tracts and slave narratives, descriptions of the torture of African Americans include the famous 'Letter IX' of Crèvecoeur's *Letters from an American Farmer* (1782), which has the narrator coming upon the horrific scene of an enslaved man hanging in a cage exposed to the elements to die.[12] In this strain of the racial Gothic, the slave's body is described as abjectly victimized, and his injuries are gruesomely detailed; but his race is not foregrounded as in the Imperial Gothic. Instead, we can observe how the narrator actually identifies with the humanity of this dehumanized body in a sort of mimetic sympathy – his own body is gripped by trembling and terror, as paralyzed (for a moment) as the enslaved man is immobilized in his cage.

In an even more gothic twist on the theme of racial torture, some stories show African American characters themselves becoming morally deformed through their experience of trauma. A striking example of this can be found in Victor Séjour's 'The Mulatto' (1836), a story that was published in Paris by a young Black man from New Orleans who went on to become a celebrated playwright in France. The story takes place in pre-Revolution Haiti and tells of a young enslaved man named Georges whose father is, unbeknownst to him, his own enslaver. Georges saves his father's life during an attempt on it, but his enslaver's brief gratitude does not prevent him from deciding to seduce/rape Georges's wife. Repulsing his advances, she causes him to fall and is condemned to hang for striking a white man. Georges pleads in vain for her life and then runs away to plot his revenge in the mountains after she is executed. He returns three years later and coolly poisons his master's new wife and decapitates him. However, in keeping with the gothic fascination with body parts and the macabre, the master's head continues speaking an instant after death, revealing that Georges has killed his own father. The despondent Georges shoots himself, adding his own body to those of his victims, thrusting home Séjour's point that slavery turns into monsters potentially everyone it touches, enslavers and enslaved alike twisted into cruelty either by power or by pain.

Another recurrent aspect of race examined by the American Gothic brings us back to the ideas of racecraft as a form of ideological witchcraft and of racial 'blood' as a macabre metaphor for racial identity. One of the uncanny specificities of how race operates in the United States is the way it can be invisible on people's bodies but still present 'inside' their bodies or genes. Notions of racial 'impurity' have been legally and discursively formalized, most notoriously in the 'one drop rule' established by *Plessy* v. *Ferguson* in the 1890s. One result of these conceptions has been an entire tradition of anxiety about somatic visibility and invisibility of racial markers such as skin colour, thick or fine hair, flat or thin noses, small or generous lips, among others. The situation of African Americans with few or no visible traces of their 'black blood' was so complex and uncomfortable for whites – for instance, light-skinned enslaved women were highly prized for sexual relations, making their plight all the more wretched – that the term 'tragic mulatto' emerged during the course of the century.

One of the most poignant gothic stories about such a situation concerns a mixed-race character who is not aware that his mother is of African descent. In Kate Chopin's 'Désirée's Baby' (1893), Armand, a wealthy and temperamental slave owner marries a beautiful young woman and has a child with her. When the baby begins to show signs of 'darker' features, Armand accuses his wife of mixed ancestry and drives her out of their house with the child. While burning her and the baby's effects he discovers a letter from his mother to his father expressing thanks that their son will never know that she 'belongs to the race that is cursed with the brand of slavery'.[13] In other words, Armand himself is Black but has managed to escape its visible 'brand' upon his features. The physical signs of what in the United States is still called 'race' (based on the racist assumption that only non-white people possess race) had skipped a generation and stamped its seal upon his baby's body.

Writers in the twentieth century have used the Gothic to examine and challenge these perverse and ghoulish effects of racialism. For instance, Ralph Ellison invoked the trope of invisibility in his novel *The Invisible Man* (1952), suggesting that African Americans were as invisible to white Americans as ghosts:

> I am not a spook like those who haunted Edgar Allan Poe; nor am I one of your Hollywood-movie ectoplasms ... I am a man of substance, of flesh and bone, fiber and liquids ... I am invisible, understand, simply because people refuse to see me ... Like the bodiless heads you see sometimes in circus sideshows, it is as though I have been surrounded by mirrors of hard, distorting glass.[14]

The narrator adopts a series of gothic tropes (the spook, the ectoplasm, the disembodied head) to describe the invisibility of African Americans as human beings to the white people around them, who see nothing more than the colour of their skin (or a racial type, if the person happens to be a phenotypically light-skinned African American).

## The Gendered Body

The final category of somatic categorisation that has been essential for the American Gothic is gender, by which I mean both the male/female dichotomy and the straight/queer binarism that emerged at the end of the nineteenth century. Female bodies in particular have been haunting the American Gothic since the nineteenth century. The social ideology that divided

American bodies into strictly differentiated and even allegedly 'opposite' sexes created many tensions and contradictions that were imaginatively explored by gothic authors. Defined by the Separate Spheres doctrine as ethereal 'angels of the house' while their reproductive capacity was ruthlessly channelled and policed according to male needs, women often appeared in the Gothic as frail victims but also on occasion as unexpectedly resilient and resourceful agents. Their bodies oscillate between inspiring desire and fear, much like the often unstable, unnatural, and abjected bodies of queer subjects.

No discussion of women in the Gothic American can avoid a close look at the work of Edgar Allan Poe, whose pages are full of female bodies both as abject victims ('The Black Cat', 'The Murders in the Rue Morgue', 'Berenice') – whose skulls are bashed in with axes, whose heads are severed with razors, and whose teeth are pulled out of their still-living bodies – and as potentially monstrous women whose bodies refuse to stay dead or even stay the same. Besides the vaguely vampiric Ligeia – who seems to invade and appropriate the body of her successor – and the uncanny Morella – who likewise seems to return in the body of her own daughter – the cataleptic Madeline in 'The Fall of the House of Usher' presents a particularly interesting example of the unpredictability of the female body. Mere days after the arrival of the nameless narrator at Usher's house, his sister Madeline, who seems to float around the mansion in a ghostly and ethereal way – almost a parody of the Victorian 'angel in the house' stereotype – takes ill and dies. As it turns out, she is not dead but in a temporary coma from which she awakens in her tomb, at which point her wispiness gives way to an unprecedented physicality. Struggling for days with the heavy door of the tomb, she finally escapes and finds her brother, with 'blood upon her white robes, and the evidence of some bitter struggle upon every portion of her emaciated frame'.[15] Usher, it turns out, has been hearing her desperate struggles for days and ignoring them, too unnerved to help, but now even more terrified of her rightful anger. Upon seeing her gory appearance, he succumbs both to his own fears and to her very physical presence: 'For a moment she remained trembling and reeling to and fro upon the threshold – then, with a low, moaning cry, fell heavily inward upon the person of her brother, and in her violent and now final death-agonies, bore him to the floor a corpse' (335). In a typically Poe-esque reversal, Madeline's angelic body has become monstrous: heavy, violent, and dangerous. In this way, Poe reminds us – with both anxiety and ambivalence – that women's bodies often cannot be contained within the corseted role of frail and obedient angel dictated by ante-bellum sexual ideology.

Louisa May Alcott goes even further than Poe in deconstructing the deadly double standards and double binds constraining women's place and agency in nineteenth-century society. Alcott's *Behind a Mask, Or, a Woman's Power* (1866) is an American Gothic twist on the British *Jane Eyre* (1847) by Charlotte Brontë, developing upon the theme of the governess whose socially awkward status – as both servant and gentlewoman at once – magnified and made visible the paradoxical status of all middle-class women, who were expected to perform physical and emotional labour in the home around the clock while maintaining the appearance of polite ladies of leisure. Alcott takes Brontë's resourceful heroine and makes her into a con-woman, American-style, who lies and manipulates herself into wealth and a title by marrying the patriarch of the house. A consummate actress acutely aware of what is expected from a woman, Jean Muir plays everyone according to their particular prejudices, but the narrative makes clear that she ends up being a good and loyal wife to her older husband. The narrative also mentions that she had once been a sweet and trusting girl but became hardened through disappointment and awareness of the precariousness of a woman's position in Victorian society: An unmarried woman of a certain age not willing to do sexual work simply cannot survive. Her ruse in the story consists of passing – with the help of makeup, false teeth, and an expert performance of girlishness – as a nineteen-year-old ingenue when she is in fact 'a haggard, worn, and moody woman of thirty at least'.[16] While thirty might not seem so old now, Jean Muir is depicted as a monster: After her 'mobile features' settle into their natural expression, 'weary, hard, bitter', she drinks alcohol from a vial and uncovers 'her breast to eye with a terrible glance the scar of a newly healed wound' (142). Her body at thirty is described as worn out, hard, scarred, sexualized (the exposed breast), prone to drink, and so old that she needs to spend all her time when she is not alone hiding her face 'behind a mask'. The fact that she will be a kind and caring wife for her elderly husband gives the story a seemingly happy ending, as if even Alcott did not realize that Jean Muir's fate – of having to hide her true features and true self for the rest of her married life – is more of a life sentence to a permanent performance than a happily-ever-after.

Gender also runs through American gothic fiction in terms of sexuality and the question of queer bodies. This is the tacit subject of Herman Melville's great gothic novel, *Pierre* (1952), several of Henry James's short stories, Edith Wharton's ghost story 'The Eyes' (1910), Sherwood Anderson's uncanny 'Hands' (1919), and Shirley Jackson's *The Haunting of Hill House* (1959), to name just a few. One of the most important examples is James Baldwin's *Giovanni's Room* (1956), which is an extended

American Gothic exploration of internalized homophobia and the cultural injunction to keeping queer bodies hidden or in the 'closet'. The first-person narrator is a young American man who has a passionate affair with a young Italian while living in Paris. When his girlfriend returns from a trip to Spain several months later, he leaves Giovanni, who slips into drug abuse and prostitution and finds himself awaiting execution for the murder of a wealthy patron-client.

The novel is a complex study of queer shame and the way that the narrator finds the desires of his body both uncontrollable and monstrous. It uses the Gothic to explore the fundamental mystery and uncanniness of desire: something that comes from within our bodies and deepest selves but that we may experience as alien and even horrifying when we live in a homophobic culture. This is what happens to the narrator after his first queer sexual experience as a teenager. Waking up in the morning and looking at his lover, he sees the body, which seemed so beautiful at first, change into a monstrosity as the social reality of homophobia overwhelms him: 'That body suddenly seemed the black opening of a cavern in which I would be tortured till madness came.'[17] Later in the novel, in a Parisian bar frequented by a queer clientele, the narrator sees a gender-ambiguous person, and all the fear and anxiety of his own failure to perform manhood according to social rules erupt into a description of this person's body that is striking for its rhetoric of abjection:

> Now someone whom I had never seen before came out of the shadows toward me. It looked like a mummy or a zombie – this was the first, overwhelming impression – of something walking after it had been put to death. ... It carried a glass, it walked on its toes, the flat hips moved with a dead, horrifying lasciviousness ... It glittered in the dim light; the thin, black hair was violent with oil, combed forward, hanging in bangs; the eyelids gleamed with mascara, the mouth raged with lipstick. The face was white and thoroughly bloodless with some kind of foundation cream; it stank of powder and a gardenia-like perfume.[18]

Here the narrator's discomfort with his own gender issues takes the form of a projection of a series of dehumanising gothic tropes: a mummy, a zombie, an 'it'. We notice that the narrator focuses obsessively on parts of the body: toes, hips, hair, mouth, and eyelids, and finally odour. The passage is terrifying – not only for how scared the narrator is by this person, who turns out to be a kind of Cassandra figure in the narrative – but even more so for the violently dehumanising and monster-ising effect of this description. We can see here how the 'failure' of queer bodies to fit the existing somatic categories of sexual opposition generates both horror and abjection, threatening in every instance to undo the humanity of queer subjects as well as women who fail to perform their nearly impossible social roles correctly.

## Conclusion

The American Gothic offers a rich corpus through which to explore the complex dynamics of somatic categorisation and hierarchy in the United States. Able-ness, health, race, gender, and sexuality are all qualities that shape the fluctuating boundaries of normative versus monstrous embodiment. The historical antecedents of the American Gothic already demonstrated an intense preoccupation with racial hierarchy, discipline, and semiotics – looking to the body for signs of evil and sin, justification for slavery and genocide, and enforcement of normativity and exclusion. From the eighteenth century to the present, the gothic genre has worked both with and against the major fault lines of somatic classification in American culture, with non-white and women writers often appropriating the genre in order to trouble and subvert body-based determinisms and epidermal myths.

### NOTES

1 Juana María Rodriguez, *Sexual Futures, Queer Gestures and other Latina Longings* (New York: New York University Press, 2014): 26.
2 This genealogy is even more interesting if we consider Nancy Armstrong's thesis that the English novel was itself strongly influenced by the American captivity narrative. In 'Captivity and Cultural Capital in the English Novel', she writes, 'nothing so much as the English variant provided the principle of continuity consolidating Samuel Richardson, Jane Austen, and Charlotte Brontë in a single literary tradition' (*Novel: A Forum on Fiction* 31, no. 1 [Summer 1998]: 373–398, 373).
3 Karen E. Fields and Barbara J. Fields, *Racecraft: The Soul of Inequality in American Life* (London: Verso, 2012), 19.
4 Charles Brockden Brown, 'Arthur Mervyn, Or, Memoirs of the Year 1793', in *Three Gothic Novels*, ed. Sidney Krause (New York: The Library of America, 1998), 346.
5 Edgar Allan Poe, 'The Masque of the Red Death', in *Poetry and Tales*, ed. Sidney Krause (New York: Library of America, 1984), 485–490, 485.
6 Fritz Gysin, 'John Edgar Wideman's "Fever"', *Callalloo* 22, no. 3 (Summer 1999): 715–726, 715.
7 John Edgar Wideman, 'Fever', in *The New Gothic: A Collection of Contemporary Gothic Fiction*, ed. Bradford Morrow and Patrick McGrath (New York: Vintage Books, 1991), 269–300, 269.
8 Eugenia de LaMotte, 'White Terror, Black Dreams: Gothic Constructions of Race in the Nineteenth Century', in *The Gothic Other: Racial and Social Constructions*

*in the Literary Imagination*, ed. Ruth Bienstock Anolik and Douglas L. Howard (Jefferson, NC: McFarland & Co., 2004), 17–31, 17.

9 Fields and Fields, *Racecraft*, 19

10 Christina Sharpe, *Monstrous Intimacies: Making Post-Slavery Subjects* (Durham, NC: Duke University Press, 2010), 3.

11 H. P. Lovecraft, 'The Call of Cthulhu', in *H. P. Lovecraft: Tales*, ed. Peter Straub (New York: The Library of America, 2005), 167–196, 179.

12 J. Hector St. John de Crèvecoeur, 'Letter IX: Description of Charles-Town; Thoughts on Slavery; On Physical Evil; A Melancholy Scene', in *Letters from an American Farmer and Other Essays*, ed. Denis D. Moore (Cambridge: President and Fellows of Harvard College, 2013), 129.

13 Kate Chopin, 'Désirée's Baby', in *American Gothic: An Anthology 1787–1916*, ed. Charles Crow (Malden and Oxford: Blackwell, 1999), 339–342, 342.

14 Ralph Ellison, *The Invisible Man* (New York: Signet Books, 1952), 3.

15 Edgar Allan Poe, 'The Fall of the House of Usher', in *Poetry and Tales*, ed. Patrick Quinn (New York: Library of America, 1984), 317–336, 335.

16 Louisa May Alcott, 'Behind a Mask: Or, a Woman's Power', in *American Gothic: An Anthology 1787–1916*, ed. Charles Crow (Malden: Blackwell, 1999), 136–196, 142.

17 James Baldwin, *Giovanni's Room* (New York: Library of America, 1998), 226.

18 Ibid., 251.

# 5

COLLEEN GLENNEY BOGGS

# Bodies at War

In "The Valley of the Shadow" (a chapter that draws its title from Psalm 23, "The Good Shepherd"), the March family of Louisa May Alcott's *Little Women* (1868) takes leave of Beth after her long illness:

> Seldom except in books do the dying utter memorable words, see visions, or depart with beatified countenances, and those who have sped many parting souls know that to most the end comes as naturally and simply as sleep. As Beth had hoped, the "tide went out easily," and in the dark hour before the dawn, on the bosom where she had drawn her first breath, she quietly drew her last, with no farewell but one loving look, one little sigh. ... When morning came ... the spring sunshine streamed in like a benediction over the placid face upon the pillow – a face so full of painless peace that those who loved it best smiled through their tears, and thanked God that Beth was well at last.                                                                                                (391–392)

At first glance, this scene has nothing to do with war. Even though much of the book takes place during the Civil War, there are no references to the things we would expect from war literature – no soldiers, combat, weapons, or wounds. The tone is sentimental and religious, not realist and secular or even profane. The scene focuses on women and gentleness, highlighted by such alliterations as the "spring sunshine streamed" and "face ... full" of "painless peace." The passage does not portray men's strength or masculinized heroism. And yet I want to start here, to suggest that this scene is not only a Civil War scene, but one that illuminates a key means by which American literature grapples with representations of the body at war: It focuses on white women's suffering as an affirmation of national innocence.

Although the passage is ripe with allegory, verbal devices, and familiar tropes, Alcott's description also claims to be an accurate portrayal of the process by which a living body becomes a corpse. The paragraph's opening disclaimer is important: In distancing itself from "books," *Little Women* denies its own status and pretends to offer the reader direct participation in the scene that unfolds. The "books" and cultural conventions criticized are those codified in other texts, from which *Little Women* distinguishes itself. As Drew Gilpin Faust has shown, literature before the Civil War had developed a cultural script that she describes as an ars moriendi, an art of dying.[1] Surrounded by loved ones at home, ill persons offered final words that affirmed their religious convictions and marked their soul's release into the afterlife. The Civil War tested these conventions, and *Little Women* is offering reassurances in response to the new realities, under which such a peaceful death was far from many Americans' experiences. How healing such a scene would have been to readers still coming to terms with the violent destruction of hundreds of thousands on Civil War battlefields far from home and family! And from our perspective, how far from reality. We have inherited from the Civil War's aftermath an expectation that literature both captures and fails to capture the horrors of conflict. Instead of peaceful deathbed scenes that leave the body intact, we might expect the fragmentation of bodies by modern weapons, or their mutilation by combatants, both of which I will discuss momentarily. For now, I want to pause over Walt Whitman's famous dictum that "the real war will never get into the books."[2] Alcott seems to echo that sentiment when she distances her writing from "books," and yet her book thereby claims to portray accurately wartime suffering and death. This is war fiction at its most powerful – fiction that rewrites the war itself as a scene of domestic intimacy, not violent conflict. With American war literature, we are dealing with a corpus of writing that finds its greatest strength in the refusal of its topic.

In drawing attention to books, Alcott makes Beth's death real to her readers; at the same time (and perhaps paradoxically), she reaffirms her reader's understanding that Beth's death is a healing fiction. Although Beth is not a combat casualty, Alcott goes out of her way to make clear that she is a war casualty. First published in 1868, *Little Women*'s plot unfolds in the absence of Mr. March, who has gone off to serve as chaplain in the Union army. When the pater familias falls ill, Marmee goes to retrieve him from the miserable conditions of a Washington hospital, conditions which Alcott knew all too well from volunteering in such hospitals. Meanwhile, the March girls learn to care for one another as well as for the sick and poor in their neighborhood. The Civil War is reimagined through an ethics of care. Continuing the good services that their mother had rendered the immigrant Hummel family at the beginning of the book, the sisters bring their impoverished neighbors food and regularly check on their needs. But in Marmee's absence, this task falls more and more to Beth, so it is Beth in whose arms the Hummels' baby dies of scarlet fever. While Meg and Jo have had the illness in the past and are hence immune, Beth falls gravely ill and never fully regains her health. Her death, then, is an indirect result of a war that called away both parents. Even more so, it is the result of a war in which her sisters, at a crucial moment, did not follow their parents' good example and neglected to care for others. In a novel structured around the Christian allegory of John Bunyan's *Pilgrim's Progress* (1678), the allegory of Beth's death is downright heavy handed: Her sisters' failure to do their duty to one another, to their community and, by extension, to their nation causes her martyrdom and death. Beth's body is tied to the ethics of women's wartime work and the consequences of its neglect. Jo especially blames herself for having killed her sister. The body's health is deeply dependent on the relationship to and actions of others. Far from thinking about the body as autonomous, Alcott emphasizes the fact that the body is relational and that the challenge of war lies in restoring familial ties, a task for which wartime literature is uniquely suited. Through this narrative, she also offers what we may nowadays consider a feminized if not feminist reinvention of the body politic: Instead of using the concept in an abstract way that imagines the state as a virtual entity, Alcott insists on the impact that the "politic" has on the "body" of Beth and her sisters. She literalizes the "body" but also allows the "politic" to be reinvented as an ethics of mutual care. Beth's long decline reminds us that war's effects on the body are not limited to the war years but have a temporality of their own, one that the long arc of fiction is particularly suited to capture.

In American war literature, the body is poised between the term's double-meaning, both living being and dead matter. There is now a whole sector of the US Military dedicated to so-called Mortuary Affairs, a branch of the armed services that was not in place during the Civil War, when many bodies remained strewn across battlefields for days and were hastily buried by neighboring civilians. No provisions had been made at the Civil War's outbreak to deal with the dead and wounded. Nursing, too, was at first ad hoc, with care for the body professionalized during the conflict only under Clara Barton's guidance. Particularly horrific were the numerous wounds that resulted in field-hospital amputations. Oliver Wendell Holmes gave expression in May 1863 to the way in which these injured bodies changed the American landscape: "Not two years since, the sight of a person who had lost one of his lower limbs was an infrequent occurrence. Now, alas! there are few of us who have not a cripple among our friends, if not in our own families."[3] For Elaine Scarry, the injured body itself becomes a text in that wounds become "'fiction-generating' or 'reality-conferring'": "a source of apparent reality for what would otherwise be a tenuous outcome, holding it firmly in place until the postwar world rebuilds that world according to the blueprint sketchily specified by the war's locus of victory."[4] In the long run, bodies injured in war changed how Americans thought about disability – moving away, when it came to wounded veterans, from tropes of the freakish and grotesque.

But staples of the horrific that gothic literature had offered to the nineteenth-century imaginary remained available to writers and echo to this day. In *Redeployment* (2014), Phil Klay includes a story called "Bodies," narrated by a soldier in Mortuary Affairs who serves in the second Iraq War. The story opens with the narrator drawing attention to the fictional nature of his first-person accounts: He explains how he adapts what he says to his audience. When people ask about the narrator's deployment, "I'd tell them lies. 'There was this hajji corpse,' I'd say, 'lying in the sun. It'd been there for days. It was swollen with gases. The eyes were sockets. And we had to clean it off the streets.'"[5]

A bit later, a lieutenant colonel comes along to help him load the body onto a truck. Drawing attention to the fact that he is weaving a tale, the narrator notes

> "But the bag rips on the edge of the truck's back gate, and the skin of the hajji tears with it, a big jagged tear through the stomach. Rotting blood and fluid and organs slide out like groceries through the bottom of a wet paper bag. Human soup hits him [the colonel loading the body] in the face, running down his mustache." If I'm telling the story sad I can stop there. (54)

The narrator's story conforms to a set of expectations, as he constantly makes clear by explaining how he tells the story differently depending on his audience. Those expectations revolve around the grossness of the body at war, the dehumanizing effects of the war on a body that has been left out in the sun so long that its skin has begun to separate. Crucially, the body no longer has a face – the "eyes were sockets," and there is no looking at this corpse as anything other than dead, gross matter. That grossness also transfers to the next scene, where the body rips and splatters the lieutenant colonel "in the face." He himself is defaced by the war. But as Klay's narrator insists, this is not a story about the reality of war; it is a fictionalized account.

The particular emphasis of this fictional account on defacement is crucial for how American literature draws on depictions of the body to examine war ethics. Alcott insistently focuses on the face when she refers to "beatified countenances," as well as Beth's "one loving look" and her "placid face . . . a face so full of painless peace that those who loved it best smiled through their tears." The face is crucial to Beth's encounter with death and her family's encounter with her. The full importance of this face-to-face encounter becomes clear when we contrast Alcott's depiction with this scene from Stephen Crane's *Red Badge of Courage* (1895):

> He reached a place where the high, arching boughs made a chapel. He softly pushed the green doors aside and entered. Pine needles were a gentle brown carpet. There was a religious half light. Near the threshold he stopped, horror-stricken at the sight of a thing. He was being looked at by a dead man who was seated with his back against a columnlike tree. The corpse was dressed in a uniform that once had been blue, but was now faded to a melancholy shade of green. The eyes, staring at the youth, had changed to the dull hue to be seen on the side of a dead fish. The mouth was open. Its red had changed to an appalling yellow. Over the gray skin of the face ran little ants. One was trundling some sort of a bundle along the upper lip. The youth gave a shriek as he confronted the thing. He was for moments turned to stone before it. He remained staring into the liquid looking eyes. The dead man and the living man exchanged a long look.[6]

Crane opts to represent war through realism (an attempt to capture objectively what occurs) and naturalism (the form of realism that relies for its worldview on a pseudo-scientific model of evolution). The scene is carefully constructed so as to replicate the sanctity of the home portrayed in Alcott's novel. Henry Fleming enters a "chapel" through a "door," and the interior is covered with a "gentle brown carpet" suffused in a "religious half light." This space of sanctity is ruptured by "the sight of a thing." Beth offers her "farewell" via "one loving look." Here, the youth is "being looked at by a dead man." The passive voice describes the youth as the object of the gaze, giving the "dead man" the agency of looking. Yet the horror of this scene comes from its reciprocity: "The dead man and the living man exchanged a long look." That look is crucial for how philosophers such as Jacques Lacan or Julia Kristeva think about the familiar and the horrific, as well as the power of language to mediate between them. In Crane, the "other" is a rotting corpse. Given the fact that this corpse wears a faded version of the youth's uniform, he is a projection of the youth's own feared fate of an unnoticed death in which his body will become a mere "thing." The body in American war literature is familiar, familial, and interpersonal; yet it threatens to lapse into its opposite – unfamiliar, estranged, impersonal – jeopardizing the very notion of personhood. For the American philosopher Judith Butler, this kind of bodily vulnerability is a way of rethinking ethics. Focusing on another unburied corpse, namely that of Antigone's brother Polyneices in Sophocles' tragedy, she argues that the physical vulnerability of human beings is a shared condition and that such "precarious life" forms the ethical base for understanding our common humanity.[7]

The texts of antiquity resonate not just for Butler but also in one seemingly minor detail for Crane, when he depicts the dead body leaning against a "columnlike tree." Given the passage's spatial detail, this architectural image invokes the neoclassicism that defined the built landscape of the early republic. The classical reference also connects with Crane's emphasis on the way texts shape expectations of battle that differ from soldiers' experiences. Describing Henry's attitudes at the beginning of the war, the text notes,

> From his home his youthful eyes had looked upon the war in his own country with distrust. It must be some sort of a play affair. He had long despaired of witnessing a Greeklike struggle. . . . He had burned several times to enlist. Tales of great movements shook the land. They might not be distinctly Homeric, but there seemed to be much glory in them. (3)

Homer's *Iliad* and *Odyssey* as well as Virgil's *Aeneid* – widely read in American literary education to this day – have shaped Henry's understanding of war. Worried that the Civil War is merely a game, he longs for "Greeklike struggle" and wants to participate in "great movements" that offer "glory." Crane enables us to understand that the Civil War is complicit with distorting a desire for narrative into a desire for war: Henry abandons his despair "of witnessing" and becomes an active participant in the conflict when the "great movements" of the war are spun into "Tales." Instead of the literary not measuring up to the real, Henry initially fears that the real cannot measure up to the epic.

Herman Melville's Civil War poem "On the Slain Collegians" best captures the cultural impact of epic heroism:

> The liberal arts and nurture sweet
> Which give his gentleness to man –
> Train him to honor, lend him grace
> Through bright examples meet –
> That culture which makes never wan
> With underminings deep, but holds
> The surface still, its fitting place,
> And so gives sunniness to the face
> And bravery to the heart; what troops
> Of generous boys in happiness thus bred –
> Saturnians through life's Tempe led,
> Went from the North and came from the South,
> With golden mottoes in the mouth
> To lie down midway on a bloody bed.[8]

Depictions of war are utterly misleading. They offer versions of "honor" and "grace" that are incompatible with the "bloody bed" of war. Melville indicts literature for recruiting "generous boys" with "golden mottoes," boys who "lie down" on the battlefield. His reference to the "golden mottoes in the mouth" also invokes the role that poetry played during the war action, as soldiers marched off singing patriotic lyrics. The most famous song of the American Civil War started off as "John Brown's Body" and was repurposed by Julia Ward Howe to become the "Battle Hymn of the Republic," a transition from the body to the body politic that illustrates Melville's outrage over heroic, national symbolism masking the human costs of conflict.

\* \* \*

All the examples I have offered so far raise a bigger question, namely whose bodies matter and whose deaths count in American war literature. As different as the scenes in Alcott, Crane, and Melville are from one another, they share a focus on the importance of white bodies and either ignore or (in the case of Klay's hajji corpse) outright denigrate racial others. This focus on white bodies shows how war literature tends to valorize whiteness as American and racializes as well as deprecates "others." That racialization and denigration adhere even in the very way we define war and war literature, when we focus by-and-large on the armed conflict between nation-states and military units. That definition does not encompass asymmetrical warfare. It does not account for the genocides perpetrated against Native Americans. Nor does it shed light on the violence inflicted on African Americans in the Middle Passage, under slavery, and under current conditions of environmental "slow violence" and carceral injustice.[9] What, then, is the role of racial "others" in American war literature? And how does American literature address war's ability to racialize the body?

In American literature, race by and large determines whose actions are portrayed as heroic, and whose sufferings count. Even those white writers concerned with the violence of genocide and slavery perpetuated this phenomenon. Take for instance the scene on which Alcott models Beth's death, the demise of "Little Eva" in Harriet Beecher Stowe's *Uncle Tom's Cabin* (1852). Like Beth, Eva is weighed down by the society that surrounds her, and she internalizes the ills of slavery: "Children do not usually generalize; but Eva was an uncommonly mature child, and the things that she had witnessed of the evils of the system under which they were living had fallen, one by one, into the depths of her thoughtful, pondering heart."[10] Eventually, those ills of slavery take her life, and she becomes a victim of the racist society in which she lives. But her life and death become the focus in this novel, in a sense appropriating the suffering of Black Americans for white women or girls and turning their bodily ailments into indictments of wrong that nonetheless reaffirm their own "racial innocence."[11] To the extent that Black suffering finds any acknowledgment, it takes on a form that negates armed resistance and soldierly heroism. Drawing on Christian iconography, Stowe's novel depicts Tom's violent end as martyrdom, his self-sacrifice alleviating white readers' fears of Black insurrection and violence. This portrayal carries into Civil War literature, where African Americans often display wartime heroism as a form of pacifism and self-sacrifice. For instance, Frances E. W. Harper's poem "A Story of the Rebellion" (1885) depicts an unnamed African American soldier as a "hero" when he sacrifices himself to save a group of soldiers. Harper draws on his self-effacement to make him Christ-like when he says, "I have no offering but my life."

However, Harper and other African American authors also use such depictions to highlight Black contributions to war. Complicit as such depictions might seem with white abolitionist writings, they are double-voiced. African American writers drew on the body of the Black martyr to argue for the very thing that he was denied: freedom. Harper plays with tropes dating back to the American Revolution's conception of freedom and agency, which so frequently represented the sacrifice of white bodies as whitening freedom itself. This racialization of the body politic via the bodies of white people made race a basis for national frames and ideologies. That is to say, race became ingrained in American intellectual and political life as something that predetermines the meaning of bodily actions: Under systemic racism, the same actions executed by a white or a Black body have different meanings.

Perhaps the clearest account of this problematic appears in the *Narrative of the Life of Frederick Douglass* (1845), which grapples with the question whether violence perpetrated against African Americans calls for responses of violence. Noting the futility of such self-defense when he describes how enslaved women and men were killed without their murderers being brought to justice, Douglass also recounts his own fight with the overseer Covey and describes it as a pivotal moment in which he reclaimed his standing as a man that the institution of slavery had denied him. Often read as an account of his acquisition of literacy, the *Narrative* is a far more radical text that shows how literacy was inadequate to liberate Douglass from bondage and portrays his physical confrontation with Covey as the truly liberatory moment. Addressing his readers, Douglass notes: "You have seen how a man was made a slave; you shall see how a slave was made a man."[12] By depicting such conflict, texts like the *Narrative* can produce a profound intervention into Whitman's dictum that "the real war" will never make it into the books. While documenting the necessity and justification for violent Black resistance, Douglass' Narrative reveals how the racially motivated violence against nonwhites amounts to asymmetrical warfare.

Having declined the opportunity to join John Brown at Harper's Ferry, Douglass spent the years of the American Civil War recruiting African American troops for the Union Army. Effectively using the army as a means of claiming de facto citizenship when African Americans remained excluded de jure till the passage of the 14th Amendment (1866), warfare also offered a means of using the depiction of African American soldiers to lay claim via their bodies – that is, via the very basis of their previous exclusion – to the abstractions of citizenship. At the war's outbreak, African Americans were barred from armed service because of their race. That quickly changed. While militias considered race a "disability" and excluded nonwhites, the Union's growing need for troops had made the mustering of African Americans as soldiers a necessity and reality by 1864. African American writers engaged with the meanings of that sea change: For instance, in J. Madison Bell's "The Black Brigade" (1864),[13] the standard-bearer of an African American regiment spurs on his comrades. Modeled after the epitome of the white-male heroic ethos expressed in Alfred, Lord Tennyson's widely popular "The Charge of the Light Brigade" (1854), the standard bearer emerges as a war hero:

> And thus he played the hero's part,
> Till on the ramparts of the foe
> A score of bullets pierced his heart,
> He sank within the trench below.[14]

Portrayed as a "hero," his death spurs on his comrades to the kind of violent action denied the formerly enslaved: "His comrades saw, and fired with rage."

The literary strategy that Douglass and poets such as Bell pioneered –using depictions of African American bodies to show the violence perpetrated against them, of armed Black resistance against that violence, and of the capacity for wartime actions to transform the abstractions of legal representation and legal personhood – is one whose tremendous costs Toni Morrison explored in *Home* (2012).[15] Centering her novel on Frank, an African American veteran of the Korean War, Morrison links his posttraumatic stress disorder to the war abroad but connects it even more to the anti-Black violence at home that propels him into war in the first place. As with the Civil War, the Korean War changed – in theory – how warfare and the racialization of bodies intersected: In 1948, President Harry S. Truman signed an executive order that integrated the military. Morrison's novel makes clear that this move toward desegregation of the armed services does not change but, if anything, further enflames racist domestic violence. Moreover, it makes African Americans complicit in the racialization of Asian peoples and in the violence enacted in Korea, then later in Vietnam. Picking up from Alcott and others the central trope of home as the locus of, rather than alternative to, wartime settings, Morrison connects the combat experience of Frank Money with the violence of eugenics that his sister Cee experiences in domestic service, all the while using their displacement by a racist mob from their childhood home and the brutality of lynching to show the multiple ways in which Black bodies experience violence as a condition of American life.

That sense of the constant presence that spectacular violence has in the lives of African Americans stands in marked contrast to the expatriation of violence that we see in the most prominent twentieth-century American literature, namely in the prose of Ernest Hemingway. Locating most of his works abroad in Europe and Africa, Hemingway pioneered a form of writing – almost journalistic in tone yet attentive to characters' stream-of-consciousness – that by and large eliminated the sentimental tradition of war writing in favor of an emotionally distanced plain prose expressive of a particular form of masculinity. Recollecting the killing of civilians in *For Whom the Bell Tolls*, the partisan Pilar recounts

> I saw the hall full of men flailing away with clubs and striking with flails, and poking and striking and pushing and heaving against people with the white wooden pitchforks that now were red and with their tines broken, and this was going on all over the room while Pablo sat in the big chair, his shotgun on his knees, watching, and they were shouting and clubbing and stabbing and they were screaming as horses scream in a fire. And I saw the priest with his skirts tucked up scrambling over a bench and those after him were chopping at him with the sickles and the reaping hoods and then some one had hold of his robe and there was another scream and another scream and I saw two men chopping into his back with sickles while a third man held the skirt of his robe and the priest's arms were up and he was clinging to the back of a chair.[16]

Hemingway creates this scene as one of direct (Pilar) and indirect (the characters who are listening; the reader) witnessing. Using verbal repetition, he makes "I saw" a statement of profound ambiguity. The scene that we readers "see" is one of unrestrained violence. In that sense, we are bearing witness. The fact that we are witnessing something that happened behind closed doors puts the unseen violence of war into the literary record. And yet, at the same time, Hemingway's skillful insertion of Pablo's passivity and complicity with this violence puts our witnessing in a different light: Are we, like Pablo, at the center of this violence and complicit with it? This raises possibilities of an ethics or morality that the text by and large withholds. The description offers the possibility of restorative justice but then also intimates that there is no such thing – just a witnessing that pivots between making visible and making complicit.

Much as we associate such a bleak view with the advent of modernism and twentieth-century warfare, there is a longer history in which amorality was racialized, as Native American "cruelty" was contrasted with white "compassion." Take this scene from James Fenimore Cooper's *The Last of the Mohicans* (1826). When a woman resists giving up her shawl, a "savage" instead grabs her baby and

> his bantering but sullen smile changing to a gleam of ferocity, he dashed the head of the infant against a rock, and cast its quivering remains to her very feet. For an instant the mother stood, like a statue of despair, looking wildly down at the unseemly object, which had so lately nestled in her bosom and smiled in her face; and then she raised her eyes and countenance toward heaven, as if calling on God to curse the perpetrator of the foul deed. She was spared the sin of such prayer for, maddened at his disappointment, and excited at the sight of blood, the Huron mercifully drove his tomahawk into her own brain. The mother sank under the blow, and fell, grasping at her child, in death, with the same engrossing love that had caused her to cherish it when living.[17]

The scene imagines the face-to-face encounter of the mother–child bond and of the ethical gaze; but, here, that encounter is violently undercut and destroyed by the infant's defacement. The mother at that moment turns the gaze that the infant can no longer reciprocate "toward heaven." Drawing on the iconography of Mary and Jesus, and especially on the depictions of Mary's grief that make up the artistic tradition of the pietà, the scene depicts the very core of an embodied bond that revolves around spirituality and holiness, a point that is underscored when the mother calls "on God." The scene sanctifies the body of the victims and, by extension, their whiteness. Pure to the end, the mother's prayerful supplication for the murderer's death is cut short, leaving her free of "sin." The Huron's action is "merciful" only in its impact and not in its intention, since he acts from a sense of "maddened" disappointment and "excited" blood lust. Acting from impulse, the Huron is the exact opposite of the life-transcending love that the mother's body expresses even in death. Her "engrossing love" can carry over even into her own death.

These descriptions serve not only as a depiction of white martyrdom; they also serve to contrast with the "savage," a word that even when used as a noun implicitly doubles as an adjective. That double function is important: In American war literature, racialized bodies are marked as savage, and savagery racializes bodies. By contrast, whiteness is not just a physical but also a moral condition. The depiction of Native Americans as "savage" serves to reduce them entirely to physical beings and to deny them the capacities of reason or emotion; their humanity itself is at stake as their depictions veer into animalization. Cooper describes an all-out massacre that follows the mother's death:

> More than two thousand raving savages broke from the forest ... The flow of blood might be likened to the outbreaking of a torrent; and as the natives became heated and maddened by the sight, many among them even kneeled to the earth, and drank freely, exultingly, hellishly, of the crimson tide.[18]

Note the wording of this passage, depicting Native Americans as "savages" and "raving," defined by an animalized or "instinctive" physical ferocity. Such animalization defines nonwhites by an embodiment absent of any humanity. We reach the nadir of that depiction when native Americans drink blood and enjoy the "crimson tide." A perversion of the sacrificial body of Christ, which is offered up in the rite of the Eucharist, the slaughter of these bodies is a "hellishly" enacted ritual of cannibalism.

That treatment of "others" as bodies and the denial of their humanity lies at the core of settler-colonial warfare, as Native writer William Apess powerfully describes. In recalling his own family history, Apess initially mentions almost casually that his "grandfather was a white man and married a female attached to the royal family of Philip, king of the Pequot."[19] This mention of his ancestry takes on another dimension, however, when he circles back to his cross-racial lineage in his account of "the wars between the whites and the natives" (4). Holding off on telling the story of King Philip, which is "generally known," Apess notes that

> it will suffice to say that he was overcome by treachery, and the goodly heritage occupied by this once happy, powerful, yet peaceful people was possessed in the process of time by their avowed enemies, the whites, who had been welcomed to their land in that spirit of kindness so peculiar to the red men of the woods. But the violation of their inherent rights, by those to whom they had extended the hand of friendship, was not the only act of injustice which this oppressed and afflicted nation was called to suffer at the hands of their white neighbors – alas! They were subject to a more intense and heart-corroding affliction, that of having their daughters claimed by the conquerors, and however much subsequent efforts were made to soothe their

sorrows, in this particular, they considered the glory of their nation as having departed. (4)

Published in 1829, three years after *The Last of the Mohicans*, this assessment is a searing indictment of Cooper. Whereas Cooper depicts Native Americans as the perpetrators of deceit, Apess depicts them as the victims of "treachery." Instead of portraying them as bloodthirsty, Apess insists that they were "happy" and "peaceful," and that they expressed those characteristics by welcoming whites in a "spirit of kindness." Insisting that whites had betrayed the "hand of friendship" they had been offered, Apess sees this violation of hospitality as aligned with the "violation of their inherent rights," with such rights not being those of their territorial sovereignty only but also those of family and kinship bonds. Where both texts focus on the impact war has on the bodies of women, Apess demonstrates that settler-colonialism is a violence against Native women's bodies and that that violence continues to express itself in acts of bodily harm. When his grandmother beats him to near death, Apess explains her actions as the far-reaching impact of the violence of settler-colonial warfare. While American literature is a powerful tool for perpetuating the violence of othering in depictions of bodies in warfare, it is also an important tool for disrupting and countering those myths. Apess puts the lie to the commonplace that "War trauma studies ... really begin with the Great War."[20]

This chapter's overarching claim, that we must think about the body in American literature as a body marked by war, risks making all American literature war literature. That is not the risk of this argument as much as it is the risk of reckoning with the named as well as the unnamed wars of American history and reading the literature that contributed to and commented on these conflicts. American bodies are multiply defined by war; it is that multiplicity that literature not only expresses but also creates, as it tries to grapple with the real wars that never make it into books, as well as those wars that do.

## NOTES

1 Drew Gilpin Faust, *This Republic of Suffering* (New York: Alfred A. Knopf, 2008), 10.
2 Walt Whitman, *Complete Poetry and Collected Prose*, ed. Justin Kaplan (New York: Library of America, 1982), 778.
3 Oliver Wendell Holmes, "The Human Wheel, Its Spokes and Felloes," *Atlantic Monthly* (May 1863), 574.
4 Elaine Scarry, *The Body in Pain: The Making and Unmaking of the World* (New York: Oxford University Press, 1985), 121.

5 Phil Klay, "Bodies," in *Redeployment* (New York: Penguin Books, 2014), 54.

6 Stephen Crane, *The Red Badge of Courage* (New York: Dover Publications, 1990), 35.

7 Judith Butler, *Antigone's Claim: Kinship between Life & Death* (New York: Columbia University Press, 2002), and *Precarious Life: The Powers of Mourning and Violence* (New York: Verso, 2004).

8 Herman Melville, "On the Slain Collegians (1866)," *Words for the Hour: A New Anthology of American Civil War Poetry*, ed. Faith Barrett and Cristanne Miller (Amherst: University of Massachusetts Press, 2005), 285.

9 Rob Nixon coined the term in *Slow Violence and the Environmentalism of the Poor* (Cambridge, MA: Harvard University Press, 2013).

10 Harriet Jacobs, *Uncle Tom's Cabin*, www.gutenberg.org/files/203/203-h/203-h.htm.

11 See Robin Bernstein, *Racial Innocence: Performing American Childhood from Slavery to Civil Rights* (New York: New York University Press, 2011).

12 Frederick Douglass, *Narrative of the Life of Frederick Douglass*, https://docsouth.unc.edu/neh/douglass/douglass.html; 65–66.

13 J. Madison Bell, "The Black Brigade," http://scholarlyediting.org/2013/editions/aa.18640206.4.html#note1.

14 Ibid.

15 Toni Morrison, *Home* (New York: Vintage Books, 2012).

16 Ernest Hemingway, *For Whom the Bell Tolls* (New York: Scribner Classics, 1940), 139–140.

17 James Fenimore Cooper, *Last of the Mohicans*, www.gutenberg.org/files/940/940-h/940-h.htm.

18 Ibid.

19 William Apess, *A Son of the Forest and Other Writings* (Amherst: University of Massachusetts Press, 1997), 3.

20 Alex Vernon, "Introduction" to *Teaching Hemingway and War* (Kent, OH: The Kent State University Press, 2016), 1–12, 2.

# 6

## SONY CORÁÑEZ BOLTON

# Decolonizing the Body in Multiethnic American Fiction

### Introduction: Hybrid Origins of Conquest

Multiethnic American fiction frequently centers "hybrid" bodies within locales and stories that draw on multiple ethnicities, languages, and national traditions. By focusing on these bodies, it challenges a national aesthetic formalism that would command conformity and assimilation, unearthing the hybrid genealogies that subtend embodiment across borders. Put differently, by representing embodiments that derive meaning from the interstitial spaces between national projects, such literature decolonializes the seemingly constitutive relationship between the nation-state and the bodies that compose the populations subjected to its political mandates. "Multiethnic" as a literary category contravenes any articulation of a cohesive national identity grounded in notions of the body with faithful monolithic origins.[1]

Notions of the bounded, legible body are as old as the concept of race, whose provenance can itself be traced to the "discovery" and conquest of the Americas. When attempting to give a decolonial account of multiethnic bodies – and when attending to the decolonial work performed by multiethnic fiction – we should start with those racial narratives produced around the epoch of the Cortesian Conquest that continue to shape the experience and representation of multiracial subjects in American letters. Prominent among these narratives was that of Dominican friar Bartolomé de las Casas, who in 1542 presented an ethical quandary to colonists about the relationship between racialized embodiment and metaphysical humanity, arguing that the "soul" was not possessed by (or within) European bodies alone. This mattered because, during conquest, the value of the human body was tied explicitly to judgments about its interior metaphysical contents. Soulless bodies could be destroyed, dispossessed, and exploited for their labor. The tension between judgments of the inherent value of human beings as something intrinsic to them was bound up with judgments about their exterior as, contra Las Casas, physical difference began to indicate interior value through the framework of race.

As Jamaican philosopher Sylvia Wynter claims, we see this tension play out in the sixteenth-century Valladolid debate (1550–1551) between Las Casas and Spanish philosopher Juan Ginés de Sepúlveda.[2] To say that the Indian body had a soul capable of redemption was to challenge genocidal campaigns of conquest, applying to them a moral religious scrutiny they had not previously faced.[3] Yet these debates about the humanity of indigenous people came only several decades after the genocidal Cortesian Conquest of what was then called "New Spain." While the Indian body possessed a soul, for European settlers the enslaved Black body constituted the soulless measure against which other definitions of human embodiment gained traction. Such a system linked bodies through ideological systems of contrast such that racialized bodies were defined in relation to the meanings ascribed to others. Race and racialization are always multiethnic, and the relation between slavery and settler colonialism is a flashpoint in a genealogical understanding of "multiethnicity" traced to the formation of racialized labor hierarchies dating back to conquest. Your "race" determined what kind of labor you would perform: The darker your complexion the more menial your labor; the more menial the labor your body performed, the more valueless your body was considered. Latin American sociologist Aníbal Quijano has called this labor relation of race the "coloniality of power."[4]

This racial hierarchy turned not only on the conceptual linkage of Blackness to menial labor and whiteness to wage labor, as Quijano has argued. What is also striking is the advent of new racial taxonomies for groups that did not exist prior to colonialism – namely, mestizos – in an effort to simultaneously racialize bodies and distance them from Blackness. "Mestizo" typically connotes a racial mixture between European and indigenous. Mestizo nation building produces a national body whose foundation is transatlantic slavery and indigenous appropriation. As I'll discuss more below, relational "multiethnic" racialization becomes even more relevant in the nineteenth century with the mass migration of Chinese and South Asian migrant laborers (called "coolies") to the Americas. When viewed as a corollary to slavery and anti-Blackness, philosophical incorporation of the "indio" into an expanded definition of the human in the early modern period sheds light on this dynamic between slavery, settler colonialism of indigenous peoples, and later labor migrations from Asia.

The organization of this chapter allows us to trace this dynamic. In the next section, I reflect on the varying definitions of "multiethnic" in North America, South America, and the Borderlands. While the meanings of this term are moving targets, homing in on what multiethnic means helps in our understanding of how human bodies' meanings shift over time and geography in relation to slavery and settler colonialism. The meanings of the body and its representations are shaped by the relationship between these violent and racist systems of colonialism. In the second section, on Filipinx American Literature, I track the mixed-race logic of mestizaje (English: miscegenation) to explore how intermediary racial subjects, like Filipinx Americans, derive embodied meaning at the intersection of multiple racial imaginaries. In the third section, I turn to Asian migration and Asian embodiment to further flesh out how human bodies and their purported value shift in response to political and economic realities. Asians and Asian racialization serve as intermediary bodies solidifying the myth of monolithic and discrete racial embodiment. By centering the American meanings of Asian embodiment, I hope to dispel that myth. I conclude by thinking about the crossroads of Black and Asian embodiment.

## Multiethnicity

In its US American context, the invocation of "multiethnic" as a category of literature can call to mind a liberal understanding of racialization that prioritizes assimilation.[5] Hence the very difference upon which ethnic categorization becomes meaningful and beneficial constitutes a conceptual liability. Discerning readers may note the paradox of this: ethnic categorization that relies on the precise definition of racial difference while simultaneously trumpeting the erasure of that difference through American assimilation. Some scholars and artists have perhaps cynically concluded that the implicit reader of these multiethnic narratives is white and normative.[6] Such critiques suggest that a diverse panoply of writers has been compelled to represent ethnic experience for an unnamed white reader, a pattern underscoring how liberal multiculturalism works in tandem with US racialization and the dominant desire to protect whiteness from contamination. White encounters with multiethnic literature all too easily prove the virtue of American assimilation while shielding whiteness from foreign incursion through its invisibility. As a category, "multiethnic" serves as a meaningful encounter with literature and difference while also being born from the deeply sedimented histories of segregation and racial violence.

North American multiethnicity differs from its political articulations in other parts of the Americas. Spanish colonialism identified indigenous peoples as subjects of the Spanish crown. Anglo-American colonial settlements constructed white identity in opposition to Indians that precisely were not subjects of the British crown. The former resulted in more diverse racial mixtures of people and modern-day nation-states that reflect that difference.

89

The latter articulated "whiteness as property" defined through its avowed distancing from Indians, who were seen as part of sovereign nations at once separate from and subjected to British colonial rule.[7] Attending to the differences of multiethnicity in different parts of the Americas allows us to examine how different imaginaries shape who belongs to the national body; the legal and political processes that segregated different bodies in varied geographic and physical space; and the differing histories that lead to the production of mixed race bodies or the maintenance of singular "pure" racial groups.

This does not mean that indigenous communities were "eliminated" from the US racial imaginary. Patrick Wolfe makes the counterintuitive argument that the complete eradication of indigenous peoples in white-settler nations (the United States, Australia, and Canada) runs counter to the assertion of settler nationalism.[8] That is to say, such nations preserve Indian culture through iconography and myth. Consider that the foundational colonial essay on US Manifest Destiny by Frederick Jackson Turner, "The Significance of the Frontier in American History" (1894), metaphorically integrates the Indian body into the white-settler body:

> [The frontier] finds him (the American pioneer) a European in dress, industries, tools, modes of travel, and thought. It takes him from the railroad car and puts him in the birch canoe. It strips off the garments of civilization and arrays him in the hunting shirt and the moccasin. It puts him in the log cabin of the Cherokee and Iroquois and runs an Indian palisade around him ... He must accept the conditions which it furnishes, or perish, and so he fits himself into the Indian clearings and follows the Indian trails.[9]

What was once a white body in European dress is transformed into one that dons the hunting shirt and moccasin, physically traversing the frontier as an Indian would. Such a logic carries on into the present in the form of Indian mascots of sports teams. This differs from the almost obsessive histories of racial segregation of Black people from whites through informal and legal means. Despite such a distinction, however, the slave-holding political economy historically works in tandem with native elimination.[10] Studying both in isolation misses crucial ways that racial groups were differentiated relationally. Together, transatlantic slavery and indigenous elimination connect the stories of multiethnicity across the Americas, shaping how racialized bodies, either as imagined constructions or material entities, have been read and understood.

As many familiar with histories of US expansionism will know, when the United States achieved its goals of Manifest Destiny to acquire the Southwest and the West coast, it didn't stop. Multiethnic as an analytic must attempt to view the historical progression of transatlantic slavery and Indian removal to eventual transpacific empire building. Significantly, this included the colony of the Philippines following the Spanish-American (1898) and Filipino-American Wars (1899–1902). The Philippines, being a former colony of Spain, also invites questions regarding the project of racial mixture endemic to Latin American nations known as mestizaje in an Asian context. I now turn toward multiethnic embodiment as it is represented in Filipinx diasporic writing.

## The Mestizo Body in Filipinx American Literature

In telling a multiethnic story about American literatures that can get at the multifarious meanings of the American body, I perhaps unexpectedly turn to Filipinx American fiction to begin thinking through a hemispheric American account that might reconcile the distinct histories of racial incorporation and exclusion – mestizaje and its perennial defense of eurocentrism, on the one hand, and US-style segregation in the historical service of the consolidation of whiteness, on the other. While not exceptional compared to other post-colonial sites, the Philippines and its diaspora formed in response to the consecutive imperial projects of first Spain and then the United States. The Philippines and its diaspora therefore experienced and contended with both racial circumstances and thus gives us a vista into both.

One text that takes advantage of the Philippines' mix of mestizaje and segregationist histories in order to stretch the analytical possibilities of American multiethnicity is Filipino American Brian Ascalon Roley's novel *American Son* (2001). Set in a post-riot Los Angeles in early 1990s California, the novel tells a coming-of-age narrative of its queer protagonist Gabriel, a mixed-race white and Filipino youth. Gabriel's queerness is never actualized through a coming-out narrative in which he confesses to gayness per se. Instead, the novel tells a more complicated story of a character attempting to make sense of a nonheteronormative identity within a Borderlands context in which different ideas of mestizaje commingle from the Pacific and the US-Mexico corridor. Multiethnicity unsettles the solidity and stability of both racial and sexual identification:

> Suddenly I notice my reflection in the mirrored glass and it appears so obviously Asian I almost stop in my tracks. My eyes look narrow, and my hair straight and coarse and black. He must be blind. I have slender Asian hips, and my cheekbones are too high. The way the sunlight hits my face you cannot even make out my eyes. My eyes jerk away. Everyone will be able to tell. I might even look Mexican, but not white.[11]

Even light obscures rather than reveals. Evidently "Asian" characteristics written on the very body of the Filipino American are diluted within the racial landscape of the American Borderlands. What is compelling about Roley's novel is its refusal to demand conformity and assimilation from its protagonist, to cast its protagonist's body within extant racial categories in the United States, or to transcend the obstacle that the ethnic difference such racial identity presents to accessing the so-called American Dream. David Palumbo-Liu has argued that much multiethnic fiction presents its protagonist with an eccentric ethnicity that is an obstacle to American inclusion, building toward correcting that eccentricity and thus demonstrating to a normative reader that the American Dream works. According to Palumbo-Liu, this assimilation narrative centers whiteness as the value to which we must strive and centers whites as the ideal readers. *American Son* eschews this kind of assimilative narrative: "I might ... look Mexican, but not white." Rather than a vertical assimilation "upward," Roley emphasizes an affinity horizontally toward Mexicanness. The mestizo history of the Philippines as a former Spanish colony reshapes commonsense Asian American narratives of racial embodiment in the US Borderlands, also a site of Spanish colonization. The reflection that Gabriel appraises in the mirror is so "obviously Asian" that if others do not see it they must be blind. Ironically, sunlight does not illuminate his face completely, rather it obscures his eyes. Also his "slender Asian hips" give an impression of a racialized erotic desire for a body that cannot be completely defined.

The queerness of Roley's characterizations turns on an infidelity to racial identification that resonates with Chicana feminist Gloria Anzaldúa's notion of a "mestiza consciousness."[12] That is to say, Gabe's construction of sexual knowledge around his queerness is inseparable from the racial ambiguity that his body furnishes within a borderlands imaginary of Los Angeles that has just experienced violent race riots. The acquittal of LAPD officers after their brutal video-recorded attack of Rodney King forms the unspoken racial background of *American Son*'s depiction of the borderlands of Los Angeles in the early 1990s. Neither these riots nor King is mentioned directly in the novel; nevertheless, they should inform our understanding of Asian and Latinx embodiment in the US Southwest.

Writing specifically about the context of the US Southwest, Anzaldúa's *Borderlands/La frontera* attempts to think through a Chicano Spanglish, queer, and feminist identity that is simultaneously outside of US American identity and Mexican national identity. She articulates a Chicana identity outside of Anglo American understandings of Americanness and that was not completely commensurate with Chicano national identity. However, a "mestiza consciousness" – which, for Anzaldúa, is always an embodied practice – wrestles with the contradictions of such an outsider status by not proposing resolution. Instead, Anzaldúa embraces contradictions. She writes of la mestiza that,

> In perceiving conflicting information and points of view, she is subjected to a swamping of her psychological borders. She has discovered that she can't hold concepts or ideas in rigid boundaries. The borders and walls that are supposed to keep the undesirable ideas out are entrenched habits and patterns of behavior; these habits and patterns are the enemy within. Rigidity means death. Only by remaining flexible is she able to stretch the psyche horizontally and vertically. La mestiza constantly has to shift out of habitual formations; from convergent thinking, analytical reasoning that tends to use rationality to move toward a single goal (a Western mode), to divergent thinking, characterized by movement away from set patterns and goals and toward a more whole perspective, one that includes rather than excludes. The new mestiza copes by developing a tolerance for contradictions, a tolerance for ambiguity. She learns to be Indian in Mexican culture, to be Mexican from an Anglo point of view... nothing is thrust out ... nothing rejected, nothing abandoned. Not only does she sustain contradictions, she turns the ambivalence into something else.[13]

The above citation may be one of the greatest critical insights that Anzaldúa has given to ethnic studies, critical theory, queer, and feminist thought. From it we can link the mestizo embodiment of Filipinx Americans in the US Borderlands with the queer mixed-race subjectivity of the Chicana border subject. Rather than a teleological understanding of identity unfolding and developing toward a unitary and unified construction of belonging, la mestiza's racial and sexual mixture "sustain[s] contradictions," encouraging a "tolerance for ambiguity" that seems out of place for the strategic essentialism of political movements even if (or perhaps especially if) they are coalitional. From a literary standpoint this points to the intersection of political identification with literary categorization under the rubric of "multiethnic" as well as the phenomenological reality of ethnic filiation, kinship, and heritage. In this way, the borderlands of Anzaldúa's queer Chicana imaginary helps us tease out a multifaceted understanding of Asian American embodiment of characters in Ascalon Roley's Filipinx-Chicanx narrative while also offering tools for understanding how to take up space when you feel racially misrecognized and out of place.

At the same time, mestizaje as a cultural discourse operates within a matrix of eugenic thought undertheorized in *Borderlands/La frontera*. Borrowing from Grace Hong and Roderick Ferguson's formulation, I suggest that within the "multiethnic" aesthetic framework of mestizaje we can locate the "strange affinities" between Asian American and Latinx subjects. Locating this matrix within a more hemispheric American structure we can delineate connections between Asian, Latinx, and Black American subjectivities locating the "intimacies between continents."[14] Mestizaje represents a cultural logic of hybridity that has been philosophically significant in nation and state building in the Americas. Perhaps the most famous and notable of this discourse is José Vasconcelos's essay La Raza Cósmica (1925).[15] Drawing on eugenic conceptions of what historian Alexandra Stern would call "better breeding," Vasconcelos gestured toward a "fifth race" of humanity that would represent the conglomeration of all the (from his perspective) currently known races of humankind: white European, Asian, Indian, and African.[16] These would meld together into a new hybrid identity that would transcend racial difference and result in the ideal citizen-subject. I would note the similarity with the US American style liberal multiculturalist discourse that also avers to transcend racial difference through color blindness and a strong belief in a pro forma equality acquired during the Civil Rights Movement. However, rather than a racial hybridity as racial transcendence we observe a functionalized and imposed desire to assimilate into an ideal US American whiteness. This could be said to be the case in some of the American states of South or Central America, but it is perhaps more accurately captured as a mestizo attachment to what Aníbal Quijano called "eurocentrism."[17] Critical Ethnic Studies scholarship in the United States attempts to formalize decolonial theories through trenchant critiques of the neoliberal carceral state and the historical structure of settler colonialism. These typically theorize the antagonistic force positioned against human equity as "white supremacy" rather than specifically euro-centrist thought.[18]

Both Latin American eurocentrism and US American white supremacy are permutations of a similar settler-colonial ideology that seeks to eliminate the native from the nation through its assimilation into a national body (mestizaje) or through legal exclusions from citizenship (white-settler nationalism). In the tradition of Latin American critical theory spearheaded by the likes of formidable scholars like Quijano, Sylvia Wynter, Fernando Ortiz, and Walter Mignolo is the critique of the palpable historical forces of eurocentrism as an instrumental ideology in the structure of the "coloniality of power."[19] Rather than formal colonialism, "coloniality" describes the ideological entrenchment of extractive capitalist and European discourses that bleed over into the contemporary modern era since the time of conquest. In a similar vein, because the colonial period's formal end does not mean that its influence cannot be ascertained today, scholars like Ann McClintock have argued that the "post" in "postcolonial" is a misnomer.[20] It is within these conceptual differences in analyzing complementary colonial forces in a "multiethnic canon" of literary works reflecting the colonial aftermath of

British and Spanish imperialisms that I locate a reading practice that decolonizes the body. Toward this end, I now turn to thinking about Asian embodiment in the Americas.

## Asia in the Americas

Inscribed within the very figure of the mestizo body is a racial hybridity that complicates monolithic racial embodiment. Mestizaje is a racial form of the human and also an aesthetic cultural form shaping literary representation. Perhaps surprisingly Asian Americanist critique has attempted to problematize the explanatory framework of mestizaje for its eurocentric, anti-indigenous, and anti-Black biases. The figure of the Asian and the discourse of the Orient have facilitated unique and important critiques that destabilize mestizaje as the only logic through which we can understand the American body. Asian American Studies scholars have started to give a deeper account of the connections between the global coolie market, the transatlantic slave trade, plantation economics, and mestizaje discourse in Latin America – a region where Asians are American in quite a different way than in North America. This work is significant as it problematizes the construction of a mestizo body through the ways that Asian coolie labor was adopted to replace emancipated Black slave labor in the mid to late nineteenth century.

What might be controversial for some is the use of theories of racial formation in the US context to understand Asian racialization in Latin America. Why this works, I think, is that "Oriental," coolie, or Asian bodies are always rendered foreign presences and never citizens. While very different historical processes mark Asian racialization in different parts of the Americas, the end result of foreignness is similar. Thus as a part of the effort to give a decolonial reading of the body I will similarly center though not overdetermine the Asian body as a node around which we can ask productive questions about the body and its representations, offering us different insights into how Latin American/Latinx diasporic literature represents racial formations in the interstices between nations. The Caribbean is one such hybrid context that unexpectedly connects to the Philippines and the mysterious "Orient."

The Dominican diaspora, as represented in Junot Díaz's novel *The Brief and Wondrous Life of Oscar Wao* (2007), is born from traumatic histories and toxic family dynamics that are themselves products of the Trujillo dictatorship (1930–1961). My focus here is on the textured representations of Díaz's marginal Black femininities, whose articulation is contextualized within oblique citations of the Asia/Pacific. Beli Cabral, Oscar Wao's mother, a Black "prieta" woman who lived under the Trujillato, animates discussions of racialized misogynies and the violent patriarchy of dictatorial and imperial rule. Black femininity becomes a conduit through which the traumas of dictatorship are transmitted diasporically, and yet it is also the avenue through which healing and a robust critique of the compulsive omissions of empire can be elucidated. These Black diasporic identifications can be understood through an almost surreptitious connection and citation of the Philippines and China through the diasporic kaleidoscope of memory:

> In later years Beli would lament that she had ever lost touch with her "chinos." They were so good to me, she moaned to Oscar and Lola. Nothing like your worthless esponja of a father. Juan, the melancholic gambler, who waxed about Shanghai as though it were a love poem sung by a beautiful woman you love but cannot have. Juan, the short sighted romantic whose girlfriends robbed him blind and who never mastered Spanish (though in later years when he was living in Skokie, Illinois, he would yell at his Americanized grandchildren in his guttural Spanish, and they laughed at him, thinking it Chinese).[21]

While implicit in the scene above, the image of an aging man speaking "guttural Spanish" rendered a burden to his "Americanized grandchildren" is clear. The totality of his experience as an Asian "American" subject is submerged and forgotten due to American assimilation. Here Asian America occludes the Caribbean and the Black-Asian intersections that reflect migratory realities to a "New World" shaped by the genocidal, settler-colonial, and plantation histories emblematic of "fukú" (the curse-like energy that follows Oscar Wao's family in their trials and tribulations). And yet, it is precisely through the traumatic formation of the Dominican American diaspora that a person like Juan Then can be recuperated such that we can regard him. Then's memory and remembering are truncated by the deficiency and gutturalness of his Spanish; he is thus misunderstood by his Asian American grandchildren and is, by extension, misunderstood by Asian American Studies. How might Filipinx Studies, with its attentiveness to Latinx concerns, account for such a subject? How might Asian American Studies account for the Hispanic Caribbean and Black diasporic subjectivity?

Díaz's novel helps us to think through some of the problems inherent in Latin American mestizaje discourses, which would fail to account for subjects like Beli Cabral and Juan Then. This ambitious and empathic literary representation mirrors the problem of foundational colonial American definitions of race, which experienced seismic redefinition in the political economic transition from slave to "free labor."[22] This is where the question of Asia and the Orient enter the equation of hybrid embodiment. Asian Americanist scholars like Lisa Lowe, Jason Oliver Chang, and Ana Paulina Lee focusing on case studies of coolies in the Caribbean, the Chinese in

Mexico, and the Japanese and Chinese in Brazil, respectively, have all similarly analyzed how mestizaje coopted a nationalized form of indigenous identity at the expense of Black and Asian freedom. In this way, according to Chang, mestizaje operates like a category of racial whiteness not unlike white supremacist statecraft in the United States. At the very least, the ways that race relations play out in the larger Americas draw from the political economic transitions of American nations from enslaved Black labor to free coolie labor, whose economic benefits are extracted by a eurocentric mestizo national who lays claim to sovereign authority through a putative reformed Indianness.

Such multiethnic encounters should then animate our interest in bodies that don't behave like they're supposed to. A multiethnic body performatively instantiates histories that do not intuitively map onto what is normatively expected. Perhaps in a different context than what literary theorist Siobhan Somerville intended, such hybrid bodies "queer the color line."[23] The hybridity of such wild bodies convokes a queerness that I argue can decolonize literary imaginaries of the American body. Drawing on Gloria Anzaldúa's feminist border framework of the "borderlands" and a "mestiza consciousness," I suggest that in order to achieve the aim of decolonizing the body in fiction, we must contend with how certain texts thread the borders between different national, linguistic, historical, and ethnic traditions. Hybridity for Anzaldúa connotes a weaving back and forth between different geopolitical environments to produce a subjectivity that is multiply marked. *Borderlands/La frontera* then cannot always be properly considered US American, and even less certain is its categorization as Mexican literature. The text is both and is neither. Chicana feminist culture and identity are produced in the encounter with both traditions in both Spanish and English or with neither in the form of Spanglish. Anzaldúa appears to produce a third space that exceeds the national boundaries of the United States and Mexico – a "consciencia mestiza" is born.

## Conclusion: Queering Vietnam

By way of conclusion I center two writers – Jessica Hagedorn and Martin Luther King – who famously brought the cultural formation of Southeast Asia into American popular and political consciousness. These writers respectively refract the representation of Filipinx and Vietnamese embodiments through the prism of Black liberation, furnishing a multiethnic vista that doesn't render Asian and Black bodies interchangeable in literature but rather intimately connects the violence enacted on racialized bodies to a broader global structure.

Filipina author Jessica Hagedorn's *Dogeaters* is a queer diasporic Filipino text that represents metropolitan Manila as a borderlands of multiple colonial encounters, with Spanish heritage, Hollywood, and Black American popular culture all mingling to produce what the reader might understand as a Filipino hybridity.[24] Many Filipino American literary critics have focused, with good reason, on the novel's narrator, the Filipina mestiza Rio Gonzaga. However, the story of another mestizo figure brings together *Dogeaters'* seemingly incommensurate racial histories through the unexpected presence of his raced body. Joey Sands is a queer Black Filipinx sex worker who is the offspring of an African American solider stationed at the Subic Naval Base, decommissioned in 1992, and a Filipina sex worker. Hagedorn frames the introduction to Joey's Blackness through a colonial representation of Filipino indigeneity. Hagedorn cites Jean Mallat's 1846 illustrated book *The Philippines: History, Geography, Customs, Agriculture, Industry, and Commerce of the Spanish Colonies in Oceania.* We come to know Joey by way of African America, through Mallat's ethnological gaze:

> The most inaccessible lairs of these wild mountains are inhabited by a great number of those small Negroes called "Negritoes" whom we spoke about earlier; sometimes they are chased out of their homes, taken prisoners, the youngest among them to be raised by inhabitants in their homes until they reach the age of reason, in the meantime being used for diverse chores, after which they are set free. One of our friends owned one which he gave to us; he was called Panchote, was not lacking in intelligence and was most of all very mischievous.[25]

As one can surmise from Mallat's work, the Philippines had/has its own group of indigenous "Negroes." These "negritos," from the Spanish meaning "little black people," are the Aetas or Itas. They are an indigenous group of hunter-gatherers who have formed complex communities in the mountainous regions of the Philippine island of Luzon. While Joey doesn't claim tribal membership as an Ita, his African American Blackness is resignified within the colonial landscape of the Philippines.

We later come to understand the additions of Black American cultural referents throughout the novel (Nat King Cole, Eartha Kitt, rustbelt cities in the US North like Detroit, Donna Summer, Disco, Blues, and Motown) as framing a different genealogy of Blackness that is reflected distinctly in the body of Joey Sands. Filipino identity is shifted by Blackness as Joey's Filipino body resituates our understanding of Blackness through ethnological indigenous frames of reference. The result is a productive, though subtle, critique of the problematic sexual economies that arise surrounding US military bases, constructing a hybrid identity that is the product of sexual imperial violence and a "mestiza consciousness" that can speak against the grain of the colonial. Hagedorn's novel obliquely references critiques made by a robust Black internationalism dating from the early twentieth century and perhaps culminating with Dr. Martin Luther King, Jr.'s stunning speech "Beyond Vietnam." King is relevant here because of the ways that he extended the domestic framing of US civil rights to the global arena of imperial war in Southeast Asia.

King's global political worldview gestures toward a multiethnic literary theory useful in questioning how we locate and periodize canons of literature. The vital histories of civil rights discourse in the United States at times occlude the fact that King was a global thinker. Domestic framings of Blackness may stand in contradistinction to the racial histories of mixture and hybridity that characterize many Latin American cultures; indeed, King showed us that Black radical thinking can do as much outside of the United States as within. "Asia" seems to figure otherwise even though both the ghosts of transatlantic slavery and the coolie system historically and philosophically shape American hybridity, whether in North or South America. King made the perpetual foreignness of Asia resonate with the more familiar struggles of Black liberation in which we might locate a coherent American experience. The transatlantic slave trade and indigenous elimination might seem counterintuitive historical formations that have little to do with the construction of Asian American fiction; nevertheless, King's moving statement in "Beyond Vietnam" that "taking the black young men who had been crippled by our society and sending them eight thousand miles away to guarantee liberties in Southeast Asia which they had not found in southwest Georgia and East Harlem" was not something that he could reconcile with his political philosophy of nonviolence. His opposition to the Vietnam War and his compassionate concern for "little brown Vietnamese boys and girls" is, to my mind, a pivotal flashpoint in Asian American history and renders King's work, in this context, a canonical interlocutor in Asian American cultural critique.[26] The violence of imperial war and the traumatic history of slavery form a historical screen upon which we can understand the body in a far more global and inclusive way. The Asian and Black bodies that suffer the violences that King responds to are both imbedded in the historical realities of cold war militarism and civil rights discourse – these are not discrete spheres but rather part of what we could call a multiethnic history of American embodiment.

The literary archive and the stakes of understanding a multiethnic fiction in the American tradition would seem to avow unexpected connection and affiliation across bodies that we imagine to be constitutively different. It is instructive to blend different theoretical traditions, in the service of studying literature in a more global encounter, that may not typically have open lines of scholarly communication. As might be apparent in the analyses of the partial literary archive furnished in this essay, I am curious about the ways that Asian American, Latinx, and Latin American Studies and Black thought have complementary although very distinct understandings of "America" as a political formation. The framework of hybridity serves as a productive crossroads facilitating these connections. Mestizaje and other forms of racial mixture represent a fruitful though curious blending of the different racial histories, colonialisms, and migratory realities that construct American identity and the ways American letters shape our understanding of American bodies.

## NOTES

1 Grace Kyungwon Hong and Roderick A. Ferguson, *Strange Affinities: The Gender and Sexual Politics of Comparative Racialization* (Durham, NC: Duke University Press, 2011).

2 Sylvia Wynter, "Unsettling the Coloniality of Being/Power/Truth/Freedom: Towards the Human, after Man, Its Overrepresentation – An Argument," *CR: The New Centennial Review* 3, no. 3 (2003): 257–337, https://doi.org/10.1353/ncr.2004.0015.

3 Bartolomé de las Casas and Stafford Poole, *In Defense of the Indians; the Defense of the Most Reverend Lord, Don Fray Bartolomé de Las Casas, of the Order of Preachers, Late Bishop of Chiapa, against the Persecutors and Slanderers of the Peoples of the New World Discovered across the Seas* (DeKalb: Northern Illinois University Press, 1974).

4 Aníbal Quijano and Michael Ennis, "Coloniality of Power, Eurocentrism, and Latin America," *Nepantla: Views from South* 1, no. 3 (2000): 533.

5 Jodi Melamed, *Represent and Destroy: Rationalizing Violence in the New Racial Capitalism* (Minneapolis: University of Minnesota Press, 2011).

6 David Palumbo-Liu, *Asian/American: Historical Crossings of Racial Frontier* (Stanford, CA: Stanford University Press, 1999); Toni Morrison, *Playing in the Dark: Whiteness and the Literary Imagination* (New York: Vintage Books, 1993).

7 Cheryl I. Harris, "Whiteness as Property," *Harvard Law Review* 106, no. 8 (1993): 1707, https://doi.org/10.2307/1341787.

8 Patrick Wolfe, "Settler Colonialism and the Elimination of the Native," *Journal of Genocide Research* 8, no. 4 (December 1, 2006): 387–409, https://doi.org/10.1080/14623520601056240.

9 Frederick Jackson Turner, "The Significance of the American Frontier," in *Rereading Frederick Jackson Turner* (New Haven: Yale University Press, 1994), 33. Turner "The Significance of the Frontier in American History" (1894), 33.

10 Iyko Day, "Being or Nothingness: Indigeneity, Antiblackness, and Settler Colonial Critique," *Critical Ethnic Studies* 1, no. 2 (2015): 102–121, https://doi.org/10.5749/jcritethnstud.1.2.0102.

11 Brian Ascalon Roley, *American Son* (New York: W. W. Norton & Company, 2001), 90.

12 Gloria Anzaldúa, *Borderlands: The New Mestiza = La Frontera* (San Francisco: Aunt Lute Books, 2012).

13 Ibid., 101.

14 Lisa Lowe, *The Intimacies of Four Continents* (Durham, NC: Duke University Press, 2015).

15 José Vasconcelos, *La Raza Cósmica Misión de La Raza Iberoamericana: Notas de Viajes a La América de Sur* (Paris: Agencia mundial de librería, 1925), http://hdl.handle.net/2027/pst.000008497192.

16 Alexandra Stern, *Eugenic Nation: Faults and Frontiers of Better Breeding in Modern America*, 2nd ed. American Crossroads: 17 (Oakland: University of California Press, 2016).

17 Quijano and Ennis, "Coloniality of Power, Eurocentrism, and Latin America."

18 Andrea Smith, "Heteropatriarchy and the Three Pillars of Settler Colonialism," in *The Color of Violence: The INCITE! Anthology*, ed. Andrea Smith et al. (Cambridge, MA: South End Press, 2006), 68–73.

19 Quijano and Ennis, "Coloniality of Power, Eurocentrism, and Latin America."

20 Anne McClintock, "The Angel of Progress: Pitfalls of the Term 'Post-Colonialism,'" *Social Text* no. 31/32 (1992): 84, https://doi.org/10.2307/466219.

21 Junot Díaz, *The Brief Wondrous Life of Oscar Wao* (New York: Riverhead Books, 2007), 104.

22 Lowe, *The Intimacies of Four Continents*; Jason Oliver Chang, *Chino: Anti-Chinese Racism in Mexico, 1880–1940* (Champaign: University of Illinois Press, 2017); Ana Paulina Lee, *Mandarin Brazil: Race, Representation, and Memory* (Stanford, CA: Stanford University Press, 2018).

23 Siobhan B. Somerville, *Queering the Color Line: Race and the Invention of Homosexuality in American Culture*. Series Q. (Durham, NC: Duke University Press, 2000).

24 Jessica Tarahata Hagedorn, *Dogeaters* (New York: Penguin Books, 1991).

25 Ibid., 41. My emphasis.

26 Martin Luther King, "Beyond Vietnam," The Martin Luther King, Jr., Research and Education Institute, July 23, 2014, https://kinginstitute.stanford.edu/king-papers/documents/beyond-vietnam.

# 7

FRANCES TRAN

# Science Fiction's Humanoid Bodies of the Future

Tracing the origins of the word "science" from the Latin "scientia," or "knowledge," illuminates the stakes of science fiction as a genre that offers insight into multiple competing, even contradictory, forms of knowing. I begin here to underscore how this Latin root makes perceptible the boundaries that have been constructed around what constitutes "science" and, by extension, science fiction. It throws into relief the violent legacies out of which Enlightenment conceptions of humanity, science, and knowledge developed through the subjugation and colonization of purportedly savage, unknowing "others." By recognizing how our generic expectations often depend on westernized definitions of science and technology, I hope to create room in what follows to challenge these parameters and elaborate a more nuanced understanding of the relationship between science fiction and embodied difference. I ask, in other words, what forms of science (fiction) are remaking bodies and whose bodies get to count as human(oid)? How is the future narrated – on whose terms, with what techno-scripts, and in which worlds?

Confronting science fiction as a fraught, predominantly white, heteronormative genre, shaped by themes of space colonization and militarized warfare, suggests why many scholars have gravitated toward its cousin, speculative fiction.[1] Cultural theorists such as Aimee Bahng, Alexis Lothian, Sami Schalk, and Shelley Streeby provide trenchant arguments about not only how speculative fiction connotes a more capacious category (encompassing conventional forms of sci-fi alongside fantasy, horror, magical realism, etc.), but also how it enables an interrogation of the value hierarchies attached to hegemonic concepts like science and reason.[2] In positing that a westernized version of science represents just one mode of knowledge production, these critics demonstrate how speculative fiction attunes us to myriad ways of knowing the world that can bring into sharper focus the lived realities of marginalized subjects. In addition to illuminating how racialized and gendered bodies have been used as test subjects and tools for the realization of technological, medical, and scientific advancements, their work demonstrates how speculative fictions that center minoritized voices prompt us to redefine what constitutes progress, prosperity, and futurity.

Walidah Imarisha and adrienne marie brown, coeditors of the anthology *Octavia's Brood* (2015), have gone even further in calling for visionary fiction as an alternative framework. They explain: "'Visionary fiction' is a term we developed to distinguish science fiction that has relevance toward building new, freer worlds from the mainstream strain of science fiction, which most often reinforces dominant narratives of power."[3] Guided by the premise that the imaginative capacity to compose science fiction draws on the same energies needed to materialize more equitable worlds, Imarisha and brown present visionary fiction not just as a literary genre but as a vital, ongoing, antiracist, decolonial, and feminist project. In doing so, they underscore that science fiction is an embodied experience:

> And for those of us from communities with historic collective trauma, we must understand that each of us is already science fiction walking around on two legs ... For adrienne and myself, as two Black women, we think of our ancestors in chains dreaming about a day when their children's children would be free ... [T]ogether they dreamed of freedom, and they brought us into being.[4]

These words highlight how science fiction encompasses bodily realities – lived experiences of abduction, alienation, and otherness – as well as the possibilities that come out of creative acts of survival, new forms of relationality, kinship, and community. By reminding us that this kind of science fictional practice has brought purportedly impossible futures into being, Imarisha and brown underscore the material stakes of a genre that has often been denounced as frivolous entertainment and mere escapism. They show how visionary science fiction is not about leaving material realities behind but involves creating the conditions of possibility for liberation and transformative justice.

I open with this overview of the contested space science fiction occupies alongside formulations like speculative fiction and visionary fiction to thematize the difficulty of providing a coherent entry point into an essay on science fiction's humanoid bodies of the future. Because questions of privilege, power, and positionality have played and continue to play an important role in shaping popular perceptions of the genre, this chapter situates an analysis of common tropes and representations of embodiment in science fiction to accentuate their embeddedness within histories of racialization, gendered and sexual exploitation, colonialism, and neocolonialisms. In an effort to foreground the stories of those who have been excluded from dominant narratives of the future, I draw on texts that resist legibility within narrow conceptions of "hard sci-fi" as works necessarily grounded in scientific theory, rationality, and plausibility. Troubling what gets to count as science, technology, and science fiction is, after all, one way of living up to the aims of a genre that purports to expand our understanding of the possible, a project with profound implications for how we come to think, know, and navigate the worlds we inhabit.

## The Stickiness of Corporeality

Science fiction offers seemingly limitless possibilities for exploring alternative embodiments, from technological enhancement and genetic modification to mutation, aliens, and multispecies assemblages. By depicting forms of hybridity that blur the relationship between humans, machines, nonhuman animals, and extraterrestrials, the genre destabilizes our conception of what constitutes the human body and, thus, the very idea of the human. At the same time, recognizing "the human" as a category that derives meaning through historical practices of exclusion demands that we temper the celebratory rhetoric around the mutability of bodies in science fiction. Attending to the writings of women and people of color attunes us to what I call the "stickiness of corporeality," which underscores how the bodies that proliferate this work bear traces of historical violence – enslavement, coloniality, and genocide – and cannot easily morph or disappear even in science fictional landscapes.

W. E. B. Du Bois's short story "The Comet" (1920) makes perceptible how corporeality and the inequities embedded in skin and flesh continue to stick to minoritized subjects in ways that belie the creative freedom associated with science fiction. The story takes as its point of departure a post-apocalyptic event triggered by the titular comet. In the wake of this devastation, we meet two survivors in New York City: Jim, a Black man who was protected from the blast because he had been sent down to the lower vaults of a bank to retrieve old records – a job deemed "too dangerous for more valuable men" – and Julia, a white woman who had been developing photographs of the comet in her dark room and finishes only to be greeted by scenes of death.[5] The two gauge each other warily:

> She had not noticed before that he was a Negro. He had not thought of her as white ... Yesterday, he thought with bitterness, she would scarcely have looked at him twice ... She stared at him. Of all the sorts of men she had pictured as coming to her rescue she had not dreamed of one like him. Not that

he was not human, but he dwelt in a world so far from hers, so infinitely far, that he seldom ever entered her thought.[6]

This passage highlights the subhuman status attached to Blackness. Even as Julia admits, "Not that he was not human," this double negative alongside her imagination of Jim living in a world "so infinitely far" from hers makes him into an alien. Reflecting on popular fascination with aliens in science fiction, Octavia Butler notes, "In our ongoing eagerness to create aliens, we express our need for them, and we express our deep fear of being alone in a universe that cares no more for us than it does for stones or suns or any other fragments of itself. And yet we are unable to get along with those aliens who are closest to us, those aliens who are of course ourselves."[7] Her words capture how science fiction introduces readers not only to aliens from outer space but also to those we create in our own midst. We see this in the way Julia puts Jim at a distance from everyday thought and, consequently, at a distance from the human. Following Butler, we might read "The Comet" as a story about two characters struggling to negotiate their fear of being alone in an uncaring universe, a condition that illuminates social divisions and lived experiences of alienation, even as it creates grounds for a coming together through difference.

Amidst their grief, Jim and Julia contemplate the role they would play in the continuation of the human species, remaking the story of Adam and Eve to suggest the possibility of a hybrid, if heteronormative, future. This tantalizing glimpse of a "race to be," of new forms of relationality, intimacy, and humanity is, however, interrupted by the discordant sound of a car horn, a sharp "'Honk! Honk!'" that returns us to a world we thought had been destroyed.[8] We learn that only New York was impacted by the blast and there are other survivors, including Julia's father and her fiancé Fred. While she rejoins her family, Jim is accosted with barely contained hostility. Saidiya Hartman's reading of this moment foregrounds the cruelty with which Jim is reminded of his corporeality: "Fixed under their gaze and dissected in the hot glare of white hatred and electric lights, he is a shrinking dazed figure. *Nigger* is repeated to make visceral the violence that accompanies the restoration of the world ... The clock has been turned back, and once again he is barred from the human."[9] Here, racial slurs and threats of lynching, coupled with the fear stirred by the physical presence of Jim's Black body, underscore the impossibility of escape for minoritized subjects from the conditions and histories attached to their corporeality.

In its refusal to portray a romanticized alternative, "The Comet" dramatizes how science fiction that captures the experiences of those regarded as less-than-human aliens cannot be read as easy escapism. This is emphasized by the story's ending, where Jim also reconnects with his family. The reunion we witness is, however, incomplete because the "brown, small, and toil-worn" woman who approaches Jim, presumably his wife, carries "the corpse of a dark baby."[10] The "sob of joy" he utters as they come together is weighed down by the body she drags forth.[11] By closing on this jarring image, Du Bois asks that we linger on the corpse this woman carries to remember the countless Black children whose lives were and continue to be cut short. In doing so, "The Comet" not only illuminates the stickiness of corporeality but also invites us to view the body – even a corpse – as a site of contestation, a refusal of historical amnesia that demands we confront past violence and persistent injustices. After all, we only have to think about the eerie resonances between the end of this story and the image of Black mothers and caregivers holding on to the bodies of their deceased children, demanding justice for lives murdered as a result of the police brutality and systemic racism that fuels the Black Lives Matter movement today.

## The Revolutionary Potential of "Bodyminds"

The sensual, embodied differences of minoritized subjects arguably represent the defining justification for their exclusion from the category of "the human." Viewed as unthinking brutes, who are ruled by base bodily senses and emotions rather than the rationality of the mind, their value has been linked primarily to the body as a site for the extraction of resources, labor, and profit. Visionary science fiction at once attunes us to such violent histories of racialization and asserts how the body figures as a vital medium for resistance. Sami Schalk's articulation of "bodyminds" offers a generative framework; recognizing what she describes as the "inextricability of mind and body" prompts us to challenge the mind/body divide that has been used to denigrate and dehumanize minoritized subjects as animals, aliens, objects, and others.[12] It also insists that revolution needs to happen through the transformation of both simultaneously.

Sabrina Vourvoulias's novel *Ink* (2012) transports readers to a near-future dystopic United States where anyone with a recent immigration history is tattooed with a different-colored barcode designating their respective citizen, permanent resident, or temporary worker status. These state-authorized surveillance markers, imprinted on the bodies of so-called "inks," demarcate them as perpetual aliens. Yet, even as this biopolitical management occurs, Vourvoulias gives readers hope through a movement that acquires increasing momentum and urgency. In a world where immigrants are incarcerated in inkatoriums and forced to undergo sterilization procedures that have haunting resonances with historical practices of internment and eugenics, she demonstrates how these wounded subjects attune us to new modes of embodiment, care, and kinship that manifest as magic.

Through one character's deep connection to the land, another's affinity for the written word, and nahuales – Mayan spirit animals that protect the protagonists – Vourvoulias illuminates the messy, affective entanglements that escape biopolitical control and point to other ways of knowing the world. In so doing, she does not position magic as the antithesis to science but rather challenges us to reevaluate the lines we have drawn between these purportedly different categories of knowledge, not to mention the generic boundaries between science fiction and fantasy. In the novel, we encounter magic as the skills and powers ordinary people possess; computer hacking, a chemistry degree, journalism, painting, and faith all figure as magic these myriad characters contribute to the resistance movement. That some of this magic – including the production of a synthetic type of "instaskin," used to help inks capable of "passing" cover up their tattoos and avoid detection – would fall under dominant (Western) conceptions of science, moreover, compels readers to question the hierarchies of value that allow only certain forms of knowledge to count as science. By refusing to abide by such hierarchies, Vourvoulias pushes us toward a more capacious worldview that allows magic and science to be regarded as one and the same, embodied knowledges that can be mobilized not only for control but also to bring better worlds into being.

Attending to the fantastical shapeshifting nahaules in *Ink* serves as an important reminder of the multiple planes on which revolutions must be waged. The nahaul's insistence that *"What happens on this layer affects all layers,"* in reference to the spiritual battle they wage against darkness and chaos, underscores that the resistance we enact in and through the imagination is just as material as what occurs on the ground.[13] In this sense, Vourvoulias's portrayal of the body as a site of revolutionary potential encompasses not just the physical frame but also mental, emotional, and spiritual recesses that animate struggles for social justice.

Schalk's notion of "bodyminds" also finds potent depiction in N. K. Jemisin's story "Walking Awake" (2018). Most widely known for her Hugo-award-winning *Broken Earth* trilogy, Jemisin's writing is animated by a desire to combat the erasure of Blackness and minoritized difference in science and speculative fiction. In a 2013 blog post, she reflects on the violence of these exclusions, asking: "Why did I have to travel to the margins of speculative fiction to see anything of myself? Why was it easier to find aliens or unicorns than people of color or realistic women?"[14] To address this absence, she fills her writing with rich depictions of intersectionality that attune readers to the experiences of multiply marginalized subjects. In "Walking Awake," Jemisin transports us to a futuristic Earth dominated by a parasitic alien species humans have been taught to regard as "Masters," a not-so-subtle allusion to histories of chattel slavery. In the world of the story, humans are divided into two roles: caregivers and hosts, with the former in charge of nurturing the latter until a Master requests a replacement because they want to "wear" a different skin. Told from the perspective of Sadie, a caregiver in "the Northeast Anthroproduction Facility," we learn caregivers are chosen because they possess "imperfect" bodies.[15] Diagnosed at a young age with bipolar disorder, Sadie knows she should appreciate her current position: "No Master would have anything less than a perfect host. They could have sent her to Disposal, or the plantations. Instead, Sadie had been given medicines to stabilize her erratic neurotransmitters."[16] Recognizing that there are worse alternatives allows Sadie to justify her complicity within the system, to be grateful even as she lies to the children in her charge about the bliss that awaits them as hosts.

Jemisin's depiction of Sadie as a caregiver invites readers to reflect on the racialized, gendered, and able-bodied assumptions attached to this work. By presenting us with a disabled protagonist who appears not as the object but agent of care as well as a woman whose caretaking labor facilitates the dispossession of children's bodies, Jemisin refuses easy binaries. Sadie cannot be comfortably viewed as either victim or oppressor. Through her conflicted perspective, we grasp that what is broken is not Sadie's bodymind but the unequal and inhospitable world she inhabits. Although Jemisin never clearly identifies Sadie's race, the way she views freedom as a dangerous dream invites connections to histories of enslavement and alludes to the racialized dimensions of affective labor (domestic service, nursing, and other forms of caretaking work disproportionately carried out by minoritized subjects).

In the story, Sadie's transformation begins after she is forced to turn over Enri, a young boy she loves deeply, as a human host for a Master whose current body "could last twenty years more, easily."[17] After Enri's body is overtaken, he visits Sadie in her dreams, sharing the truth behind the Masters' origins as man-made laboratory specimens that have surpassed and now dominate their creators. Although this science fictional trope is not new, Jemisin's compelling depiction of disability attunes us to the revolutionary potential of bodyminds. We learn dreaming is the one symptom of Sadie's disorder that could not be managed with medication. Like the magic that pervades Vourvoulias's *Ink*, dreams are the excess that cannot be contained. By connecting these dreams to why Sadie has been marked "unfit" to serve as a host, Jemisin challenges normative views of disabled persons as weak and incapacitated. At the same time, she prevents any facile idealization of the disabled subject; the revolution does not come easily or without loss. It is also a battle Sadie cannot wage alone. Drawing strength from Enri and the children who animate her dreams, Sadie realizes that to destroy the Masters, she must murder a human host. This leaves the parasitic "alien" with no other choice but to take on her imperfect, disabled body, which she opens to "Enri and the others. A thousand, million memories of terrible death, coiled and ready to be flung forth like a weapon."[18] By giving herself over so this "dream of death" can take hold through her to "the Master that took her, through every Master in every body," Sadie performs the ultimate act of care.[19] The decision to sacrifice herself, body and mind, represents a commitment to facilitate conditions of possibility beyond her lifespan for the creation of more equitable worlds. As Jemisin, through Sadie, contends, "No revolution without blood. No freedom without the willingness to die."[20]

### Of "Common Cyborgs"

In addition to deconstructing the mind/body hierarchy that has been used to variously denigrate and dehumanize minoritized subjects, visionary science fiction prompts us to rethink the relationship between the body and technology. In particular, the pervasiveness of the figure of the cyborg in popular culture prompts us to consider how humans can be remade through scientific and technological advancements and, by extension, how humanity itself might be redefined. Donna Haraway's seminal "A Cyborg Manifesto" (1985) elaborates how the cyborg functions as a generative theoretical framework. Recognizing the ubiquity of cyborgs in science fiction and our social landscape, Haraway posits the cyborg as a transgressive, boundary-blurring figure:

> From one perspective, a cyborg world is about the final imposition of a grid of control on the planet ... about the final appropriation of women's bodies in a masculinist orgy of war ... From another perspective, a cyborg world might be about lived social and bodily realities in which people are not afraid of their joint kinship with animals and machines, not afraid of permanently partial identities and contradictory standpoints.[21]

This passage illustrates Haraway's attentiveness to the cyborg's troubling origins in projects of domination; it also makes a case for reading the cyborg otherwise as a figure that attunes us to the possibilities of transgressed boundaries, unexpected combinations, and kinship that crosses species divides. The potent forms of blending and fusion the cyborg enables, Haraway argues, allow us to shift from a politics organized around singular identity categories to a coalitional politics based on affinity rather than sameness. Despite her compelling articulation of the cyborg as a figure for feminist and antiracist politics, Haraway has been taken to task for neglecting the very "lived social and bodily realities" she champions above.

Jillian Weise offers an illuminating critique of Haraway's essay in "Common Cyborg" (2018). She writes, "Haraway's manifesto lays claim to cyborgs ('we are all cyborgs') and defines the cyborg unilaterally through metaphor," a perspective that discounts the fact that "Disabled people who use tech to live are cyborgs."[22] Weise's powerful assertion, "Our lives are not metaphors," reminds us that science fictional tropes like that of the cyborg do not just populate futuristic landscapes but are part of people's daily lived realities.[23] Attending to the material existence of cyborgs further complicates Haraway's aim to position her project as part of a "utopian tradition of imagining a world without gender."[24] Although she demonstrates how the cyborg can challenge violent divisions created through the construction and performance of gender, following Weise and disability scholars like Alison Kafer and Rosemarie Garland-Thomson compels us to confront how disabled persons – especially women – whose reliance on technology makes them cyborgs, are also violently ungendered and desexualized in ways that refuse to recognize their humanity and womanhood – that is, their existence as desiring and desirable subjects.

The speculative poetry of Leah Lakshmi Piepzna-Samarasinha, a queer disabled author, affirms in equal parts the pain and suffering she endures daily because of fibromyalgia but also the pleasure, beauty, and joy of her body. In her poetry, we find vivid unabashed depictions of the satisfaction she gets from using vibrators, dildos, and Facebook, a merging of flesh, bodily fluids, and technology that can be read as a form of cyborg sex. She writes in "dirty river girl" (2015):

> When I flare I go in my bed and I fuck myself so hard. I close
> all the doors and I make myself come, over and over again.
> Sometimes I jerk off, read library books and look at Facebook at
> the same time. my cock in my pussy and my vibrator on my clit
> stays there forever. sometime I just hover there in that place with
> no coming for hours, and there is no pain, just me being the slut
> that kept me alive.[25]

In this passage, Piepzna-Samarasinha illuminates a vision of the cyborg that sharply contests the figure at the center of Haraway's politics; here, we encounter a proudly gendered and sexualized disabled woman who revels in the technologies that bring her gratification. The erotic language she employs represents a powerful affirmation that she is a living, breathing woman who has found a way to claim a future for herself, a future often denied to disabled subjects in a world where disability continues to be viewed as akin to death.

In addition to the lived experience of disability, Haraway's "A Cyborg Manifesto" fails to address the historically racialized dimensions of the cyborg. She writes, "Ironically, it might be the unnatural cyborg women making chips in Asia and spiral dancing in Santa Rita Jail whose constructed unities will guide effective oppositional strategies."[26] Although Haraway acknowledges the lives of women in the developing world whose bodies are exploited to sustain global capitalism, positioning these "unnatural cyborg women" at the center of an oppositional politics essentializes them and disregards the long-lived histories of racialization that have made minoritized subjects into cyborgs. Karen Tei Yamashita's novel *Tropic of Orange* (1997) brings together both magical realist and science fictional elements to challenge dominant perceptions of the cyborg as a futuristic being. One of the central characters Yamashita introduces is Arcangel, a performance artist who has lived for centuries. As an embodiment of the spirit of Latin America, numerous holes, stains, and scars score his flesh, a corporeal violence that represents the physical inscription of histories of suffering, inequality, and colonial conquest. It is through Arcangel that we are reminded of the abuses inflicted on laborers from the global south, their treatment as *"human washing machines, / human vacuums, / human garbage disposals,"* which underscores how the cyborg is not a futuristic figure but one deeply rooted in historical and ongoing practices of racialization.[27]

Visionary science fiction deepens our understanding of what it means to inhabit the world as a cyborg, to grapple with the dispossession of one's body, its transformation into technology and tool. Charles Yu's story "Standard Loneliness Package" (2012) transports readers to a near future in which a technological advancement that enables the transference of emotions has created a booming industry, where workers in developing countries are paid paltry sums to feel the negative emotions of wealthy inhabitants from developed nations. We follow the nameless protagonist who works in one such call center in India, experiencing other people's bodily pain for money – from a root canal and broken leg to heartbreak and loss – as he struggles to sustain a modest living that depends on ignoring his own bodily needs and desires. The technology Yu describes points to the vampiric nature of capitalism and forms of neocolonialism occurring today through labor exploitation and organ trafficking, which repeat the trauma and violation of colonial conquest. In "Standard Loneliness Package," the bodyminds of those involved in this "emotional engineering" industry have been so deeply overtaken that they are robbed of the intimacy and right to experience the depth of their own feelings.[28] This makes the ending all the more jarring when the narrator's one moment of sensory bodily release comes from using the technology to watch and feel his lover fling herself off a cliff into the ocean, an act that underscores the attenuated agency left to such subjects in a world that profits from racialized cyborg labor.

The speculative futures, technologies, and embodiments we encounter in the work of authors like Piepzna-Samarasinha, Yamashita, and Yu therefore compel us to confront the cyborg not just as a theoretical figure for politics but as a living being and embodiment that pervades our material world.

## Visionary Science Fiction and the Future

I have reflected at length on how the writings of women and people of color call into question the humanoid bodies that proliferate in science fiction, those that possess human shape and characteristics but nonetheless continue to be placed at a distance from "the human," as cyborgs, robots, and aliens. In closing, I want to address the emphasis this essay's title places on humanoid bodies of the future. Most of the texts described above invite us into science fictional landscapes not drastically removed from our material realities today; the bodies we encounter, aside from the occasional fantastic tech, are not futuristic in ways we might anticipate. What, then, does the invocation of these bodies as part of "the future" offer us?

Samuel Delany has famously argued that "Science fiction is not 'about the future.' Science fiction *is in dialogue with the present*."[29] In this regard, we might read the refusal to present legibly futuristic bodies in the writings of Du Bois, Jemisin, Vourvoulias, and Yu as an enjoinder to reckon with the disjuncture between our assumptions of what the future should look like and those figures that have been historically excluded from such futures. As Delany suggests, these authors mobilize science fictional tropes to bring into sharper focus the forms of inequality and structural injustice that too often manifest as background noise in our everyday lives. Through the cognitively estranging settings and characters we encounter in works like "The Comet," *Ink*, "Walking Awake," and "Standard Loneliness Package," we are confronted with the corporeal effects of racism, xenophobia, ableism, and exploitation that not only dehumanize minoritized subjects but rob them of agency over their bodies.

Recognizing the ways in which science fiction dialogues with the present, however, does not get at the importance of insisting that the humanoid bodies we encounter in visionary science fiction are part of the future. To claim them as such is to admit the ongoingness of processes of racialization, exclusion, and alienation that contribute to the reproduction of structural inequities; it is to understand that social violences like slavery and coloniality are not "past" but continue to manifest in the present and, by extension, will manifest in our future under different names and practices – as mass incarceration, policing, environmental racism, and more. Aimee Bahng demonstrates in *Migrant Futures* (2018) how the future is colonized through the manipulation of "financial instruments [that] work precisely toward actualizing the future in order to monetize and profit from it," through the use of expendable bodies to build gleaming skyscrapers on which our visions of the future are predicated, even as these workers are written out of those futures.[30] Yet, Bahng also emphasizes that the future "exists as absolute uncertainty" and, as such, "can never be fully colonized."[31] To claim the humanoid bodies we encounter in visionary fiction as part of the future is, therefore, to emphasize the "endless multiplicity of futures," the potential for worlds better and more just than those we inhabit, where embodied differences are not used to divide but can serve as grounds for the articulation of new modes of relationality, solidarity, and kinship.[32]

## Coda: On the Science Fictional Quality of What Could Have Been

To assert the importance of claiming the future for minoritized subjects does not mean to forget the past. While my essay has been about, to cite its title, "Science Fiction's Humanoid Bodies of the Future," this coda elaborates how, for women and people of color, imagining better futures often depends on negotiating histories of violence, oppression, and inequality. It might also entail reimagining these histories that are not quite past. While Black feminist science fiction author Octavia Butler is most widely known for her *Xenogenesis* trilogy, *Parable* series, and short stories set in futuristic postapocalyptic landscapes, one of her most influential novels is *Kindred* (1979). It tells the story of Dana, an African American woman living in twentieth-century Los Angeles, who is pulled uncontrollably into the past by her ancestor Rufus, a white enslaver who owns a plantation in the antebellum south. Through Dana's involuntary time travels readers are forced along with her into a rude awakening, that despite her knowledge of a future where slavery has been abolished, she is wholly unprepared to deal with the forms of racialized and gendered violence her female ancestors endured during a time when being a Black woman was to be vulnerable in ways difficult to imagine. Gabrielle Bellot notes:

> Butler was inspired to write *Kindred* partly because she had heard so many young black Americans minimizing the horrors of slavery and claiming that if *they* had been enslaved, they simply wouldn't have tolerated this or that. Such

naïveté ... upset Butler. She wanted to write a novel that showed such young people what it might feel like to become a slave: not merely to teach them the brute facts about this American institution, but to show them, on the page, teeth getting kicked out, backs being torn open from whips, white slaveholders casually attempting to rape black women ...[33]

Reading *Kindred* expands our field of vision; we learn that for all of Dana's knowledge, her ability to read and write, to bring back in time maps and other modern conveniences enslaved Africans had no access to, she nonetheless fails to escape at every turn. Butler's use of the science fictional trope of time travel consequently immerses us in a past conditional temporality of what could have been that brings into jarring focus the costs and consequences of resistance, and prevents any easy romanticization of her protagonist.

From the opening lines of the prologue – "I lost an arm on my last trip home. My left arm" – we know *Kindred* will end in pain and loss.[34] Even so, the weight of all that happens in the intervening chapters cannot prepare us for the haunting conclusion where Dana, who finally strikes up the courage to stab Rufus, is abruptly brought back to her present in LA:

> I was back at home – in my own house, in my own time. But I was still caught somehow ... From the elbow to the ends of the fingers, my left arm had become a part of the wall. I looked at the spot where flesh joined with plaster, stared at it uncomprehending ...
> I pulled my arm toward me, pulled hard.
> And suddenly, there was an avalanche of pain, red impossible agony!
> And I screamed and screamed.[35]

This vivid depiction of how Dana's body is violently, irreversibly transformed through her time travels points to how the past continues to imprint itself on the bodyminds of minoritized subjects. We see the transgenerational impact of enslavement on Dana, a free Black woman living in post-Civil Rights Era America. When asked why she chose to begin and end *Kindred* with Dana's fractured body, Butler notes, "I couldn't let her return to what she was, I couldn't let her come back whole ... Antebellum slavery didn't leave people quite whole."[36] Butler's words can also be extended to us as readers of *Kindred* and visionary science fiction, for the experience of engaging these texts should not leave us whole. The violences and inequities they attune us to are part of a world we have inherited; they are the foundations on which the present and our futures are necessarily built. By inviting us into the past, *Kindred* offers neither escapism nor nihilism; instead, it demonstrates how looking back, learning how to connect the dots between antebellum slavery, Jim Crow segregation, the prison-industrial complex, and unprovoked forms of police brutality and murder of Black people occurring in the streets today, is precisely what we need to sketch alternative ways of moving forward. Unlike the forms of futurism that propel racial capitalism relentlessly ahead into already colonized futures, visionary science fiction remains grounded in the memories of historical and persistent injustices that fuel struggles for transformative redistributive justice.

## NOTES

1 The term "speculative fiction" is not entirely free of controversy. Because it has acquired significant cultural capital in academia, speculative fiction has been criticized as an intellectual category mobilized to obscure the pop culture roots of science fiction, thereby turning a form of "low art" into a respectable object of study for literary scholars.

2 See Aimee Bahng, *Migrant Futures* (Durham, NC: Duke University Press, 2018); Alexis Lothian, *Old Futures* (New York: New York University Press, 2018); Sami Schalk, *Bodyminds Reimagined* (Durham, NC: Duke University Press, 2018); Shelley Streeby, *Imagining the Future of Climate Change* (Oakland: University of California Press, 2018).

3 Walidah Imarisha, Introduction to *Octavia's Brood*, ed. Walidah Imarisha and adrienne marie brown (Oakland, CA: AK Press, 2015), 4.

4 Ibid., 5.

5 W. E. B. Du Bois, "The Comet," in *Dark Matter*, ed. Sheree R. Thomas (New York: Warner Books, 2000), 5.

6 Ibid., 9.

7 Octavia Butler, "The Monophobic Response," in *Dark Matter* (New York: Warner Books, 2000), 415–416.

8 Du Bois, "The Comet," 15, 16.

9 Saidiya Hartman, "The End of White Supremacy, An American Romance," *BOMB Magazine* no. 152 (June 5, 2020), https://bombmagazine.org/articles/the-end-of-white-supremacy-an-american-romance/, emphasis original.

10 Du Bois, "The Comet," 18.

11 Ibid.

12 Schalk, *Bodyminds Reimagined*, 5.

13 Sabrina Vourvoulias, *Ink* (Framingham, MA: Crossed Genres Publications, 2012), 108, emphasis original.

14 N. K. Jemisin, "How Long 'til Black Future Month," *N. K. Jemisin* (September 30, 2013), http://nkjemisin.com/2013/09/how-long-til-black-future-month/.

15 N. K. Jemisin, "Walking Awake," in *How Long 'Til Black Future Month?* (New York: *Orbit*, 2018), 216.

16 Ibid., 217.

17 Ibid., 214.

18 Ibid., 233.

19 Ibid.

20 Ibid.

21 Donna Haraway, *A Cyborg Manifesto: Science, Technology, and Socialist-Feminism in the Late Twentieth Century* (Minneapolis: University of Minnesota Press, 2016), 15.
22 Jillian Weise, "Common Cyborg," *Granta* (September 24, 2018), https://granta.com/common-cyborg/.
23 Ibid.
24 Haraway, *Cyborg Manifesto*, 7.
25 Leah Lakshmi Piepzna-Samarasinha, "dirty river girl," in *Bodymap* (Toronto: Mawenzi House, 2015), 33–34.
26 Haraway, *Cyborg Manifesto*, 14.
27 Karen Tei Yamashita, *Tropic of Orange* (Minneapolis, MN: Coffee House Press, 1997), 200, emphasis original.
28 Charles Yu, "Standard Loneliness Package," in *Sorry Please Thank You* (New York: Pantheon Books, 2012), 4.
29 Samuel R. Delany, "Dichtung und Science Fiction," in *Starboard Wine* (Middletown, CT: Wesleyan University Press, 2012), 165, emphasis original.
30 Bahng, *Migrant Futures*, 12.
31 Ibid.
32 Ibid., 12.
33 Gabrielle Bellot, "Octavia Butler: The Brutalities of the Past Are All around This," *lithub.com* (October 17, 2017), https://lithub.com/octavia-butler-the-brutalities-of-the-past-are-all-around-this/, emphasis original.
34 Octavia Butler, *Kindred* (Boston: Beacon Press, 1979), 9.
35 Ibid., 261.
36 Randall Kenan, "An Interview with Octavia E. Butler," *Callaloo* 14 (Spring 1991): 498.

# 8

STEPHANIE CLARE

# Contemporary North American Transgender Literature

## Realness, Fantasy, and the Body

On December 19, 2019, J. K. Rowling, the British author of the popular Harry Potter series, tweeted her support of the view that it is impossible to change one's sex. "Sex is real," she claimed, and, by extension, immutable. Rowling was not writing in a vacuum. The notion of biological sex, its fixity and binary structure, is called upon time and again, often to dismiss claims for transgender rights. Faced with this context, a prominent response to Rowling's tweet deserves attention. Both *The Washington Post* and *The New York Times* published essays by transgender writer-activists who explained how disappointed they were by Rowling's position, especially given their attachment to her books. These essays, by Jackson Bird and Charlotte Clymer, claim that transgender living brings something akin to magic into the world – not because transgender bodies are somehow magical but rather because transgender vitality and community in a cisnormative, transphobic world pushes daily against the perceived limits of the real.

A series of contemporary North American transgender novels have also adopted magic, fantasy, and the supernatural into their narratives, at once playing with the genre of memoir and moving beyond its realism. For instance, Kai Cheng Thom's 2016 *Fierce Femmes and Notorious Liars: A Dangerous Trans Girl's Confabulous Memoir* begins with the protagonist explaining how she wants to write a new transgender memoir, one that is not about the white, wealthy, suffering character who waits her turn, and then transitions, marrying the "prince or the football player."[1] Her story will be different: "kick-ass and intense with hot sex and gang violence and maybe zombies and lots of magic" (3). A few pages later, the confabulous memoir describes a day when at least sixty gigantic mermaids beach themselves, dying on the shore (11). Fantastic elements return throughout the text. Similarly, Jordy Rosenberg's 2018 *Confessions of the Fox* deploys magical motifs within the context of memoir: Dr. Voth discovers an autobiographical manuscript that tells the tale of transmasculine Jack Sheppard who, in eighteenth-century London, hears the voices of objects brought to life.

Publishers ask the professor if the manuscript is authentic, a fairy tale, or a hoax, and Dr. Voth ultimately refuses to answer.[2] Andrea Lawlor's 2017 *Paul Takes the Form of a Mortal Girl* likewise features magical elements. The text is clearly a historical novel: It archives 1990s American queer, lesbian, and gay culture. At the same time, however, it describes a magical, shapeshifting protagonist, who – reminiscent of Virginia Woolf's *Orlando* – can morph his body at will, taking on different sexed forms.[3] Fantasy appears in contemporary transgender literature beyond the novel form as well, such as in Julian K. Jarboe's 2020 collection of short stories, *Everyone on the Moon is Essential Personnel* and Cameron Awkward-Rich's 2016 book of poetry, *Sympathetic Little Monster*.[4]

This chapter provides an overview to prominent understandings of embodiment that have developed in transgender studies, focusing especially on the field's critique of normative and objectifying conceptions of the sexed body, conceptions that are often granted the status of the real. It then turns to the analysis of the deployment of fantasy in contemporary North American transgender literature, reading *Fierce Femmes and Notorious Liars*. I explain how transgender writing has often been limited to realism and to the memoir form in particular. Texts have been under pressure to perform authenticity and truthfulness so as to claim realness, however what counts as true embodiment has often been weaponized against transgender people. The plethora of fantastic elements in contemporary transgender literature rejects the strategy of representing truthful embodiment and instead takes hold of the imagination as a practice of freedom and a method for creating community. These texts highlight how bodies take shape in the intertwining of matter and meaning. They also suggest that attention to trans embodiment need not focus on questions of personal identity and truthful embodiment, but rather on the social contexts that shape embodied experiences.

## But What Is "Transgender Literature"?

Before beginning, it is worth clarifying what I mean by "transgender" and "transgender literature." The word "transgender" is often traced to its emergent use in the 1960s and 1970s in the United States. It was a self-descriptive term that people gave to themselves as they lived in a gender other than the one they were assigned at birth and also rejected medical intervention.[5] The term, however, gained widespread currency beginning in the 1990s especially in the work of Leslie Feinberg. For Feinberg, "transgender" is an umbrella term, referring to a "wide range of 'gender outlaws,'" people who define themselves in many ways, but share and value an experience of gender variance and gender transitivity.[6] This use of the term has been taken up in activist and academic circles and has been institutionalized, for instance in Susan Stryker and Paisley Currah's 2014 founding of *TSQ: Transgender Studies Quarterly*. "Transgender" tends to be preferred over "transsexual," which is often understood as a pathologizing, medical term that is exogenic to transgender communities.[7]

That said, as Avery Tompkins explains, "transgender" does not cover "the widest possible range of gender variation," and, some argue, it has become tied to "binary notions of transness," referring only to "trans men and trans women rather than to those who contest the gender binary."[8] In addition, the term "transgender" can reproduce hierarchies of race and class and function as a form of epistemic colonization because it posits itself as a modern and correct understanding of gender transitivity over and against alternatives, such as models that do not separate gender from sexuality, alternatives that are less prominent among white, American middle-class people.[9] As a result, in the place of "transgender," the Global Action of Trans* Equality, among other organizations and people, advocates for the use of the term "trans,*" claiming that the asterisk "signals greater inclusivity of new gender identities and expressions and better represents a broader community of individuals."[10] Trans* is meant to include indigenous and non-European gender/sexual formations such as two-spirit, fa'afafine, and hijra, as well as nonbinary gender identities, although some argue that the asterisk is unnecessary, and that "trans" (or even "transgender") can have the same meaning as "trans*."[11]

In comparison to "transgender," which has been taken up in contemporary psychology, medicine, social work, and law, "trans" seems to refuse the capture of such official discourse and currently in the United States is often – though certainly not always – a preferred term of self-definition.[12] For this reason, in the pages that follow, I use the term "trans" to describe people unless authors explicitly refer to themselves differently.

Yet following Stryker and Currah, I strategically use the term "transgender literature" and not "trans* literature" or "trans literature" to signal that I am interested in gender variance and transitivity rather than all forms of transness (such as, for instance, transnational).[13] By "transgender literature" I mean literature written by trans-identified writers, literature that explores the relations between transness and aesthetics while explicitly attempting to reach audiences that are trans or transliterate.[14] I frame my analysis of literature in identitarian terms so as to center trans-identified people in the analysis of transness. This is important because of the history of queer theory, which has often used the analysis of trans-related phenomena for the purpose of developing queer theories of gender that do not always attend to the lived, embodied experience of trans people.[15] My centering of trans writers is one method to write about transness in a way that draws major-itarian conclusions without having actual trans people disappear into alle-gories or metaphors, and without having trans bodies become the site for the abstract theorization of sex and gender in ways that do not attend to often more pressing issues facing many trans people, issues still having to do with embodiment such as access to physical safety, healthcare, and material security.

## Prominent Approaches to Embodiment in Transgender Studies

One central idea frames transgender studies' approach to the body: That which is taken as a natural form of embodiment is actually normative. Bodies are never pure of construction or technology. Related to this argu-ment is a critique of the concept of biological sex, a concept that either strips bodies of their lived condition (a condition that includes felt sense) or that violently treats humans as objects. Finally, transgender studies has traced how the history of the concept of binary sex is intertwined with the history of scientific racism, which has often figured people of color as less sexually differentiated, and hence evolutionarily backward. Nonetheless, the field has considered how gender undifferentiation and transitivity can be and have been reclaimed as a source of freedom or condition of possibility.

Transgender studies begins in a critique of scientific understandings of sex, gender, and gender non-normativity, a critique that significantly problem-atizes the assumption that the "real body" is an empirically apprehensible, natural, material thing. Many narrate the field as emerging with Sandy Stone's influential 1991 essay "The Empire Strikes Back: A Posttranssexual Manifesto."[16] This essay develops a critique of the already-existing dis-course surrounding "transsexuality," notably sexological work such as Harry Benjamin's. Stone argues that sexology has limited the narratives available for transness, pathologizing non-normative embodiments of gender and seeking to administer and contain gender non-normativity. She analyzes the effects of this discourse on existing popular memoirs written by self-identified male-to-female transsexual people who transitioned in the 1930s, 1950s, and 1970s. These narratives often reproduce gender norms, Stone argues. This is because they are shaped by their authors' desires to be recognized as authentic women. Instead, Stone calls for the production of new narratives produced by trans-identified people, narratives that do not efface one's transition, but rather challenge the belief that "only one body per gendered subject is 'right' and all other bodies are wrong." Such narra-tives interrupt "the binary phallocratic founding myth by which Western bodies and subjects are authorized."[17]

Stone's critique of the science of "transsexuality" has implications for theorizing embodiment. In calling for new narratives, Stone implies that scientific discourse, such as sexology, does not have a monopoly over the truth of the body. In fact, Stone's focus on narrative and sexology highlights how experiences of embodiment as well as actual materializations of the body are mediated by the narratives we can tell. She identifies, for instance, how Benjamin's account of transness shaped trans people's accounts of themselves, especially as they sought recognition as really trans so as to gain access to medicalized technologies. Finally, Stone implies that that which is taken as empirical reality or scientific fact – such as the belief that there is only one body per gender – can be normative.

Stone's focus on narrative has been influential and taken up by other prominent scholars in the field, such as Jay Prosser. Prosser argues that "transsexuality is always narrative work, a transformation of the body that requires the remolding of the life into a particular narrative shape."[18] One must, Prosser explains, construct a "transsexual narrative" before materially transitioning, and thus the "resexing of the transsexual body is made possible through narrativization."[19] Prosser's argument, which builds on Stone's, implies that embodiment, especially trans embodiment, materializes in the intertwining of matter and discourse, each never pure of one another. This is certainly not to say that corporeality is meaningless, and that physical transformation is somehow misguided. Prosser insists that the desire to physically transform one's body "reveals the extent to which embodiment forms an essential base to subjectivity; but it also reveals that embodiment is as much about feeling one inhabits material flesh as the flesh itself."[20]

Prosser's work draws attention to the body as it is lived, that is to say, to a body endowed with form and feeling. His approach might therefore be understood as phenomenological, a method with significant implications for theorizing "sex" that has become influential in transgender studies, for instance in work by Henry Rubin and Gayle Salamon.[21] Phenomenology, especially writing by the French philosopher Maurice Merleau-Ponty, insists that the body is always lived, and to live with and as a body is to have a body image that cannot be abstracted from the body itself. In other words, there is no sex beyond body image; sex is always accompanied by an image that cannot be dismissed as inessential to it.[22] In addition, to understand that sex is always lived is to allow that, as it is lived, it transforms. The ways that sex and gender are lived transform the body itself. To argue that there is a truth or realness that exists beyond this situation is to reduce the body to a thing rather than to understand embodiment within the life world of which it is always a part.[23]

In this view, rather than treat sex as prediscursive and presocial, and therefore somehow more objectively real, we might understand "sex" as produced through violent social relations that strip the body of subjectivity, treating humans as bare life. The understanding of sex as pure biological matter has recently been historicized in C. Riley Snorton's *Black on Both Sides* (2017). Snorton argues that the differentiation between sex and gender can be traced to J. Marion Sims nineteenth-century gynecological experiments on enslaved women, including Anarcha, Betsey, and Lucy. In Sims framework, these women are understood as sexed, and therefore experimentation on them is deemed to yield conclusions that could help treat white women. And yet, while sexed, the enslaved women are not figured as gendered, which is to say they are not granted the social positionality of women, a positionality that would have their bodies shielded from visibility. This sexed but ungendered position legitimates violence against them. In other words, in Snorton's analysis of Western science, "sex" as material facticity is constituted through the violence of slavery. It is not a "natural" condition of bodies.[24]

Critically, none of these arguments should be read as rejections of the use of science and technology. In sometimes choosing to take hormones and at other times choosing surgery, some transgender subjects strategically use scientific techniques to make their bodies. Such technical arts are part of a range of gender-making practices everyone performs. As Dean Spade and Nikki Sullivan argue, we all engage in practices that shape our bodies inside and out, practices such as dress, exercise, and diet that produce ourselves as gendered subjects.[25] In her 1994 formative essay "My Words to Victor Frankenstein above the Village of Chamounix," Stryker builds a similar argument. She explains that – much like the monster in Mary Shelley's *Frankenstein* – her own body, as a transgender woman, is a product "of medical science. It is a technological construction."[26] Inhabiting, even claiming, the position of the monster, Stryker shares an important message with those who denigrate her on the basis of her constructed embodiment: "You are as constructed as me; the same anarchic womb has birthed us both."[27] The assignation of sex at birth is a moment of this construction, and behind or before that construction, Stryker posits a vital materiality, "the chaos and blackness from which Nature itself spills forth."[28] In this view, all embodied subject positions are constructions, even if some are considered natural. And yet beyond this "nature," there exists a fundamental chaos, an unformed potentiality or vitality with which Stryker aligns herself.

Transness might then come to index a metaphysical realm of mobility and becoming, one that provides the condition for individual embodiment.

Claire Colebrook offers such a vision of "trans": a primordial "not-yet-differentiated singularity from which genders, race, species, sexes, and sexualities are generated in a form of relative stability."[29] She asks that we understand trans people as expressing a "more profound transitivity that is the condition for what became known as *the* human."[30] Marquis Bey picks up on Colebrook's framing, while also drawing on Black and Black feminist scholarship, especially the work of Fred Moten and Hortense Spillers. They argue that "trans* is black and black is trans*."[31] This is, of course, not to argue that everyone who identifies as trans* is Black or vice versa. Rather, Bey figures Blackness and trans*-ness as "differently inflected names for an anoriginal lawlessness that marks an escape from confinement and a besidedness to ontology."[32] People who identify as Black and/or trans* index a prior "foundational condition of those fugitive identificatory demarcation," a form of race and gender fugitivity, a "movement of flight, of escape ... from the confines of ontological pinning down."[33] Bey's and Colebrook's visions resonate with Stryker's embracing of the connection between trans people and the "chaos and blackness from which Nature itself spills forth."[34] They all point to an ungovernable movement beyond or underneath that which is and suggest that formed bodies are unseated by a vital materiality that always escapes capture.

It is important to remember, however, that the condition of sex and gender undifferentiation has often been ascribed to people of color as part of a project of white supremacy. Differentiated, binary gender embodiment has often been read as a sign of evolutionary progress and tied to middle-class whiteness, for instance in the work of the sexologist Havelock Ellis.[35] As Jules Gill-Peterson traces, early twentieth-century intersex medicine – from which transsexual medicine emerges – understood embryonic life as sexually plastic. Intersex embodiment was then framed as a form of atavistic, arrested development. In this vision, white bodies were figured as having a greater capacity to take on the form of binary sex, and black and brown bodies were figured as "less evolved sexually, and thereby less worthy of medical care."[36]

Overall, transgender studies has critiqued the status given to "biological sex" and has argued that sex is always lived and accompanied by an image that cannot be theorized as inessential to it. The field has examined the interweaving of bodily materiality and narrative. In addition, it has shown how the status given to sexual dimorphism has been tied to projects of white supremacy, which have legitimized racial hierarchies by claiming that people of color, and especially Black people, are either ungendered or do not inhabit binary sex. Finally, the field has insisted that all bodies are constructed. Beyond that construction is a vital materiality that can never be contained and that is somehow connected to freedom. Across these arguments, the "real body" is not an unconstructed one, nor is it a body stripped of experience.

This brief overview lays a groundwork for interpreting the fantastic in contemporary North American transgender writing. In the next section, I use *Fierce Femmes and Notorious Liars* as an example, showing how the text lays claim to the power of the imagination and the para-ontological while unseating the discipline and legibility of the "real." The text is an especially useful case study because of the continued attention it gives to questions concerning violence, community, work, and wealth. This disrupts any attempt to read transgender literature to develop an abstract theory of sex, gender, or embodiment that does not address questions of embodiment having to do with trans survivability and livability. In fact, the novel clearly underlines how survivability is not enough. *Fierce Femmes and Notorious Liars* seeks to promote communal, embodied trans and especially trans of color thriving through the production of fantastic narrative.

## Confabulation, Fantasy, and the Body

"I don't believe in safe spaces," begins *Fierce Femmes and Notorious Liars*. "They don't exist. I do, however, believe in dangerous stories" (1). Directly addressing the reader, the first-person narrator describes these stories as ones that get inside your head, disrupting the ordinary and interrupting what is accepted as reality: The stories "bend and twist the air as they crackle off your tongue, making you shimmer with glamour" (1). In twisting the air, the stories create new spaces, and, in making you shimmer, they adorn your body, bringing you into the realm of the fabulous and the spectacular. Thom relates these stories to freedom: They "blast the stained sheets off your filthy bed" and send your "secrets ... shrieking outside, overjoyed to be finally set free" (1). And while Thom figures the telling of these stories as a process of coming "out of the closet" (1), they are less about revealing a truth so much as about the creation of something fantastic, something that provides a sense of hope, a break in the everyday, and an embodiment of glamor. In Thom's telling, these narratives become embodied because they shape the somatic experience of the body itself, "making you," for instance, glamorous (1).

*Fierce Femmes* frames itself as one of these dangerous stories. It tells the tale of an unnamed Asian North American narrator who leaves her family because, as she puts it, "I was always wild at heart, and I wanted to be a girl" (8–9). The narrator moves to the Street of Miracles in the City of Smoke and Lights where she finds a trans femme community of mostly trans women of color. When one femme is murdered, the community falls apart as members disagree about how best to respond. Some, including the narrator, begin a street gang, the Lipstick Lacerators, who fight back with violence. Ultimately, however, the violence is self-destructive. The community finds healing through communal self-care: an open-mic night and the sweetness of a homemade cake.

*Fierce Femmes* breaks from a tradition of transgender writing that has often been confined to realism and to the memoir or autobiographical form in particular, a tradition exemplified by texts such Christine Jorgensen's 1967 *Christine Jorgensen: A Personal Autobiography*, Jan Morris's 1974 *Conundrum*, and Jane Fry's 1974 *Being Different: The Autobiography of Jane Fry*. More recent examples include Janet Mock's 2014 *Redefining Realness: My Path to Womanhood, Identity, Love and So Much More* and Caitlyn Jenner's 2017 *The Secrets of My Life*. Many transgender autobiographies tell the story of passage from the "wrong" to the "right" body, from dysphoria to alignment, from misrecognition to recognition. Given that public discourse has often focused on the truthfulness (or lack thereof) of transgender embodiment, the narratives are understandably concerned with demonstrating the authenticity of the author's gender identity. Telling the right story of one's life (and especially one's childhood and adolescence) in a convincing, heart-felt way (and hence becoming an autobiographical story-teller) has been a requirement for gaining access to care, for being seen as authentic and real, and for gaining rights.[37] There is also a market for sensational, spectacular, romantic stories of tribulation followed by personal triumph, stories that individualize being transgender rather than articulating a critique of gender normativity and compulsory gender identification.[38]

In contrast, *Fierce Femmes* announces itself as a memoir, but it does not deploy the genre's typical realism. It borrows tropes from fantasy, myth, and fairy tale, reclaiming the spectacular for trans audiences. The text directly addresses a trans audience, "trans girls like you and me" (1). It is more interested in what stories can do for its audience than in how authentically they might represent reality: "What really matters," the book concludes, "isn't whether something is true or false, maybe what matters is the story itself: what kinds of doors it opens, what kinds of dreams it brings" (187). *Fierce Femmes* also breaks from the tradition of trans memoir because the text does not dwell on gender identity or bodily transformation. In other words, *Fierce Femmes* is important for its depersonalization and depsychologization of trans and trans of color literature. It asks to be read as a memoir, but a memoir that does not focus on the experience of gendered embodiment in terms of one's personal identity, an experience often narrated to prove one's realness. Instead, the text brings attention to what we might understand as situated gendered embodiment: experiences of violence, the creation of community, access to public space, and, centrally, the creation of narrative.[39] It is not interested in what is real but rather in what fantastic stories can help to support and build trans and trans of color community.

*Fierce Femmes* is especially interesting because a central undecidability structures the text: It is unclear whether the story takes place in a world similar to ours, with the exception of some fantastical elements, or whether the story takes place in our world but is simply being told by an unreliable narrator. For example, the first few pages describe the protagonist watching a white, rich, celebrity trans woman on television. The woman gives a speech about "believing in yourself," and the crowd responds with a standing ovation (3). The narrator feels angry but does not want to hate a fellow "sister," and so, "instead of kicking" the television, she blows it a kiss (4). The kiss turns into a spark that explodes the screen into "a thousand razor shards" that magically transform into "crimson butterflies" (4). Especially because of the book's title, it is easy to read this scene as a "confabulation," a psychiatric term for fabricated, imaginary stories that compensate for memory loss, for instance following trauma. In this case, however, the story might not exactly be compensatory so much as simply better, describing the narrator as she might want to be seen or as she might want to be. This scene might also be read as an allegory for racial dynamics within trans community: Trans women of color are often pressured to overlook if not pardon racism and white privilege in order to build lifesaving, trans community.[40]

And yet not all the moments of fantasy in the text are easily interpreted as confabulations. Take, for instance, a scene that features gigantic mermaids the size of oil tanks beaching themselves. When the narrator and her sister try to save them, the mermaids speak back, "Eeeerrrrgghhnuuuurrgghfff" (15). While this might certainly be interpreted as a confabulation, it is more readily understood as a moment that signals we are in a (slightly) different world because there is no apparent reason why the narrator would not be telling the truth here. This reading is especially convincing given the book's opening critique of prominent narratives of transfemininity, narratives that posit themselves as realist but, in fact, borrow on the tropes of fairy tales: "The stories are told in this way," Thom writes,

> Everyone look at this poor little trans girl desperate for a ~~fairy godmother~~doctor to give her boobs and a vagina and a pretty face and wear nice dresses! Save the trans girls! Save the whales! Put them in a zoo!

> It's actually a very old archetype that trans girl stories get put into. ... We're like Cinderella, waiting to go to the ball. Like the Little Mermaid, getting her tail surgically altered and her voice removed, so that she can walk around on land. (2–3)

The phrase "save the whales" brings attention to the agency of those doing the saving. It frames the agentic actor as good without having that actor consider the larger structures that make the futurity of whales (and other creatures) precarious, and without considering the savior's complicity in those very systems. A similar structure shapes popular narratives of trans and trans women of color. In contrast, the huge beached mermaids, unlike the whales-to-be-saved and unlike the Little Mermaid, are clearly agentic and have a voice. They bring attention to the pollution that has made their habitat unlivable; they refuse the help of saviors who are primarily interested in themselves. In this reading, the beached mermaids are less the effect of an unreliable narrator than part of the author's world-building project, a project that seeks new narratives, narratives that do not aim to be realistic (while covering over their fictional elements) but rather that own the imagination and seek new stories for living in the world.

The book's mobilization of fantasy alongside its unreliable narrator points to the power of nondisclosure. Providing a transparent account of one's gender identity has been and is especially fraught within the context of trans of color lives, where visibility quickly falls into the biopolitics of surveillance and control.[41] Faced with a context of proving one's realness, *Fierce Femmes* simply opts out: "I am a trans girl," the narrator writes, "danger and lies and emptiness flow electric under my skin" (60). Thom withholds an account of interiority, leaving it opaque: a realm of danger, lies, emptiness, and electricity. The electric current might be equated with Colebrook's and Bey's conceptualization of transness as the condition of an ungovernable, para-ontological, or metaphysical vitality, here orthogonally embodied in a trans of color girl who tells fabulous, imaginary tales. In keeping the narrator unnamed, the story becomes less about the development of a singular person or an account of true feeling; rather, the protagonist slides into the realm of the archetype and the general. This realm creates new mythologies that render trans and trans of color living not simply more possible, but also, quite simply, better.

This is certainly not to say that the text opens to the possibility that transgender embodiment is somehow not real or that the text repeats the treatment of trans women of color as metaphors or allegories for something else and thus calls their material existence into question. Instead, the novel is just not interested in proving reality. It breaks down the distinction between bodies and fantasy, the real and the unreal. *Fierce Femmes* highlights how what is taken as real or authentic is often overlaid with ideology and myth. The book seizes upon the power of storytelling and the creation of myth in the development of new trans communal worlds. These myths become part of embodied experience; they shape one's experience of one's own body in the world, with others.

## Fantasy, Myth, and the Mundane

I have focused on the deployment of fantasy in contemporary transgender literature, but, in conclusion, it is worth recognizing that another strand of this literature exists, as exemplified by Juliet Jacques's *Trans: A Memoir* and also Imogen Binnie's 2013 novel *Nevada*. These texts focus not on the spectacular or the fantastic, as in *Fierce Femmes*, but on the mundane. Andrea Long Chu reads Jacques' memoir as a phenomenology, an account of first-person, present-tense embodied experience, and calls for more such narratives, narratives that focus on the mundane present tense, refusing the story of passage from the "wrong" to the "right" body.[42] And yet a problem with phenomenology is that it often cannot account for the ways in which experience is put into language, or, even more strongly, it often hides the ways in which what is taken as "true experience" has been shaped by language, discourse, ideology, or myth.

This is clear in *Nevada*. Binnie, much like Thom, explicitly frames *Nevada* in distinction to popular narratives of transness: "Trans women in real life are different from trans women on television," Binnie writes. "For one thing, when you take away the mystification, misconceptions and mystery, they're at least as boring as everybody else."[43] In distinguishing itself from television, *Nevada* frames itself as more real, and the reality it represents is quite simple: Trans people are not particularly different or unique, and certainly not magical. Trans people work jobs, buy bagels, and commute to work. Readers of *Nevada* are often in the head of the transfeminine protagonist, Maria, in the present tense. The book has no clear sense of development and offers little resolution. It does not describe a passage from the wrong body to the right body but might be read as exploring the survivability of what is wrong, including or especially the wrong society. The text therefore is very close to the phenomenological approach Chu calls for, an approach that calls for attention to what it feels like to be embodied in the world. *Nevada* seems to depart sharply from the turn to fantasy I have analyzed thus far.

But *Nevada* demonstrates an awareness we find in Thom's novel as well. While Nevada is committed to realism, the book explores how mythology comes to shape reality: Once again, narrative and materiality intertwine. Maria goes on a road trip, taking on the American, white-settler-colonial search for herself. Traveling West, she leaves behind her beloved bicycle, where she in fact feels most at home in her body, and, on the road, Maria ultimately finds nothing. Significantly, however, her decision to leave was shaped by the American myth. Thus, both *Nevada* and *Fierce Femmes* show how reality is shaped by myth and fantasy. Trans community, vitality, and survivability require new myths, new fantasies we can embody – even as or especially because trans bodies are real.

## NOTES

1 Kai Cheng Thom, *Fierce Femmes and Notorious Liars: A Dangerous Trans Girl's Confabulous Memoir* (Montreal: Metonymy Press, 2016), 2. Subsequent references to this text will be parenthetical.
2 Jordy Rosenberg, *Confessions of the Fox* (New York: One World, 2018), xiii.
3 Andrea Lawlor, *Paul Takes the Form of a Mortal Girl* (New York: Vintage Books, 2017).
4 Julian K. Jarboe, *Everyone on the Moon Is Essential Personnel* (Maple Shade, NJ: Lethe Press, 2020); Cameron Awkward-Rich, *Sympathetic Little Monster* (Los Angeles: Ricochet, 2016).
5 Susan Stryker and Paisley Currah, Introduction to *TSQ: Transgender Studies Quarterly* 2, no. 1 (2015): 5; David Valentine, *Imagining Transgender: An Ethnography of a Category* (Durham, NC: Duke University Press, 2007), 32.
6 Leslie Feinberg, "Transgender Liberation: A Movement Whose Time Has Come," in *The Transgender Studies Reader*, ed. Susan Stryker and Stephen Whittle (New York: Routledge, 2006), 206.
7 For a notable departure from this argument, see Andrea Long Chu and Emmett Harsin Drager, "After Trans Studies," *TSQ: Transgender Studies Quarterly* 6, no. 1 (2019): 106–109.
8 Avery Tompkins, "Asterisk," *TSQ: Transgender Studies Quarterly* 1, no. 1–2 (2014): 27.
9 See Valentine, *Imagining Transgender*, 5; Katrina Roen, "Transgender Theory and Embodiment: The Risk of Racial Marginalization," *Journal of Gender Studies* 10, no. 3 (2001): 257.
10 Tompkins, "Asterisk," 27.
11 For a beautiful, evocative analysis of the asterisk, see Marquis Bey, "The Trans*-ness of Blackness, the Blackness of Trans*-ness," *TSQ: Transgender Studies Quarterly* 4, no. 2 (May 2017): 284. For a definition of "transgender" that is quite similar to my definition of "trans*," see Susan Stryker, "My Words to Victor Frankenstein above the Village of Chamounix: Performing Transgender Rage," *GLQ: A Journal of Lesbian and Gay Studies* 1 (1994): 251. For an argument against the use of the asterisk, see "Why We Used Trans* and Why We Don't Anymore," *Trans Student Educational Resources* at www.transstudent .org/asterisk. Thank you to Sam Stone for bringing this website to my attention.
12 "Why We Used Trans*," *Trans Student Educational Resources*.
13 Stryker and Currah, Introduction, 17.
14 My framing of transgender literature draws on Helen Hok-Sze Leung, "Film," *TSQ: Transgender Studies Quarterly* 1, no. 1–2 (2014): 86–89.

15 For a prominent example of this argument, see Jay Prosser's and Jian Neo Chen's critiques of Judith Butler's reading of the film *Paris Is Burning* (dir. Jennie Livingstone) in *Bodies That Matter* (New York: Routledge, 1999). Jay Prosser, *Second Skins: The Body Narratives of Transsexuality* (New York: Columbia University Press, 1998), 45–55; Jian Neo Chen, *Trans Exploits: Trans of Color Cultures and Technologies in Movement* (Durham, NC: Duke University Press, 2019), 36. See also Viviane K. Namaste, *Invisible Lives: The Erasure of Transsexual and Transgendered People* (Chicago: University of Chicago Press, 2000); Emma Heaney, *The New Woman: Literary Modernism, Queer Theory, and the Trans Feminine Allegory* (Evanston, IL: Northwestern University Press, 2017); Chu and Drager, "After Trans Studies," 110–111; and Gabby Benavente and Jules Gill-Peterson, "The Promise of Trans Critique: Susan Stryker's Queer Theory," *GLQ: A Journal of Lesbian and Gay Studies* 25, no. 1 (January 2019): 24–26.

16 This essay was first presented at a conference in 1988 and first published as Sandy Stone, "The Empire Strikes Back: A Posttranssexual Manifesto," in *Body Guards: The Cultural Politics of Gender Ambiguity*, ed. Julia Epstein and Kristina Straub (New York: Routledge, 1991), 280–304. I will be citing the revised and updated version that appeared in *Camera Obscura* in 1992: Sandy Stone, "The Empire Strikes Back: A Posttranssexual Manifesto," *Camera Obscura* 10, no. 2 (1992): 150–176.

17 Stone, "The Empire Strikes Back," 166.

18 Prosser, *Second Skins*, 4.

19 Ibid., 5.

20 Ibid., 7.

21 Henry S. Rubin, "Phenomenology as Method in Trans Studies," *GLQ: A Journal of Lesbian and Gay Studies* 4, no. 2 (1998): 263–281; Gayle Salamon, *Assuming a Body: Transgender and the Rhetoric of Materiality* (New York: Columbia University Press, 2010); Gayle Salamon, *The Life and Times of Latisha King: A Critical Phenomenology of Transphobia* (New York: New York University Press, 2018).

22 Rubin, "Phenomenology as Method," 268–271.

23 Salamon, *Assuming a Body*, 93.

24 C. Riley Snorton, *Black on Both Sides: A Racial History of Trans Identity* (Minneapolis: University of Minnesota Press, 2017), 17–54.

25 Dean Spade, "Mutilating Gender," in *The Transgender Studies Reader*, 315–332, and Nikki Sullivan, "Transmogrification: (Un)Becoming Other(s)," in *The Transgender Studies Reader*, 552–564.

26 Stryker, "My Words," 238.

27 Ibid., 241.

28 Ibid., 251.

29 Claire Colebrook, "What Is It Like to Be a Human?," *Transgender Studies Quarterly* 2, no. 2 (2015): 228.

30 Ibid.

31 Bey, "The Trans*-ness," 278.

32 Ibid.

33 Ibid., 279.

34 Ibid., 251.

35 See Sally Markowitz, "Pelvic Politics: Sexual Dimorphism and Racial Difference," *Signs* 26, no. 2 (Winter 2001): 389–414. See also Hortense Spillers, "Mama's Baby, Papa's Maybe: An American Grammar Book," *Diacritics* 17, no. 2 (July 1987): 65–81; and Kyla Schuller, *The Biopolitics of Feeling: Race, Sex, and Science in the Nineteenth Century* (Durham, NC: Duke University Press, 2018).

36 Jules Gill-Peterson, "Trans of Color Critique before Transsexuality," *TSQ: Transgender Studies Quarterly* 5, no. 4 (November 2018): 610.

37 See Spade, "Mutilating Gender," 321; Prosser, *Second Skins*, 110–112; Stone, "The Empire Strikes Back," 160–162. I thank my student April Clark for her thesis and insights into contemporary psychological research on transgender youth. Clark develops a trans critique of this research's interest in determining which youth are "authentically transgender."

38 Juliet Jacques, *Trans: A Memoir* (London: Verso, 2015), 299; Prosser, *Second Skins*, 129.

39 Borrowing from Jacques, *Trans: A Memoir*, 76, and Andrea Long Chu, "The Wrong Body: Notes on Trans Phenomenology," *TSQ* 4, no. 1 (2017): 141–152, we can conclude that *Fierce Femmes* brings attention to the experience not of the "wrong body" but of the wrong society.

40 Thank you to my student Sora Hong for this convincing reading.

41 Gill-Peterson, "Trans of Color Critique," 613.

42 Chu, "The Wrong Body," 150–151.

43 Imogen Binnie, *Nevada* (New York: Topside Press, 2013), 4.

PART II

# Critical Methodologies

# 9

XINE YAO

# Feminist Theory, Feminist Criticism, and the Sex/Gender Distinction

"In literature I sensed the possibility of the integration of feeling/knowledge, rather than the split between the abstract and the emotional in which Western philosophy inevitably indulged," writes Barbara Christian in her foundational discussion about Black feminist literary theory.[1] While she critiques the veneration of theoretical abstraction, Christian, too, pushes against the biologically reductive, eurocentric preoccupation of white French feminist theorists who fixate on "the female body as the means to creating a female language."[2] Wary of producing a monolithic feminist literary theory herself, she draws our attention to the intertwined problems that emerge when we ask whose bodies, writings, theories, labors, experiences are centered. As Christian's essay illustrates, feminist theory provides multitudinous convergent and divergent ways to understand bodies and their relations to and through the world via what has been variously termed "gender" and "sex." To only define feminist theory as by women and for women ignores traditions from manifold configurations of histories, cultures, and politics that place different weight on the term "women" as they seek to comprehend, to critique, to survive, and to reimagine the world.

Amid this multiplicity, it can be tempting to ascribe to the clear distinction between sex as natural, indisputable embodiment and gender as artificial, contingent social construct. This division between sex and gender, however, is more a political convenience than an accurate account, traceable to certain schools of feminist thought in the 1970s, which borrowed from the development of sexological terminology a few decades prior. More recently, the instability of the sex/gender divide, which unsettles the definitional clarity of both concepts, has presented opportunities for feminist methodologies to question categories of identity, forms of expression, and structures of power writ large along far-ranging lines of inquiry, such as the ontological, ethical, and epistemological. Indeed, as the work of Christian and many other Black, Indigenous, and other feminist of color theorists reminds us, the exclusionary preoccupation with "sex" and "gender" as keywords obscures how they are articulated through racial difference and other regulatory norms of state and colonial power that seek to govern and produce bodies and populations. The body, privileged as the location of interiority, agency, and subjecthood, is always a metonym for more. As the signature feminist slogan declares, the personal is political.

Thus, this chapter cannot claim to be exhaustive but begs to be read in relation to others in this volume. It offers an account of a few generative clusters of discursive genealogies organized around contested terms attributed to bodies. I open with a preliminary overview of feminist interrogations of the definitions of "sex" and "gender" to foreground the inadequacies of addressing them as abstract universals. The structure of the chapter then bifurcates into questions of the natural and the unnatural as opposing regulatory principles that create, manage, authenticate, and abject differences. By focusing on the natural and the unnatural instead as analytical lenses, we can follow entangled lines of feminist inquiry about bodies drawn into orbit around the poles of this primary dualism that is near-synonymous with other related binaries that structure power. In this way, we may observe a few illustrative feminist tactics that seek to strategize from where they are situated on the different sides of this opposition, placing pressure from these positions in order to undermine that hegemonic dichotomization. To word it bluntly, when it comes to sex, there is no such thing as the merely biological; when it comes to gender, there is no such thing as the merely sociocultural. The tension between the literal and the literary perhaps is aptly suited to addressing the blurry distinctions between sex and gender in their fixity and fluidity as a jumping-off point for an abbreviated account of feminist struggles to claim the body is essential but not essentialist.

## "Sex" and "Gender": Distinctive and Indistinguishable

In *The Coquette; or, the History of Eliza Wharton* (1797) by Hannah Webster Foster, the word "sex" recurs, but the word "gender" is absent. The epistolary seduction novel fictionalizes the notorious death of an elite white New England woman who gave birth to a stillborn child out of wedlock: This is the material "fact" upon which the title page proclaims the narrative is founded. Eliza's seducer Peter Sanford is the first to use the word "sex" during his expression of desire for Eliza, which affirms a binary antagonism between men and women: "But I fancy this young lady is a coquette, and if so, I shall avenge my sex, by retaliating the mischiefs she meditates against us," he plots.[3] Eliza herself hopes to her other suitor that epistolary communication may enable more fluid relations: "The knowledge and masculine virtues of your sex may be softened, and rendered more diffusive by the inquisitiveness, vivacity, and docility of ours; drawn forth and exercised by each other."[4] Nonetheless, her mourning best friend closes the novel with a moral injunction "for the sake of my sex in general."[5] What are the functions of "sex" when characters discuss their relationships if the modern nongrammatical sense of "gender" would not become commonplace for at least another century? Even if that meaning were retroactively imposed, the anachronistic delineation between "sex" and "gender" in the literary rendition of one woman's tragic fate is difficult to discern: Lines are blurred between what is nature and what is being naturalized. From one exaggerated perspective, is it the biological inevitability of the body's sex as the underlying point of origin for all relations, or, from the polar opposite view, is it the sociocultural mutability of gender all the way down molding the body?

I choose this example from early American literature to gesture broadly toward some of the complexities that arise from a basic exercise to isolate "sex" and "gender." Although it should be noted that feminist interrogations of the body as a locus of regulatory power precede poststructuralism and often emerge from other intellectual genealogies, nonetheless, for many critics, Michel Foucault's definition of "biopolitics" operates as a useful referent. Politics is not confined to the formal public arena: Foucauldian biopolitics covers the workings of political power over life itself, thereby providing a heuristic for understanding the policing of sex, gender, and sexuality as key features of the regulation of individual bodies and populations. Gayle Rubin's sex/gender system identifies and explains these biopolitical dynamics: The system transmutes the matter of biological sex via society into cultural gender that then feeds back into the processes of sex. The system acts as an analytical framework for examining women's oppression and the organization of feminist politics by borrowing critically from Marxism, anthropology, and psychoanalysis to discuss social economies, forms of reproduction, and modes of production. Existing methodologies on their own are insufficient since they can themselves operate as oppressive ideologies that, at best, have neglected endemic sexism. Generally, in models such as Rubin's, sex constitutes the embodied, definitive foundation onto which the contingency of acculturated gender is constructed. Despite this useful distinction, Rubin herself imagines how feminism and the sex/gender system should move beyond a focus on women to the overall disruption of regulatory sex roles and sexualities. She concludes, "The dream I find most compelling is one of an androgynous and genderless (although not sexless) society, in which one's sexual anatomy is irrelevant to who one is, what one does, and with whom one makes love."[6] There will be sex, but anatomy will not be normative.

The insistence on gender over sex often remains the prevailing feminist principle: This strategy invests in the mutability of gender against the entrenchment of sex as the basis of arguments for sociopolitical transformation. In this vein, Judith Butler's early discussion of the performativity of gender continues to be misread as the claim that gender is constructed, and therefore it is illusory and can be willfully chosen and altered. In their subsequent intervention about how bodies matter, Butler takes issue with an entirely constructivist approach to gender that dismisses sex as simply gendered, thereby downplaying the body and its constitutive violences. As they ask, "What are the constraints by which bodies are materialized as 'sexed,' and how are we to understand the 'matter' of sex, and of bodies more generally, as the repeated and violent circumscription of cultural intelligibility?"[7] They do not want to cede sex and the body as critical domains for feminist politics, nor to deny their material salience. Nature and sex have histories, but that does not negate them. To return to "sex" in *The Coquette*, we can see that sex matters, not as a bodily given or static condition, but as a materialized process that consolidates, naturalizes, and gives the effect of solidity for the overall conditions of legibility – but also, conversely, illegitimacy – of embodied identities. Although shaped by abjection, exclusion, and other regulatory pressures, the repetition of performativity is testimony to these incomplete processes of materialization that can never fully compel bodies to be obedient to the norms that produce them or to the citations that make them intelligible. Rather than arguing over what is fantasy and what is reality in terms of sex and gender, Butler asks, what "if 'sex' is a fiction, it is one within whose necessities we live, without which life itself would be unthinkable?"[8] While they use "fiction" here in a broad sense, it is worth noting that among their choice of materials to discuss Anglo-American accounts of gender, Butler turns to reading American literature. Willa Cather's fictions, for instance, enable them to consider the links between sexuality and gender through the entanglements of identification and desire for queer attachments, the workings of names, and representation of body parts. Likewise, for Butler, Nella Larsen's *Passing* demonstrates that sexual difference does not precede racial difference; citing Black feminist critics, Butler emphasizes how the novel retheorizes how sexual norms are articulated through racial regimes.[9]

Historians of science further complicate the ahistorical conflation between the body and sex as a neutral definitional premise by unveiling the shifting contextual construction of the categories of somatic sex. Careful attention to the archive can disrupt commonplace logics which guide how we read. Thomas Laqueur, for instance, overturns the assumption that sex is primary and gender secondary: He claims that before the Enlightenment the reverse was true, so that gender was the "real" essence, whereas sex, or the body, was the manifestation.[10] Bodies are gendered, and Anne Fausto-Sterling looks at how sexing the body is also a process in modern science's focus on biological criteria: from genitals to chromosomes to sex hormones to the behavioral and developmental. She follows the construction of scientific knowledge about sex from features physically manifest on the body's exterior to those activities and principles presumed located within the body that are deduced by outcome and taken as expression. Fausto-Sterling nuances the conversions of the sex/gender system through Elizabeth Grosz's illustrative use of the Möbius strip. Sex and gender are on different sides of the strip, but rather than nature versus nurture, the conundrum of the Möbius is that the flat ribbon is twisted and joined at the ends to make a complete circuit: Both sides are seamlessly continuous with one another so that tracing the exterior surface to the interior leads outside again.[11] The Möbius strip presents another way of thinking about sex and gender as integrated puzzle, not dualistic dichotomy. I suggest that this metaphor testifies to how the literary does not simply represent concepts but constitutes the very form of thinking. Attempts to isolate and distinguish "sex" and "gender" in relation to characters' bodies are reductive, obscuring far more interesting dimensions of the terms' force and malleability in contested processes of literary meaning-making.

## The Question of "Natural" Embodiment

Barbara Christian concludes her discussion of Black feminist literary theory with an excerpt from Audre Lorde's "Poetry Is Not a Luxury." This citation enacts her refusal to establish a single set method for approaching texts and instead affirms how each literary work suggests its own approach. Here Lorde affirms a sensitive and disciplined approach to feelings as the precursor for creative and radical thinking that is not abstracted from embodied experience. Poetry is not a luxury for women because poetry allows for the articulation of new possibilities when current language is inadequate: "Poetry is not only dream and vision; it is the skeleton architecture of our lives. It lays the foundations for a future of change, a bridge across our fears of what has never been before."[12] Like many other feminist thinkers, Lorde challenges the Cartesian dualism of mind over body that maps onto other oppressive binaries. She seeks to reorder the hierarchy of the sensorium by reclaiming the feeling body as a site of knowledge. By asserting that poetry is the "skeleton architecture of our lives," Lorde invokes a somatic structural metaphor consonant with her other writings foregrounding corporeal embodiment as a site for pleasure, creativity, and change. This sense of the body aims to be nonreductive, much as her celebration of the erotic as a resource, way of knowing, and mode of living rebuts the understanding of the erotic as confined to the physically sexual.

In this section I give an account of some of the approaches that feminist theorists have taken to assess, to reconceptualize, and, sometimes, to reclaim the body by repurposing associated terms like "feeling" and "nature" that naturalize the hegemonic paradigm of differences in the American cultural imagination. The stigmatization of the body accomplishes political and symbolic work: For instance, through an ecofeminist lens Annette Kolodny investigates the metaphor of the landscape as the feminized body in relation to the colonization of the United States, or fat studies critic Susan Bordo unpacks the representative meanings of weight and appetites for idealized and denigrated gendered bodies. As ample scholarship by scholars like Nina Baym shows, even genres tied to the body – like sensationalism, melodrama, and sentimentalism – are gendered as aesthetically and morally suspect.[13]

Nonetheless, feminists turning to the natural body as a site of authority to redress the hierarchy of oppressions sometimes fail to consider that the demarcation of "nature" itself constitutes a settler-colonial imposition of a prelapsarian idea of innocence. Indigenous feminism calls for a resurgent reorientation to the world that would decolonize Western ideas of the body, feelings, and nature; critiquing moralistic equivalences between Indigeneity and environmentalism, Kim TallBear (Sisseton-Wahpeton Oyate) cautions against reproducing romanticized colonial ideas that narrowly homogenize the diversity and flux of environmental practices specific to different Indigenous peoples.[14] Similarly, many Indigenous literary scholars assert the need for criticism appropriate for Indigenous works informed by the thinking and practices of their respective nations. To this end Dian Million (Tanana Athabascan) argues for "felt theory" to account for the affective, feminist narrative methods enacted by Indigenous women in North America, creating the language that allows them to explore the painful facets of their colonization. An epistemic disruption is required to unsettle academic colonial discourses that gatekeep the communal felt knowledges of Indigenous literary, historical, and oral traditions, relegating such scholarship that actively participates in these important traditions to the restricted, invalidated category of the "feminine." Native narratives and scholars, according to Million, are dismissed by settler-colonial apparatuses because they do not bracket the subjective or the emotional. As she remarks, "But what is objective except Western science's own wet dream of detached corporeality?"[15] In contrast to that colonial compartmentalization of life from the world, Leanne Simpson (Ojibwe) reflects upon Indigenous feminist and

Two-Spirit/LGBTQ perspectives on the centrality of "relationships with each other and with plant and animal nations, with our lands and waters and with the spiritual world" that ground Indigenous understandings of sovereignty and nationhood.[16] For Simpson, considerations of gender and bodies cannot be extricated from *Kina Gchi Nishnaabeg-ogaming*, the phrase shared by an Elder Gidigaa Migizi from Waashkigamaagki, which roughly means "the place where we all live and work together."[17] Thus, the Indigenous women and Two-Spirit/LGBTQ people organize around the concept of individual and collective "sovereign bodies" routed through land in a material, spiritual network of relationships.[18]

Examinations of gendered subjugation in the American context must also contend with the legacies of chattel slavery. Few analyses of embodiment have been as generative as Hortense Spillers's Black feminist theorization of "flesh" in contradistinction to "the body" as fundamental to the American symbolic order. Before the discursive body of the individual subject, there is the bare fact of the flesh: The system of enslavement violated captive Black people on the level of flesh itself, a complete objectification that made them nonsovereign, that is to say, available to all manner of violences sexual, scientific, and otherwise. Under chattel slavery, children born from a Black mother legally inherited her enslaved status, thereby disrupting white patriarchal familial norms of gender, naming, and kinship without conferring upon her any actual matriarchal authority, since she and her children were still subjected to enslavers. Spillers reads narratives of enslavement by Harriet Jacobs and Frederick Douglass to trace how "ungendered" flesh was vulnerable to "a gigantic sexualized repertoire that may be alternately expressed as male/female" and to assert that Black people, particularly Black women, were denied "gendering" because they did not have access to domesticity and its cultural fictions as the privileged realm wherein these processes are legitimized.[19] This legacy continues to inform the alleged deviance of the matriarchal African American family and Black people in general. Rather than calling for Black access to the categories of normative gender, Spillers asks how this ongoing history provides a counternarrative with the potential for radically different empowerment. Her analysis of flesh and ungendering opened up space for Black queer and trans studies; indeed, using Spillers's terms, trans theorist C. Riley Snorton further intervenes into the insights of Judith Butler by highlighting how Black enslavement provided the conceptual and material context for the development of scientific knowledge about the distinction between sex and gender. Although flesh was the raw material for this brutal historical consolidation, Snorton – like Spillers – sees flesh as the possibility for alternative modes of being and other forms of gender.[20]

We can consider these Indigenous senses of embodied relations and Black feminist meanings of "flesh" when reading what Cherríe Moraga and Gloria Anzaldúa call "theory in the flesh" in their defining woman of color anthology *This Bridge Called My Back*, which brings together Latinx, Black, Indigenous, and Asian feminists. In explicit dialogue with Lorde, the collection gathers poetry, essays, interviews, manifestos, and personal testimonies to explore the intersecting axes of domination – such as racism, sexism, homophobia, and class – nuanced by the textures of lived experience informed by culturally specific, but still entangled, histories in order to articulate a US Third World feminist consciousness that troubles the borders of the nation-state and deliberately turns away from mainstream feminism by privileged white women and toward solidarity with the shared but distinct struggles of women of color across the world. Included are the Combahee River Collective's iconic Black feminist statement; Lakota activist Barbara Cameron's meditations on Indigeneity, homophobia, and racism; Merle Woo's letter to her mother articulating a Yellow Feminism in concert with other Third World feminisms; and Norma Alarcón theorizing Chicanx literature by reclaiming Aztec history to critique universal humanism. Moraga and Anzaldúa state, "A theory in the flesh means one where the physical realities of our lives – our skin color, the land or concrete we grew up on, our sexual longings – all fuse to create a politic born of necessity."[21] These collected writings perform the difficult work of solidarity across difference and are driven by a politic that addresses oppression and liberation through the material and the spiritual.

## The Question of Unnatural Embodiment

"The transsexual body is an unnatural body," declares trans theorist Susan Stryker: "It is the product of medical science. It is a technological construction. It is flesh torn apart and sewn together again in a shape other than that in which it was born."[22] On the other end of the American cultural imagination, the unnatural and artificial – dichotomized as the opposite of the natural and real – constitutes a realm of meanings through which feminist criticism has interrogated and reimagined the body. This section addresses a number of the insightful ways feminist critics have reassessed, and tapped into, ambivalence and even antagonism to the organic body and its claims to wholeness, which are so frequently weaponized to police the purported naturalness of gender roles and the self-evident validity of biological sex. Instead of trying to plead for inclusion into that natural order, Stryker embraces the unnatural monstrosity attributed to trans women by trans-exclusionary radical feminists who cling to an unexamined commitment to biological sex that determines strict categories of proper gender expression. Much as we have seen feminist thinkers rupture processes of naturalization by putting pressure on "nature," others have salvaged the vilification of the unnatural and artificial. In lieu of organic wholeness, they have found and created space for the partial and prosthetic. This critical tendency lends itself to conceptual schools like new materialism and posthumanism, with their emphasis on syntheses between bodies of all sorts, but refuses the persistent hegemonic tendency towards the erasure of differences in these fields; instead, feminist theorists, for example, take advantage of the confluence of these intellectual threads to present provocative observations that illuminate and expand overlapping sites of inquiry, such as critical race studies and disability studies.

The influences of speculative fiction run through much of this theorizing. Originally delivered as a performance piece at California State University, Stryker's text uses Mary Shelley's *Frankenstein* to cast herself as the paradigmatic science fiction monster. Originally a protest against the annual meeting of the American Psychiatric Association that officially classified trans identity as a medical disorder, the speech expressed "a transgender aesthetic" that disrupted taxonomies of genres, styles, and genders on a formal level while being simultaneously embodied by Stryker dressed in "genderfuck drag" in defiance of the norms of the academic conference.[23] This American performance art draws upon the interpretation generally held by scholars that the monster of the classic British novel is Frankenstein's projection of all that he disavows. Since some feminist arguments for trans exclusion cast trans people as Frankenstein's monster or as generally monstrous, Stryker speculates that this comparison similarly illuminates how they are positioning the figure of the trans person as negation to attempt to repudiate what they cannot accept in themselves. Thus she situates herself in relation to her interlocutors by reworking the novel's scene above the village of Chamounix wherein the monster confronts Victor Frankenstein with its own account of its creation, explaining its anger. The manifesto combines activism, queer and feminist theory, literary criticism, cultural studies, personal experience, and poetry into an assemblage that expresses, akin to the rebellious monster, a rage that refuses to grieve her alleged unnaturalness. The trans body apprehends the violence of the gendering process writ upon all flesh, revealing the artifice of nature and the kinds of politics that depend upon fixed identities. For Stryker, interventions into medical and cultural discourses must be through language, for, while language is "the scalpel that defines our flesh," her fury can deform it and thereby rewrite herself.[24]

One significant precedent for Stryker's work, and, indeed, many other provocations reclaiming the nonhuman and the unnatural, is Donna Haraway's landmark 1985 essay "A Cyborg Manifesto." Grounded in the struggle for socialist-feminist liberation, Haraway explores science fiction to skewer myths of organic wholeness while proudly affirming blasphemy as critical orientation and irony as playful political strategy. Like other feminist theorists we have encountered, she insists that fiction is not simple escapism: After all, "women's experience" is both a collective fact and fiction fabricated by international women's movements for political agendas. "A cyborg is a cybernetic organism, a hybrid of machine and organism, a creature of social reality as well as a creature of fiction," defines Haraway, viewing the postgender figure's unruly amalgam as a powerful means of rupturing the imposed boundaries of hegemony, including that between reality and fiction in order to contribute to that feminist project.[25] The dichotomy of nature versus culture is not so easily seen as a matter of the exploitation of one or the return to the other (in this vein we have already seen Kim TallBear trouble easy moves to moral superiority through claims to nature that reproduce narrow ideas of Indigenous authenticity). Science fiction writers like Octavia Butler, Samuel R. Delany, James Tiptree, Jr., and Joanna Russ theorize cyborgs; she enumerates technological advancements at every possible scale that signify the cyborg's subversions of the existing order. Simultaneously, the cyborg is an analytic framework for apprehending our embodied, social realities and a fiction that generates imaginative possibilities. By including technology and the nonhuman, Haraway augments Foucauldian biopolitics through the potential of a cyborg politics that includes cyborg gender; indeed, she asserts that we are all cyborgs. Haraway identifies three deterministic structural dualisms that the cyborg transgresses: the human and the animal, the organic and the machinic, the material and the immaterial. Such cyborg disruptions, she acknowledges, can and do reflect the consolidation of planetary domination by a capitalist, militaristic politics based upon masculinized violence against women's bodies. Nonetheless, Haraway urges progressive politics to move beyond the reiteration of the dichotomy between the natural and unnatural, and instead to see the potential for how the cyborg's fusions gesture toward more expansive kinships and nonessentialist identities, and to make space for contradictions.

White women – and here she includes herself – have been forced to realize "the non-innocence of the category 'woman.'"[26] She gives credit to the work of women of color for the positing of a political response that does not reconsolidate a new unified identity dependent upon a natural standpoint but rather is built upon affinities and coalition. Via readings of Cherríe

Moraga and Lorde she claims that women of color are cyborgs and that writing is a cyborg technology. Cyborg imagery invokes another way to understand our bodies other than as organic, unified embodiment, and to imagine possibilities beyond dualisms that do not rely upon the discourse of reproductive sex. The unnatural provides revolutionary alternatives: as she famously concludes, "I would rather be a cyborg than a goddess."[27]

Who has access to such a choice? Haraway cites Black and Chicanx feminists, while "the cyborg" has inspired the work of subsequent theorists like Jasbir Puar. However, in her original essay there are no contributions from thinkers speaking for "the unnatural cyborg women making chips in Asia," whose images she invokes.[28] As poet Cathy Park Hong writes ironically, "We're so post-racial we're silicon."[29] The pervasiveness of such techno-Orientalist tropes informs the investments of noted Asian American feminist theorists in investigating alien, inorganic bodies that trouble national boundaries. Thanks to Lisa Lowe, the field has had a long commitment to hybridity, multiplicity, and heterogeneity as keywords to disrupt the presumed wholeness of identities and linear, biological affiliations.[30] Drawing upon the influences of poststructuralism, Kandice Chuh made the important claim that Asian American critique is a "subjectless discourse," which preceded queer theory's similar declaration, suggesting a disciplinary tendency to question the organic coherence of the body.[31]

To Rachel C. Lee, fragmented bodies have a particular salience in Asian American aesthetic production and politics, an intervention of race, queer, feminist, and postcolonial studies into new materialisms and science and technology studies. Among Asian Americans there was a historical tendency to insist on a synecdochal relationship between body parts and the coherent racialized body for ethical, political, and moral arguments for a return to the putative original state of organic, whole personhood. Anxiety about this fragmentation is traceable to worries about the cohesion of the identity formation of "Asian American," its associated literary tradition, and the disciplinary field. For Lee, however, representations of divisible corporeality and pliable biology in literature and biotechnology provoke a posthuman challenge to humanistic frameworks by considering, and even reveling in, bodily fragments, patterns, and ecologies instead of the idolization of somatic wholeness. This disturbs but does not abandon the biological; in fact, the value of tactics of anthropomorphization can point to the dynamics of materiality distributed at different scales and via infrastructures rather than the classic assertion of indivisible embodiment.[32]

The problem of Asian feminine embodiment produced by these discourses poses, for Anne Anlin Cheng, the possibility of an account of racialization radically different from Spillers's conception of the flesh. By comparison, the mute figure of the "yellow woman" is ornamental: "a style, promising yet supplanting skin and flesh, an insistently aesthetic presence that is prized and despoiled."[33] Cheng's "ornamentalism" evokes Orientalism, commodification, and objectification to address a synthetic, aestheticized gendered embodiment that is curiously abstracted and disembodied. As she explores through literature, and visual and material culture, this ornamental embodiment is transferrable and material, constructed and prosthetic. Although she contrasts this artificial racialized person-making with Spillers's 'flesh' as different modes of racialized gender, nonetheless, she stresses they are not essentially linked to racial identities, that is, exclusive properties of 'Asiatic' versus Black womanhood. To this end, Cheng closes with a reading of ornamentalized Black flesh in Toni Morrison's *Beloved* to show how such polarized processes may still relate to each other in an overall system of differentiated racialized gender subjugation that seeks to flatten out meaningful comparative analysis. In contradistinction to the usual feminist analysis of objectification, Cheng attends to how objects are made into people to challenge one of the standard assumptions of many feminist readings and the category of human personhood. Thus, Asian Americanist and trans scholars are among those feminist critics who help us reevaluate the "unnatural."

## Conclusion

To make space for a plurality of Black feminist literary critical approaches, Barbara Christian questions the boundaries between theory and literature, reminding us that although certain literatures and discourses are minoritized, in no way are they actually minor. An aim of this chapter has not been to model feminist theory through American literature, or American literature through feminist theory, but to draw attention to the proliferation of feminist theorizations of the body when we refuse to keep theory and literature segregated. Christian validates narrative forms and literary language as "both sensual and abstract" modes of theorizing.[34] Along with broadening our scope for different registers and modes of feminist critique, I take her insight to emphasize the interplay of aesthetic form and embodied form within feminist readings that trouble rigid categorizations of "sex" and "gender." For instance, Sandy Stone's foundational essay on trans studies suggests approaching "transsexuals" as a "genre – a series of embodied texts whose potential for productive disruption of structured sexualities and spectra of desire has yet to be explored."[35] To stretch our scales of reference even further for thinking about genre, philosopher Sylvia Wynter calls attention to how the obsession with universality obscures the multiplicity of the "genres" of being human: "We are simultaneously storytelling and biological beings."[36] Gender is but one member class of genre – it is always already a verb, not a noun.[37]

Feminist theory can inspire us to better apprehend bodies in dynamic relation rather than attempting to classify qualities like gender according to constraining taxonomies. In her reflections that preface the fourth edition of *This Bridge Called My Back*, Moraga proposes a generous but critical methodology for reading the anthology as a counterarchive several decades later: to acknowledge the datedness, which registers the temporal moment and geographies that shaped their political, creative consciousness. While thanking the subsequent generations who continue to challenge the definitions of womanhood and lesbianism that were the basis for the collection, Moraga notes that a few contributors themselves have now come to different minoritarian gender identifications as trans men or gender nonconforming. Openness to diversities of queer desire and gender identities does not obviate the original emphasis of the collection: as she maintains,

> The body – that site which houses the intuitive, the unspoken, the viscera of our being. – this is the revolutionary promise of 'theory in the flesh;' for it is both the *expression* of evolving political consciousness and the *creator* of consciousness, itself.[38]

Approaching American literature through feminist theory means reckoning with how debates about sex and gender reflect the nation-state's historical and ongoing policing of bodies through the imposition of these categories, not limited to that national geographical context but also to the violence of American cultural imperialism on the global scale. According to Moraga and the other contributors, writing not only records but enacts this incarnated theory.

## NOTES

1 Barbara Christian, "The Race for Theory," *Cultural Critique* 14, no. 6 (1987): 72, https://doi.org/10.2307/1354255.
2 Ibid., 75–76.
3 Hannah W. Foster, *The Coquette* (New York: Oxford University Press, 1797), 18.
4 Ibid., 47.
5 Ibid., 167.
6 Gayle Rubin, "The Traffic in Women: Notes on the 'Political Economy' of Sex," in *Deviations: A Gayle Rubin Reader*, ed. Gayle Rubin (Durham, NC: Duke University Press, 2011), 61.
7 Judith Butler, *Bodies That Matter: On the Discursive Limits of "Sex"* (London: Routledge, 2017), x, https://doi.org/10.5840/intstudphil199830414.
8 Ibid., xv.

9 Butler acknowledges their indebtedness to Black feminist literary criticism such as Hazel V. Carby, *Reconstructing Womanhood: The Emergence of the Afro-American Woman Novelist* (Oxford: Oxford University Press, 1988), and Deborah E. McDowell, Introduction to *Quicksand and Passing*, by Nella Larsen (New Brunswick, NJ: Rutgers University Press, 1986).

10 Thomas W. Laqueur, *Making Sex: Body and Gender from the Greeks to Freud* (Boston: Harvard University Press, 1990).

11 Anne Fausto-Sterling, *Sexing the Body: Gender Politics and the Construction of Sexuality* (New York: Basic Books, 2000).

12 Audre Lorde, *Sister Outsider: Essays and Speeches* (Berkeley, CA: Crossing Press, 1984), 38.

13 Kolodny, *The Lay of the Land: Metaphor as Experience and History in American Life and Letters*; Bordo, *Unbearable Weight: Feminism, Western Culture, and the Body*. For a starting point on reconsidering the gender bias of American literary criticism see Baym, *Woman's Fiction*.

14 Kim TallBear, "Review: All Our Relations: Native Struggles for Land and Life by Winona LaDuke," *Wicazo Sa Review* 17, no. 1 (2002): 234–242.

15 Dian Million, "Felt Theory: An Indigenous Feminist Approach to Affect and History," *Wicazo Sa Review* 24, no. 2 (2009): 73.

16 Leanne Betasamosake Simpson, "The Place Where We All Live and Work Together: A Gendered Analysis of 'Sovereignty,'" in *Native Studies Keywords*, ed. Stephanie Nohelani Teves, Andrea Smith, and Michelle H. Raheja (Tucson: University of Arizona Press, 2015), 18.

17 Leanne Betasamosake Simpson, "Indigenous Resurgence and Co-Resistance," *Critical Ethnic Studies* 2, no. 2 (2016): 18.

18 Walter Benjamin, "Surrealism. The Last Snapshot of the European Intelligentsia," *New Left Review* 108 (1978): 225–239.

19 Hortense Spillers, "Mama's Baby, Papa's Maybe: An American Grammar Book," *Diacritics* 17, no. 2 (1987): 77.

20 C. Riley Snorton, *Black on Both Sides: A Racial History of Trans Identity* (Minneapolis: University of Minnesota Press, 2017).

21 Cherríe Moraga and Gloria Anzaldúa, eds., *This Bridge Called My Back: Writings by Radical Women of Color*, 4th ed. (Albany: State University of New York Press, 1981), 19.

22 Susan Stryker, "My Words to Victor Frankenstein above the Village of Chamounix: Performing Transgender Rage," *GLQ: A Journal of Lesbian and Gay Studies* 1, no. 3 (1994): 238, https://doi.org/10.1215/10642684-1-3-237.

23 Ibid., 237.

24 Ibid., 250.

25 Donna J. Haraway, *Simians, Cyborgs and Women: The Reinvention of Nature* (New York: Routledge, 1991), 149.

26 Ibid., 157.

27 Ibid., 181.

28 Ibid., 154; Jasbir Puar, "'I Would Rather Be a Cyborg than a Goddess': Becoming-Intersectional in Assemblage Theory," *PhiloSOPHIA* 2, no. 1 (2012): 49–66.

29 Cathy Park Hong, *Minor Feelings: A Reckoning on Race and the Asian Condition* (New York: Random House, 2020), 7.

30 Lisa Lowe, "Heterogeneity, Hybridity, Multiplicity: Marking Asian American Differences," *Diaspora: A Journal of Transnational Studies* 1, no. 1 (1991): 24–44.
31 Kandice Chuh, *Imagine Otherwise: On Asian Americanist Critique* (Durham, NC: Duke University Press, 2003); Helena Grice and Crystal Parikh, "Feminisms and Queer Interventions into Asian America," in *The Cambridge Companion to Asian American Literature*, ed. Crystal Parikh and Daniel Y. Kim (New York: Cambridge University Press, 2015), 169–182.
32 Rachel C. Lee, *The Exquisite Corpse of Asian America: Biopolitics, Biosociality, and Posthuman Ecologies* (New York: New York University Press, 2014).
33 Anne Anlin Cheng, *Ornamentalism* (New York: Oxford University Press, 2019), 1.
34 Christian, "The Race for Theory," 68.
35 Sandy Stone, "The Empire Strikes Back: A Posttransexual Manifesto," *Camera OBscura* 10, no. 2 (1992): 165.
36 Katherine McKittrick, *Sylvia Wynter: On Being Human as Praxis* (2015), 29, https://doi.org/10.1017/CBO9781107415324.004.
37 Ibid., 33.
38 Moraga and Anzaldúa, *This Bridge Called My Back*, xxiv.

# 10

THOMAS CONSTANTINESCO

# Reading Bodies and Textual Materialities

Reading "leaves no trace; its product is invisible," or so Susan Stewart argues in *On Longing*, theorizing reading as an immaterial activity of the mind, implicitly divorced from the body.[1] Sometime in 1865, as the Civil War was drawing to a close, Emily Dickinson came to a different conclusion in a short poem contesting such an ethereal conception of reading. The poem rehearses, rather cryptically, a scenario that had become tragically familiar in many households on both sides of the conflict, the reading of a letter announcing a soldier's death and the devastating grief that the news of this loss caused in the surviving relatives:

> He scanned it – Staggered –
> Dropped the Loop
> To Past or Period –
> Caught Helpless at a sense as if
> His Mind were going blind –
>
> Groped up, to see if God were there –
> Groped backward at Himself
> Caressed a Trigger absently
> And wandered out of Life –[2]

Dickinson emphasizes both the textual materiality of the letter and the intensely embodied nature of the act of reading it. Barely registering the distinctive "Loop" of the cursive script, all the while indexing it, the reader in the poem is transfixed, however, by the letter's "Past" tense and closing "Period," legible as material intimations of the terrible finality of its undisclosed contents. The reading is cursory – a mere glancing over the lines – yet Dickinson's initial verb zooms in on the reader's eyes moving quickly across the page as a prelude to the bodily collapse that follows. The first dash punctures the opening line and materializes the unarticulated shock of death, while linking together the two segments of the line and the respective body parts they designate – the scanning eyes and the staggering legs – eventually framing the psychosomatic breakdown which the line describes as an effect of the readerly act. With its arresting trope of an embodied "Mind ... going blind," the first stanza's concluding line further insists that reading is a matter of the body rather than an intellectual act, while the second stanza continues to foreground the reader's body, as his groping hands vainly attempt to reach for "God" and then get a grip of "Himself," before yielding to a macabrely eroticized suicidal wish, where the "Trigger" to be "Caressed" figures the reader's desire to be reunited with his son in death imagined as an eternal embrace.

Dickinson's scene of traumatic reading sets the stage for many of the questions this chapter wishes to consider, at the crossroads of the material text and the reading body. In *Theories of Reading: Books, Bodies, and Bibliomania*, Karin Littau contends that the history of reading is underwritten by "a split" between two traditions: One "tends to regard reading as a reducibly mental activity," whereas the other "[assumes] that reading literature [is] not only about sense-making but also about sensation."[3] She further claims that the development of literary criticism in the modern period progressively led to a conception of the reader as a disembodied figure, as abstract as that of the writer itself, and argues instead for a corrective theory of reading as a relation between two bodies, that of the text and that of the reader. Dickinson's poem surely speaks to Littau's material concerns. Configuring reading in terms of haptics as well as optics, it attends both to the physicality entailed in the performance of reading and to its consequent bodily affects, understood as constitutive of the reading experience. Through the image of the "Mind ... going blind" and the purposeful suppression of the letter's all-too predictable contents, Dickinson centers reading as trafficking in sensation rather than sense-making. In this regard, the uncertainty of God's presence testifies to the reader's skepticism for the possibility of a theodicy that would help make "sense" of his son's death and of his grief as part of a Providential design. By pitting immediate corporeal sensations against the doubtful promise of spiritual reward, Dickinson tilts the scales in favor of reading-as-decoding – a deciphering of the textual algorithm which has to do with the brain and the body – over reading-as-interpretation, where meaning-making would be the preserve of the mind. The poem thus builds on the historically split sense of the word "reading," which names simultaneously the experience of interpreting and of scanning a text.[4] It also reflexively encourages its own readers to think about what Garrett Stewart has called "the somatics of reading," asking them to consider the mirroring relation between the reader in the poem and the reader of the poem.[5] How indeed should this lyric be "scanned"? What rhythms do its prosodic and syntactic "Period[s]" require and put in motion? These are questions of and for the body, even if one takes silent reading, as opposed to reading aloud, as a paradigmatic modality. As Stewart argues, reading "is always a putting in of body time": It mobilizes "the internal somatic register of the reader," which includes "the invisible level of the subvocal enunciation incident to reading, with its own inhibited musculature and phonation."[6] As a figuration of embodied reading calling attention to the physicality of its own reading protocol, then, Dickinson's poem literally performs Roger Chartier's notion that "[r]eading is not uniquely an abstract operation of the intellect: it brings the body into play."[7]

Yet in describing the reading experience as one of wounding, and in particular of blinding, Dickinson's compressed lyric also reveals the fantasy of able-bodiedness that implicitly underwrites many conceptions of embodied reading and that disability scholarship has taught us to complicate. The evidently sighted reader of the first line is imagined, by the second stanza, as a blind or blinded reader for whom reading becomes exclusively a matter of touch. Dickinson thus references not only various bodily ways of reading – through sight and touch, through the eyes and the hands – but also the many reading bodies that may be excluded from a theory of reading that would privilege the able body as a mode of embodiment, marking it invisibly as a form of abstract, and paradoxically disembodied, nonidentity. Writing in 1976, well before the advent of disability studies, French novelist Georges Perec noted a similar paradox. "We read with eyes," he observed, only to turn his attention to all those who do not, beginning with "blind people, who read with fingers," as well as "those who are being read to" and who read with the ears. We also read with the hands, he continued, except for "the one-armed, who can't turn the pages."[8] As Perec's self-corrections suggest, approaching reading as a technique of the body often relies on silent assumptions of able-bodiedness. Thinking about embodied literacies in the plural rather than the singular, about the diversity of reading bodies and the range of physical gestures required in the act of reading, therefore becomes a way to enter into one of those "emergency zones of which all we know is that we don't know very much, although we sense we might learn a great deal from them were we to take it into our heads to pay them some attention."[9]

Heeding Perec's invitation while restricting its investigations to American literary history, this chapter asks what we might learn from paying attention to the body as such an "emergency zone" where reading takes place. What is the purchase of emphasizing reading as an embodied practice for Americanist literary criticism? In what follows, I offer a threefold answer. The first is literary historical; the second, methodological; and the third, interpretive. The first two are animated by a centrifugal pull toward extending and decentering the field, while the third is driven by a somewhat contradictory, centripetal movement. From a literary historical standpoint, insisting on the bodily economies of reading facilitates the emergence of alternative timelines and models of periodization by shifting the focus to readerly communities largely occluded from more canonical histories of literature and of reading. From a methodological perspective, attending to the reading body helps redescribe reading as a sensory experience, one which is often involuntary. This reorients the conversation toward reading as aesthetic response and away from reading as interpretation and critical mastery over the text, in keeping with the recent postcritical turn in literary studies, whose proponents advocate a shift away from the hermeneutics of suspicion which have driven so many readerly endeavors for the past forty years.[10] One may nonetheless wonder how taking into account the somatic nature of reading might contribute to our understanding of literary texts. Accordingly, the final section of this chapter takes up ways in which an emphasis on reading as a bodily practice helps to make sense of the texts we read.

## Reading by Touch

Leafing through the multivolume *A History of the Book in America* reveals a gap between the wealth of knowledge regarding the production and circulation of books and the relative dearth of information about actual reading practices, between books as material objects and the ways in which readers interacted with them.[11] The first accounts of reading in colonial America for instance, especially of reading the Bible, rarely emphasize the body and conventionally focus on the heart as the disembodied locus of Protestant spirituality. When they do, it is often to dismiss the material conditions and physical circumstances of reading as irrelevant, if not suspect, and certainly distinct from actual or true reading. Doing so, they effectively restrict reading to an act of the mind, while relegating to the margins of literary history those readers who engaged in alternative, more capacious ways of reading. In *A briefe and true report of the new found land of Virginia* (1588), for example, Thomas Harriot describes the Algonquians' relation to the Bible as dangerously sensual, as opposed to the abstract, spiritual form of reading that he recommends and that informs his own evangelism:

> Manie times and in euery towne where I came ... I made declaration of the
> contentes of the Bible; that therein was set foorth the true and onelie GOD, and
> his mightie woorkes, that therein was contayned the true doctrine of saluation

through Christ, with manie particularities of Miracles and chiefe poyntes of religion, as I was able then to vtter, and thought fitte for the time. And although I told them the booke materially & of itself was not of anie such vertue, as I thought they did conceiue, but onely the doctrine therein contained; yet would many be glad to touch it, to embrace it, to kisse it, to hold it to their brests and heades, and stroke ouer all their bodie with it; to shewe their hungrie desire of that knowledge which was spoken of.[12]

Harriot separates the "contentes" of the book, containing God's "true doctrine," from its material form, which is deemed immaterial to the process of revelation, and even a source of sinful behaviors. From this perspective, the racialized conflict between Christianity and paganism, between civilization and barbarity, between the white, English preacher and the native Algonquians he is at pains to convert, is implicitly framed within the terms of an intra-European conflict between Protestant scripturalism and Catholic idolatry. At the same time, the very idealization of meaning over form, of spirit over matter, hinges on "the book as a prop and a locus of [Harriot's] authority," as suggested by his repeated emphasis on God's law being "set foorth" "therein": however dematerialized, the book remains the material repository of religious orthodoxy and colonial power.[13] Besides, the passionate reading modeled by the Algonquians evidences, despite Harriot's disavowal, a metonymic continuity between their devotion to the material object and the evangelical doctrine of love that the Bible teaches. While the highly eroticized handling of the book being touched, embraced, kissed, held, and stroked may index idolatry and mysticism, it also registers a profoundly intimate, personal relation to the Bible, which aligns ultimately, if unexpectedly, with Harriot's own Protestantism. This scene of haptic reading is thus legible in terms of what Mark Amsler has called "affective literacy," which configures reading as involving a range of "emotional, somatic, activity-based relationships with texts."[14] It also attests the complexity of devotional reading practices in colonial America, where "heart piety" was often complemented by what Matthew Brown has termed "hand piety" and "eye piety," where touch and sight participated actively in "sensory, performance-based" forms of spirituality.[15] It further frames the Bible as a "scriptive thing," to borrow Robin Bernstein's phrase, that is, as "an item of material culture that prompts meaningful bodily behaviors."[16] It finally foregrounds an instance of early Native American literacy as an alternative, embodied form of reading to the dominant Anglo, abstract tradition. This helps to expand our understanding of readerly communities in colonial America, while reframing our notion of what constitutes the experience of reading as one that also involves touching the book and being touched by it.

This early and eventually marginalized instance of reading by touch calls attention, by contrast, to the longer history of reading in America, but also elsewhere in the Western world, as predominantly spiritualized and intellectual. In the United States, this history reached one of its high points in the Romantic period with the development of New England Transcendentalism. According to the standard critical narrative, Transcendentalism privileged spirit over matter as a function of its idealist philosophy. It also theorized reading as a visual activity. Emerson's master trope of the "transparent eyeball" reading the invisible presence of the divine in the material signs of nature speaks eloquently to the structure of disembodiment encoded within the primacy of ocular reading.[17] It also reveals the teleological hermeneutics that subtends it and that purports to uncover "the highest spiritual cause lurking, as it always does lurk, in these suburbs and extremities of nature."[18] As Erica Fretwell recently argued, however, the historical overemphasis on reading as an act of vision that would render book, body, and world ultimately transparent has had the paradoxical effect of obscuring "other scripts," as well as other histories of reading practices, and of excluding them from the critical conversation.[19] Yet the nineteenth century also "witnessed the birth of reading *as* touch," with Louis Braille's invention in 1824 of a reading system of raised dots for the blind.[20] Fretwell traces the American side of that transatlantic history of digital reading throughout the nineteenth and early twentieth centuries, where braille competed with other systems of raised print, and she maps out the constitution of "an American para-canon" available to blind readers, one which included already anthologized texts and authors, from the Bible and Shakespeare to Longfellow, Emerson, and Hawthorne, as well as more personal and subversive literary productions in the form of private correspondences, diaries, and scrapbooks.[21]

Besides adding to our comprehension of which books and texts were circulated and read, by whom, and under what material conditions across the nineteenth century, the history of tactile reading also provides an alternative theoretical model for thinking about literary history and the discipline of literary studies. While sighted readers of English and other Western languages are accustomed to reading linearly from left to right, blind readers read through a radial movement of both hands across the page. As Fretwell observes: "Unlike the forward eye movements of reading inkprint, with embossed print hands move outward in opposite directions, return to meet at an ever-sliding center, then move outward again, and so on."[22] Such radial dynamics, afforded by centering the discussion on the tactility of reading, help to complicate the linear vectorization that usually underwrites literary historical narratives. They also configure reading as a critical nexus at the intersection of various "lines of thought" and disciplinary practices branching out within literary studies and the humanities, from print culture to media history, reading history, canon history, aesthetic form, and disability studies.[23]

## Sense and Sensation

In "Neurodiversity and the Revision of Book History," Gillian Silverman observes that the critical strategy which consists in confronting the history of the book, the history of reading, and disability studies "is not simply a way of expanding the field – making room for more readers and more reading practices – it is also a means of decentering the discipline of language and literary studies, which still suffers from ... 'meaning fetish[ism].'"[24] Focusing on a series of contemporary autistic readers and writers, she explores their sensory relation to language and suggests that their intensely embodied attention to the material properties of words is not dissimilar to that of "language poets, avant-garde minimalists, conceptual writers and book artists," all of whom are engaged in "extrainterpretive" approaches to texts.[25]

Jonathan Lethem's 1999 neuronovel-cum-detective fiction *Motherless Brooklyn* offers an adjacent example. Its protagonist, Lionel Essrog, has Tourette's syndrome, a neurological condition that causes him to make involuntary, socially disruptive sounds and movements. His linguistic tics are a feature of his narrative voice, as well as a major impediment in his attempt to solve not only the manifest murder of his employer and surrogate father, private eye Frank Minna, but also the latent mystery of his mother-lessness, which the novel's title gestures toward. They also resist interpret-ation by a literary critic that would pass off as a sleuth or analyst, precisely because "from a strictly neuropsychiatric perspective, the attribution of any kind of meaning to the tic would be an error."[26] Frustrating the interpretive logic of narrative fiction at both the diegetic and narrative levels, Lionel's ticking compulsion is often spurred by his sonic and linguistic environment:

> "Who you trying to protect, Daffodil? Minna's dead." ...
> "Dickety Daffodil! Dissident Chocophile! Laughable Chocodopolus!"
> "Ah, I heard it all before."
> "Likable lunchpone, veritable spongefist, teenage mutant Zendo lungfish, penis Milhaus Nixon tuning fork." ...
> "Somebody killed Frank."
> "Are you accusing Tony?"
> "Accusatony! Excusebaloney! Funnymonopoly!" I squeezed my eyes shut to interrupt the seizure of language.[27]

What matters in these exchanges is the sheer excess of energy that the tics manifest, as well as a deeply sensory relation to language, where the material properties of words and letters trump their possible meanings to give the text its associative and neuropoetic momentum.

Whereas Silverman describes as distinct the two benefits that her approach of reading as a haptic experience affords, separating between "expanding" and "decentering" the field of literary studies, I believe that these moves are in fact related. The ambition to "[make] room for more readers" and the desire to make reading more about sensation than interpretation strike me as forming two sides of the same methodological coin, which consists in shifting the conversations animating the field away from the narrow circle of professional readings and readers as unrepresentative of, and largely at odds with, the diversity of reading practices among the wider public. From this perspective, Silverman's approach may be taken to fall within the category of the "postcritical," understood as an umbrella term encompassing alternative ways to relate to literary texts than through the exclusive prism of critical interpretation. It has become a commonplace to pit the close, deep reading – suspicious by default – that literary scholars routinely engage in against the supposed superficiality and naïveté of lay readers, opposing reading for meaning to reading for pleasure, knowledge to feeling, mind to body. It has increasingly become a commonplace too to lament this rift as oversimplifying and to investigate, if not the continuum between professional and ordinary reading practices, at least "their messy entanglement."[28] To be sure, the many critiques of critique which have flowered in recent years, and their attendant valuation of what Michael Warner has called "uncritical reading," evidence literary critics' growing anxiety of irrelevance in what is arguably a difficult time for the humanities at large.[29] More pointedly, the disenchantment with critique reveals a growing frustration with a conception of reading as detached, unfeeling, and therefore largely disembodied, by contrast with the more passionate involvement with books that common readers are often said to display. This is all the more paradoxical as critique purports to attend to the multifarious ways in which ideologies of race, gender, and class leave their disciplinary mark on bodies and souls alike. The more the body of the other is at the center of critical attention, it seems, and is made the locus of interpretation, the more that of the critical reader recedes into the background.

Nina Baym's compelling exploration of readerly "responses to fiction in Antebellum America" offers a case in point.[30] Surveying a wide range of literary reviews published in the periodical press before the Civil War, from accounts of *Jane Eyre* to *The Mysteries of Paris*, she notes how popular reading was often metaphorized as consumption, as drinking and eating, and its effects assimilated to a form of bodily intoxication, whether this was deemed a motif of praise or of censure. This corporeal relation to literature speaks more generally to a cultural phenomenon identified as "novel-fever," which spread across Europe and the United States from the middle of the eighteenth century to the mid-nineteenth century, fueling a debate around the pathologization of literature and its supposed dangers on the reader's sanity of body and mind.[31] Implicit in this debate and its literary historical presentation is a distinction between popular, embodied reading and professional detachment, whereby the critic occupies a vantage position predicated on an assumption of disembodiment that allows her to remain at a safe distance from the feverish contagion she describes. One way of challenging this assumption, and of complicating, if not of bridging, the perceived gap between professional and common readers, has been to highlight the embodied dimension that underwrites readerly practices across the board. This means to insist on the aesthesis, rather than the noesis, of reading as the bedrock of our affective attachments to literature. More accurately, it is to suggest that intellectual meaning is also a function of embodied feeling, as many recent studies in the field of Victorian literature demonstrate.[32]

In one of her latest elaborations of what "postcritical" reading might look like, Rita Felski turns to "the language of mood" as a way to describe the physical and intellectual operations entailed in the act of reading. Reflecting on our affective, embodied response to a text, she argues, helps to attend to the formal and aesthetic features and strategies that fashion our receptive mood and condition, at least in part, our interpretive gestures.[33] For an Americanist literary scholar, Felski's emphasis on mood sounds an eerily Emersonian note and recalls what Stanley Cavell has described as Emerson's articulation of an "epistemology of moods" in his 1844 essay "Experience": "Life is a train of moods like a string of beads, and, as we pass through them, they prove to be many-colored lenses which paint the world their own hue, and each shows only what lies in its focus. ... We animate what we can, and we see only what we animate."[34] While Emerson initially conceptualizes moods within the optical regime under which his Transcendentalism operates, as "lenses" through which we "see" and "animate" the world, he is quick to acknowledge the embodiedness of moods, their origin in "temperament" and "sensibility," but also their susceptibility to "pleasure," "pain," and "the state of the blood."[35] However impatient and frustrated he may be at times with temperament as "a prison of glass which we cannot see," his philosophy of moods nonetheless provides a helpful, if unexpected, template with which to reconsider the methods of our trade and to think about the affective and bodily labors that simultaneously enable and constrain our reading practices.[36]

## Haptic Hermeneutics

We read from the body. While this provides an answer to the "where" of reading (Where does reading take place?), it poses the larger question of what we might learn from it. What is the interpretive payoff of insisting that reading is also and always embodied? How does this insight allow for a different, reenergized tack on the texts we customarily read and teach, especially by some of the more anthologized authors of the American literary canon? Sari Altschuler has recently taken up this issue, by choosing to return to *The Scarlet Letter* from the threefold perspective of disability studies, material textuality, and haptic reading.[37] Hawthorne was familiar, Altschuler demonstrates, with the Boston Perkins School for the Blind and the work of its founding director, Dr. Samuel Gridley Howe. In 1841, his soon-to-be wife, Sophia Peabody, was asked to craft a bust of Laura Bridgman, a pupil of Howe's and the first deafblind person in the United States to learn how to read and write. The following year, Hawthorne himself was commissioned to write a biography of Bridgman. While he never produced it, visually impaired readers and teachers populate many of his children's stories, from *Biographical Stories* (1842) to *A Wonder-Book for Girls and Boys* (1851), and Howe's regular exhibitions of Bridgman, halfway between the child prodigy and the freak, may have inspired *The Blithedale Romance* (1852). Hawthorne's interest in the question of reading by touch thus provides a way to reconsider competing modes of apprehension of the letter in *The Scarlet Letter*. While obviously a visual sign – and a highly, if contradictorily, symbolic one at that – Hester Prynne's letter "A" is also tactile, and Pearl progressively intuits its meaning by literally touching, grasping, and clutching it, just as Arthur Dimmesdale, who compulsively "press[es] his hand over his heart" throughout the novel, painfully experiences the bodily imprint of the letter.[38] Ultimately, however, the novel complicates the opposition between visual and tactile reading by foregrounding the stigmatizing power of the gaze, asking readers to reflect on the ways their own seemingly detached, visual readings also "scorch," "brand[]," and "sear," and inevitably so.[39] The haptic pedagogy of *The Scarlet Letter* – grounded in the letter's insistent materiality, which editions of the novel for blind readers literally perform – reveals therefore the inextricability of sight and touch, while dramatizing the deeply embodied ways we read and are being read.

In the conclusion of her essay, Altschuler encourages other, parallel lines of inquiry and wonders, for instance, "how Emerson's early experience with visual impairment and eye surgery shaped his insistence on the importance of vision to experience or how blind education affected that work" and how, conversely, we might locate an Emersonian haptic pedagogy of reading.[40] Emerson's epistemology of moods, as a way of being in the world and as a model for a theory of embodied reading, may indeed provide a way forward. In *Nature* for instance, as I already noted, Emerson's triumphantly optimistic mood is at once intensely visual and fantasmatically disembodied. It is also darkened sometimes by intimations of physical disability:

> In the woods, we return to reason and faith. There I feel that nothing can befall me in life, – no disgrace, no calamity, (leaving me my eyes,) which nature cannot repair. Standing on the bare ground, – my head bathed by the blithe air, and uplifted into infinite space, – all mean egotism vanishes. I become a transparent eye-ball; I am nothing; I see all; the currents of the Universal Being circulate through me; I am part or particle of God.[41]

The anxiety of blindness that haunts this famous passage undermines the dream of immaterial and omnipotent vision which seeks to counteract it, just as it dogged Emerson after his vision started to fail him while a student at Harvard in 1825, causing him to undergo surgery. It also helps to uncover as illusory the fantasy of abstract disembodiment that commands an understanding of reading the world or a text as a purely visual activity. The opening paragraphs of "Experience" further press this point, as they stage a ghostly speaker unable to see or touch the world yet forcefully desiring to do so. "All things swim and glitter," Emerson writes, lamenting "this evanescence and lubricity of all objects, which lets them slip through our fingers then when we clutch hardest," for "there is at last no rough rasping friction, but the most slippery sliding surfaces."[42] By emphasizing the physicality of our dreamed relation to the world, this scene of thwarted access figures antiphrastically a model of reading as "rough rasping friction" with the matter of both the world and the text, which contrasts with *Nature*'s transparent reading and which Emerson foregrounds by exhibiting the materiality of his own writing, with its complex play of anaphoras, alliterations, and assonances. The speaker of "Experience" thus offers the reader of the essay an inverted image of her own readerly activity as material contact between body and text. "We live amid surfaces, and the true art of life is to skate well on them," Emerson later writes in the same essay, eventually imaging and performing reading as bodily exertion, as the art of skating across the page.[43] Engaging in a haptic hermeneutics therefore offers a double reward: Centering on the somatics of reading illuminates anew Emerson's complex engagement with embodiment and materiality, while attending to the function of the body in Emerson's Transcendentalism contributes to thinking about reading as an always already embodied practice.

\* \* \*

In *Dreaming by the Book*, Elaine Scarry observes:

> Verbal art, especially narrative, is almost bereft of any sensuous content. Its visual features . . . consist of monotonous small black marks on a white page. It has *no* acoustical features. Its tactile features are limited to the weight of its pages, their smooth surfaces, and their exquisitely thin edges. The attributes it has that are directly apprehensible by perception are, then, meager in number. More important, these attributes are utterly irrelevant, sometimes even antagonistic, to the mental images that a poem or novel seeks to produce . . ..[44]

Compare this with Andrew Piper's diametrically opposed description of the eminent graspability of books, printed or digital:

> Whether it is the soft graininess of the page or the resistant slickness of the screen, the kinetic activities of swiping instead of turning, the postural differences of sitting back versus up, tilting our heads down or forward, grasping with our hands or resting our hands on, the shape of folded sheets versus the roamable, zoomable, or clickable surfaces of the electronic screen – all of these features (and many more) contribute to a different relationship to reading, and thus thinking.[45]

Echoing the contrast between Susan Stewart's invisible reading and Dickinson's embodied scanning with which this chapter began, Scarry's and Piper's accounts register antithetical traditions of reading that have informed the history of reading from the outset as the critical pendulum has alternatively swayed in one direction or the other. One tradition emphasizes the virtually immaterial "verbal art" of writing, while the other insists on the materiality of the book object. At the heart of this split lies a disagreement over what to make of the "small marks on a white page." In one instance, these marks quickly disappear behind, and are even erased by, the "mental images" they "produce," whereas in the other, they remain lingering material inscriptions where meaning inheres, as they require the reader's bodily and intellectual labors simultaneously. In one instance, reading is a way of looking, whereas, in the other, it is also a way of touching, both literally and tropologically. American literary history is legible through the prism of this opposition between the optics and the haptics of reading.

The purpose of this chapter has not been to discard the former in favor of the latter, but rather to demonstrate their inextricability and to suggest some of the historical, methodological, and interpretive affordances that may come from paying attention to the bodily dimension of our reading practices. Not only does this reveal the longer history of tactile reading, but it also helps to reperiodize American literary history by foregrounding alternative timelines organized around different technological innovations to those catering to able-bodied readers. By emphasizing the postures and gestures required for reading to take place as well as the affective and bodily effects produced by reading, a shift to the body further directs the conversation toward reading as a sensory-based performance, pushing back against a long dominant conception of reading as an essentially intellectual hermeneutic practice. Yet accenting sensation may not come at the cost of sense-making. Rather, it may serve as an invitation to grapple with the singular materiality of the literary text and to reflect on the critical value of hapticality as the conjoined locus of writerly endeavor and readerly interpretation, a reciprocal touching of auctor and lector through the complex mediation of the text, much like the mutual, if elusive, embrace that Walt Whitman imagined, performed, and playfully frustrated all at once:

Whoever you are, holding me now in hand, . . .

. . . thrusting me beneath your clothing,
Where I may feel the throbs of your heart or rest upon your hip,
Carry me when you go forth over land or sea;
For thus merely touching you is enough, is best,
And thus touching you, would I silently sleep and be carried eternally.

But these leaves conning you con at peril,
For these leaves and me you will not understand,
They will elude you at first and still more afterward, I will certainly elude you,
Even while you should think you had unquestionably caught me, behold!
Already you see I have escaped from you.[46]

## NOTES

1 Susan Stewart, *On Longing: Narratives of the Miniature, the Gigantic, the Souvenir, the Collection* (Durham, NC: Duke University Press, 1993), 14.
2 Emily Dickinson, *The Poems of Emily Dickinson: Reading Edition*, ed. R. W. Franklin (Cambridge, MA: Belknap Press, 1999), F994.
3 Karin Littau, *Theories of Reading: Books, Bodies, and Bibliomania* (Cambridge: Polity, 2006), 3.
4 *Oxford English Dictionary*, 3rd ed., s.v., "read."
5 Garrett Stewart, *The Look of Reading: Book, Painting, Text* (Chicago: University of Chicago Press, 2006), 77.
6 Ibid., 3, 87, 95.
7 Roger Chartier, *The Order of Books: Readers, Authors, and Libraries in Europe between the Fourteenth and Eighteenth Centuries* (Stanford, CA: Stanford University Press, 1994), 8.
8 Georges Perec, "Reading: A Socio-physiological Outline" (1976), in *Species of Spaces and Other Pieces*, ed. and trans. John Sturrock (London: Penguin, 1999), 175, 178.

9 Ibid., 174.

10 Rita Felski, *The Limits of Critique* (Chicago: University of Chicago Press, 2015).

11 David D. Hall et al., eds., *A History of the Book in America*, 5 vols. (Chapel Hill: University of North Carolina Press, 2000–2010).

12 Thomas Harriot, *A briefe and true report of the new found land of Virginia* (London, 1588), E4r–v.

13 Bradin Cormack and Carla Mazzio, *Book Use, Book Theory: 1500–1700* (Chicago: University of Chicago Press, 2005), 6–7.

14 Mark Amsler, "Affective Literacy: Gestures of Reading in the Later Middle Ages," *Essays in Medieval Studies* 18 (2001): 83.

15 Matthew Brown, *The Pilgrim and the Bee: Reading Rituals and Book Culture in Early New England* (Philadelphia: University of Pennsylvania Press, 2007), xii.

16 Robin Bernstein, *Racial Innocence: Performing American Childhood from Slavery to Civil Rights* (New York: New York University Press, 2011), 71.

17 Ralph Waldo Emerson, *Nature*, in *Essays and Lectures*, ed. Joel Porte (New York: Library of America, 1983), 10.

18 Ibid., 69.

19 Erica Fretwell, "1833–1932: American Literature's Other Scripts," in *Timelines of American Literature*, ed. Cody Marrs and Christopher Hager (Baltimore: Johns Hopkins University Press, 2019), 21–36.

20 Andrew Piper, *Book Was There* (Chicago: University of Chicago Press, 2012), 9, emphasis in the original.

21 Fretwell, "1833–1932," 26.

22 Ibid., 23.

23 Ibid.

24 Gillian Silverman, "Neurodiversity and the Revision of Book History," *PMLA* 131, no. 2 (2016): 309.

25 Ibid.

26 Jennifer Fleissner, "Symptomatology and the Novel," *NOVEL: A Forum on Fiction* 42, no. 3 (Fall 2009): 390.

27 Alexander Lethem, *Motherless Brooklyn* (New York: Vintage, 2000), 156, 175.

28 Rita Felski, "Postcritical," in *Further Reading*, ed. Matthew Rubery and Leah Price (New York: Oxford University Press, 2020), 143.

29 Michael Warner, "Uncritical Reading," in *Polemic: Critical or Uncritical*, ed. Jane Gallop (New York: Routledge, 2004), 13–38.

30 Nina Baym, *Novels, Readers and Reviewers: Responses to Fiction in Antebellum America* (Ithaca, NY: Cornell University Press, 1984).

31 Michael Millner, *Fever Reading: Affect and Reading Badly in the Early American Public Sphere* (Durham, NC: University of New Hampshire Press, 2012).

32 See "Further Reading."

33 Felski, "Postcritical," 139–141.

34 Ralph Waldo Emerson, "Experience," in *Essays and Lectures*, 473; Stanley Cavell, "An Emerson Mood," in *Emerson's Transcendental Etudes*, ed. David Justin Hodge (Stanford, CA: Stanford University Press, 2003), 20–32.

35 Emerson, "Experience," 474.

36 Ibid.

37 Sari Altschuler, "Touching *The Scarlet Letter*: What Disability History Can Teach Us about Literature," *American Literature* 92, no. 1 (2020): 91–122.

38 Nathaniel Hawthorne, *The Scarlet Letter*, in *Collected Novels*, ed. Millicent Bell (New York: Library of America, 1983), 222.

39 Ibid., 180, 191, 193.

40 Altschuler, "Touching *The Scarlet Letter*," 114.

41 Emerson, *Nature*, 10.

42 Emerson, "Experience," 471, 472, 472.

43 Ibid., 478.

44 Elaine Scarry, *Dreaming by the Book: Imagining under Authorial Instruction* (New York: Farrar, Straus, & Giroux, 1999), 5.

45 Piper, *Book Was There*, x.

46 Walt Whitman, "Whoever You Are Holding Me Now in Hand," in *Leaves of Grass and Other Writings*, ed. Michael Moon (New York: W. W. Norton, 2002), 99–100.

# II

ERICA FRETWELL

# How to Read Disabled Bodies in History

"Do we have a body – that is, not a permanent object of thought, but a flesh that suffers when it is wounded, hands that touch?" philosopher Maurice Merleau-Ponty asks.[1]

People with disabilities have long known the answer: yes. "Disability" refers to a wide range of experiences and embodiments socially designated as abnormal: physical impairments (e.g., limb difference), cognitive and neuro-sensory conditions (e.g., autism spectrum disorder), mental health (e.g., depression), chronic as well as terminal diseases (e.g., diabetes and cancer), physiological disorders (e.g., dwarfism), and a life outside the labor market (e.g., receiving state benefits). As this catalog suggests, disability is "more fluid than most other forms of identity in that it can potentially happen to anyone at any time," and so gathers together "people who may not agree on a common definition or on how the category applies to themselves and others."[2] Bipolar disorder, hirsutism, and the "hardness of hearing" that accompanies senescence are all experienced differently and amass uneven weight as they crosscut axes of race, gender, sexuality, and class. Yet they all share the condition of inhabiting a world not built around or for bodily and behavioral variation, a world that only sparingly, and even then begrudgingly, makes accommodations. The itinerancies of language reflect the diversity and contingency of disability experience: "Disfigured," "ugly," "feeble-minded," "affliction," "invalid," "handicap," "freak," "idiot," "monstrous," "lame," and "queer" move in and out of the archive, designating bodies that inhabit "zones of indistinction and exception,"[3] surfacing those lives hidden from view by publics beholden to the fantasy of normalcy.

While disability identity is notable for its flexibility, until recently the dominant paradigm for understanding it was quite rigid. From the seventeenth through the mid-twentieth century, the "medical model" framed disability as a personal burden to be overcome. Insisting that disability is a problem that only the impaired individual can correct, it stigmatized whole classes of people living on the frayed edges of the labor market while pathologizing others as inherently damaged. The medical model underwrote the disciplinary institutions, such as charity organizations and asylums, that served liberal biopower. With the ability both to "reason" and to conduct industrial labor now requisite for social membership, nation-states managed the lives of heterogenous peoples – children, people of color, immigrants, and women – as disabled noncitizens and/or dependent subjects. From temperance societies to racial uplift by the "talented tenth," the reform movements of the eighteenth and nineteenth centuries sought to "fix" allegedly defective members of the population.[4] And when that failed, the state took another tack: using forced sterilization, anti-miscegenation laws, and incarceration to segregate those classified as obstacles to market productivity and civilizational progress from the "fit" subjects whose lives the state had a vested interest in protecting and maximizing.

The formation of disability studies in the late twentieth century, powered by post-1968 disability rights activism, forcefully discredited the medical model. The "first wave" of disability scholarship replaced this pathologizing discourse with a social model of disability: the idea that disability abides in the built environment, not in the body. The problem is not a person's visual impairment but the culture that reifies a normal body as one with 20/20 vision. From pedestrian signals that lack audio notifications to workplace requirements for medical exemptions and the stairs that shut out those using wheelchairs and strollers, it is society that is disabling. Advancing the social model with the tools of poststructuralism, disability scholars uncovered the narrative construction of disability. Rosemarie Garland-Thomson, Mary Klages, and Lennard Davis have powerfully argued that the strategies for representing disability as pathological serve to shore up normative embodiment.[5] Disability is a repository of stock representations that both inflect the function of narrative and act as a "master trope" for conflict and ideological errancy. David Mitchell and Sharon Snyder famously called this appropriation of disability a "narrative prosthesis," the "crutch upon which literary narratives lean for their representational power, disruptive potentiality, and analytical insight."[6] From the peg leg that signifies Captain Ahab's totalizing evil in Herman Melville's *Moby-Dick* (1851) to the illness that makes Beth March a sympathetic figure in Louisa May Alcott's *Little Women* (1868–1869), narrative prosthesis stages disability only to relegate it to the background – mise-èn-scene rather than meaningful engagement with the material significance of "complex embodiment."[7]

Building on this important body of work, more recent disability studies scholarship – termed "Disability Studies 2.0" by Leonard Cassuto[8] – moves the analysis of disability beyond representation and into the domain of worldmaking. Scholars such as Georgina Kleege, Ellen Samuels, and Ralph

Saverese have put pressure on the social model by calling attention to the phenomenological, aesthetic, and political potentialities – irreducible to biological and social domains – of disability experience.[9] Disability is the lived reality of marginalization and an inherently creative activity. It makes something in and of the world, such as new models of caregiving and community, new practices of kinship and inclusion, and new bodily and artistic practices that, for Petra Kuppers, hold "a wide variety of experiences and structured impositions in moments of precarious productive imbalance."[10] Second-wave disability studies, keyed to the affective and environmental entanglement of bodies and things, takes up the inventive interdependencies of disabled being to illuminate what "limitation" can open up for our literary histories: new aesthetic forms, new kinds of authorship, new print cultures.[11] Reading the disabled body in literature, then, is no mere search for "another other,"[12] but rather requires an attentiveness to disability as a, if not the, primary locus where bodies become legibly different (and differentially legible) in the teeth of racialization, gendered sexualization, and class.

This chapter sketches out one way to read disability: as a genre. While genre typically denotes a set of formal conventions that structure the relation between reader and text, queer and feminist scholars have fruitfully reframed genre as a social convention. An identity is a genre "like an aesthetic one," Lauren Berlant argues, because "it is a structure of conventional expectation that people rely on to provide certain kinds of affective intensities and assurances."[13] For Berlant, femininity is a genre built around normative attachments that preclude structural change. I consider disability slantwise: as the genre through which embodied indeterminacy is lived, and therefore a genre that queries the generic (the conventional, normal, average) as such. Rather than rehearse well-told stories of subject formation through narratives of disability, we might read for the fluid modes of relation that reframe disability as narrative. This chapter offers an extended reading of phantom limbs to elucidate the indeterminate attachments and embodied indistinctions that disability makes socially legible.

## The Body in Phantom Pain

Disability is everywhere in nineteenth-century US literature, from Georgiana's birthmark in Nathaniel Hawthorne's "The Birth-Mark" (1843) to Union veteran Berthold Lindau's missing hand in William Dean Howells's *A Hazard of New Fortunes* (1890). But how do we read for the disabled bodies that have fallen below the threshold of our critical perception? Rather than adopt the Foucauldian medical gaze that lodges expertise in the beholder, that scans the literary corpus for readily apparent "defects," we might consider those bodies that lie beyond the reach of empirical observation. Disability proves over and over again the epistemological insufficiency of vision in statist attempts to catalog and manage subjects. When bodily difference operates at the level of perception (rather than physicality or phenotype), the Cartesian dualism – mind over matter – that liberal selfhood presupposes starts to collapse. Indeed, the phantom limb prompts the question: How does disability trouble the very concept of "body"? The literary body or corpus of the phantom limb suggests some possibilities.

Often experienced by people with limb loss, the phantom limb is a feeling that takes up space, a psychological attachment to a body part that is no longer physically attached. Ambroise Paré first described post-amputation sensation in the sixteenth century, but Civil War contract surgeon and nerve specialist S. Weir Mitchell systematically studied and named it: "phantom limb." An epistemic and ontological crisis ensued. Is the phantom limb "real" or in the amputee's head? If the latter, then what's not to say that physical limbs are also "in the head"? Or that our bodies are in our head? That is precisely what aptly named twentieth-century neurologist Henry Head determined when the phantom limb led him to formulate the body image as the mental image of the body in time and space. If the body image is "the body in the head," then later neurologists determined that the phantom limb constitutes a "body image disturbance": The mind has not yet adjusted to limb loss and so continues to send sensory signals. A disturbance that made the body image possible, the phantom limb is part of a long history of cultural institutions taking a concept, technique, or technology (like the telephone) originally made for disabled bodies, redeploying it for nondisabled bodies, and retrofitting it as "mainstream" knowledge.[14] In ways both idiomatic and material, disability is the ghost in the machine. Gothicism inscribed in its name, the phantom limb literalizes that haunting: medicine shadowed by the "wild facts" that lie beyond its regime of compulsory visibility.[15] The body is, perhaps, less a unified structure than a set of affective attachments to the idea of the body as a unified structure.

Confounding Western distinctions between mind and body, fact and fiction, reality and representation, the phantom limb is not objectively verifiable but is subjectively felt. It is also a fiction – a psychological limb, a mental representation that prompts the feeling of a limb that is not physically attached to the body. How do you go about proving the reality of an ideational body part? You might write a fictional story that resembles factual research. That's what Mitchell did. His story "The Case of George Dedlow," presented as the titular narrator's self-reported case study of his amputations and ensuing phantom pain, appeared in the *Atlantic Monthly* in 1866; audiences initially mistook it for the real thing, starting up a collection for Dedlow and seeking an audience with him at the Philadelphia hospital where the story is set. The generic indeterminacy the story solicits nicely reproduces the epistemic crisis (how do I know what is real?) and ontological crisis (am I me?) that Dedlow, rendered a quadruple amputee by wartime wounds and infections, experiences.

A hospital patient who has lost "four fifths of my weight," Dedlow meditates on the existential deficit that his physical deficit generates:

> I found to my horror that at times I was less conscious of myself, of my own existence, than used to be the case. ... I felt like asking someone constantly if I were really George Dedlow or not. ... At times the conviction of my want of being myself was overwhelming and most painful. ... Would such a being, I asked myself, possess the sense of individuality in its usual completeness? ... I thus reached the conclusion that a man is not his brain, or any one part of it, but all of his economy, and that to lose any part must lessen this sense of his own existence.[16]

Amputating the body means amputating the soul. If having one-fifth a body means having one-fifth a self, then one might not "count" as a person at all. The psychological effect of amputation is resolutely political: Dedlow here embodies the "peculiar dialectic between embodiment and abstraction in the post-Enlightenment body politic."[17] The liberal rhetoric of citizenship enshrines white manhood as capable of transcending the body, even as cultural discourses have "invested the core of citizenship in the whole, white male body."[18] The ideal citizen leaves his body behind to inhabit the lofty plane of reason, while the normate subject has a virile and healthy body. But when disembodiment is lived rather than ideal (unmarked, universal), it diminishes rather than enhances whiteness and masculinity. For Dedlow, being physically bodiless is a problem, not a privilege. The fact that he, a self-described "fraction of a man," has lost four-fifths his weight conjures the political calculus against which he had fought: slavery's reduction of Black people to three-fifths personhood – its "amputation" of the Black body.[19] Amputation marks a loss of whiteness because it marks a loss of whiteness's "natural" properties: agency, autonomy, and self-possession.

Dedlow's disability – only partly visible – lodges Blackness at the center of medicine's mind-body problem: whether pain is mental or material, a hallucination, or an objective reality.[20] During treatment at the US Army Hospital, Dedlow discovers that when a limb "is cut off, the nerve trunks which led to it and from it ... are made to convey ... impressions which are as usual referred by the brain to the lost parts."[21] But medicine offers no palliative for the sensation of legs. This failure is marked in the story's generic shift from realist description to sensationalist spectacle. Dedlow seeks healing in Spiritualism, an American religious movement predicated on the belief that the living can communicate with the dead. Spiritualism cannot physically reattach Dedlow's physical limbs to his body, but it might make him existentially "whole" again. In a scene suspended between disbelief and comic relief, he joins a male "eclectic doctor," a female spirit medium, and an "authoress of two somewhat feeble novels" at a spiritualist meeting:

> "Will it please [the spirits] to say how they are called in the world of spirits?"
> Again came the irregular raps – 3, 4, 8, 6; then a pause, 3, 4, 8, 7.
> "I think," said the authoress, "they must be numbers. . . . I will write them," she said, and, doing so, took up the card and tapped the letters. The spelling was pretty rapid, and ran thus as she tapped, in turn, first the letters, and last the numbers she had already set down:
> "UNITED STATES ARMY MEDICAL MUSEUM, Nos. 3486, 3487."
> The medium looked up with a puzzled expression. "Good gracious!" said I, "they are my legs – my legs!"
> What followed, I ask no one to believe except those who, like myself, have communed with the things of another sphere. Suddenly I felt a strange return of my self-consciousness . . . I arose and walked across the room on limbs invisible to them or me.[22]

This spectacle of ambulatory reunion humorously literalizes the phantom limb. The internal spirits are now external ghosts, invisible yet manifestly there. The repeated exclamation of "my!" realigns Dedlow's body and body image, marking a return of autonomy and self-possession. However, the reunion is short-lived. "My legs were going, and in a moment I was resting feebly on my two stumps on the floor. It was too much. All that was left of me fainted and rolled over senseless," the fictitious case concludes.[23] Dedlow is left alone, as feeble and feminized as the novels of the "authoress." In heavy-handed fashion Mitchell insists that spiritualism has no legs to stand on. A memory that painfully throbs, the phantom limb is a mental fiction, not an objective fact.

Yet Mitchell's nonfictional case studies suggest it is a mental fact. In his essay "Phantom Limbs" (1871) and handbook *Injuries of the Nerves and their Consequences* (1872), what Mitchell's patients "really feel" is not at all that different from what Dedlow "falsely" felt. "There is something almost tragical, almost ghastly, in the notion of these thousands of spirit limbs haunting as many good soldiers," Mitchell lamented.[24] These "ghostly members" are fictions of bodily presence so convincing as to make the real body seem illusory; they have a "distinctly material" presence that "betrays" the amputee in the middle of embodied action.[25] In one case, when a "gallant fellow, who had lost an arm at Shiloh," went riding, "he used the lost hand to grasp the reins, while with the other he struck his horse. He paid for his blunder with a fall," and, in another, a "poor fellow, at every meal for many months, would try to pick up his fork, and failing would be suddenly seized with nausea."[26] These "absurd mishaps" involve virile men who are victims of a mental "hoax" that only experience can debunk. Rather than unmask the phantom limb as a mental fiction, these medical cases end up certifying a truth with which Mitchell was not entirely comfortable: There is no easy distinction to be made between internal experience and external phenomena, between mental life and material life, between invisible and visible embodiment. Fictional limbs are facts in their own right

"The Case of George Dedlow" established the formal and conceptual parameters that later writers used in their own attempts to interrogate the internal reality of "external" oppression and violent dislocation. In conjunction with the emergence of the phantom limb at the nexus of medical history (the increased survival rate for amputation) and national history (the US Civil War), the racial calculus underlying Dedlow's phantom pain suggests that disabled embodiment does not simply converge with but actively organizes experiences of racialization. The phantom limb is, after all, a sensation arising when two realities "occupy the same space and time, one the ghostly double of the other's absence."[27] To this end, the phantom limb reverberates with another psychological theory of an elementally fragmented self: W. E. B. Du Bois's formulation of double consciousness as a distinctly Black feeling, the "peculiar sensation" of seeing yourself through the eyes of another, of the African American "I" experienced in the third-person.[28] The phantom limb and double consciousness are not the same, but they are not dissimilar either: embodied conditions marked by self-alienation. Following the "nonevent of Emancipation" and at the height of the "eugenic Atlantic," both phenomena name real bodies with imaginary extensions: the invisible limb extending from the physical body; the "second sight" of an internalized white sensorium that allows African Americans to experience themselves from the outside.[29] Double consciousness too is a "body image disturbance," a deviation from the psychosomatic norm, that discloses the centrality of disability to what Du Bois called "the problem of the color line."[30]

How might disabled embodiment organize Black inner life? Mitchell's writings frame the phantom limb as the unincorporated excess of amputation and, further, racialize that excess. In the decades following the federal abandonment of Reconstruction in 1877, the phantom limb offered fertile grounds for exploring Black subjectivity as a condition of alienation. The peculiar disability that the phantom limb names, in postbellum African American writing, is inextricably tethered to racialized and sexualized flesh. Building on Black feminist thinker Hortense Spillers's theorization of flesh as the lost experience of the wounded Black body – constitutively marked through and for violence – under chattel slavery, Nirmala Erevelles has further posited that flesh is an originary impairment that lodges disability at the center of Black life.[31] As Bryan Wagner shows, twentieth-century philosophers like Frantz Fanon have likened Black being under colonial modernity to amputation and the phantom limb to the "false consolation" of accepting one's condition of oppression.[32] Yet scholars like Saidiya Hartman consider the phantom limb a powerful trope for the "violent discontinuities" and the "experience of loss and affiliation" activated by chattel slavery. From Hartman's perspective, these traces of memory function in a manner akin to a phantom limb, in that what is felt is no longer there."[33] The phantom limb is a lived condition centered not on fictional or simulated wholeness but instead on "the recognition of the amputated body in its amputatedness."[34] The phantom limb moves across material and metaphorical registers to signify the brokenness that is the condition of Black cultural memory's possibility. The phantom limb marks a disabled embodiment that is simultaneously Black because it names the dis- and re-membering of the Middle Passage; it feels where feeling ought not to be; and it refuses any notion of a stable empirical reality.

Take, for instance, Frances Ellen Watkins Harper's novel of racial uplift, *Iola Leroy* (1892). Set during and shortly after the Civil War, the novel tracks the eponymous heroine's discovery of her African ancestry and subsequent enslavement, then her emancipation and work as a Union army nurse, and finally her successful effort to reunite her once-fragmented Black family. While the novel's focus on Iola's development into a race woman operates in the key of the Bildungsroman, Harper attends equally to the bodily practices that register the "haunting inheritance" of enslavement, in Avery Gordon's words, at the preconscious level of sensation.[35] At the center of this embodied haunting is the juxtaposition between African American hero Tom Anderson and white army surgeon Dr. Gresham. The doctor's "armless sleeve" indexes his heroic sacrifice and, in turn, allows him to lay claim to the "strong arm of the Government" as a prosthetic for remediating his injured masculinity – mainly by trying to save the mixed-race Iola "from a fate worse than death," being legally categorized an African American.[36] With his armless sleeve and his white savior fantasies, Gresham is both weak in body and paternalistic in soul. In direct contrast stands Tom Anderson, whose unspecified "physical defects" bar him from army service during the Civil War, even as his "herculean strength" allows him to actually save Iola from a fate worse than death: being raped by her enslaver.[37] After saving Iola, the "defective" Tom feels "as if every nerve in his right arm was tingling to strike a blow for freedom."[38] In the space of a clause, the "tingling" limb transforms from a sign of injured white masculinity into a sensation allied with Black heroism. Tom's arm is in service not to the nation but to the race.

*Iola Leroy* displaces the phantom limb (allied to Dedlow's and Gresham's whiteness) with a *phantom* phantom limb. A "tingling" arm suggests a phantom limb – and yet Tom is not an amputee because he has both arms. Tom is experiencing what feels like phantom pain. The tingling arises from a physical arm that feels as if it had been amputated and then perceptually reattached. Phrased differently: If a phantom limb is a "mental" arm that feels physically real, Tom's "phantom" phantom limb is a physical arm that feels like it is "in his head." According with Du Bois's conceptualization of the "two-ness" of African American being, Tom's arm(s) suggest that to be Black is to be one's own phantom body. This phantasmal-feeling body makes possible the "blow for freedom" that thrusts the Black body into a more promising future. And so when Iola's uncle Robert later avows that he wants "the young folks to keep ... their right arms strong, to fight the battle of life manually, and take their places alongside of every other people in this country," the strength of their "right arms" derives not from the "strong arm" of the US government – symbolically tied to Dr. Gresham's amputated arm – but from the "tingling" arm of Black agency that the figure of the "defect" conjures.[39] *Iola Leroy* revalues Blackness as an indeterminate being, always double and other than itself, generating feelings that exist despite anaesthetizing biopolitical protocols that reject the capacity of non-white subjects to feel.[40]

Insofar as the phantom limb marks "a felt advance beyond severance and limitation that contends with and questions conventional reality, that it is a feeling for what is not there that reaches beyond as it calls into question what is," in Nathaniel Mackey's words, *Iola Leroy* foregoes physical sacrifice (empty sleeves) in favor of the racial gift of doubled embodiment – "the capacity for feeling which holds itself apart" from the "numb contingency" of slavery – as the basis of racial progress.[41] But if, for Harper, Tom's "defect" is in fact a gift, a surfeit of sensation that extends the Black body beyond itself, writers like Charles Chesnutt consider the perils of this otherwise promising model of embodiment. His conjure tale "Po' Sandy" (1888) is itself a doubled body, featuring an outer Reconstruction frame narrated by a carpetbagger and his wife, John and Annie, and an inner antebellum story narrated by the formerly enslaved trickster Uncle Julius, who "doubt[s] in his own mind ... whether he had a right to think or to feel."[42] The inner story, as told to John and Annie by Julius, involves an enslaved person named Sandy whose labor is so frequently sold to other enslavers that a conjure woman transforms him into a pine tree, so that he can stay rooted near his wife Tenie. As a result, Sandy has two bodies. What follows is a series of movements across human and nonhuman registers: A woodpecker pecks a hole in tree-Sandy that carries over as a scar on human-Sandy, and when later tree-Sandy is chopped for turpentine, "de nex' time Sandy wuz turnt back [to human] he had a big skyar on his lef' leg."[43] The scars are a reminder that tree and human body are not distinct but unitary. Sandy embodies the fungibility of human and nonhuman life. With both human limbs and tree limbs mutilated, conjuring proves not an escape hatch from slavery but an extension of it, because as it turns out the natural world is as subject to the violence of extraction under racial capitalism as people are.

Sandy lives a "real" life as an enslaved human and an "unreal" life as a ghostly yet materially felt thing, which we might call phantom lumber. A trope for objects that feel, phantom lumber extends the "twoness" of Black life to include not only the categories of "American" and "Negro" but also being and thing. Sandy's ligneous body and human body are ghosts that haunt each other. Given that trees were a central tool for and icon of lynching in the postbellum period, tree-Sandy materializes how Western humanism cuts off Black people from consciousness itself. When Sandy's enslaver orders tree-Sandy to be chopped down and turned into lumber for building a kitchen, this is a lynching. The chopping of tree-Sandy stands in for the systematic murder of Black people by hanging (and sometimes by fire), which "began on tree limbs" and that, in contrast to the victim's spasmodic motions, lent the tree an aura of "immobility and seeming immortality (since the lynched ghost forever resides in its limbs)," Sandy Alexandre writes.[44] Sandy's dual embodiment posits Black men as living matter to be both mutilated and murdered as well as the material of their own mutilation and murder, a hanging tree.

Yet Julius recalls that when tree-Sandy is taken to the sawmill to be refined into lumber, "all de sweekin', en moanin', en groanin', dat log done it w'iles de saw wuz a-cuttin' thoo it ... Dey greased de saw, but dat didn' stop de fuss; hit kep' right on."[45] Ultimately, the lumber that "wuz sawed ou'n' de tree w'at Sandy wuz turnt inter, is gwine ter be ha'nted tel de las' piece er plank is rotted en crumble' inter dus.'"[46] The rhythms and cadences of Sandy's squeaks, moans, and groans draw attention to Black expressive life as multiply composed and performative. Understood as the ghostly presence of the physical body's absence, phantom lumber marks the persistence of

Black life. Sandy exists outside the bounds of normative embodiment to haunt the former plantation – a phantom feeling that is neither comforting nor redemptive but does enact a kind of sensory interference jamming the machinery of white supremacy. In its radical extension of body parts into the nonhuman world, the phantom limb/lumber in "Po' Sandy" frames Black life as the refusal not to feel. Rather than strive for wholeness or coherence, Chesnutt as well as Harper trouble the notion of the generic body – invisible pain at once an effect of the abuses of white supremacy and a trope for what Mackey calls the "creative reconstruction" of Black life.[47]

This creative reconstruction speaks forcefully to why the phantom limb is a uniquely literary kind of body: a mental representation that mediates both the body's physical relation to time and space and the subject's affective relation to the historical present. Across medical and literary fictions, the psychical fiction called the phantom limb evinces pain, especially chronic pain, as its own kind of body. Although thinking phenomenology "beyond" the phantom limb, Michael Snediker is instructive for considering the disintegrative force of phantom pain: The "ontologizing iterations of pain only serve to deteriorate the self, as though the interiority that pain installed were its own. It is for itself. This is where a phenomenology of pain opens onto object-oriented ontology, registering the humbling incongruity of this thing that both is and isn't one's own flesh."[48] From Dedlow's phantom limbs to Tom Anderson's "phantom" phantom limb and Sandy's phantom lumber – each a "disintegrative force" and a body in its own right, that "is for itself" – fiction reconceives the body as an experience of "humbling incongruity" with the object world, ever inflected by the asymmetries of power consolidated under racial capitalism.

### Beyond the Margins

The phantom limb is a disability that calls the very ontology of "the body" into question, and its literary representation suggests some ways for rethinking disability as a convention or a genre that affectively reattaches people outside of dominant subject formations. But keeping company with the phantoms that haunt the twinned concepts of disability and embodiment is the rather phantasmal "body" of disability worldmaking. Of late, a number of critics have turned their attention to the productive crises of reading, writing, and publication that disability activates. Clare Mullaney, for instance, persuasively argues that physical constraint plays a crucial role in Emily Dickinson's poetic production – constraint not simply in terms of her alleged agoraphobia but the scraps of paper that were her medium of writing.[49] Likewise, we might consider the causalgia that exempted Henry James from the Civil War, and how this "obscure hurt" radiates throughout his literary corpus and organizes novels like *The Bostonians* (1885), itself a kind of Civil War battle reenactment.[50] Nathaniel Hawthorne's interest in deafblind celebrity Laura Bridgman, who mastered tactile reading, underwrites the figuration of Pearl as an artist in *The Scarlet Letter*.[51] And as a final example that comes full circle, Mitchell himself suffered from hand tremors that not only made writing a difficult affair but also materialized, and quite spectacularly embodied, the epistemological shakiness of the phantom limbs he studied.

In addition to turning our attention to the canonical authors whose disability or, in the case of Hawthorne, engagement with disabled public figures played an important role in their literary production, it is equally important to excavate the disability writing long occluded by ableist constructions of authorship. Helen Keller herself, after all, was frequently charged with "plagiarism" precisely because her authorship was a collaborative one, undertaken alongside her mentor and companion Anne Sullivan and editor John Macy. At the same time, disability fruitfully reconstellates literary criticism and periodization around the nonprint literatures disabled bodies produced. How might people have adapted literature and letters to their bodies, rather than the other way around? Consider "armless wonder" Ann E. Leak, who used her toes for writing, crocheting, and sewing.[52] Reading Leak's body as an authorial one requires moving past the margins and off the printed page itself. How does literary history change when we decenter manuscript and ink-print? What new stories emerge when we shift our critical gaze to novel mediums like craftwork, the knitted and woven objects that many disabled and/or poor people created for purposes that cannot be reduced to strictly utilitarian? What varieties of human experience, what storytelling and aesthetic techniques, come to the fore when the materiality of disability takes hold in the study of US literature?

Taking a cue from phantom limbs, one approach might be to pivot from the visual and toward the tactile or haptic – a key sensory modality "experienced with particular force in the disabled body."[53] Touch is a "sense of the individual as a collection of self-determined feelings that exist to attach, to feel another person," and thus "echoes a central principle of disability activism: human identity is a phenomenon of self-with-others, not of atomized individuals existing only for their own advancement."[54] The haptic, the tactile, is a sense of permeability, of fluctuation and reversibility, of spatial and morphological inconsistency that suggests new identities, new genres, grounded in experiences of exposure to and immersion in others, as the case of Ann E. Leak suggests. The radical horizontality – even as it crosscuts the biopolitical fractalization of race, gender, sexuality, and class – that tactility and haptics offers up might model a literary history organized around the knotty, rhizomatic entanglements that disabled bodies both initiate and instantiate.

## NOTES

1 Maurice Merleau-Ponty, *The Visible and the Invisible*, trans. Alphonso Lingis (Chicago: Northwestern University Press, 1969), 137.
2 Rachel Adams, Ben Reiss, and David Serlin, *Keywords in Disability Studies* (New York: New York University Press, 2015), 5–6.
3 Andrea Stone, "The Black Atlantic Revisited, the Body Reconsidered: On Lingering, Liminality, Lies, and Disability," *American Literary History* 24, no. 4 (2012): 815.
4 See Todd Carmody, "In Spite of Handicaps: The Disability History of Racial Uplift," *American Literary History* 27, no. 1 (2015): 56–78.
5 See Lennard Davis, *Enforcing Normalcy: Disability, Deafness, and the Body* (New York: Verso, 1995); Rosemarie Garland-Thomson, ed., *Extraordinary Bodies: Figuring Disability in American Culture and Literature* (New York: Columbia University Press, 1997); Mary Klages, *Woeful Afflictions: Disability and Sentimentality in Victorian America* (Philadelphia: University of Pennsylvania Press, 1999).
6 David Mitchell and Sharon Snyder, *Narrative Prosthesis; Disability and the Dependencies of Discourse* (Ann Arbor: University of Michigan Press, 2001), 49.
7 See Tobin Siebers, *Disability Theory* (Ann Arbor: University of Michigan Press, 2008).
8 Leonard Cassuto, "Disability Studies 2.0," *American Literary History* 22, no. 1 (2010): 218–231.
9 See Georgina Kleege, *More than Meets the Eye: What Blindness Brings to Art* (Oxford: Oxford University Press, 2018); Ellen Samuels, *Fantasies of Identification: Disability, Gender, Race* (New York: New York University Press, 2014); Ralph Saverese, *See It Feelingly: Classic Novels, Autistic Readers, and the Schooling of a No-Good English Professor* (Durham, NC: Duke University Press, 2018).
10 Petra Kuppers, *Disability Culture and Community Performance: Find a Strange and Twisted Shape* (New York: Palgrave Macmillan, 2011), 93.
11 See Susan Schweik, *The Ugly Laws: Disability in Public* (New York: New York University Press, 2009); Erica Fretwell, "1833–1932: American Literature's Other Scripts," in *Timelines of American Literature*, ed. Cody Marrs and Christopher Hager (Baltimore: Johns Hopkins University, 2019).
12 Catherine Kudlick, "Disability History: Why We Need Another 'Other,'" *The American Historical Review* 108, no. 3 (2003): 763–793.
13 Lauren Berlant, *The Female Complaint: The Unfinished Business of Sentimentality in American Culture* (Durham, NC: Duke University Press, 2008), 4.

14 For the disability history of communication media, see Mara Mills, "Deaf Jam: From Inscription to Reproduction to Information," *Social Text* 28, no. 1 (2010): 35–58.

15 William James, "The Hidden Self," in *Essays in Psychology*, ed. B. Frederick and B. Fredson (Cambridge, MA: Harvard University Press, 1983), 249.

16 S. Weir Mitchell, "The Case of George Dedlow," *The Atlantic Monthly* 18, no. 105 (July 1866): 8.

17 Lauren Berlant, "National Brands/National Body," in *The Phantom Public Sphere*, ed. Bruce Robbins (Minneapolis: University of Minnesota Press, 1993), 112.

18 Megan Kate Nelson, *Ruin Nation: Destruction and the American Civil War* (Athens: University of Georgia Press, 2012), 169.

19 Mitchell, "Case," 11.

20 For a further elaboration of the phantom limb as it straddled the mind-body problem, see Erica Fretwell, *Sensory Experiments: Psychophysics, Race, and the Aesthetics of Feeling* (Durham, NC: Duke University Press, 2020).

21 Mitchell, "Case," 6.

22 Ibid., 10–11.

23 Ibid., 11.

24 S. Weir Mitchell, "Phantom Limbs," *Lippincott's Magazine* (December 1871), 564.

25 Ibid., 565.

26 Ibid.

27 Elizabeth Grosz, *Volatile Bodies: Toward a Corporeal Feminism* (Bloomington: Indiana University Press, 1994), 72.

28 W. E. B. Du Bois, "Strivings of the Negro People," *Atlantic Monthly* 80 (August 1897), 194.

29 Saidiya Hartman, *Scenes of Subjection: Race, Terror, and Self-Making in Nineteenth-Century America* (New York: Oxford University Press, 1997). On the "eugenic Atlantic" as the nineteenth- and twentieth-century emergence of race and disability as mutual scientific projects of human exclusion, see Mitchell and Snyder, *Cultural Locations of Disability* (Chicago: University of Chicago Press, 2006).

30 See W. E. B. Du Bois, *The Souls of Black Folk* (Chicago: AC McClurg, 1903).

31 Nirmala Erevelles, *Disability and Difference in Global Contexts: Enabling a Transformative Body Politic* (New York: Palgrave Macmillan, 2011), 39. See Hortense Spillers, "Mama's Baby, Papa's Maybe: An American Grammar Book," in *Black, White, and in Color: Essays on American Literature and Culture* (Chicago: University of Chicago Press, 2003).

32 Bryan Wagner, *Disturbing the Peace: Black Culture and the Police Power after Slavery* (Cambridge, MA: Harvard University Press, 2009), 112.

33 Hartman, *Scenes of Subjection*, 73.

34 Ibid., 74.

35 Avery Gordon, *Ghostly Matters: Haunting and the Sociological Imagination* (Minnesota: University of Minnesota Press, 1997), 200.

36 Frances E. W. Harper, *Iola Leroy, or, Shadows Uplifted* (Philadelphia: Garrigues Brothers, 1892), 59.

37 Ibid., 40.

38 Ibid.

39 Ibid., 170.

40 See Simon Strick, *American Dolorologies: Pain, Sentimentalism, and Biopolitics* (Albany: State University of New York Press, 2015), and Kyla Schuller, *The Biopolitics of Feeling: Race, Sex, and Science in Nineteenth-Century America* (Durham, NC: Duke University Press, 2017).

41 Nathaniel Mackey, *Discrepant Engagement: Dissonance, Cross-Culturality, and Experimental Writing* (Cambridge: Cambridge University Press, 1933), 235, 236. On Blackness and phantom limbs, see alsoVera Kutzinski, "Wilson Harris's Phantom Bodies: Re-Reading the Subject," in *Theater of the Arts: Wilson Harris and the Caribbean*, ed. Hena Maes-Jelinek and Bénédicte Ledent (New York: Brill Rodopi, 2002)

42 Charles Chesnutt, "Dave's Neckliss," in *The Conjure Woman and Other Conjure Tales*, ed. Richard Brodhead (Durham, NC: Duke University Press, 1993), 124.

43 Charles Chesnutt, "Po' Sandy." In *The Conjure Woman and Other Conjure Tales*, 49.

44 Sandy Alexandre, *The Property of Violence: Claims to Ownership in Representations of Lynching* (Jackson: University of Mississippi Press, 2012), 27, 70.

45 Chesnutt, "Po' Sandy," 50.

46 Ibid., 57.

47 Mackey, *Discrepant Engagement*, 169.

48 Michael Snediker, "Phenomenology beyond the Phantom Limb: Melvillean Figuration and Chronic Pain," in *Melville's Philosophies*, ed. Branka Arsic and K. L. Evans (New York: Bloomsbury, 2017), 159.

49 Clare Mullaney, "'Not to Discover Weakness Is the Artifice of Strength': Emily Dickinson, Constraint, and Disability Poetics," *J19: The Journal of Nineteenth-Century Americanists* 7, no. 1 (2019): 49–81.

50 Henry James, *Notes of a Son and Brother* (New York: Scribner's, 1914), 298.

51 See Sari Altschuler, "Touching *The Scarlet Letter*: What Disability History Can Teach Us about Literature," *American Literature* 92, no. 1 (2020): 91–122.

52 See Ann E. Leak, *The Autobiography of Miss Ann E. Leak, Born without Arms* (Philadelphia: Barclay, 1871).

53 Janet Price and Margrit Shildrick, "Bodies Together: Touch, Ethics, and Disability," in *Disability/Postmodernity: Embodying Disability Theory*, ed. Mairian Corker and Tom Shakespeare (London: Continuum, 2002), 68.

54 Sarah Chinn, "Feeling Her Way: Audre Lorde and the Power of Touch," *GLQ* 9, no. 1–2 (2003): 195.

# 12

ANNA HINTON

# How to Read Disabled Bodies Now

## *Crip-of-Color Critique*

Eli Clare's groundbreaking memoir *Exile and Pride: Disability, Queerness, and Liberation* (1999) examines the intersections of class, queerness, and disability. Clare, influenced by queer women of color, disrupts the boundaries between gender identity, sexuality, and disability, demonstrating how these various identities are hopelessly entangled. For Clare, "[g]ender reaches into disability, disability wraps around class; class strains against abuse; abuse snarls into sexuality; sexuality folds on top of race ... everything finally piling into a single human body."[1] Clare articulates how queer/crip theories of the body disrupt normalcy and refuse easy answers as they question and blur the boundaries of identity and agency. Clare's work is foundational to the subfield of disability studies called crip theory. Crip theory, as Robert McRuer articulates in his foundational book *Crip Theory: Cultural Signs of Queerness and Disability* (2006), exposes the linkages between compulsory heterosexuality and what he coins compulsory able-bodiedness. In *Crip Theory*, McRuer is wary of disability inclusion. Instead, he emphasizes the contradiction that neoliberalism celebrates difference even as it ushers in greater inequality and less regulation of corrupt systems.[2] Crip identity resists such celebration and instead relishes its position at the margins.

Crip, like the queerness that influences, informs, and, often, intersects with it, is an in-your-face political stance. As Caitlin Wood explicates in their introduction to *Criptiques*, a collection of crip writing,

> Crip is my favorite four-letter word. Succinct and blunt, profane to some, crip packs a punch. Crip is unapologetic. Audacious. Noncompliant. Crip takes pleasure in its boldness and utter disinterest in appearing "respectable" to the status quo. It's a powerful self-descriptor, a cultural signifier, and a challenge to anyone attempting to conceal disability off in the shadows. Crip is anti-assimilationist and proud of it. Crip is outspoken with no patience for nonsense. Crip is my culture and it's where I want to be.[3]

Crip counters the neoliberal diversity imperatives that recognize certain performances of inclusion as profitable, resulting in increased representation of marginalized subjects while simultaneously scaling back civil rights gains, such as in 2017 when Congress attempted to pass the education and reform act, which would have made it even more difficult to file lawsuits against businesses in noncompliance with the Americans with Disabilities Act (ADA).[4] Moreover, crip has become a home for those with contested disabilities, what Anna Mollow has called "undocumented disabilities." Not only does crip further wrest power away from the medical community to define and delineate the lives of disabled people, but, as Mollow asserts, it "disrupts accepted conceptions of disability."[5] Crip is also where conversations about the thorny relationship between trauma and disability emerge while still embracing and affirming disability.

Contradictions within disability studies further illuminate the contestatory focus on inclusion. In 2006, Christopher M. Bell lambasted the field for its faux diversity, remarking,

> it is disingenuous to keep up the pretense that the field is an inclusive one when it is not. ... I would like to concede the failure of Disability Studies to engage issues of race and ethnicity in a substantive capacity, thereby entrenching whiteness as its constitutive underpinning. In short, I want to call a shrimp a shrimp and acknowledge Disability Studies for what it is, White Disability Studies.[6]

With Bell's work as editor of and contributor to *Blackness and Disability: Critical Examinations and Cultural Interventions* (2012) and the emergence of critical race and disability scholars like Cynthia Wu, Nirmala Erevelles, Michelle Jarman, Sami Schalk, and Therí Pickens, to name a few, the field's whiteness has ebbed, especially with the emergent subfield of Black disability studies. Black disability studies, as Therí Pickens argues, demands that we "reach outside of both Black Studies and Disability Studies ... to create new paradigms."[7] Doing so requires representational detective work, recovering disability in the figures we already study and embracing more marginal figures, as well as recovering the Black presence in disability movements. Black disability studies also requires expanding what falls under the umbrella of disability. While disability studies theoretically understands disability in an expansive way, in practice the field has, to its detriment, privileged visible, physical disabilities, including in groundbreaking work about disability in American literature such as Rosemarie Garland-Thomson's *Extraordinary Bodies: Figuring Physical Disability in American Culture and Literature* (1997). As Sami Schalk argues, however, "disability rights communities must expand to recognize and value the experiences of

those with non-apparent and chronic disabilities such as asthma and diabetes, which are overrepresented in communities of color."[8] Finally, and
perhaps most importantly, Black disability studies tackles the issues of
violence and disability, such as debilitating state violence like police
brutality, on which disability studies scholars have had little to say.

There is much overlap between crip theory and Black disability studies,
and the two fields came together in what a 2016 round table with Julie
Minich, Jina B. Kim, and Sami Schalk coined "crip-of-color critique."
Building on its predecessor, queer-of-color critique, this method of understanding disability reclaims, theorizes, and examines how queer women of
color feminist writer activists engage radical disability politics, though they
may not identify their work as such. Crip-of-color critique allows us to
identify and reclaim these women's intellectual and activist work because,
as Julie Minich explains, it "emphasizes its mode of analysis rather than its
objects of study."[9] This shift recognizes that there is much work concerned
with disability that does not align with what we recognize as critical disability studies: "work that objectifies disability; places it under the medical gaze;
pathologizes it; deploys it as a device of characterization; or uncritically
treats it as a metaphor for decay, decline, or failure."[10] Moreover, many
women of color do activist work that "advocat[es] a radical politics of
corporeal variation and neurodiversity" – such as "protests against racialized disparities in health, education, and policing; struggles for environmental justice and reproductive freedom; HIV/AIDS and fat activism" – that
has gone unrecognized and unnamed as such.[11] Whereas other ethnic
American scholarship "envisions liberation primarily in terms of self-
ownership and bodily wholeness," crip-of-color critique, Jina B. Kim
explains, "instead asks what liberation might look like when able-
bodiedness is no longer centered."[12] This shift, for Kim, "honors vulnerability, disability, and inter/dependency, instead of viewing such conditions as
evidence of political failure or weakness."[13] Moreover, crip-of-color critique
turns our attention toward the most vulnerable populations and how "the
state, rather than protecting disabled people, in fact operates as an apparatus
of racialized disablement."[14]

I've argued elsewhere that disability studies has shied away from conversations about disability and violence because of its understandable political
commitment to positive representations of disability that move away from
understanding disability as tragedy. Instead, "the field has sought to divorce
disability from discourses about suffering, and rightly so, affirm disabled
identity while challenging societal attitudes that devalue disabled life evident
in obstacles such as environments inhospitable to disabled bodies."[15] The
issue, however, is "that the experiences of becoming disabled for those who

occupy multiple marginalized positions must be elided."[16] Those stories of becoming disabled as a violent consequence of nonwhite, noncismale, nonstraight, nonabled embodiment do not fit the political narrative of disability as a positive identity and must be repressed. Many potential disability archives have, until recently, been circumscribed, dismissed, or ignored. Crip-of-color critique reclaims these archives by diving into conversations about violence while also celebrating how race, class, ethnicity, sexuality, gender identity, and nationality add to crip identity.

In this chapter, I use crip-of-color critique, along with interventions in literary disability studies and aesthetics, to closely read novels by Toni Morrison, Leslie Marmon Silko, and Virginia Grise. These texts reflect a choice to privilege works of American literature by women of color who embrace a crip politics without necessarily claiming crip. First, I will discuss the antirespectability crip politics of Eva Peace in Morrison's second novel *Sula* (1973). Next, I will put Silko's *Almanac of the Dead* (1991) in conversation with the recent turn in crip studies to feminist technoscience. Finally, I analyze Grise's crip performance manifesto *Your Healing Is Killing Me* (2017) through what I call a crip technoscience of the Spirit.

## Desiring Disability: Crip Characters and Crip Aesthetics in Toni Morrison's *Sula*

Morrison's entire oeuvre features complex, audacious, noncompliant, unapologetic crip Black women. In *Sula*, the titular character's grandmother emerges as a dominant (and at times domineering) character. After her husband leaves her to raise their children alone on just a few food items, Eva chooses to leave them with a neighbor for over a year, when she returns with "two crutches, a new black pocketbook, and one leg," suggesting that Eva's amputation is connected to her current financial stability.[17] Though Eva's choice to become an amputee was, as Rosemarie Garland-Thomson reminds us, a limited choice, Eva is not the pitiable or tragic disabled figure that typically haunts American literature.[18] "Physical disability" in Morrison's oeuvre "neither diminishes nor corrupts Morrison's extraordinary women; rather, it affirms the self in context," and, for Eva specifically, "disability augments her power and dignity, inspiring awe and becoming a mark of superiority, a residue of ennobling history."[19] For Garland-Thomson, Black American women writers like Morrison present "the body as a site of history and identity is at once burden and means of redemption."[20] *Sula* represents Eva Peace's disability as a method of relating that welcomes disability and rejects respectability, crips disability tropes, fosters crip community, and demands we pay attention to the Spirit.

In *Crip Theory*, Robert McRuer asks us to consider what it would mean to welcome and embrace disability.[21] Eva Peace is an answer to his question. Not only does she welcome and embrace disability as a viable and lively alternative to abject poverty, but she also refuses performances of compulsory able-bodiedness and heteronormativity. Though on a fundamental level desiring disability is equated with desiring a measure of financial freedom, Eva flirts with tropes of the welfare queen by refusing to disavow narratives that she chose disability for economic reasons only to create an alternative economy based on interdependence and care. In this alternative economy, Eva creates a space for crip culture to emerge. In her boarding home, people across marginalized identities come together. They are what Morrison identifies as the "pariahs" of society. Unlike acceptable marginalized neoliberal subjects that seek a degree of assimilation and integration into hegemonic society, they prefer their life at the margins. Eva "adopts," names, and cares for the three Deweys who turn out very short at a fully developed height of forty-eight inches tall and refuse to socialize with anyone outside of each other. Eva never tries to force Tar Baby, a racially ambiguous white-skinned character who experiences periods of depression and suicide ideation, into sobriety. Instead, she gives him space yet regularly checks in and offers care. It is not simply that she comes to embrace her disability, but she also creates community around it, including a community of romantic interests. Like the texts Robert McRuer analyzes in "The World Making Potential of Contemporary Crip/Queer Literary and Cultural Production" (2017), Eva "rejects mainstream culture's ableist belief that disability is neither desirable nor desiring."[22] Whereas disabled women and older women are often desexualized in American culture at large, Eva – an older disabled woman – has a "regular flock of gentlemen callers"; yet she never remarries. [23] These admirers revel in her one remaining leg and in the absence of the other, yet Eva's disability is never fetishized. She encourages suitors yet refuses sex. She coaches other women in their affairs with men. Moreover, she offers no criticism of her daughter's promiscuity. In *Sula*, Eva evolves from the traditional values of marriage and motherhood that left her destitute to what the novel calls manlove, a queercrip understanding of (a) sexual and romantic relating and desire as nonpossessive, generous, and mutually empowering.

Eva performs crip as she evokes then frustrates common stereotypes around Black disabled womanhood. I have already briefly discussed how she recalls and then challenges the tropes of the welfare queen and the desexualized older disabled woman. She also frustrates the common reading of disability as absence in Black women's literature. For example, she directs our attention toward the absence of her leg only to shore up instead the presence of empowered disability. Significantly, Eva crips tropes about disability and narrative. Though Eva's sudden disability creates a desire for the story about it, Eva frustrates this desire. For instance, while Ato Quayson notes that she neither confirms nor denies stories about how she became one-legged – ultimately arguing that the vague details around her accident and the nature of her disability are meant to draw "attention away from it as an object" – he fails to note how this frustrates and teases, even, the commonly accepted idea that disability must inaugurate narrative.[24] Morrison uses the desire to narrativize disability to characterize Eva as a griot and trickster figure. She is the limping Eshu.

*Sula* not only features crip writing but it also reflects a crip aesthetic, one particular to writers who present characters that navigate race, sexuality, gender, class, and disability. Similar to Morrison, Octavia E. Butler's novels, as Therí Pickens observes, all feature disabled Black women. Pickens highlights this significance, explaining that "to understand identity as central to the story is to understand that same identity (or set of identities) as central to the aesthetics of storytelling."[25] Or in the words of Garland-Thomson, "shape structures story."[26] Pickens argues that novels that address the intersections of class, gender, race, sexuality, and disability force writers to develop narrative structures that privilege "open-ended conclusions that frustrate the narrative cohesion associated with the novel form, intricate depictions of power that potentially alienate the able-bodied reader, and contained literary chaos that upends the idea of ontological fixity."[27] I agree with Pickens that one finds similar aesthetics in novels by other women of color, including Morrison's body of work. I add that, in Morrison's and other women of color's writing, such an aesthetics is enacted through the influence of non-Western spiritualities.

For example, Eva Peace "upends ontological fixity" in her characterization as a goddess-like figure. She also signifies on multiple disabled African and African-derived deities, from the limping trickster Eshu to the limping keeper of the crossroad Papa Legba in Vodun. These deities are complicated and contradictory, much like Eva, who, for example, loves her son enough to kill him. Yet, these deities are reverenced. In syncretic spiritual systems like Vodun, they are even welcome to "mount" or possess one's body.

Morrison presents not just intricate but also subtle depictions of power that frustrate the (white) able-bodied reader. Morrison centers the worlds and worldviews of the mostly Black characters that inhabit her works. She refuses to privilege the white gaze, so whiteness, including white people, often remains at the margins of her text. Whiteness's presence instead registers in the details of the characters' material realities, like how all-Black communities – such as The Bottom in *Sula* – become so. Interestingly, Ato Quayson reads Morrison's depictions of race, such as these material and structural realities, as "sociological" but not her representations of disability.[28] Quayson instead reads Morrison's representation of disability as symbolic, as "quasi-mythical."[29] Quayson is not incorrect, but ableism, too, is a subtle yet structuring presence in her characters' world. That Eva must craft a makeshift wheelchair speaks not only to her crip technological ingenuity but also to her very real need for access, which she, for whatever reason, cannot acquire from other sources. Eva survives a jump from a second-story window, yet she nearly dies from her injuries as she waits for care in a hospital hallway. Moreover, both race and disability are central to the experiences of her characters, so Morrison often gives both race, particularly Blackness, and disability an air of magic, myth, and legend. This is mainly because, as she centers Black worldviews, she also centers Black cosmologies, African-derived understandings of time, place, good, and evil. Even in reference to *Sula* Morrison claims that the people of The Bottom understand evil according to African spiritual systems, which in general encompass religion, science, ethics, and so on, where evil occupies a different ethical and moral space than in (white) Western paradigms. Understanding these cosmologies is essential to understanding Morrison's intricate depictions of power dynamics and place. This underscores that physical disability in Morrison's novel is embraced, celebrated, and reverenced.

### Beyond Cure: Resistance and Feminist Crip Technoscience in Leslie Marmon Silko's *Almanac of the Dead*

Morrison's creative solutions to accessibility in *Sula* gesture toward a history between communities of color and medical professionals where access to care and accommodations cannot be taken for granted. Indeed, though Black and brown bodies have been pathologized by medical communities as deviant, used for illegal and unethical medical experimentation, and turned into synecdoches for illness and disease in the cultural imagination, Black and brown people have been excluded from health insurance and healthcare or healthcare that isn't compromised by unexamined and unchecked racial biases. For instance, unfettered access to Black women's enslaved bodies was instrumental in ushering in the rise of modern gynecology, and yet, to this day, Black women across class lines have the highest maternal and infant mortality rates. There is little research on Black mothers injured and debilitated by the gynecological system from a crip perspective. Consequently, health activism has been a crucial element of women of color's activism and one of the primary places where progressive disability politics emerge. Though activists often seek access to the medical community, as with Audre Lorde's and Gloria Anzaldúa's health activism,[30] they maintain a healthy skepticism of medical discourse that pathologizes disabled bodies. In this section, I look to a recent turn toward feminist technoscience in crip studies for reading paradigms that allow us to examine how women of color writers in the United States understand the relationship between identity, disability, community, and technoscience.

Kelly Fritsch, Aimi Hamraie, Mara Mills, and David Serlin, in their introduction to their special edition of *Catalyst*, on Crip technoscience,

> assert an understanding of crip technoscience that builds upon the ways that crip theory, and critical disability studies more broadly, have emphasized an anti-assimilationist disability politics – not only through disability activism but also through the material and social practices of disability world-building. As a result, crip technoscience engages with rather than eschews the relationships, activisms, and products of engineering, design, and other technoscientific practices.[31]

This is significant, as they note, because "crip technoscience emphasizes difference and embodiment at the core of disability politics while affirming an open rather than hostile relationship to technoscience, often regarded as anathema to disability politics."[32] Despite this, the editors are aware that disability has a thorny relationship with technoscience, since "'disabled peoples' activist practices can be ... commodified or appropriated by technoscience."[33] In what follows, I contemplate the politics of crip identity, resistance, and technoscience in Silko's novel *Almanac of the Dead*.

Silko's *Almanac of the Dead* features a cadre of queer and disabled characters that demonstrate the limitations of disability as identity. As Michelle Jarman argues, "Silko deploys disability and queer identities to complicate authenticity in two important ways: first, to expand borderland notions of hybrid identity; and second, to ironically expose the cultural erasures of eugenic histories connected to homosexuality and disability-erasures that mirror and complicate current identity politics of border theory."[34] For Jarman, Silko's work reveals that identifying with a hybrid identity doesn't make one immune to eugenics perspectives or necessarily "value difference."[35] In short, Silko engages crip-of-color critique as methodology.

*Almanac of the Dead* is as much about world destroying as it is about world building. Indeed, justice, including disability justice, in the novel involves destroying systems of power that have repressed and erased discredited Indigenous ways of knowing. The novel presents the worst of ableism, sexism, racism, and capitalism and then challenges and upsets them. For instance, like Eva Peace, Lecha, as a crip character, seems to play into pejorative narratives around disabled embodiment only to contest these perceptions, particularly the trope of the disability con. As Ellen Samuels informs us, the idea of people pretending to be disabled for charity was a popular image and trope in the mid-twentieth century.[36] Lecha returns home from work as a psychic on the television circuit and tells everyone, including doctors, that she has cancer, thus her need for a wheelchair and use of prescription pain relievers. She then hires Seese, a person who manages drug addiction, as her aide. Seese believes that Lecha is addicted to Demerol. Many in the narrative suspect that Lecha does not need her wheelchair and are dubious about her status as someone dying from cancer. They are right. Lecha doesn't need a wheelchair, and she doesn't have cancer. Lecha is not a disability con because she does use drugs for pain management. Only, the source of Lecha's pain is one deemed illegitimate by scientific communities: She is slowly dying from her psychic abilities. Similar to rhetoric about how we think of cancer, Lecha's body is consuming itself.

Lecha's character draws our attention to the radical politics against the hegemony that diagnoses can assume even within critical disability communities. Crip scholars and activists question and resist the need for diagnosis as they navigate lack of diagnosis or a diagnosis of contested illness, such as fibromyalgia, environmental toxins, and other "undocumented disabilities." The trope of the disability con has material consequences in the lives of disabled people living at the margins of diagnosis, revealing the limitations of current legal remedies, such as the ADA. Without a disability documented by medical professionals, accommodation in mainstream spaces is not possible. Access to quality care is limited. Lecha's actions are less con and more a creative, if strategically dishonest – a trickster's – solution to the healthcare system.

While dominant understandings of disability and technoscience figure disabled people as "object[s] of innovation discourse, rather than as a driver of technological change," characters like Lecha and Trigg in *Almanac of the Dead* upend this idea, simultaneously challenging the notion that disability identity results in action toward disability liberation.[37] Though Lecha appears, on the surface, to embody the disability con, Trigg's less contested disability identity doesn't lead him to any investment in justice, including disability justice. Trigg acquired a spinal cord injury as a young adult, which turned him into a "wheelie," a derogatory term for wheelchair users amongst some of the characters in the novel. Trigg is obsessed with walking again and with capitalist-driven wealth acquisition. He invests his money in property and plasma centers, acquiring the former for reduced rates by opening the latter in neighborhoods to depreciate property values. Trigg also invests in advanced stem-cell research and illegal organ harvesting.

He fancies himself better than the Black and brown people and people with addictions who take advantage of his plasma centers.

Trigg's sections offer poignant critiques of ableist systems and attitudes. He mocks able-bodied people who ask obvious or insulting questions. He has sexual desire and does and can have sex, which surprises many able-bodied people. He becomes disabled right before the passage of the ADA, so he remarks on accessibility before and after. Yet, Trigg, problematically, perpetuates harm against disabled people. He lures unsuspecting people with addictions or houselessness into his plasma centers, where he drains them dry and collects and sells their organs. His racism and sexism are abhorrent. He is obsessed with being cured and overcompensates for feeling emasculated in his chair with his wealth and sexual prowess. Trigg skirts the line between the medical model of disability, or what Hamraie and Fritsch distinguish as disability technoscience versus crip technoscience, illuminating the potential issues in feminist crip technoscience, issues scholars are still working through. Though Trigg is disabled, he is deeply invested in the able-bodymind, patriarchy, capitalism, and racism, revealing the need to move away from disability as identity to disability as method and politics.

Yet, in Trigg's section, through his diaries' representation of his relationship with Max Blue, we see hints of the desire for a world otherwise. Michelle Jarman reads his diaries, which make up a chapter of the text, as evidence that he embodies narcissism.[38] I add that they become a way of expressing a desire for crip community that is built into the form of the novel. Max Blue is another crip character. After an accident, Max becomes paralyzed and a wheelchair user. Like Trigg, he abhors his condition. Unlike Trigg, Max is "cured"; he "recovers" his ability to walk. However, Max experiences what Eunjung Kim calls "curative violence": cured paralysis leaves him impotent, a less obvious disability that gets erased within the discourse of cure.[39] Yet Max's new disability refuses erasure. It is how Max meets Trigg, as Trigg is Max's wife Leah's lover. Trigg is Max's prosthetic dick. Where Max cannot feel arousal, nor manage an erection, no matter how hard he tries, Trigg takes pride in his sexual stamina and relishes his mental orgasms. For Max, Trigg represents his inverted double, an alternative history/reality, what Max could have been. Max, not Leah, reads Trigg's diaries, though Trigg had given them to her. I read Max's obsession with Trigg as a desire for the community of "wheelies" both Trigg and Max neglect in favor of their investment in able-embodiment through neoliberal (bio) capitalism. Through Trigg and Max, in *Almanac of the Dead*, neoliberal capitalism is tethered to compulsory able-bodiedness. However, even as characters embody anti-crip politics, formal and aesthetic elements of the novel affirm crip methodology.

Through Trigg, the novel critiques the relationship between disability and technoscience. Yet while it exhibits a deep distrust of the biomedical industry, *Almanac of the Dead* does not fully eschew technoscience. Instead, it offers up an Indigenous crip alternative, what I am calling a crip technoscience of the Spirit. Putting conversations of crip technoscience with various conversations about spirituality in women of color's writing, I will briefly introduce this term through a final reading of *Almanac of the Dead* and elaborate upon it as I move to Latinx playwright Grise's manifesto, *Your Healing Is Killing Me*.

Scholars such as Gay Wilentz, Ann Folwell Stanford, and Rebecca Tillet have discussed how Indigenous characters use spiritual knowledge. I add that we should consider these epistemologies as a technology against Western scientific/industrial technology that would be used against them. Harvesting the knowledge and magic of non-Western spiritual traditions is an essential theme in women of color's writing. Wilentz argues that Silko positions divorce from sacred knowledge as a cultural and personal injury that must be healed in order to move forward and fight against oppressive forces.[40] As Christina Garcia Lopez argues of Latinx writers, "spirituality dramatically shapes our experiences of and approach to concrete social conditions"; therefore, "spirituality matters because it affects not only *what* we think we are, but also *how* we are."[41] I identify such spirituality as a crip technology because the spiritual is considered, in the worlds of the texts and many groups that practice them, discredited embodied knowledge. Like Hamraie and Fritsch, I see it instead as a realm of knowledge production encompassing philosophy, ethics, history, medicine, and technology that facilitates "politicized practices of non-compliant knowing-making: world-building and world-dismantling practices *by* and *with* disabled people and communities that respond to intersectional systems of power, privilege, and oppression by working within and around them."[42]

Take Lecha's gift, for example. She uses her visions to both help and harm those who seek her services, and she uses her gift to destroy the cisnormative, heterosexist, racist ableist capitalist destructive society. Another example of crip technoscience of the Spirit is when Lecha travels to Alaska and meets an "old Yupik woman," who also has spiritual gifts.[43] The old woman "realized the possibilities in the white man's gadgets" and harnessed her power to disrupt them, causing planes for corporations who want to destroy the land to crash.[44] In *Almanac of the Dead*, crip technoscience of the Spirit is used to subvert and destroy white Western technoscience. Crip technoscience of the Spirit becomes decolonization in action, a reclaiming of ancient knowledge to destroy worlds and rebuild them.

## Crip Technoscience of the Spirit and *Your Healing Is Killing Me*

Virginia Grise's *Your Healing Is Killing Me* is, according to the back cover,

> a performance manifesto based on lessons learned in San Antonio free health clinics, and New York acupuncture schools; from the treatments and consejos of curanderas, abortion doctors, Marxist artists, community health workers, and bourgie dermatologists. One artist's reflections on living with post-traumatic stress disorder, ansia, and eczema in the new age of trigger warnings, the Master Cleanse, and crowd-funded self-care.

Yet, expressed throughout the text, in ways that resonate with people of color populated communities, is a deep fear of the medical-industrial complex. An analytical frame is needed to explore what it means for a Chicanx woman writer to begin in these spaces. This necessitates an exploration into the spiritual. Non-Western spiritualities become paradigms for creating alternative cosmologies that allow writers to reenvision liberation. This vision, as articulated by Grise, is a crip one, despite its connection to the medical-industrial complex. Indeed, it is within crip techno spaces that spiritual practices, particularly magic, unmake and remake worlds.

The performance, which I witnessed at Cara Mía Theatre located in Dallas, Texas, is a one-woman show featuring a queer, fat Chicanx woman who performs the movement sequence illustrated in the print version of the manifesto. The performance crips who we imagine can occupy space. Florinda Bryant, the actress, sweats, breathes heavily, moves – all acts of embodying space denied fat women of color. The theatre turns into a spiritual space as the audience is given a copy of the choreography and encouraged to join in the healing movements in whatever ways their bodies allow. Through the rhythm and flow of the yogalike poses, body and spirit merge together in community. Like Morrison's and Silko's novels, Grise's performance manifesto takes up crip of color themes like violence, disabled embodiment, queerness, activism, and creative technoscience that emerges in marginalized spaces.

In *Your Healing Is Killing Me*, crip technoscience of the Spirit is a more viable and accessible mode of decolonization. The blurb snidely remarks that "Capitalism is toxic but the Revolution is not in your body butter," implying that current trends in self-care are not what crip of color activists like Audre Lorde had in mind when she asserted that self-care is radical. Actually, like Lorde, Grise imagines crip technoscience of the Spirit as a means of world building and ensuring futurity amid Black and brown death. In her life writing, Lorde redefines survival. While disability technoscience suggests that physical survival through medical intervention is the only ideal outcome, Lorde believes otherwise. As she faces her mortality with a cancer diagnosis, she asserts, "Our battle is to define survival in ways that are acceptable and nourishing to us meaning with substance and style."[45] For Lorde with, "Racism. Cancer. In both cases, to win the aggressor must conquer, but the resisters need only survive. How do I define that survival and on whose terms?"[46] Survival is Lorde's ability, even after her health fades and she dies, to continue working toward meaningful change through her legacy. A crip technoscience of the Spirit becomes the mechanism through which she can engage this meaningful change, particularly through African-based ontological paradigms that view the world of the living and spirit as continuous and conversant. Within this worldview, one survives as long as there is someone there to still speak one's name.

Similarly, *Your Healing Is Killing Me* deploys a crip technoscience of the Spirit to ensure the continuation of a movement. Toward the end of the manifesto, the protagonist has a dream that internationalist and small-bookstore owner Ràul, who died in 2008, visited her in a dream and told her to call Rene, his protégé and current owner of his store, Resistencia. She calls for Rene but is told he is "gone." Fearing that Rene, too, has transitioned, she is relieved then astonished to learn that Rene is not only alive but also in New York City, not far from where she lives. They meet, and Rene tells her that Fred Ho wants to meet her. When she meets the radical activist and composer, who at this time is dying of cancer, Ho tells her that he wants her to write about Russel "Maroon" Shoatz as part of his campaign to free Shoatz from solitary confinement. In *Your Healing Is Killing Me*, we get Shoatz's story "and what it means to be a Maroon, what it means to be free, for us to be free, in the 21st century."[47] As the protagonist relates, "Within two months, Maroon had been freed from solitary confinement ... Two months after that Fred died." [48] The visit from the spirit in her dream is the catalyst for a meeting with Ho before he dies. He is able to pass on the story of Maroon, which, like the Almanac in Silko's novel, holds sacred cultural information for liberation. In the midst of the precarity of crip of color life, crip technoscience of the Spirit enables a futurity unfulfillable by medical technology.

## NOTES

1 Eli Clare, Aurora Levins Morales, and Dean Spade, *Exile and Pride: Disability, Queerness, and Liberation*, reissue ed. (Durham, NC: Duke University Press, 2015), 143.
2 Robert McRuer, *Crip Theory: Cultural Signs of Queerness and Disability* (New York: New York University Press, 2006), 3.
3 Caitlin Wood, *Criptiques* (Mineral Point, WI: May Day, 2014), 1–2.

4 See Rebecca Cokley, Rebecca Vallas, and Eliza Schultz's "The Quiet Attack on the ADA Making Its Way through Congress," Center for American Progress, www.americanprogress.org/article/quiet-attack-ada-making-way-congress/.

5 Anna Mollow, "Criphystemologies: What Disability Theory Needs to Know about Hysteria," *Journal of Literary & Cultural Disability Studies* 8, no. 2 (July 5, 2014): 187.

6 Christopher M. Bell, "Introducing White Disability Studies: A Modest Proposal," in *The Disability Studies Reader*, ed. Lennard J. Davis, 2nd ed. (New York: Routledge, 2006), 275.

7 Therí A. Pickens and Howard Rambsy II, "Outliers and Out Right Lies; or How We 'Do' Black Disability Studies," *Cultural Front: A Notebook on Literary Art, Digital Humanities, and Emerging Ideas* (blog), August 7, 2012, www.culturalfront.org/2012/08/outliers-and-out-right-lies-or-how-we.html.

8 Jane Dunhamn et al., "Developing and Reflecting on a Black Disability Studies Pedagogy: Work from the National Black Disability Coalition," *Disability Studies Quarterly* 35, no. 2 (May 19, 2015), http://dsq-sds.org/article/view/4637.

9 Julie Avril Minich, "Enabling Whom? Critical Disability Studies Now," *Lateral* 5, no. 1 (May 2016), https://doi.org/10.25158/L5.1.9.

10 Ibid.

11 Ibid.

12 Jina Kim, "Toward a Crip-of-Color Critique: Thinking with Minich's 'Enabling Whom?,'" *Lateral* (blog), May 15, 2017, https://csalateral.org/issue/6-1/forum-alt-humanities-critical-disability-studies-crip-of-color-critique-kim/.

13 Ibid.

14 Ibid.

15 Anna Hinton, "A War of Minds Waged against Bodies: The Political Activist as Prisoner and Patient," *Anthurium: A Caribbean Studies Journal* 15, no. 2 (September 23, 2019): 2, https://doi.org/10.33596/anth.380.

16 Ibid., 2.

17 Toni Morrison, *Sula*, reprint ed. (New York: Vintage, 2004), 34.

18 Rosemarie Garland-Thomson, *Extraordinary Bodies: Figuring Physical Disability in American Culture and Literature* (New York: Columbia University Press, 1997), 214. See also Sharon Snyder and David Mitchell, "Disability Haunting in American Poetics," *Journal of Literary & Cultural Disability Studies* 1, no. 1 (May 1, 2007): 1, https://doi.org/10.3828/jlcds.1.1.2.

19 Garland-Thomson, *Extraordinary Bodies*, 215.

20 Ibid., 196.

21 McRuer, *Crip Theory*, 207.

22 Robert McRuer, "The World Making Potential of Contemporary Crip/Queer Literary and Cultural Production," in *The Cambridge Companion to Literature and Disability*, ed. Clare Barker and Stuart Murray (Cambridge: Cambridge University Press, 2017), 142.

23 Morrison, *Sula*, 41.

24 Ato Quayson, *Aesthetic Nervousness: Disability and the Crisis of Representation* (New York: Columbia University Press, 2007), 104.

25 Therí A. Pickens, "Octavia Butler and the Aesthetics of the Novel," *Hypatia* 30, no. 1 (February 1, 2015): 168, https://doi.org/10.1111/hypa.12129.

26 Rosemarie Garland-Thomson, "Shape Structures Story: Fresh and Feisty Stories about Disability," *Narrative* 15, no. 1 (2007): 113–123.
27 Pickens, "Octavia Butler and the Aesthetics of the Novel," 168.
28 Quayson, *Aesthetic Nervousness*, 86–87.
29 Ibid., 104.
30 See Audre Lorde's *The Cancer Journals*. Special ed. (San Francisco: Aunt Lute Books, 1997) and *A Burst of Light: Essays* (Ithaca, NY: Firebrand Books, 1988); and Gloria Anzaldúa's *Borderlands: The New Mestiza* (San Francisco: Aunt Lute Books, 2007).
31 Kelly Fritsch et al., "Introduction to Special Section on Crip Technoscience," *Catalyst: Feminism, Theory, Technoscience* 5, no. 1 (April 1, 2019): 1–10, https://doi.org/10.28968/cftt.v5i1.31998.
32 Ibid.
33 Ibid.
34 Michelle Jarman, "Exploring the World of the Different in Leslie Marmon Silko's *Almanac of the Dead*," *MELUS* 31, no. 3 (2006): 148.
35 Ibid., 149.
36 It is an anxiety that continues to haunt society as people take pictures of and sometimes act in a hostile manner against those who do not perform disability according to the cultural imagination. Most often this involves ambulatory users of mobility aids or those with invisible disabilities who park in reserved spots. This is a display of feigned concern for actual disabled bodies when it is an able-bodied exercise of policing disabled bodies, of being the arbiters of who qualifies as disabled and what is acceptable disabled behavior, as people rarely maintain that same fervor in fighting for actual disability justice. This is a prime example of the neoliberal diversity McRuer theorizes.
37 Aimi Hamraie and Kelly Fritsch, "Crip Technoscience Manifesto," *Catalyst: Feminism, Theory, Technoscience* 5, no. 1 (April 1, 2019): 4, https://doi.org/10.28968/cftt.v5i1.29607.
38 Jarman, "Exploring the World of the Different in Leslie Marmon Silko's *Almanac of the Dead*," 153.
39 Eunjung Kim, *Curative Violence: Rehabilitating Disability, Gender, and Sexuality in Modern Korea* (Durham, NC: Duke University Press, 2017).
40 Gay Alden Wilentz, *Healing Narratives: Women Writers Curing Cultural Dis-Ease* (New Brunswick, NJ: Rutgers University Press, 2000).
41 Christina Garcia Lopez, *Calling the Soul Back: Embodied Spirituality in Chicanx Narrative* (Tucson: University of Arizona Press, 2019), 4.
42 Hamraie and Fritsch, "Crip Technoscience Manifesto," 4–5.
43 Leslie Marmon Silko, *Almanac of the Dead: A Novel* (New York: Simon and Schuster, 2013), 152.
44 Ibid., 155.
45 Audre Lorde, *A Burst of Light*, 95.
46 Ibid., 99.
47 Virginia Grise, *Your Healing Is Killing Me* (2017), 77.
48 Ibid., 77.

# 13

LINDSEY GRUBBS

# Health Humanities, Illness, and the Body in American Literature

Among the medical texts in early American physician Benjamin Rush's library was a copy of Daniel Defoe's 1722 novel *A Journal of the Plague Year*. Three years before his own encounter with a devastating 1793 yellow fever outbreak in Philadelphia, Rush penned in the volume, "For the instruction, & entertainment I have received from this book, I am truly thankful."[1] Rush underlined and marked key passages as well, including one about a physician combating disease with garlic, tobacco, and vinegar, and compiled an index including entries like "Origin of the plague," "State of morals after the plague," "The number who died of the plague & in what months," and "Effects of terror." Gleaning medical and social information about disease from this fictionalized account, Rush demonstrates how tightly literary and medical knowledge were intertwined in the early United States.

   Although literature and medicine professionalized separately across the nineteenth and twentieth centuries, the past decades have seen a renewed focus on their connections. In the 1960s and 1970s, new procedures like organ transplantation and in vitro fertilization as well as revelations of unethical research like the Tuskegee Syphilis Study proved that medicine's technical capacities were outpacing its ethical ones. A swell of texts from the humanities grappled with the limits of medicine, including now-classic works like Ivan Illich's *Medical Nemesis*, Susan Sontag's *Illness as Metaphor*, and the first edition of the still commonly used *Principles of Biomedical Ethics* by Tom Beauchamp and James Childress.[2] Medical centers began hiring literary scholars in the 1970s to find applications for literary texts and methods that might "humanize" medical practice and improve the "moral sensibilities" of physicians-in-training.[3] This endeavor became the medical humanities. Today, many scholars speak instead of health humanities to include a broader array of health professions and to acknowledge that health goes beyond the clinic.[4] Prefixing "critical" to medical or health humanities denotes work drawing on fields including disability studies, queer theory, critical race theory, and environmental humanities to consider the politics of health.[5] The field is expanding rapidly: In 2000, there were fifteen undergraduate programs in health humanities (ranging from majors to minors to concentrations), and, in 2020, there are 102, with more in development.[6]

Work in the health humanities takes many, often competing, forms: It may seek to "humanize" the clinical space; to "disrupt, broaden and embellish what are taken to be the overly reductive, materialist and scientistic definitions of human experience promoted by biomedicine"; or to take on a more "entangled" approach, in which scholars work across disciplines – perhaps even in the lab or clinic – allowing themselves to shape and be shaped by collaboration and experiment.[7] Within the context of the health sciences, health humanists may work to denaturalize medical ideology, demonstrating the historical and cultural contingency of ideas about health. In the context of literary scholarship, however, they may reemphasize the materiality of the body. The approach is not homogeneous, though, and, beyond the "health humanities" as such, many literary scholars examine representations of health, illness, and embodiment, or use methodologies like close reading on medical texts.

The assumption that narrative impacts the body underpins much health humanities scholarship. Among the most canonical texts of the field are physician-anthropologist Arthur Kleinman's *The Illness Narratives*, which argues for "the recurrent effect of narrative on physiology, and of pathology on story," and sociologist Arthur Frank's *The Wounded Storyteller*, which offers several archetypal narratives through which people make sense of illness.[8] This interdisciplinary emphasis on narrative makes literary analysis an essential method for the field. Foundational works by literary scholars such as Kathryn Montgomery Hunter and Rita Charon brought expertise in the analysis of texts, subtexts, and genres to bear on clinical stories. Working in a medical center, Hunter listened for narrative, metaphor, and other "literary" features, pointing out that "much of the central business of caring for patients is transacted by means of narrative."[9] Charon argues that skill in literary analysis benefits the patient–provider relationship, improving attention, empathy, and care.[10]

Beyond the clinic, literary scholars ask many questions about narratives of health and illness. Noting that humanities programming in medical contexts often uses the texts of literary scholarship (short stories, poems) more than its analytic methods, Sari Altschuler asserts that the health humanities must turn "from matters of feeling to methods of knowing."[11] For Altschuler, the humanities offer a perspective "informed by historical precedent, structural understanding, and an ability to dwell in ambiguity" (203). Literary critics, Elaine Showalter writes, may be particularly well suited to tracing the "prototypes, archetypes, and plots" of illness as it moves "from the clinic to the library, from the case study to the novel, from bodies to books, from page to stage and screen."[12] Medicine can shape literature, as Cynthia Davis demonstrates in her book on late nineteenth- and early twentieth-century medicine and aesthetics, and literature can shape medicine, as in Priscilla Wald's argument that narratives of illness can shape the path of disease.[13] Medicine has been used to reify differences between people, as Diane Price Herndl outlines with the nineteenth-century trope of the "invalid woman," but it can also reveal resistance to this marginalization, as in Britt Russert's exploration of how African Americans articulated antiracist science through their own cultural production in the nineteenth century.

Through examples spanning the eighteenth century to the twenty-first, this chapter asks how the lens of the health humanities offers new ways to read the body in American literature, emphasizing how health is entwined with gender, race, and disability. I begin by reading for contagion in the early American novel to introduce beliefs about the relationship between literature and the body. I turn next to Charlotte Perkins Gilman's often-studied 1892 story "The Yellow Wall-Paper" to show how health humanities scholars add to earlier feminist interpretations. Finally, I present recent calls for the field to look beyond empathy to confront structural injustice, which I illustrate through readings of recent books of poetry by Bettina Judd and Kwoya Fagin Maples that link contemporary medical racism to the historical pathologization of Black women.

## Reading Narratives of Contagion

Ann Jurecic notes that work in the medical humanities "demonstrates the limits of social constructionist practices that sharply separate the social and the biological."[14] The interplay between social and biological is perhaps nowhere more obvious than in epidemic disease, and studies of contagion in literature reveal the centrality of disease narratives to the formation of an imagined "American" body. Cristobal Silva's *Miraculous Plagues* takes its title from John Winthrop's seventeenth-century claim that the epidemics devastating Indigenous populations on the East coast providentially transformed wilderness into colonial property, and shows how colonists used these narratives to assert bodily – and moral – superiority.[15] Examining the nineteenth and twentieth centuries, Priscilla Wald shows how national identity is solidified through discourses of contagion, as "The interactions that make us sick also constitute us as a community." Not merely theoretical, narratives of contagion shape the course of disease: "As they disseminate information, they affect survival rates and contagion routes. They promote or mitigate the stigmatizing of individuals, groups, populations, locales (regional and global), behaviors, and lifestyles, and they change economies."[16] Contagion also has aesthetic implications. In *Viral Modernism*, Elizabeth Outka calls for a "radical reframing" of the body in Modernism by centering the often neglected 1918–1919 influenza epidemic rather than the First World War. She suggests modernist plotlessness, long sentences, and vague characters "provided the ideal form to represent the pandemic's presence and indeed helped shape that very form."[17] Reading for illness can offer a fresh look at literatures often periodized through war, and reveal how disease narratives can be politicized and even weaponized.

Health humanities approaches to Charles Brockden Brown, often called America's first professional novelist, have advanced the understanding of the body in early American literature, clarifying how social life becomes embodied. Brown wrote in a world profoundly shaped by illness. Living through New York's recurring yellow fever epidemics in the 1790s, Brown worked alongside his friend and roommate Elihu Hubbard Smith, a physician working on America's first medical journal, the *Medical Repository*.[18] In 1798, shortly after Brown began his novel *Arthur Mervyn; or, Memoirs of the Year 1793*, Smith died during an outbreak that sickened Brown as well.[19] In the preface to the novel, Brown asserts fiction's value for interpreting illness. In addition to inspiring medical and political change, the epidemic "furnished new displays of the influence of human passions and motives" to the "moral observer" – a role he claimed as author. In *Arthur Mervyn*, he plans "to weave into an humble narrative, such incidents as appears to him most instructive and remarkable" and claims it as a "duty" to favorably impact morals through this representation.[20]

This "moral" aim was not only psychological, as imagination was believed to shape the body. As Justine Murison writes, the assumption was "that fiction, whether moral or licentious, can infiltrate the reader – get beneath her very skin to shake her nerves and upset her physiology."[21] Imagination was powerful, and within the novel, panic about yellow fever caused "lingering or mortal diseases" in distant populations.[22] As Altschuler and Bryan Waterman have noted, Brown's novel thus serves a medical function by counteracting potentially fatal rumors and encouraging right conduct.[23] Those who read the novel could prepare for the horrors of illness and control their physical and moral response to the epidemic more successfully.

Contagion clarifies the bodily stakes of community bonds, so writing about epidemics allowed Brown to illuminate social networks, linking personal and social pathologies. The novel opens with a physician finding Mervyn ill and nursing him back to health. Only upon recovery does he share the story that constitutes the novel. Although the epidemic doesn't arrive until midway through the novel's first volume, this fevered frame insists that readers think of Mervyn's earlier journeys through the lens of coming disease. Mervyn is from the country and goes to the city to find work: He is overwhelmed, losing his money and even his shoes as he encounters unexpected expenses and frauds. When he finds employment, it is with Welbeck, who makes his living through lying and forgery. The novel thus develops the most common themes of the time, demonstrating the dangers of urban life and the constant risk of deception. These dangers are not transformed but clarified by the coming of infectious disease, as even family relations are shown to be unreliable. Mervyn records, "Wives were deserted by husbands, and children by parents. ... The chambers of disease were deserted, and the sick left to die of negligence."[24] Disease in the novel does not fundamentally alter society but renders existing fault lines visible and thus offers scholars reading for contagion a clear expression of cultural values.

If, as Maureen Tuthill suggests, one of the primary questions of the early American novel is about the balance between social cohesion and self-interest, the answer given by *Arthur Mervyn* requires a more detailed break-down about who is included in that society. Almost one-tenth of Philadelphia's 55,000 residents died during the 1793 outbreak, and 17,000 more fled the city. Because the upper classes could more easily evacuate, working-class residents faced disproportionately high mortality.[25] At one point, Mervyn goes to help someone and notices that, "The style and articulation denoted the speaker to be superior to the class of servants. Hence my anxiety to see and to aid him was increased."[26] In privileging such a "superior" sufferer, Mervyn reinforces social hierarchy.

Racial divisions were even more stark. Rush incorrectly theorized that African Americans were immune to yellow fever, and so should care for the ill and the dead.[27] This idea was propagated by Matthew Carey, who claimed these workers took advantage of the ill. Represented as immune and exploitative, Derrick Spires writes, "black Philadelphians come to represent the corruptive elements at work during the crisis."[28] Black Philadelphians offered their own medical counter-narratives, and the year after Carey's pamphlet, Absalom Jones and Richard Allen's *A Narrative of the Proceedings of the Black People during the Late and Awful Calamity in Philadelphia in the Year 1793* refuted both claims of immunity and charges of corruption. *Arthur Mervyn*, however, solidifies these stereotypes, as a Black driver and two white "undertakers" rove the city gathering corpses (and seemingly creating new ones).[29] Mervyn himself is mistaken for dead after being attacked by a "tawny" nurse stealing from the dying man he was supposed to help. For Black Philadelphians in the 1790s, narratives that wrongly attributed immunity had concrete effects on who was expected to do the deadly work of caring for the ill. Stories of disease like those offered by Carey, Brown, Jones, and Allen shaped the physical experience of readers who understood themselves as physiologically susceptible to imagination, and also of people marginalized by these narratives. Health humanities approaches to *Arthur Mervyn* reveal how illness shapes literature, offer authors and critics a powerful lens for examining the social body, and clarify the embodied consequences of narrative.

## Reading the "Madwoman"

Medicine gained professional and cultural authority across the nineteenth century, in part by making scientific claims about innate deficiencies in the bodies and capacities of marginalized people, including women, Indigenous people, and people of African descent.[30] By following the paths these medical ideas – and resistance to them – took through medical, literary, and popular texts, health humanities scholars help expose how discourses of the body were weaponized against certain populations and how cultural production of the marginalized offered alternatives. In the late nineteenth century, for example, many physicians believed in the biological inferiority of women. Popular science held that bodies had limited energy, and, if women exercised their minds, it would deprive their reproductive system of needed energy.[31] When George Miller Beard proposed the new diagnosis of "Neurasthenia," he cited five causes for this "American Nervousness": "steam power, the periodical press, the telegraph, the sciences, and the mental activity of women."[32] Physician S. Weir Mitchell developed a "rest cure" for women, which in its most extreme form required remaining totally still and eating tremendous amounts of food to build up healthful fat and blood.[33] Mitchell's medical theory assumed women's fundamental inequality, and he argued that doctors had special insight into gender as they know from experience "how near to disorder and how close to misfortune [woman] is brought by the very peculiarities of her nature."[34]

Because of this history, medicine was a popular topic of early feminist literary critics, and Charlotte Perkins Gilman's 1892 story "The Yellow Wall-Paper" was a popular text. Gilman wrote "The Yellow Wall-Paper" after being treated by Mitchell for nervousness. In the story, a young mother becomes progressively insane while given a version of the rest cure by her physician-husband. Feminist critics argued that medical misogyny could drive women to insanity or read the narrator as gaining the "limited freedom of madness which ... constitutes a kind of sanity in the face of the insanity of male dominance."[35] In Gilman's text, it is only through insanity that the narrator is able to free the woman lurking behind the wallpaper – trapped in the nursery as she is – and claim power over her prone husband.

Feminist scholarship's critiques of power and objectivity underlie much work in the health humanities. The turn toward health humanities as such, however, reveals a different orientation to the body than feminism alone, in part by emphasizing illness as literal rather than figurative. In her foundational work on illness metaphors, Susan Sontag rails against the metaphorical use of illnesses like cancer and AIDS. She writes, "Nothing is more punitive than to give a disease a meaning – that meaning being invariably a moralistic one."[36] More recently, scholars have critiqued the use of madness as symbol, arguing that viewing mental illness without accounting for its material reality risks perpetuating stereotypes.[37]

Because health humanists often privilege patient experience, they might also emphasize Gilman's active resistance to medical patriarchy. Blending the figure of physician and husband into one, the narrator suggests that "John is a physician, and perhaps – ... perhaps that is one reason I do not get well faster."[38] Her husband condemns the writing that she finds a "relief" because, "He says that with my imaginative power and habit of story-making a nervous weakness like mine is sure to lead to all manner of excited fancies" (170). By writing a compelling story in which a woman is told not to write, Gilman takes aim at the belief that women's intellectual activity was a danger, claiming it instead as a power. Many years later in "Why I Wrote the Yellow Wallpaper," she noted that she sent the story to Mitchell, causing him to change the treatment. (It probably didn't.)[39] By rigorously historicizing Gilman's own physiologic theories – in many ways similar to Mitchell's – Jane Thrailkill shows how "The Yellow Wall-Paper" does medical work, enabling the transition from somatic to psychoanalytic theories of women's mental disorder.[40] In this reading, illness is not a symbolic expression of gendered oppression but an effective argument in cultural debates about the appropriate role of medicine.

In 1989, Susan Lanser asked how scholars could reconcile the feminist themes of "The Yellow Wall-Paper" and its popularity among feminist critics (including herself) with Gilman's overt racism and advocacy for eugenic principles.[41] She wrote that it was time "to stop reading a privileged, white, New England woman's text as simply – a woman's text" (424). Health humanities provides the tools to understand how scientific rhetoric shaped social prominence. Theories of women's pathology in the nineteenth century were not applied evenly. While white women in the middle and upper classes were seen as delicate and in need of medical management, working-class white women and women of color were seen as potentially diseased and as producing too many of the wrong kind of children.[42] White feminists like Gilman fought repressive gender roles and advocated for greater autonomy in part by targeting poor, immigrant, disabled, and non-white women through eugenic campaigns.[43] These eugenic sentiments shaped and were shaped by new literary genres, like what Dana Seitler calls "regeneration narratives," which imagined white women's healthy reproduction as racial uplift.[44] Altogether, health humanities thus shows how literary fiction like "The Yellow Wall-Paper" does not just symbolically reveal oppression but actively shapes medical discourse, both for good and ill.

## Reading for Systemic Racism

In her 2020 essay, "On No Longer Being a Hysterical Woman," Nafissa Thompson-Spires recounts a lifetime of illnesses using nineteenth-century tropes: "I have always lived in the Gothic castle of my body and brain." If a planned hysterectomy eases her symptoms, she imagines, "My friends can throw me a 'Yellow Wallpaper' party and we can alternately dance and scream-cry and creep along the baseboards." Thompson-Spires thus links her personal experience to a tradition of women's illness narratives. But not only gender shapes her illness, as she negotiates "the casual and blatant racism and misogynoir and ableism directed at a chronically ill black woman living and working in predominantly white spaces." Thompson-Spires's essay draws a line between the past and present of medical racism, writing that she has previously resisted hysterectomy because of the over-sterilization of Black women, and "because modern gynecology was founded on the torture of my ancestors, used at the whims of a sado-racist who tore apart the bodies of enslaved black women and children like wishbones."[45]

First-person autobiographical writing plays a more prominent role in the health humanities than in many other literary fields. Rebecca Garden writes that the health humanities is "in essence a form of advocacy." By focusing on individual accounts of illness as opposed to diagnoses of disease, the field assumes that autobiography provides an alternative to biomedical theories of the body. (This representational advocacy, she notes, carries the risk of misrepresentation, especially when writing about communities to which you do not belong – an important consideration for those working in the field.)[46] Because it emphasizes the social components of health, health humanities has tools for analyzing and challenging racism in US healthcare. Examining the field's foundational texts and journals, however, Olivia Banner writes that the field has largely ignored writers of color and overemphasized empathy, which "can do little to overcome the racist practices and biases embedded in medicine, which are institutionally reproduced, not intrinsic to interpersonal relations." A structurally minded health humanities, she suggests, could "foster textual readings that elucidate how ideologies of race, gender, and disability inform social, political, economic, and institutional structures, which then inform health and illness."[47] Increasingly, health humanists advocate for this turn, which has already been theorized by the literary texts themselves. Examining scholarship on Audre Lorde's cancer writings and empathy, for example, Banner argues that the field misses Lorde's call for activism against the heteronormativity of medicine and environmental racism that leaves people of color disproportionately exposed to carcinogens.[48]

In recent years, two collections of poetry have taken up the legacy of "Father of American Gynecology" J. Marion Sims, who practiced the surgical techniques for which he is now celebrated on enslaved women named Lucy, Anarcha, and Betsey. Bettina Judd's *patient* (2014) and Kwoya Fagen Maples's *Mend* (2018) weave together poems in the voices of these women with poems about present-day medical trauma. Today, infant and maternal mortality are higher for Black than white women and babies – a disparity perhaps even more pronounced now than it was during slavery.[49] Maples writes, "black women are three times more likely to die after childbirth than white women, regardless of ability to pay and regardless of prenatal care. Biases toward black bodies still exist within the medical profession that lead to such an imbalance in medical care."[50] Both collections theorize how strongly the experience of living in, and medical treatment of, individual bodies is shaped by historical structures.

Poetic form does serious work in Judd's and Maples's theories of the body in systemic racism. They use nonlinearity to grapple with the past, emphasizing how histories of medical racism remain present. Many poems in *patient.* are given dates, moving between the nineteenth- and twenty-first centuries. Its opening poem locates the reader temporally: "In 2006 I Had an Ordeal with Medicine." The timelines of the poem slip, though, as each stanza blends past tense with present: "I had an ordeal with medicine and was found innocent or guilty. It feels the same because I live in a haunted house."[51] Evoking the blame placed on Black women for their own ill health, she writes of "punishment," "Like the way the body is murdered by its own weight when lynched." Analogizing illness and lynching, the speaker situates her "ordeal" historically, using irony to redirect attention to the perpetrators of violence.

Both books incorporate historical medical texts, subordinating Sims's words to the lyrical voices of the poems. Maples's epigraph opens with historical language: "The peculiarities of diseases in negroes are so distinct-ive that they can be safely and successfully treated, as a general rule, only by southern physicians, with a southern education." Judd's book also incorpor-ates nineteenth-century voices. She opens "Betsey Invents the Speculum. Fall 1845" with Sims's description of his "discovery": "Introducing the bent handle of the spoon I saw everything as no man had ever seen before" (32). Betsey's voice in the poem that follows, though, positions her as grammatical and experimental agent: "Sims invents the speculum / I invent the wincing // the *if you must* of it / the looking away // the here of discovery" (32). Claiming Betsey as the "inventor" of a new affect, Judd makes her subject rather than object of the encounter. Judd frames the collection with a similar reversal of the subject-object dyad of medical research: "The research question is: Why am I patient?" (1) With these reversals, Judd refuses the objectification of Black women.

Emphasizing the subjectivity of Anarcha, Betsey, and Lucy, Judd and Maples challenge the idolization of abusive historical figures and call for structural changes in medicine. From its very title, *Mend* implies the possi-bility of repair. After introducing Sims in the preface, Maples writes: "Dear reader, here is my wish: that you would consider how this story relates to now. . . . Maybe, reader, with further consideration, you will see how you are connected with this story. Maybe you will honor what you come to know by sharing it" (xi–xii). The volume's opening poem "The Door" clarifies medi-cine's destructive power by introducing Sims's speculum and closing with the sinking knowledge that this doctor is working to no therapeutic ends: "and she knows / she's not here / for mending" (3). The mending that does take place comes instead from care of the self and the care of a family. The final poem, "My Mother Bathes Me after I Give Birth," fulfills the promise of mending in the title, as her mother swaddles her in towels after a birth that left her daughters in the NICU. The last line of the collection reads, "her touch says I am worth tenderness" (72).

Judd, Maples, and Thompson-Spires theorize the structural racism of the healthcare system by placing it in continuity with the historical abuses that enabled the growth of the medical field. The texts refuse to allow history to be read as a narrative of medical progress, as the reader is moved back and forth between present and past at the level of the volume and the level of the poem – and sometimes even sentence – itself. They make clear that humanistic approaches to health must go beyond empathy and interpersonal relationships: These works call for structural change and historical redress. Jonathan Metzl and Helena Hansen have argued that healthcare needs to look beyond "cultural competency" frameworks that "train doctors to listen to individualized stories" and to focus instead on "structural competency," which would deemphasize how stigma is created in individual relationships to consider injustice at the level of institutions.[52]

Literary scholar and bioethicist Karla F. C. Holloway makes a similar case in her theorization of a "cultural ethics," where she argues that "narrative medicine cannot ignore the intersections and histories embedded in the thick cultures within science, medicine, law, and society that have produced the very stories that are of such interest to the field."[53] Rather than the abstraction of a "patient's story," she uses literature as a method to examine the "architectures of knowledge and its forms of production."[54] Drawing together historical and contemporary legal and bioethical cases with analyses of literary works, Holloway argues that fiction can counter the objectification of the case study genre by rendering its subjects "complex and elusive, rather than readily available."[55] Filled with a chorus of "complex and elusive" voices, shifting temporalities that demand contemporary redress for historical wrongs, and lyrical explorations of the subjectivity of those often forgotten, books by Judd and Maples demonstrate Metzl's assertion that "like any stories, structures are thus subject to revision through imagination, reparation, and transformation."[56]

## Conclusion

In Edgar Allan Poe's short story "The Masque of the Red Death" (1842), the "happy and dauntless and sagacious" Prince Prospero retreats with his court to a secluded abbey where they can wait out a dramatic "pestilence" with "all the appliances of pleasure." In the face of this disease, "A strong and lofty wall girdled it in. This wall had gates of iron." At the conclusion of a phantasmagoric masquerade ball, the personification of the Red Death appears, and the revelers all, of course, die.[57] The illusion of safety and the attempt at segregation from the diseased commoners results in the dramatic death of those who imagined they could separate themselves from the problems of the broader public. This story has struck a chord with contemporary readers and has been cited in articles about the COVID-19 epidemic taking place at the time this chapter is being written, as in *Slate*'s "The Rich Can't Hide from the Plague. Just Ask Edgar Allan Poe" and the *New York Times*'s "What Can We Learn from the Art of Pandemics Past?"[58]

Readers turn to literature to find meaning, or at least a grim familiarity, in the face of illness. Among the things that we can learn from the literature of illness is that stories can bring people together, offering a sense of connection and shared experience in difficult times. But they can also create greater distance, reifying and dramatizing difference. In the twentieth and twenty-first centuries, narratives and films about disease often begin with the "emergence" of a new outbreak in the supposedly "primitive" practices of communities in Asia and Africa.[59] And as Silva notes, although epidemics move transnationally, theoretically unifying the globe through mutual vulnerability, "pathogens reify the very nationalist impulses they undermine."[60] This xenophobia is apparent in President Trump's insistence on speaking of COVID-19 as "The Chinese Virus" or the "Wuhan Virus" – and Asian Americans have correspondingly reported an increase in racist encounters.[61]

Like Rush reading Defoe in the eighteenth century, our ideas about health and illness are shaped by the narratives we hear and read. Representations of illness reveal (and create) cultural attitudes; these attitudes and narratives are not just discursive but have real impacts on bodies and minds. Literature can promote empathy but also deny it; it can render some characters as deserving of care and others as deserving of scorn; it can revel in ambiguity or offer a dangerously simple narrative; it can challenge racism, sexism, or xenophobia, or reify it, suggesting that certain kinds of people are pathological. Literary scholars thus offer an important perspective to the health humanities, which needs to grapple with literature's capacity to stereotype as well as to "humanize" the reader.

## NOTES

1 Rush's copy of [Daniel Defoe], *A Journal of the Plague Year* (London: E. Nutt, 1722) is in the collections of The Library Company of Philadelphia. Although the volume was published pseudonymously, Rush penned in Defoe's name on page 287, and his index follows.
2 Therese Jones et al., "The Almost Right Word: The Move from Medical to Health Humanities," *Academic Medicine* 92, no. 7 (July 2017): 933.
3 Tod Chambers, "Literature," in *Methods in Medical Ethics*, ed. Jeremy Sugarman and Daniel Sulmasy, 2nd ed. (Washington, DC: Georgetown University Press, 2010), 160.
4 Jones et al., "The Almost Right Word," 934.
5 William Viney, Felicity Callard, and Angela Woods, "Critical Medical Humanities: Embracing Entanglement, Taking Risks," *Medical Humanities* 41, no. 1 (June 2015): 2–7.
6 Sarah Gentry Lamb, Sarah Berry, and Therese Jones, *Health Humanities Baccalaureate Programs in the United States* (Cleveland, OH: Case Western Reserve University, March 2020), 7.
7 Viney et al., "Critical Medical Humanities," 3.
8 Arthur Kleinman, *The Illness Narratives* (New York: Basic Books, 1988), 55; Arthur Frank, *The Wounded Storyteller*, 2nd ed. (Chicago: University of Chicago Press, 2013).
9 Kathryn Montgomery Hunter, *Doctors' Stories: The Narrative Structure of Medical Knowledge* (Princeton, NJ: Princeton University Press, 1991), 5.

10  Rita Charon, *Narrative Medicine: Honoring the Stories of Illness* (Oxford: Oxford University Press, 2008).

11  Sari Altschuler, *The Medical Imagination: Literature and Health in the Early United States* (Philadelphia: University of Pennsylvania Press, 2018), 20.

12  Elaine Showalter, *Hystories* (New York: Columbia University Press, 1997), 6.

13  Cynthia Davis, *Bodily and Narrative Forms: The Influence of Medicine on American Literature, 1845–1918* (Stanford, CA: Stanford University Press, 2000); Priscilla Wald, *Contagious: Cultures, Carriers, and the Outbreak Narrative* (Durham, NC: Duke University Press, 2008).

14  Ann Jurecic, *Illness as Narrative* (Pittsburgh, PA: University of Pittsburgh Press, 2012), 15.

15  Cristobal Silva, *Miraculous Plagues: An Epidemiology of Early New England Narrative* (Oxford: Oxford University Press, 2011), 11.

16  Wald, *Contagious*, 2, 3.

17  Elizabeth Outka, *Viral Modernism: The Influenza Pandemic and Interwar Literature* (New York: Columbia University Press, 2019), 4.

18  Bryan Waterman, "Arthur Mervyn's Medical Repository and the Early Republic's Knowledge Industries," *American Literary History* 15, no. 2 (2003): 213–247; Altschuler, *Medical Imagination*, chaps. 1 and 2. For a survey of medical and disability approaches to early American literature, see Sari Altschuler, "Medicine, Disability, and Early American Literature," in *A Companion to American Literature*, ed. Susan Belasco, Theresa Strouth Gaul, Linck Johnson, and Michael Soto (Hoboken, NJ: John Wiley & Sons, Ltd, 2020), 462–477.

19  Altschuler, *Medical Imagination*, 65.

20  Charles Brockden Brown, *Arthur Mervyn; or, Memoirs of the Year 1793* (Philadelphia: H. Maxwell, 1799), v.

21  Justine S. Murison, *The Politics of Anxiety in Nineteenth-Century American Literature* (Cambridge: Cambridge University Press, 2011), 5.

22  Brown, *Arthur Mervyn; or, Memoirs of the Year 1793*, 133.

23  Waterman, "*Arthur Mervyn's* Medical Repository," 231.

24  Brown, *Arthur Mervyn; or, Memoirs of the Year 1793*, 131–132.

25  Philip Barnard and Stephen Shapiro, Introduction to *Arthur Mervyn; or, Memoirs of the Year 1793: With Related Texts*, by Charles Brockden Brown (Indianapolis, IN: Hackett Publishing Company, 2008), xxiii. Maureen Tuthill, *Health and Sickness in the Early American Novel: Social Affection and Eighteenth-Century Medicine* (London: Palgrave Macmillan, 2016), 108.

26  Brown, *Arthur Mervyn; or, Memoirs of the Year 1793*, 193.

27  Barnard and Shapiro, "Introduction," xxiii; on racial theories of yellow fever, see Rana Hogarth, *Medicalizing Blackness: Making Racial Difference in the Atlantic World, 1780–1840* (Chapel Hill: University of North Carolina Press, 2017), chaps. 1 and 2; Altschuler, *Medical Imagination*, chap. 2.

28  Derrick R. Spires, *The Practice of Citizenship: Black Politics and Print Culture in the Early United States* (Philadelphia: University of Pennsylvania Press, 2019), 48.

29  Brown, *Arthur Mervyn; or, Memoirs of the Year 1793*, 144, 153.

30  Hogarth, *Medicalizing Blackness*; Barbara Ehrenreich and Deidre English, *Complaints and Disorders*, 2nd ed. (New York: Feminist Press, 2011).

31 Dana Seitler, "Unnatural Selection: Mothers, Eugenic Feminism, and Charlotte Perkins Gilman's Regeneration Narratives," *American Quarterly* 55, no. 1 (2003): 77.

32 Quoted in Tom Lutz, *American Nervousness, 1903* (Ithaca, NY: Cornell University Press, 1991), 4.

33 For an overview of the rest cure, see Anne Stiles, "The Rest Cure, 1873–1925," in *BRANCH: Britain, Representation and Nineteenth-Century History*, ed. Dino Franco Felluga, September 25, 2014. Mitchell did not always use the rest cure for women, and he sometimes used it for men. See Nancy Cervetti, *S. Weir Mitchell, 1829–1914: Philadelphia's Literary Physician* (University Park: Pennsylvania State University Press, 2012), 109.

34 S. Weir Mitchell, *Doctor and Patient* (Philadelphia: J. B. Lippincott & Co., 1888).

35 Susan S. Lanser, "Feminist Criticism, 'The Yellow Wallpaper,' and the Politics of Color in America," *Feminist Studies* 15, no. 3 (1989): 418. This is Lanser's summation of the interpretations of others.

36 Susan Sontag, *Illness as Metaphor and AIDS and Its Metaphors* (New York: Picador, 2001).

37 Marta Caminero-Santangelo, *The Madwoman Can't Speak: Or Why Insanity Is Not Subversive* (Ithaca, NY: Cornell University Press, 1998); Elizabeth Donaldson, "Revisiting the Corpus of the Madwoman," in *Feminist Disability Studies*, ed. Kim Q. Hall (Bloomington: Indiana University Press, 2011), 91–114.

38 Charlotte Perkins Gilman, *Herland, the Yellow Wall-Paper, and Selected Writings*, ed. Denise D. Knight (New York: Penguin Books, 1999), 166.

39 Julie Bates Dock et al., "'But One Expects That': Charlotte Perkins Gilman's 'The Yellow Wallpaper' and the Shifting Light of Scholarship," *PMLA*, 111, no. 1 (1996): 52–65.

40 Jane F. Thrailkill, "Doctoring 'The Yellow Wallpaper,'" *ELH* 69, no. 2 (2002): 525–566.

41 Lanser, "Feminist Criticism," 430.

42 Barbara Ehrenreich and Deidre English, *Complaints and Disorders*, 2nd ed. (New York: Feminist Press, 2011 [1973]), 45.

43 Seitler, "Unnatural Selection," 64.

44 Ibid., 62.

45 Nafissa Thompson-Spires, "On No Longer Being a Hysterical Woman," The Paris Review (blog), January 6, 2020.

46 Rebecca Garden, "Who Speaks for Whom? Health Humanities and the Ethics of Representation," *Medical Humanities* 41, no. 2 (2015): 77–80, https://doi.org/10.1136/medhum-2014-010642.

47 Olivia Banner, "Structural Racism and Practices of Reading in the Medical Humanities," *Literature and Medicine* 34, no. 1 (2016): 27.

48 Ibid., 31.

49 Deirdre Cooper Owens and Sharla M. Fett, "Black Maternal and Infant Health: Historical Legacies of Slavery," *American Journal of Public Health* 100, no. 10 (October 2019): 1343.

50 Kwoya Fagin Maples, *Mend* (Lexington: University Press of Kentucky, 2018), xi–xii.

51 Bettina Judd, *Patient* (New York: Black Lawrence Press, 2014), 1.

52  Jonathan M. Metzl and Helena Hansen, "Structural Competency: Theorizing a New Medical Engagement with Stigma and Inequality," *Social Science & Medicine, Structural Stigma and Population Health* 103 (2014): 128.

53  Karla F. C. Holloway, *Private Bodies, Public Texts: Race, Gender, and a Cultural Bioethics* (Durham, NC: Duke University Press, 2011), xvii.

54  Ibid., xvi.

55  Ibid., xvii.

56  Jonathan M. Metzl, "Structural Competency," *American Quarterly* 64, no. 2 (2012): 217.

57  Edgar Allan Poe, "The Masque of the Red Death," Edgar Allan Poe Museum, accessed March 24, 2020, www.poemuseum.org/the-masque-of-the-red-death.

58  Maya Phillips, "The Rich Can't Hide from a Plague. Just Ask Edgar Allan Poe," *Slate Magazine*, March 26, 2020; Megan O'Grady, "What Can We Learn from the Art of Pandemics Past?," *The New York Times*, April 8, 2020, sec. T Magazine.

59  Wald, *Contagious*, 8.

60  Silva, *Miraculous Plagues*, 9.

61  Eren Orbey, "Trump's 'Chinese Virus' and What's at Stake in the Coronavirus's Name," *The New Yorker*, accessed March 27, 2020; Cathy Park Hong, "The Slur I Never Expected to Hear in 2020," *The New York Times Magazine*, April 12, 2020.

# 14

SEAN TEUTON

# The Indigenous Body in
# American Literature

In Leslie Marmon Silko's landmark novel *Ceremony* (1977), Tayo – a
Laguna man socially disfigured by losing his mother, suffering racism, and
surviving combat in World War II – finally recovers his body by making love
with T'seh, a mysterious woman living atop a sacred mountain. As Tayo's
journey to this place becomes more mystical by the day, we come to believe
this injured man has entered a mythic land, where the Laguna rain deity
takes him into her arms and melds him to women and earth:

> He was afraid of being lost, so he repeated trail marks to himself: this is my
> mouth tasting the salt of her brown breasts; this is my voice calling out to her.
> He eased himself deeper within her and felt the warmth close around him like
> river sand, softly giving way under foot, then closing firmly around the ankle in
> cloudy warm water.[1]

In this celebrated passage, through bodily experience Tayo recovers not only
intimacy with women but indeed, through women, a relationship with
Laguna ancestral land itself. Yet while the trusting body, no longer fearing
loss, serves as the vehicle for 1970s-era calls for liberation of Indigenous
communities and lands, the passage today appears male-centered and indul-
gent of an idealized erotic Indigenous body.

In later Native-authored works, however, the Indigenous body takes
shape in more complex spaces, in which bodies, especially women's bodies,
are not only the source of sexual pleasure or maternal reconciliation, but are
also colonized, idealized, feared, or hated. Linda Hogan's *Power* (1998)
places us in the Florida Everglades, where the endangered panther aligns
with the struggle of the fictional Taiga people who, like the panther, have
been driven from their ancestral lands in the wake of conquest. Sixteen-year-
old Omishto lives in fear of her white stepfather Herm, who hunts her body
with his eyes. So when not in school Omishto spends her time with Ama, a
tribal member her mother's age who lives alone in the neighboring swamp,
on the border of Taiga land. Says Omishto: "Sometimes I love [Ama], and in

those moments I think the gap between her teeth is beautiful. But there are other times I don't even like her, and on those days I think she's ugly .... It's when I've come from school I'm most likely to find her homely and strange" (19).[2] Here the novel lays bare the colonizing force to degrade Indigenous bodies, especially through public education. Later, *Power* shares a moment with the earlier *Ceremony*, but now that bodily process of belonging to land – Indigenizing – operates more honestly; that is, in a manner that recognizes the complexity of human embodiment to include not only youthful and romantic embrace but also impaired and painful struggle, in which Indigenous bodies are often objects of colonialism. Omishto finds herself now the caretaker of Ama's home: "I fix myself a bed on the floor and I lie down, close to the earth. I am something dim inside my own memory. I know that not even the mind of the world, the heart of the waters, can distinguish the shape of what's fallen over me."[3] Omishto, described as thin and brown, escapes the city and school to revalue her Native self. The process may be as mystified as Tayo's bodily immersion in land, but, in this woman-centered event, Omishto lies not on the ground but on a floor, in a nonidealized body, and begins not with trusting but with forgetting. She releases not to an erotic moment but to the forces of the earth, who begin to reshape her in the realm of possibility and freedom. The novels above, then, express the strides in our representations of the Indigenous body, but they also stress our need to imagine more honest and realistic Native bodies to serve actual Indigenous lives and nations.

## Identity and the Native Body

To begin we must recast racist imaginings about Native bodily inferiority, a damaging colonial legacy that continues stubbornly to function in American literature to present the dichotomously perfect or fallen Indigenous body: Still today, it too often asks readers either to revere a romanticized and pristine pre-contact Indigenous body, or to pity or fear a broken, tainted, even monstrous Native body. Yet as colonialism pervades the permeable border between settler and Indigenous states, so does dominant thinking also affect the Native world, in which Indigenous people at times internalize and reproduce distorted perceptions of the ideal Indigenous body. For this reason, critique of this ideology of Indigenous corporeal perfection engenders the potential to imagine a "new" Native body, one perhaps better connected to traditional models of wellness but also more realistically and honestly placed in more inclusive literary and lived realities. With that new Indigenous body and a politics of identity and sovereign nationhood to serve it, scholars in both Indigenous and American literary studies may better theoretically justify their work for justice.

As an unavoidable source of social, sexual, and political knowledge, the Native body confounds as often as it energizes literary studies, for though the body must mediate our thoughts and perceptions about the world, it is by no means a stable agent of knowledge. The Indigenous body does political work in the very act of representing itself, resisting language that misrepresents its actual flesh with dominating words that attempt to define, contain, control, and thus colonize it. Consider the embodied lives of Native prisoners, a group of whom I taught for several years. In the United States, citizens are imprisoned less to remove a danger from society than to punish them for their convicted crimes. For this punishment, prison pursues the mind by serving up a good deal of mental anguish, but it abuses the body most visibly. From beatings and rape right down to the deprivation of nutrition, sleep, medicine, and privacy, prison brutalizes the human body beyond repair. Yet Native flesh resists: The Indigenous men with whom I worked limped lightly into the classroom by cane and smiled through lost teeth as they wrote with shaky hands.[4] Attention to the body grounds linguistically driven views that groups of bodies comprise societies in a merely constructed way. If we acknowledge identity as an embodied category, the body itself can serve identity-based struggles for social and anticolonial justice.

Scholars theorizing the body, however, often trace a critique of embodied identity that targets this acknowledgement. Tobin Siebers, to whose work this essay is deeply indebted, announces one source of resistance to theories of identity grounded in bodily realities: "[I]dentity is seen as a crutch for the person who needs extra help . . .. I use the word 'crutch' on purpose because the attack on identity is best understood in the context of disability";[5] in part, Siebers suggests, attacks on claims to embodied identities assume that bodies in need of identity claims function improperly. Other scholars, such as Linda Martín Alcoff, trace the challenge to identity back to the Enlightenment, when such philosophers as Descartes advanced a model of rational autonomy that excluded bodily function.[6] Elevating the power to reason, European thinkers often targeted non-Europeans and especially differently embodied tribal peoples as innately intellectually inferior. Rather abruptly race became inextricably tied to mental defect and defect to the social exclusion of bodies.[7] For this reason, majority bodies do not undergo the same scrutiny as minority bodies do. European bodies, with their ties to colonialism, patriarchy, and ecological destruction, remain the most empowered embodied identity the world over and seldom suffer from identity critiques. Whiteness relies on the unacknowledged privilege of occupying an unlimited, unmarked category; it does not rely on essential qualities but adapts and absorbs other groups to sustain its power. Unmarked and thus allowed to thrive in a dominant location, embodiment of white racial identity remains untouchable.[8]

From a bodily perspective, the West's centuries-long attack on Indigenous identity gains further complexity. For decades, scholars have relied on the dichotomy between civilization and savagism to best understand the European obsession with colonizing Native people.[9] More recently, the inclusion of gender in this paradigm has helped explain the Western perception of Indigenous land as a resistant woman to be subdued.[10] A theory of the body might go even further to show how Europeans, in perception and policy, viewed Indigenous people as physically defective. For centuries Western Europe operated on the medical model of the ideal body, which held that modern medicine could fix or cure defective bodies to grant minorities fuller status as human beings. On this belief, settler-colonial governments composed policies arguing either that Native people were too defective to be repaired and thus should be displaced beyond the reach of civilization, or that they were indeed within repair and that state-sponsored programs, from eugenics to medicine to education, could meet this challenge.

No Indigenous person needs reminding that altering culturally located bodily practices became and remains a primary means of destroying or "fixing" Native identities: The civilization program begun in the 1790s planned to replace Indigenous ceremonial dances with Christian kneeling and bison hunting using horse and spear with the planting of agricultural furrows dug by placing seeds behind horse and plow; the boarding and residential schools of the 1870s sought to reprogram generations of Native bodies to stop speaking their first languages and retrain them toward European speech and labor practices; the allotment legislation begun in the 1880s endeavored to transform communal peoples into individual yeoman farmers with alienable property rights; citizenship in 1924 and tribal termination and relocation in the 1950s sought finally to remove Native bodies from tribal lands. Whatever the program, Indian policy often relied on an implicit inferior-body model to justify its treatment of Indigenous people. During allotment, for instance, agents required a minimum of European blood to deem Indigenous applicants competent, trustworthy landowners. In the 1970s, the Indian Health Service (IHS) dealt with this assumed bodily inferiority through eugenics, by secretly sterilizing at least 25% of Native women patients between the ages of 15 and 44.[11]

To resist these policies, Native people embraced their traditional views of the body. More than just "wounded attachments,"[12] as Wendy Brown terms them, identities function like theories, organizing and interpreting human experience. Minority identity need not rely on essentialism for its claims, let alone notions of bodily suffering and subjugation. Instead, it is an interpretive framework for the production of knowledge; identities in fact yield theories for living in and understanding the world. Like all theories, identities can produce misguided knowledge, but they can also reform, the better to explain life's experiences. Indigenous identities connect Native people with histories and lands, families and nations that enrich and explain our lives.[13] Indigenous identities gain richness through their inextricable links to bodily practice and experience. Bodily changes, such as those that occur through aging, complicate all identities. Emphasis on bodily aspects of identity reveals more complex social locations surrounding race, gender, sexuality, nation, or land.[14] Functioning in reciprocal dialogue with Native identity, the body can only add color to our vision of the Indigenous world.

## Colonizing the Indigenous Body

Many Indigenous people who have different bodies nonetheless view their bodies in a positive light. An Ojibway woman who uses a wheelchair might enjoy her pace of life; a Comanche elder with low vision may nonetheless appreciate his different connection with the world. It can be a point of pride to love one's body just as it is. This corporeal truth reveals one of the many contradictions in our views of the body, especially in a society so often dedicated to producing the ideal body. We tend to view the existence of bodily pain as negative, for instance, but acknowledge that no alteration of the built environment will guarantee its eradication.[15] That said, the exclusion of those with disabilities cannot be tolerated in any just society. Such contradictions alert us to the social place of ideology and force us to realize the mediated nature of narratives of the body's place in society. Native people moreover struggle to free visions of the body from centuries-old ideologies casting the colonized body as defective and curable through sheer human will or the miracles of medicine. Revalued as a reciprocal component of Indigenous identity, we can retheorize the Native body to perform anticolonial resistance.

A new, anticolonial view of the Native body, however, labors beneath the problem that theories of the body always self-contradict, as in the example above, in which bodily pain cannot but must be eradicated.[16] To pose another example, we can all recall a time when we were ill. When the body serves us well enough, it seems hardly to exist. Indeed, it seems to function only as an invisible vehicle of our thought and will. But the moment an injury or illness occurs, the body suddenly takes form. The body now appears as a victim we must save, or even an enemy that we vow to appease the day we recover. That the body can be both an inconsequential cipher and a betraying villain declares a deep contradiction. Ideology attempts to resolve these contradictions through naturalizing narratives that brush over flaws in the picture of human bodily perfection. In the story produced by this ideology, human bodily pain is intolerable, for instance, and has no place in the ideal body. Those intolerant of any type of pain often state that they would rather die than have a permanent injury, or that they wish to die before aging, for ageism is also a part of this ideology. Many theorists hold little hope of overcoming such ideology, arguing that it permeates and structures a world out of which we cannot step. In his assessment of this ideology in disability studies, Siebers disagrees with these theorists, contending that, because the ideology of ability excludes the disabled from the purview of its operation, in these marginalized social locations embodied identities may make claims to knowledge about that disabling world and the society that constructs it.[17] To illustrate, consider a brief history of the perfect Indigenous body.

By the nineteenth century, earlier European views of the idealized Native body moving in harmony with nature often gave way to perceptions that the Indigenous body represented humans in an earlier state of social evolution, as imperfect anachronisms doomed to extinction in the wake of modern, perfected man.[18] Indeed, this narrative of human evolution still holds sway in settler-colonial North America, where notions of American Progress drive technology and medicine in a near desperate attempt to perfect the human body – or return it to its imagined pre-contact, prelapsarian state. Traditional notions of the Native body as not perfectible but sustainable, in fact, disrupt this Progress narrative, and place bodies within larger Native views of the environment.

Consider the watercolor paintings of John White (1540–c.1593), the first known depictions by a European of Indigenous people in North America. White served as official mapmaker and painter for the Grenville expedition to found a colony on Roanoke Island, North Carolina, in 1585. Most known among his many depictions of the Algonkian people of the Carolina coast is the portrait "The Flyer." One glance at the painting confirms the title's description; White wishes to establish for Indigenes such ethnographic categories as mother, warrior, or healer, with the "The Flyer" clearly representing the latter. But, though the painter witnessed and recorded the actual lives of Indigenous people, "The Flyer" stands more like Mercury in classic pose. Indeed, it is as if White begins with this classic form, then adorns it with dark skin, a bird headdress, an animal-skin breech cloth, and a medicine bag. The healer looks away from the viewer, docile and light of foot, his delicate hands free of weapons. In this first known depiction by a

European of an American Indigenous body, we may read all that Europeans hope to find in the New World: a new Eden where the perfect, unfallen human body thrives in innocence. The European view of the Native body as human perfection continues into the eighteenth century – in the writings of Thomas Jefferson, for example, who says we cannot "condemn the Indians of the continent as wanting genius"[19] – then moves through the nineteenth century – in the writings of George Catlin, for example, who celebrates the "tall and graceful form of a huge Indian."[20]

We find the inverse of this Edenic Indigenous body in equally prevalent images of the monstrous Indigenous body, from Shakespeare's flesh-devouring cannibal Caliban to Cooper's plotting warrior Magua to the bright-red skin and jeer of the Cleveland Indians' Chief Wahoo. At times drawing on the watercolors of John White, Flemish engraver Theodore de Bry (1528–1598) illustrated *America*, a multivolume account of the New World. Within its pages one finds the grisly depiction of Native bodily decay. Indigenes' breasts sag and jaws gape as they gnaw on themselves. In one engraving, the Tupinamba of Brazil celebrate the destruction of European bodies, the Native people themselves decomposing bodily in the process. This disability image of the Indigenous body resurges in the nineteenth-century United States, when colonial settlers wished to acquire more land and finally destroy or confine Indigenous people. Read in the midst of the 1830s Removal era, James Fenimore Cooper's *The Last of the Mohicans* (1826) presents Magua, perhaps the best-known villain in American litera-ture.[21] Over and over again, Magua's savage and hateful behavior is tied to his deformed body, in nineteenth-century terms of bodily abnormality. Cooper, however, clearly names colonialism as the cause of Magua's disab-ling alcoholism. Indeed, in the 1992 film version of the story, Hawkeye, played by Daniel Day Lewis, declares of Magua, played by Wes Studi: "Magua's heart is twisted. He would make himself into what twisted him." The invocation of a "twisted," damaged heart and body unmistakably calls up the colonizing ideology of bodies. The Native body as decayed and deformed, savage and hateful remains with us today in American mascots. Most infamously, Chief Wahoo of the Cleveland Indians jeers at his oppon-ents through bright-red skin and enormous white teeth. First used in 1947 and, after numerous social and legal protests, finally staged for retirement, Chief Wahoo may well present the most popular – and thus most internal-ized – image of the colonized Native body, one that implicitly reduces Indigenous people to defective though fierce bodily objects.

Among Indigenous portrayals of the body, from the earliest texts in oral literature, ideas about corporeal perfection invest a Native body that is challenged to see, hear, or speak, impaired at birth or wounded from war or the hunt. Recall perhaps the best-known oral narrative of the Iroquois Gayanashagowa or Great Law of Peace.[22] The prophet Deganawida or Peacemaker travels throughout the Northeast to bring warring nations together in peace. Deganawida is said to have a speech impediment and thus relies on the assistance of Hayanwatah to communicate his powerful message on humanity, reason, and governance. Though known throughout the world for their oratorical power, the Six Nations received their greatest oratorical message from an assisted person with a speech disability. Other great messages have come from speakers with hindered bodies. In his effort to unite woodland peoples against the advancing colonists, Tecumseh received divine guidance from his brother, Tenskwatawa or The Prophet, who was blind in one eye. And Sequoyah, who brought a written language to the Cherokees, was said to have been born with an impaired leg.

In other tribal traditions disability results from an accident but nonetheless confers a secret strength. In the Blackfeet story of Soatsaki or Feather Woman, as related in James Welch's *Fools Crow* (1987), the deeply scarred Poia or Scar Face reunites sky and earth people through the gift of the Sun Dance. Or consider the Crow story of Lost Boy, as told in Frank Linderman's *Pretty Shield: Medicine Woman of the Crows* (1932). At eleven years old, a boy burns his face in a fire, is permanently scarred, and leaves home from shame. Years later, some women from his community seek refuge in the mountains, where they discover Lost Boy living with the Little People in a rock wall: "Without speaking, without even looking at the women, he cut off the elk's hindquarters, shouldered the rest, as though it were nothing at all – and then stepped off the canyon's rim into the air that was streaked with sunlight."[23] In many oral traditions, a bodily obstacle paradoxically becomes a source of power.

Yet too often in the Indigenous novel, the body is idealized as a formerly beautiful, now broken, object. By participating in this romanticized vision of the previously perfect Indigenous body, Native writers risk serving the desires of mainstream readers who imagine a pristine pre-contact Indigenous body – a stranger to disease, over six feet tall, faster than a speeding arrow, able to leap tall canyons in a single bound – in contrast to the post-contact, fallen Indigenous body that cannot help but confirm the decline of Native people in North America today. Of course, Indigenes, from the stage to the arena, for profit and for joy, have frequently traded in these utopian or dystopian visions of the Native body.[24] In *House Made of Dawn* (1968), N. Scott Momaday presents a paradisial body in the character of Abel, a Pueblo man physically damaged by a police beating: "Once he could have run all day, really run, not jogging but moving fast over distances, without ruining his feet or burning himself out."[25] Momaday's imagined body glides Catlin-like over the buffaloed plains, the dream body twin of the nightmare body that emerges only pages later: "Abel's face was cut and broken .... [H]is hands ... were twisted and mangled, the thumbs splayed back and broken at the joints."[26] Foucault has argued that the premodern body bore the "natural" signs of strength and valor. In the modern age, he claims, the human body has become a piece of "formless clay,"[27] awaiting direction by the machines that transform and improve it. Scholars in Native studies will discern Foucault's unspoken timeline from the unfallen, "natural" Indigenous body to the fallen, mechanically directed Indigenous body. The end of *House Made of Dawn* shows Abel recovering his idealized Native body. In so doing, the novel appears to follow the progress narrative of the American novel, in which bodies are broken, then fixed.

In Native literature, however, the Indigenous body is still most often celebrated as a source of pleasure. Let us recall the poetic pleasure in lines about a responsive, supple body that serves as a map to new lands and ideas but is also home to lovers and even ancestors. In *A Map to the Next World* (2000), Joy Harjo enlists the Indigenous body to achieve this very heightened erotic and mystical experience: "In the dark I travel by instinct ... along your body's horizon."[28] Though justifiably enraptured by the thrill of bodily pleasure, security, and freedom, such literatures of bodily joy perhaps consciously overlook the body's inevitable physical limitations.

## The New Indigenous Body

Native writers continue to seek a "new" Indigenous body, a complex embodiment that declares and resists disabling colonialism, on the one hand, but also acknowledges the spectrum of human variation and limits to human ability, on the other. Most importantly, the impaired Indigene is reconceived as enmeshed in a broader human community that must reckon with variously embodied experiences and the knowledge these produce. Perhaps the most painful image in the Indigenous novel is that of Yellow Kidney in James Welch's *Fools Crow* (1987), the story of a Blackfeet community that, in 1870, struggles to negotiate colonial change. On Yellow Kidney's capture in a horse raid on the Crow, Crow leaders cut off his fingers and send him to wander. It is a long and mythic journey home, and Yellow Kidney is forever changed by his disfigurement. No longer able to hunt for his family nor even properly to fill his pipe, he feels emasculated and dehumanized, and descends into depression, which he describes as the "familiar tightness behind [the] eyes" of a "near-man."[29] Like Scar Face, silently he leaves his Lone Eaters community forever. But as he waits out a blizzard in a distant lodge, he decides to return: "Yellow Kidney ... had gotten used to having no fingers, but most things were still difficult .... Still, he was pleased that he could get along. Since leaving the Lone Eaters camp, he had been finding more and more that he could do things if he did them deliberately and without haste .... He no longer felt that it was necessary to go to the camp of the Spotted Horse people to die. He had lost much honor with his own people, but he no longer felt pitiful and worthless."[30]

Yellow Kidney's impairment is a painful material fact difficult to fetishize as a source of new knowledge, or as an emblem of anticolonial resistance or Native cyborg freedom. Instead, he must learn to live with both his physical pain and his mental anguish, as a person who feels dehumanized and without a community. No doubt such feelings about the condition of his body are the product of social forces that operate both through the Lone Eater community and within Yellow Kidney's own subjectivity. And yet there is something profoundly rooting about the body and its condition that troubles the way scholars describe the extremely determining mechanism of ideology on the human subject. In working to understand social ideas about the body and ability in our actual lives, we can develop a flesh theory of the self in society that better addresses what we commonly call reality. As such, theories of embodiment have much to offer Indigenous studies, a field that has also struggled to be recognized as theoretically sophisticated while community driven, or to be recognized at all.

Yellow Kidney and his damaged body test whether such figures can ever embody a celebrated boundary-busting liberation. His shocking fingerless hands make us turn away yet desire to stare, as we both identify and disidentify with his body and our own inevitable decline in bodies that wear out. Yellow Kidney displays many of the features of the resistant body – yet somehow his body does not transgress a dominant society or colonial regime. Indeed, a scholar would have to work very hard to remove Yellow Kidney from his suffering and to celebrate his resistance. This is so because the body in pain defies hasty theorization by insisting that we hear and see it as a material fact. Siebers defends this philosophical realism:

> [I] am not claiming either that the body exists apart from social forces or that it represents something more "real," "natural," or "authentic" than things of culture. I am claiming that the body has its own forces and that we need to recognize them if we are to get a less one-sided picture of how bodies and their representations affect each other for good and for bad.[31]

Such scholars make visible our own inevitable bodily changes, a visibility that new views of the body within Native literature often seek to expose.

Only recently have we begun to see individual, defective bodies not as sicknesses to be cured but as collective realities to be addressed by civil rights and access to a more livable built environment. In the same manner, scholars in Indigenous studies pay attention when Native communities ask not to be modernized and absorbed, American style, but instead call for bodily sustainability in all its manifestations. The Global Institute of Sustainability defines sustainability as "development that meets the needs of the present without compromising the ability of future generations to meet their own needs." The federal Environmental Protection Agency (EPA) defines sustainability as "the study of the interconnectedness of all things." This latter definition of sustainability aligns with Native theories of the body, in which individual progress and its accommodation are not the primary goals as much as human recognition, interdependence, and inclusive community.

In Indigenous literature, such models for body sustainability appear in characters that recognize their own corporeal fragility as part of a larger process that involves other kinsmen both young and old, and even the natural world itself. In James Welch's *Winter in the Blood* (1974), the narrator begins to discover that connection with the sightless elder Yellow Calf: "[I]t was his eyes, narrow beneath the loose skin of his lids, deep behind his cheekbones, that made one realize the old man's distance was permanent. It was behind those misty white eyes that gave off no light that he lived, a world as clean as the rustling willows, the bark of a fox or the odor of musk during mating season."[32] With his deeply sensory experience of sound and scent, Yellow Calf sustains himself as a man permanently tied to a particular piece of land. In more recent novels, Native bodies are again scarred with painful colonial histories but nonetheless often accept these wounds not as secret strengths but as realities to account for and include in our shared histories, such as in the scarred bodily past of Angela Jensen in Linda Hogan's *Solar Storms* (1995).[33] A closer look at Indigenous literature often portrays broken bodies as the consequence of labor exploitation. In David Treuer's *The Hiawatha* (2000), One-Two is permanently injured by daring to work the iron and falling hundreds of feet from the sky.[34] This disabling colonial history and its ongoing societal obstructions continue to restrict the Indigenous body. Yet when the disobedient skin finally speaks, we discover a fuller spectrum of human variation that cannot be entirely "fixed" by decolonization. Instead, Native and non-Native bodies alike feel pain through injury or age in North America as a part of complex embodiment. And ultimately it is the Indigenous community that enables a new vision of the Native body to serve the expansion of Native national sovereignty.

## An Indigenous Body to Build Indigenous Nations

In 1806, Thomas Jefferson sent Meriweather Lewis and William Clark with a letter to establish trade and diplomacy with the tribes that, in his view, resided in lands newly acquired for the United States from France. In that letter, he promised those Indian nations: "Your blood will run in our veins" (December 21, 1808). Perhaps Jefferson believed he was being generous with Indigenous people in his willingness to intermarry, thus allowing them, if only in blood, to become part of America. In the historical moment, it is a curious promise but, looking back, it is an ominous threat. It was just the beginning of what Frederick Hoxie calls "a final promise"[35] to destroy tribalism, divide and sell Indigenous lands, and absorb Native people into the mass of American society. By the passing of the General Allotment or Dawes Act in 1887, this promise was well underway in Indian Territory, and, strikingly, government leaders continued to describe the promise in terms of blood and bodies, inventing blood quantums to divide tribes into individuals, reclothed, then absorbed into the US body politic. Were it not so baleful, it would make great science fiction. Wonderfully, Indigenous people opposed allotment with a similar language of the body, in which the tribal body would remain intact by resisting its individuation, entrenching in the breast of the Native national body: "Our hearts were on the ground," as one Crow elder described the era of allotment.

On disclosing the colonization of the Indigenous body and calling for a new one, we stand at a threshold of rooting Native bodies in land, a relationship that ultimately defines indigeneity and Native national sovereignty. In other words, a sound theory of the Indigenous body is key to future Native national flourishing. In examining such a theory, we discover a language of the national body to serve national autonomy. Indigenous people and European Americans have, for centuries, employed metaphors of the body to meld relationships to land and nation. Deploying this metaphor in the Dawes Act, the US national body planned to remain intact by absorbing the individual Native person, cut off from the tribal body.

Indigenous people, across historical moments and tribal traditions, have described their sovereignty in the language of the body. After all, Native nations maintain their own traditions of marking bodies in a way that roots them in homelands, ties them to ancestors, and links them with living human and nonhuman relations. In one brief example, Navajo or Dine views of the human body recognize layers of human tissue – from bones, to organs, to muscles, to flesh – as carefully interconnected casings with spaces in between. Through these interstices ghosts or winds are said to travel, entering the body through whorls that reside on the fingertips or at the crown of the head, for example. These many body parts are composed of specific earth materials; the hair on the head is constructed of male rain, female rain, and the moisture of clouds, for example. The "moving power" in the joints and foot soles is made of rainbow and connects the Dine to Mother Earth, while the "Feather of Life" at the top of the head connects one to Father Sky.[36] Similar traditional views of the complex Indigenous body are no doubt shared across Native North America.

The nation is a body that grows from the primary relationship of the people and the land. "The earth is our mother," we hear many Indigenous ancestors say; and in such statements, the body is a literal rather than a metaphorical child of the earth. This bodily earth–birth language is affirmed in hundreds of thousands of earthen mounds in North America. While we may never know the specific reasons for Indigenous forebears to have constructed these earthworks, they were often places to return bodies to the land, via massive landmarks shaped like the body itself, or, more precisely, like the swollen, pregnant womb. When Native leaders speak of the heartbeat of the land and its representation in a drumbeat, they are using that language of the flesh to affirm the organic life of the land as a great body. Indigenous literature abounds with descriptions of Native land as a single massive body. In James Welch's *Fools Crow* (1987), for example, the Pikuni people call their mountains the "Backbone of the World."[37] In *The Way to Rainy Mountain* (1969), N. Scott Momaday made famous the Kiowa story of their "coming out," when the people, one by one, emerged through a hollow log, only to have a pregnant woman get trapped in the opening, making the nation forever smaller in number.[38] In a later piece from that text, a woman is said to be buried in a fine elk's tooth dress, in a cabinet, somewhere in the shadow of Rainy Mountain. In each story, a woman consecrates the ground with her body, which becomes the land and, indeed, comes to stand for the homeland itself. One might say these women put their nurturing power in the land, making it bear the people's sense of sovereignty.

Among other Native nations, the Indigenous body melds with the land to bring gifts. Recall the Hitchiti story that tells of the origin of tobacco. In that story, a woman and a man make love in the woods beside a fallen log. Days later, the man happens on the very spot where they had lain to discover that a strange plant had sprouted up, with a fragrant smell and small flowers. He carefully tends the plant and eventually brings it to town, where he learns from an elder how to dry and smoke this medicine for protection.[39] In one story from the Cherokee oral tradition, Selu wishes to feed her hungry people, but her children determine she is a witch and plan to kill her. Selu knows their plans and tells the boys, "when you have killed me, clear a large piece of ground ... and drag my body seven times around the circle. Then drag me seven times over the ground inside the circle, and stay up all night and watch, and in the morning you will have plenty of corn."[40] Such stories confirm again and again the power of women's bodies and the land to confirm sovereignty. In this story, the Cherokees' central female archetype, First Woman or Selu – which is also the Cherokee word for corn – consecrates the ground with her body, and wherever her body touches the earth, maize springs up – as does tobacco in the Hitchiti story. The body returns to the land to renew it. And the circular movement of Selu forms the ancient pattern for the Green Corn ceremony, when, still today, Cherokees sweep the grounds to prepare them for ceremonies of bodily renewal. Most of all, Selu's story confirms sovereign lands by placing the body in the land in ceremonial pattern, while this cycle also claims space and territory.

Among intellectuals of the Native Southeast, the body as state also figures earlier, in the writings to oppose Removal. Cherokees were well aware of the rapacity of the United States and represented it as a bodily creature bent on "eating" the Cherokee Nation, which threatened to be, as they put it, "swallowed up." The National Council declares: "The power of a State may put our national existence under its feet, and coerce us into her jurisdiction; but it would be contrary to legal right." In such body imagery, the colonial power acts like a monstrous body, attacking, eating, or crushing Indigenous nations underfoot. With this language of the body as state, Cherokee leaders implored the American nation to view their tribal sovereignty as, like the Phoenix, "rising from the ashes of her degradation and taking her seat with the nations of the earth." In one of his many editorials for the newspaper, Elias Boudnot asserts: "As long as we continue as a people in a body, with our internal regulations, we can continue to improve in civilization and respectability."[41] In this manner, Native people also employed the image of the body as a sovereign state with a seat in a future United Nations.

With this bodily language already available, Native people were able, both in fiction and address, to support and oppose the allotment of their lands. Mainstream scholars such as Lucy Maddox often wrongly suggest that the allotment was generally supported by Indigenous people.[42] But as Native scholars such as Robert Warrior point out, only a handful of handpicked elites, who comprised the Society of American Indians, accepted this so-called civilization program.[43] Those who did, strangely, employed their Indigenous bodies to serve the desires of white Americans. Charles Eastman, for example, supported the allotment and celebrated his Indian body as a universal model of masculine virtue. In *The Soul of the Indian* (1911), he writes: "The moment that man conceived a perfect body, supple, symmetrical, graceful and enduring – in that moment he had laid the foundation of a moral life!"[44]

For the sake of the bodily but also the "intellectual"[45] health of Indigenous people, scholars in Native studies should include the body as a mode of analysis, and body identity as a source of knowledge and anticolonial resistance. Viewing Indigenous North America from a bodily perspective, we discern a more complex portrait of race and empire as we challenge American Progress in American literature, but we also expand Indigenous communities not only to include but also to learn from bodily difference as a social value. With a solid understanding of the Indigenous body, we link it to ancestral lands, thereby affirming national sovereignty. Last, in embracing bodies we restore a little more pride to Indigenous people.

## NOTES

1 Leslie Marmon Silko, *Ceremony* (New York: Penguin, 1977), 180–181.
2 Linda Hogan, *Power* (New York: W. W. Norton, 1998), 19.
3 Ibid., 228.
4 Sean Teuton, "The Callout: Writing American Indian Politics" in *Reasoning Together: The Native Critics Collective*, ed. Daniel Justice, Chris Teuton, and Craig Womack (Norman: University of Oklahoma Press, 2008), 105–125.
5 Tobin Siebers, *Disability Theory* (Ann Arbor: University of Michigan Press, 2008), 11–12.
6 Linda Martín Alcoff, *Visible Identities: Race, Gender, and the Self* (Oxford: Oxford University Press, 2000).
7 Sharon L. Snyder and David T. Mitchell, *Cultural Locations of Disability* (Chicago: University of Chicago Press, 2006).
8 Sean Teuton, "Teaching Disclosure: Overcoming the Invisibility of Whiteness in the American Indian Studies Classroom," in *Identity in Education*, ed. Susan Sanchez-Casal and Amie Macdonald (New York: Palgrave, 2009), 191–209.
9 Roy Harvey Pearce, *Savagism and Civilization: A Study of the American Indian and the American Mind* (Berkeley: University of California Press, 1988).
10 Carolyn Merchant, *The Death of Nature: Women, Ecology, and the Scientific Revolution* (San Francisco: Harper and Row, 1980); Henry Nash Smith, *Virgin Land: The American West as Symbol and Myth* (Cambridge: Harvard University Press, 1950).
11 Jane Lawrence, "The Indian Health Service and the Sterilization of Native American Women," *AIQ* 24, no. 3 (2000): 400–419.
12 Wendy Brown, "Wounded Attachments," *Political Theory* 21, no. 3 (1993): 391.
13 Sean Teuton, *Red Land, Red Power: Grounding Knowledge in the American Indian Novel* (Durham, NC: Duke University Press, 2008), 1–40.
14 Corbett Joan O'Toole, "The Sexist Inheritance of the Disability Movement," in *Gendering Disability*, ed. Bonnie G. Smith and Beth Hutchison (New Brunswick, NJ: Rutgers University Press, 2004), 294–300.

15 Elaine Scarry, *The Body in Pain: The Making and Unmaking of the World* (Oxford: Oxford University Press, 1985).

16 Paul Longmore, *Why I Burned My Book and Other Essays on Disability* (Philadelphia: Temple University Press, 2003).

17 Siebers, *Disability Theory*, 8.

18 Helen Carr, *Inventing the American Primitive: Politics, Gender and the Representation of Native American Literary Traditions, 1789–1936* (New York: New York University Press, 1996).

19 Thomas Jefferson, *Notes on the State of Virginia*, ed. Frank Shuffelton (New York: Penguin, 1999), 69.

20 George Catlin, *Life among the Indians* (New York: Wentworth Press, 2019), 38.

21 James Fenimore Cooper, *The Last of the Mohicans* (New York: Bantam, 1982).

22 Paul A. Wallace, *The White Roots of Peace: The Iroquois Book of Life* (Santa Fe, NM: Clear Light, 1994).

23 Frank Linderman, *Pretty Shield: Medicine Woman of the Crows* (Lincoln: University of Nebraska Press, 2003), 190.

24 Lucy Maddox, *Citizen Indians: Native American Intellectuals, Race and Reform* (Ithaca, NY: Cornell University Press, 2005); Philip J. Deloria, "I am of the Body: My Grandfather, Culture, and Sports," in *Indians in Unexpected Places* (Lawrence: University of Kansas Press, 2004), 109–135.

25 N. Scott Momaday, *House Made of Dawn* (New York: Harper Perennial, 2018), 100.

26 Ibid., 114.

27 Michele Foucault, *Discipline and Punish: The Birth of the Prison* (New York: Vintage, 1979), 135.

28 Joy Harjo, *A Map to the Next World* (New York: Norton, 2000), 16.

29 James Welch, *Fools Crow* (New York: Penguin, 1987).

30 Ibid., 240.

31 Siebers, *Disability Theory*, 67–68.

32 James Welch, *Winter in the Blood* (New York: Penguin, 1974), 118.

33 Linda Hogan, *Solar Storms* (New York: Scribner, 1995).

34 David Treuer, *The Hiawatha* (New York: Picador, 1999).

35 Frederick E. Hoxie, *A Final Promise: The Campaign to Assimilate the Indians, 1880–1920* (Lincoln: University of Nebraska Press, 1984).

36 Maureen Trudelle Schwartz, *Molded in the Image of Changing Woman: Navajo Views on the Human Body and Personhood* (Tucson: University of Arizona Press, 1997), 78–83.

37 Welch, *Fools Crow*.

38 N. Scott Momaday, *The Way to Rainy Mountain* (Albuquerque: University of New Mexico Press, 1976).

39 John R. Swanton, *Myths and Tales of the Southeastern Indians* (Norman: University of Oklahoma Press, 1995), 87–88.

40 James Mooney, *Myths of the Cherokee* (Nashville: Elder, 1982), 244.

41 Theda Perdue, *Cherokee Editor: The Writings of Elias Boudinot* (Knoxville: University of Tennessee Press, 1983), 73.

42 Maddox, *Citizen Indians*.

43 Robert Warrior, *Tribal Secrets: Recovering American Indian Intellectual Traditions* (Minneapolis: University of Minnesota Press, 1994), 23.
44 Charles Alexander Eastman, *The Soul of the Indian* (Lincoln: University of Nebraska Press, 1980), 91.
45 Robert Warrior, *The People and the Word: Reading Native Nonfiction* (Minneapolis: University of Minnesota Press, 2005), xiv.

# 15

CHRISTINE OKOTH

# The Black Body and the Reading of Race

Commenting on her poetic engagement with *Framed by Modernism* (1996), the photographic collaboration between Carrie Mae Weems and Robert Colescott, the poet and scholar Dawn Lundy Martin remarks on how her response to the series 'illuminates modernism's yoke of representation when it comes to the black body'.[1] The three photographs which Lundy encountered at the Montclair Art Museum are presented as portraits of Colescott, but the images also include Weems in the background, nude and standing in a corner of the room. The bodies of two Black artists are subject to the technological and aesthetic frame of the photographic medium, a racialising form that is accentuated by Weems's signature black and white palette. But Weems is both behind the camera and in front of it, in a portrait that she did not have to be a part of, as though she is deliberately toying with the camera's demands for Black legibility by willingly acquiescing to them. Martin sees in the image 'a trajectory between historic representations of blackness, the representation of the female body by male artists and a unique tension between subject and object in which the lack of agency is not a devout positioning'.[2] The series invites attempts at analytical readings only to immediately reshape these attempts at analysis. In effect, the bodies of the two Black artists enact their own readings during the act of being read.

This chapter might best be understood as a snapshot of scholarly conversations around race and the body, one with a particular focus on what has come to be known as 'the Black body'. My intention in focusing on the Black body is to give an example of a critical genealogy that paints a particularly salient picture of how the real bodies of racialised people come to be replaced by a discursive composite. What this critical history demonstrates is that the analytical methods associated with reading and writing are central to the production of 'the Black body' and the continued maintenance of race and racism. One aim of this chapter, then, is to insist that the foundational gestures of literary production and literary study do not just reflect race and racism as they exist in the world but actively produce racial hierarchies. Our methods for producing and writing about culture are structured around the assumption that some bodies can and should be read more closely and more readily than others. This chapter is therefore also interested in how strategies associated with aesthetic representation refuse to let the bodies of Black people speak and in tracing where Black thinkers, writers, and artists in turn locate the terrain on which such acts of embodied theorising are possible.

The critical interventions collected in this chapter are organised around three anecdotes of racial hailing, which themselves act as a formal refrain. Though they share common concerns and raise overlapping theoretical questions, these three scenes all contribute in different ways to a broader conversation about the distinct processes that result in the making of 'the Black body'. Frantz Fanon's 'The Fact of Blackness' identifies replacement as a formal basis of racialisation; the opening of Hortense Spillers's 'Mama's Baby, Papa's Maybe' initiates a theoretical meditation on how the violent physical inscriptions of Black bodies relate to the grammatical markers of Black subjection; and Nicole Fleetwood's first viewing of Spike Lee's *Do the Right Thing* highlights the centrality of vision and visual media in the making and unmaking of the Black body.

What follows is both a primer of how the analytical unit of the Black body functions within scholarship on race and racism and a critical excursion that reveals the difficulties of attempting to pry Black personhood and real embodiment apart from the mantle of the Black body. For the purposes of this chapter, these analytical tensions might be broadly described as a constant interplay between the actual body of a racialised person and the representational schema that coalesce around that body. Though the distinction between the two can appear straightforward, it is anything but. In the case of Black people in the Americas, a historical racist substitution of the Black person with the Black body permeates economic, legal, and aesthetic representations of Black personhood. At the same time, the violent histories inscribed upon the bodies of Black people are also histories of refusal and survival. For this reason, scholarship on race and racism is often as interested in the making of the Black body as it is engaged in an effort to recognise how the real bodies of Black people interact with and subvert the discursive construct that haunts us. The critical tendencies outlined therefore oscillate between pleasure and pain, historical knowledge and contemporary performance practices, or, if you will, between the bodies of Black people and the Black body.

## I.

The racial epithet that opens Frantz Fanon's 'The Fact of Blackness' comes seemingly out of nowhere. 'Look, a Negro!' stands on the page without origin or clear direction, an insult thrown at reader, writer, or narrator by an initially anonymous, external entity.[3] In the absence of framing devices and immediate explanation, the racial slur cannot be contained once spoken, thereby subjecting the Black reader to the interpolating white gaze. This same sense of dislocation also goes some way to explain how 'The Fanonian Moment', to use Nicole Fleetwood's terms, has become a global reference point for theories of race and racialisation. Though Fanon died in the United States seeking treatment for leukaemia, he was born in the French colony of Martinique and spent much of his adult life in France and Algeria witnessing and experiencing the effects of institutionalised racism and colonialism outside of America. Even so, the opening scenes of 'The Fact of Blackness' reverberate across American literature and literary studies, influencing scholars and writers like Fleetwood, Fred Moten, Nathaniel Mackey, and John Edgar Wideman. While the critical genealogy recounted here is focused on North America and the United States, the foundational analytical gestures of American literary history also contain wider histories of colonialism and conquest that produced race on a global scale. To be sure, race has a situated history and functions according to the specific geographical, temporal, and political backdrop of the spaces in which it continues to enforce hierarchies of difference. But the experience that Fanon describes in his influential account of racialisation is often read in a variety of contexts across the Black Atlantic and beyond due to its focus on the formal composition of race and racialisation. In 'The Fact of Blackness', Fanon insists on the centrality of repetition to the production of race both within the text and outside of its bounds.

Fanon's theory of epidermalisation hinges on the central claim that racialisation dissembles and remakes the body that once granted a sense of stability to the Black man, replacing it with a discursive unit. In spite of recent attempts on the parts of Afropessimists to read Fanon's description of the 'body suddenly abraded into nonbeing' as an indication of an abrupt and complete destruction of the Black man's core epistemological and ontological principles, Fanon's formal reliance on the refrain of 'Look, A Negro!' indicates that the substitution of the Black person with the Black body is more akin to a progressive erosion or a slow encroachment of Blackness on Black corporeality.[4] While the first appearance of 'Look, a Negro!' in the text leads Fanon to the conclusion that 'the man of color encounters difficulties in the development of his bodily schema', it takes a repetition of that decisive utterance to introduce the theory of epidermalisation that Fanon is now best known for.[5] Interrupting the reconstitution of the writer's bodily schema, the second, third, and fourth iterations of 'Look, a Negro!' are what finally rupture the 'real dialectic between [Fanon's] body and the world'.[6] It is after these repetitions that Fanon describes how, 'assailed at various points, the corporeal schema crumbled, its place taken by a racial epidermal schema'.[7] The wall of self-knowledge and corporeal integrity has been breached and the floodgates of racialisation opened. The Black man finds himself suddenly 'responsible ... for [his] body, for [his] race, for [his] ancestors', weighed down by histories and narratives of racial subjection.[8] The repetition of the racial epithet finally pushes the writer towards a total crisis of embodiment, one that ultimately results in the substitution of the corporeal with the discursive.

The formal trope of racial hailing and the disaggregation of the corporeal unit repeats in more recent works that draw on Fanon's theory of epidermalisation. Harvey Young, for instance, opens his study of race and the Black body with an account of being arrested and held in a police cell after an encounter with two traffic cops. This experience of 'driving while Black' is, in Young's words, the repetition of an event that has occurred numerous times and will be repeated many more times over. In each iteration of this repetition, a different Black person experiences the feeling of being 'transformed, dislocated, incarcerated, and objectified by the continued reverberations of these repeated encounters'.[9] This repetition is a formal component of what Young defines as 'racializing projection' or the application of a racial script on different, individual bodies.[10] For Young, the Black body is a double of the real body of a Black person, a 'shadow' without clear boundaries that, in the moment of racialisation, merges with the visual presence of the subject of racialisation.[11] This choice of metaphors creates a mirror image to the prologue of Ralph Ellison's 1952 novel *Invisible Man*, in which the anonymous narrator declares that he is 'not a spook' but 'a man of substance, of flesh and bone, fiber and liquids – and ... might even be said to possess a mind'. What renders Ellison's narrator invisible is the fact that 'people refuse to see [him]'. Reprinted in layers of paint, these words reappear in visual artist Glenn Ligon's 1991 oil print *Untitled (I am an invisible man)*, which explores the textual and visual components of race and racialisation. Here, the repeated printing of black text against white background highlights how repetition reinforces the stability of the racial script, granting it the kind of structural integrity that the bodies of Black people can no longer claim.

As Ligon's work suggests, textuality's role in the production of race is more than metaphoric. Later sections of this chapter will discuss the physical inscription of race on the bodies of Black people and the tensions between discursive substitution and corporeal violence. But first, we might consider how acts of description and reading function as a means of locating race on the bodies of Black people. In her history of eighteenth-century advertisements, Sharon Block proposes that an emphasis on skin colour in advertisements describing self-liberated enslaved people is an example of how the act of 'noting ... details about some bodies and not others marked whose bodies were consistently commodified'.[12] Through the writing and circulation of 'daily racial scripts', white Americans enshrined the notion that some bodies possessed particular features where others had only generalizable traits.[13] In this formulation, racism is a process of misreading because its scripts are written as a means of providing cognitive stability to a white reader. And this cognitive stability in turn ensures that the bodies of Black people can be temporarily fixed in place, imprisoned through the deployment of demands and expectations that reappear in the guise of social norms.

Such an account of reading bodies and translating their presentation into recognizable markers of racial difference also points to a necessary critique of the central assumptions around which Fanon constructs his theory of epidermalisation. Sharon Holland's account of an initial hailing scene leads her to the conclusion that those people giving voice to the racist tropes encapsulated in the discursive entity of the Black body are engaged in 'a profound misreading of the subjects they encounter'.[14] In Holland's case, a white woman interrupts a friendly moment of intimacy between Holland and her friend's teenage daughter. When Holland partially accommodates the white woman's demands, that woman reprimands Holland with the accusation: 'to think I marched for you'.[15] Echoing Saidiya Hartman's critique of the 'burdened individuality of freedom', Holland concludes that the white woman's prior acts in support of civil rights were aimed at 'acquiring a kind of purchase on black bodies' and a right to intrude on Black women's kinship structures.[16] This particular instance of racial misreading also highlights the extent to which Fanon's account of racialisation reinforces the over-representation of masculinity and whiteness. In *The Fact of Blackness*, the source of the racial slur is eventually revealed to be a white boy on the hand of his white mother. By positioning this familial unit at the centre of an essay about corporeal displacement, Fanon grants white, reproductive, heterosexual womanhood an especially destructive power over the body of the Black man. And unlike the interaction described by Holland, in which Holland in turn identifies the white woman's own performance as a familiar script, Fanon's racialising gaze remains unidirectional. It is not met with a response from the Black person whose body is the target of the racist substitution.

Theoretical approaches that extrapolate from lived experience – of sex, gender, disability, and class – often dislodge the primacy of the Fanonian moment and sometimes directly refute its theoretical conclusions. We might therefore think of Holland's example as evidence of how the effect of racial hailing is refracted and reordered as it meets differently subjected Black people and their bodies. Simone Browne's reminder, articulated via Sylvia Wynter, that the original title of the fifth chapter of *Black Skin, White Masks* is 'L'éxperience vécue du noir' or 'The Lived Experience of the Black', points to a larger question about how embodied experience can produce a range of theoretical approaches that speak to the relationship between race and the body.[17] Blackness and the Black body are a complex amalgamation of experiences accumulated over time, and they can function as dialectical units in the theorisation of Black life as much as they can enact modes of subjection and exploitation. The body of a Black person can receive already existing racial readings, but it can also engender new ways of reading and writing race. And while the bodies of racialised people have been the subject of reading and inscription, those same bodies also perform their own readings of the people and institutions that actively produce racial hierarchies of difference.

## II.

Hortense Spillers's field-defining essay 'Mama's Baby, Papa's Maybe' opens with a list of racial scripts: 'Peaches' and 'Brown Sugar', 'Sapphire' and 'Earth Mother', 'Aunty', 'Granny', God's 'Holy Fool', a 'Miss Ebony First', or 'Black Woman at the Podium'. These are the signifiers that have acted as a discursive prison of Black womanhood or, in Spillers's words, the 'overdetermined nominative properties' within which Black women are permitted to exist.[18] This opening echoes the list of racial tropes that make up Fanon's racial epidermal schema at the exact moment of its encroachment on his bodily schema. It also parses the porous boundaries between discursive and corporeal violence and initiates a careful, theoretical excavation of the real bodies that have been repeatedly subsumed by a rampant racial script. At the centre of Spillers's essay stands the argument that the theft and captivity of Black people have rendered their bodies as 'ungendered flesh'. The distinction between 'body' and 'flesh' maps onto 'captive and liberated subject-positions' and is the foundational argument behind Spillers's consideration of how the beatings, rapes, and murders of Black people under the regime of slavery repeatedly enforced the over-representation of flesh as the primary physical and epistemic unit of blackness.[19] The flesh is a means of thinking about how the inscription of the enslaved person's being precedes any recognition of that person's body as a body.

While the discursive unit of the Black body remains central to Spillers's analysis of race and representation, her insistence on centring the physical evidence of racial readings on the bodies of Black people is a pivotal analytical step. A theory of 'hieroglyphics of the flesh' is, in effect, a necessary reminder that Stuart Hall's understanding of epidermalisation as the 'inscription of race on the skin' has both a literal and figurative dimension.[20] This oscillation between real and metaphoric, corporeal and epistemic that runs throughout 'Mama's Baby' complicates the assumption that the Black body exists largely as a discursive construct. Through the marking of real Black bodies according to the tenets of a constantly shifting racial script, the Black body attaches itself to Black people, clinging onto corporeality as an engraved reminder of racial hierarchies. This understanding of the Black body as a violent mode of grammatical inscription also highlights the commensurability of reading with acts of physical violence inflicted on the bodies of Black people. As much as the Black body exists as a pastiche of racist ideologies, the damage inflicted on the corporeal constitution of Black people is real and lasting.

From the scientific discipline of nineteenth-century phrenology to contemporary discourse around the insufficient femininity of Black athletes, the bodies of racialised people have been annotated, analysed, and interpreted both for evidence of racial difference and as part of a concomitant pursuit of generalisable scientific knowledge. Though by no means limited to this sphere, American medical science has played a particularly egregious role in the physical inscription of race onto the bodies of Black people and Black women in particular. In her ground-breaking history of American gynaecology, Deirdre Cooper Owens shows how the American medical profession relied on racial myths around differential physiology to justify the violent exploitation of enslaved women's bodies.[21] Her account of early American medicine and the crimes of J. Marion Sims reveals the extent to which the concept of the Black body relies on an immanent conceptual flexibility in which the same bodies that are thought to contain evidence of fundamental difference can still be imagined as the source of scientific knowledge about the universal human body. Putting these arguments in conversation with recent debates in Trans Studies, C. Riley Snorton highlights the representation of Sims's victims Anarcha, Betsey, and Lucy in the doctor's diaries. Snorton characterises Sims's words as 'an aperture with which to perceive how divided flesh was defined by its characteristic accessibility, its availability for viewing, exploration, and other modes of unrelenting, unmitigated apprehension'.[22] The bodies of Black people were subsequently rendered into ungendered flesh and science's raw material. These critical works demonstrate that the history of race is a history of reading bodies and that the history of science is also a history of racial reading.

When Spillers describes the flesh as 'a primary narrative', she insists that demands on legibility and availability are intertwined with the unmaking of

Black people's corporeality. Flesh names the violently enforced expectation that Black people must expose their interior lives to white observers in both a corporeal and metaphysical sense. This textual marking also effectively blocks the means through which Black people could provide the metaphysical evidence for self-knowledge that functions as a necessary step towards the articulation of personhood. This is why Édouard Glissant's insistence on 'a right to opacity' should not be understood as a universal claim for the emancipatory possibilities of unknowability, but a demand that Black people – their bodies, minds, and artistic expressions – no longer be subjected to unrelenting calls to make themselves known.[23] These gestures of opacity are not necessarily resistant to the function of the Black body. They emerge in relation to it, as both an outcome and a rejection of the racial script.

In her study of Black female corporeality, Kimberly Juanita Brown refers to a pivotal scene in Toni Morrison's novel *Beloved* to illustrate how the bodies of Black people become legible for white onlookers and how Black people engage in acts of counter-reading. Morrison's protagonist Sethe bears the scars of her enslavement on her back, a place that is hidden from her own field of vision but one that she can choose to reveal to others. Brown proposes that 'when Sethe allows others to see the scars on her back, she conceals and reveals all at once', partially reclaiming the act of reading to create a new sense of intimacy.[24] An inscription of past violations, Sethe's back is no longer a page on which race is inscribed but one that carries the history of race's inscription on the bodies of Black people. Though Sethe 'makes herself vulnerable and open to reading', she does so in a position that shields her face from those same acts of reading and interpretation.[25] Brown's analysis of *Beloved* presents the possibility of reclaiming the form of inscription for emancipatory ends. Even within the bounds of the colonial, racist, settler-state of the United States, Black people have developed reading practices that do not reproduce historical and ongoing forms of subjection. Through tactics of concealment, counter-reading, and re-writing Black people interrupt and disrupt the reproduction of the Black body's subjugating effect.

### III.

Nicole Fleetwood's study of the Black body in the visual field begins with a memory of seeing an early screening of Spike Lee's *Do the Right Thing* (1989). The racially mixed group of friends leave the screening silently, in the knowledge that the images they have just witnessed on screen have the potential to ignite not just a cultural but a political movement. Lee's film stands at the beginning of Fleetwood's study as an example of what she refers to as 'black iconicity', in which a popular image of Black people becomes representative of a generalised and generalisable idea of blackness.[26] Film, television, and photography here function as another means of making Black people and their bodies legible through the deployment of an abstract, discursive concept of blackness and the Black body. *Do the Right Thing* and its director are, however, more than abstracted signifiers because they are positioned in a field of vision that is itself always grappling with the management of blackness. Visual media constructs blackness in the eyes of the viewer as troubling or disconcerting, but this same gesture also acknowledges the threat of disruption that blackness poses to the integrity of the visual field. Fleetwood's assertion that 'the visible Black body is always already troubling the dominant visual field' therefore works in two ways; the idea of the Black body generates a demand for coercion and enclosure within the visual field, but the presence of real Black people on screen also routinely undermines the formal mechanisms of visual capture that seek to manage it.[27] Here, the visual is not immediately rendered as 'a punitive field' but as a site at which racialising abstractions and substitutions can be both made and unmade.[28]

In the American context, photography and the field of vision occupy a particularly contentious place in the history of the Black body because of their ties to the repetition and recirculation of Black pain through photographic reproduction. Leigh Raiford and Jacqueline Goldsby have each shown how visual culture has enabled the transformation of Black people and Black pain into an abstracted, consumable form.[29] Writing on the more recent circulation of video footage of police brutality, Jon L. Jackson has argued that the lack of convictions in a court of law for crimes committed against Black people by police officers is evidence of the inefficacy of the visual in the pursuit of racial justice.[30] In the work of Deborah Willis and Tina Campt, however, photography becomes more a means of connecting diasporic visual practices than a medium which reinforces the circulation of the Black body. The editors of the volume *Migrating the Black Body* advance an argument that nods towards each of these critical tendencies, proposing that scholarship on the subject of Black bodies in the visual field collected in the volume 'is interested in the interplay between black bodies as visual objects and subjects; as visual spectres and spectacles and visual spectators; as objects of visual culture and as visual producers in a transnational context'.[31] Again, the visual field, as itself a discursive site, produces the Black body as much as it serves as a means of its potential disaggregation.

In the works of E. Patrick Johnson, Jennifer Nash, and Tavia Nyong'o, the visual field also acts as both an enclosure in which Black bodies are forced into legibility and a site of subversive visual practices that play on and with the discursive entity of the Black body. Here, performance plays a pivotal role in renegotiating the terms on which visual engagement takes place. E. Patrick Johnson, for instance, suggests that 'blackness and performance are two discourses whose histories converge at the site of otherness' and that the two are connected through 'the status of the bodies that have come to be associated with them'.[32] Like performance, blackness is structured around an over-determined script that relates it to 'denigration, impurity, nature, and the body'.[33] But blackness also remakes the formal principles of performance because of its complicated history with vision and the visual field. Referring to the principle of embodied knowledge and embodied theorising, Johnson insists that, 'blackness does not only reside in the theatrical fantasy of the white imaginary that is then projected onto black bodies, nor is it always consciously acted out; rather, it is also the inexpressible yet undeniable racial experience of Black people – the ways in which the "living of blackness" becomes a material way of knowing.'[34] Wrenching the definition of performance away from the immediate sphere of the visual and its technologies of seeing/looking, Johnson considers Black performance as an act of everyday theorising that does not require the presence of a viewer to enact embodied practices. Central to this assertion is the refusal to enforce legibility on these acts of everyday performance. For Johnson, the performance of blackness that is the subject of his work is 'neither solely volitional nor without agency' and needs neither direction nor spectator.[35]

This assertion that performance encompasses a range of practices from the unconscious and quotidian to the deliberately staged and directionally performed adds further complication to any attempt to clearly distinguish the Black body from the real bodies of Black people. Through performance, the act of substitution, which Fanon describes at the beginning of this chapter, becomes something more akin to a dialectics of racialisation, in which the body is constituted not out of the interplay between the corporeal and the external world but between the corporeal and the discursive racial script. The resulting relationship to the Black body is more ambiguous than those critical approaches outlined earlier on. Performance can give credence to the racial script and rewrite the discursive tenets of the Black body at the same time.

For Tavia Nyong'o, whose work is in close conversation with other theorists of queer of colour critique such as José Muñoz, performance is a central site of theorisation of the Black body precisely because it works both with and against the regimes of the visual field. By way of Trajal Harrell's performance *Twenty Looks or Paris Is Burning at the Judson Church, Size Small*, Nyong'o develops a theory of 'critical shade', which he defines as a way to 'perform both for and against the camera'.[36] Rather than inhabiting the predetermined form of dance or adhering to a racial script of how Black queer people are expected to interpret that form, Harrell positions his body at a critical 'vantage point' from which he can both participate in and withhold from the reproduction of the Black body.[37] Invoking Huey Copeland's argument that contemporary Black artists interrogate the long-standing expectation that the Black body should appear and present itself as available to onlookers, Nyong'o identifies 'techniques of deferral, recycling, and subtle redirection' that impede the easy translation of Black performance into legible categories of fierceness or glamour.[38] In the critical writings of Jennifer Nash, the gaze of the camera also elicits contingent responses from Black performers, who simultaneously invite and retreat from that gaze. In a similar vein to Fleetwood, Nash proposes that visual culture should be treated with less outright critical suspicion and turns to the archive of pornography and pornographic performances to make the case for a critical hermeneutics of 'racial iconography'.[39] Desire, the erotic, and bodily pleasure necessitate this shift towards an understanding of racialised pornography as more than an exploitative deployment of racial scripts for the enjoyment of viewers. Though pornography 'constrains protagonists' lexicons of desire', the experience of embodied pleasure is not itself limited by the terms of the visual field.[40] Performances in racialised pornography are part of 'the meaning-making work that black women's bodies' enact on the screen'.[41] Black visual studies and Black performance studies therefore reframe the ways we can read and interpret racial scripts. Placing an emphasis on the translation, transmutation, and oscillation between the figurative and the real enables a theoretical exploration of how the real bodies of Black people theorise their own constitution in response to but also alongside the violent impositions of the discursive unit of 'the Black body'. The bodies of Black people as the targets of racism also enact theoretical knowledge about the constitution of race and racialisation.

## Conclusion

On 16 March 2015, the anonymous collective Mongrel Coalition Against Gringpo posted a statement entitled 'The Mongrel Coalition Killed Conceptualism' on their website. The now archived post was written in response to events that unfolded at the *Interruptions 3* poetry conference held at Brown University. On the second day of the conference, the conceptual poet Kenneth Goldsmith stood in front of an audience of largely white members of the literary academy and read out the autopsy report of Michael Brown, the teenager who had been murdered at the hands of a white police

CHRISTINE OKOTH

officer in Ferguson, Missouri, a year earlier. For the duration of the performance, scholars and poets watched as a white poet transformed a Black
teenager's dead body into a literary text, using a technique of textual
repurposing that had facilitated the conceptual movement's rise to prominence. Literariness – both in terms of the affectations of poetic readings and
the textual violence enacted through the rearrangement of Brown's autopsy
report – is a central target of Gringpo's critique. The collective takes particular aim at Goldsmith's 'treatment of blackness, black murder as raw material
for depraved pleasure'.[42] Using similar phrasing to the artist and writer
Hannah Black, who, in a 2017 open letter to the Whitney Museum protest-
ing white artist Dana Schutz's painting of Emmett Till's casket, demanded
that artists who were sincerely invested in anti-racist activism should 'stop
treating Black pain as raw material', Gringpo rejects the repeated extraction
of value from Black people's real lives and deaths through literary means.[43]
By declaring that 'The Murdered Body of Mike Brown's Medical Report is
not our poetry, it's the building blocks of white supremacy', the anonymous
collective therefore intervened in the process that makes the dead bodies of
Black people 'literary'.

Gringpo's statement is a fitting conclusion to this chapter on American
literary and cultural criticism's relationship to the lived experience of
embodiment because it draws attention to a series of mediations, replace-
ments, and abstractions that structure the translation of racialised violence
into literary form. Goldsmith's decision to name his poem 'The Body of
Michael Brown' exposes a foundational refusal to contend with the differences between the sphere of corporeal violence and the sphere of representation. This refusal is itself based on an initial conflation contained within the
text of the medical report. Here, the dual racist institutions of law and
medicine produce a narrative representation of a Black person's final
moments in life through the examination of that person's dead body. The
poem therefore enters into the discursive formations around Black embodiment at an odd juncture; it accepts the replacement of a person's life with a
reading of a dead body and then enshrines this substitution in the form of the
poetic text. Enabling claims to literariness, the real body of Michael Brown is
forced to protect the institution of literature, losing his life and his body once
more. Imprisoned in the poem, Michael Brown is not permitted to be more
than a discursive concept of the Black body. In refusing to use Goldsmith's
chosen title for his poem and replacing it with their own, Gringpo partially
reverse this cycle of substitutions, taking the poeticised Black body out of
citational circulation.

This recent example highlights how literary writing refers to the wholly
discursive unit of the Black body as a means of avoiding confrontation with

the real violence inflicted on the bodies of Black people. In a sense, this final instance of corporeal replacement demonstrates how physical and epistemic violence rely on those cumulative meanings of the Black body that circulate in popular and academic discourse. Through it, we can see the extent to which aesthetic strategies are themselves imbricated in the production of race and racism. But the above anecdote also points to the challenges and opportunities that bodies and embodiment pose for thinkers, writers, and artists working within and in relation to scholarship on race and racism. Every iteration of the Black body also becomes a site at which Black people engage in acts of embodied and non-embodied theorising. In a discussion about the afterlife of 'Mama's Baby', Spillers specifically critiques a scholarly landscape in which 'black people [are] treated as a kind of raw material'.[44] The critical traditions outlined above take seriously Spillers's accompanying assertion that Black people and their bodies routinely 'explain something in theoretical terms'.[45] The Black body is a shadow, a schema, and a script, but it is also a history and a theory that is bound to Black life.

## NOTES

1 'On the Black Avant-Garde, Trigger Warnings, and Life in East Hampton', interview with Dawn Lundy Martin, *Literary Hub*, 2015, https://lithub.com/on-the-black-avant-garde-trigger-warnings-and-life-in-east-hampton, accessed 25 March 2020.

2 Ibid.

3 Frantz Fanon, 'The Fact of Blackness', in *Black Skin, White Masks*, trans. Charles Lam Markmann (New York: Pluto Press, 2008), 82.

4 Ibid., 82.

5 Ibid., 83.

6 Ibid.

7 Ibid., 84.

8 Ibid.

9 Harvey Young, *Embodying Black Experience: Stillness, Critical Memory, and the Black Body* (Ann Arbor: University of Michigan Press, 2010), 3–4.

10 Ibid., 5.

11 Ibid., 7.

12 Sharon Block, *Colonial Complexions: Race and Bodies in Eighteenth-Century America* (Philadelphia: University of Pennsylvania Press, 2018), 7.

13 Ibid., 2, 7–8.

14 Sharon P. Holland, 'The Last Word on Racism: New Directions for a Critical Race Theory', *South Atlantic Quarterly* 104, no. 3 (2005): 404.

15 Ibid.

16 Ibid.

17 Simone Browne, *Dark Matters: On the Surveillance of Blackness* (Durham, NC: Duke University Press, 2015), 7.

18 Hortense J. Spillers, 'Mama's Baby, Papa's Maybe: An American Grammar Book', *Diacritics* 17, no. 2 (1987): 65.

19 Ibid., 67.

20 Stuart Hall, 'The After Life of Frantz Fanon: Why Fanon? Why Now? Why Black Skin, White Masks?', in *The Fact of Blackness: Frantz Fanon and Visual Representation*, ed. Alan Read (London: Institute of Contemporary Arts, 1996), 16.

21 Deirdre Cooper Owens, *Medical Bondage: Race, Gender, and the Origins of American Gynecology* (Athens: University of Georgia Press, 2018).

22 C. Riley Snorton, *Black on Both Sides: A Racial History of Trans Identity* (Minneapolis: University of Minnesota Press, 2017). Snorton's work is one example of the ongoing critical conversation around the connection between Trans Studies and Black Studies, recently summarised in Cameron Awkward-Rich, 'Thinking Black [Trans] Gender', *American Quarterly* 71, no. 3 (2019): 903–914. Other notable contributions include LaMonda Horton-Stallings, *Funk the Erotic: Transaesthetics and Black Sexual Cultures* (Champaign: University of Illinois Press, 2015) and Marquis Bey, 'The Trans*-Ness of Blackness, the Blackness of Trans*-Ness', *TSQ: Transgender Studies Quarterly* 4, no. 2 (2017), 275–295.

23 Edouard Glissant, *Poetics of Relation*, trans. Betsy Wing (Ann Arbor: University of Michigan Press, 1997), 190.

24 Kimberly Juanita Brown, *The Repeating Body: Slavery's Visual Resonance in the Contemporary* (Durham, NC: Duke University Press, 2015), 8.

25 Ibid., 8.

26 Nicole R. Fleetwood, *Troubling Vision: Performance, Visuality, and Blackness* (Chicago: University of Chicago Press, 2011).

27 Ibid., 6.

28 Ibid., 13

29 Jacqueline Goldsby, *A Spectacular Secret: Lynching in American Life and Literature* (Chicago: University of Chicago Press, 2006); Leigh Raiford, *Imprisoned in a Luminous Glare: Photography and the African American Freedom Struggle* (Chapel Hill: University of North Carolina Press, 2011).

30 John L. Jackson, 'Lights, Camera, Police Action!', *Public Culture* 28.1, no. 78 (2016): 3–8.

31 Leigh Raiford and Heike Raphael-Hernandez, eds., *Migrating the Black Body: The African Diaspora and Visual Culture* (Seattle: University of Washington Press, 2017), 5.

32 E. Patrick Johnson, *Appropriating Blackness: Performance and the Politics of Authenticity* (Durham, NC: Duke University Press, 2003), 7.

33 Ibid., 32.

34 Ibid., 8.

35 Ibid.

36 Tavia Nyong'o, *Afro-Fabulations* (New York: New York University Press, 2018).

37 Ibid., 34.

38 Ibid., 35.

39 Jennifer C. Nash, *The Black Body in Ecstasy: Reading Race, Reading Pornography* (Durham, NC: Duke University Press, 2014), 2.

40 Ibid., 3.

41 Ibid., 7.
42 'The Mongrel Coalition Against Gringpo', 2015, https://web.archive.org/web/20150316210242/http://gringpo.com/, accessed 26 June 2020.
43 Hannah Black, 'The Painting Must Go – Open Letter to the Curators and Staff of the Whitney Biennial', March 2017, www.artnews.com/art-news/news/the-painting-must-go-hannah-black-pens-open-letter-to-the-whitney-about-contro versial-biennial-work-7992/.
44 Hortense Spillers et al., '"Whatcha Gonna Do?": Revisiting "Mama's Baby, Papa's Maybe: An American Grammar Book": A Conversation with Hortense Spillers, Saidiya Hartman, Farah Jasmine Griffin, Shelly Eversley, & Jennifer L. Morgan', *Women's Studies Quarterly* 35.1, no. 2 (2007): 300.
45 Ibid., 300.

# 16

DELIA BYRNES

# Ecocriticism and the Body

## Ecocriticism and the Body

"Bodies tell stories."[1] So begins the fifth chapter of *Salvage the Bones*, Jesmyn Ward's 2011 novel of Hurricane Katrina's racialized landscapes. The story follows fifteen-year-old Esch Batiste, a Black teenager living in rural poverty with her family along the Mississippi Gulf Coast in the days leading up to the 2005 storm. Pregnant and caught between emerging desires as an adolescent woman and compounding responsibilities as an expectant mother, Esch utters these words as she rushes into the family's bathroom, bursting to pee, and sees her older brother Skeetah softly touching wounds on his stomach. Esch alludes to the stories revealed by her own pregnant belly and those inscribed on her brother's torso, which tell of the ravaging of his body in exchange for resources. Ward weaves these corporeal stories into a broader narrative of racialized embodiment, structural abandonment, and environmental vulnerability as they inextricably entangle in the southern United States. *Salvage the Bones* teems with references to the tenuous boundaries between human and nonhuman life, with rural Mississippi itself represented as living body: "We live in the black heart of Bois Sauvage," Esch explains as she recalls the white farmer from whom her brother had just attempted to steal dog food, "and he lives out away in the pale arteries, so I don't think he will ever come here."[2] Esch's metaphor implicates the racial geographies of the town through its segregated "black" and "pale" vessels. The phrase "black heart" gestures toward the Batiste family's liveliness – they are the surging lifeblood of the town – while simultaneously registering the state-sanctioned abandonment of their community through the throttling of vital social and material resources. On the day Hurricane Katrina makes landfall, she recalls the Mississippi government's automated telephone message to homes in the path of the storm: "If you choose to stay in your home and have not evacuated by this time, we are not responsible."[3] The juxtaposition of the state's neoliberal self-indemnification with Esch's earlier observation that, before a hurricane, "the animals that can, leave,"[4] is a stark meditation on what Christopher Lloyd refers to as "creaturely, throw-away life"[5] – the dehumanizing biopolitics through which racialized and gendered bodies come to matter in the US South.

I open with this discussion of Ward's novel to emphasize that relationships between bodies and environments are uneven, unequal, and historically situated: There is no body or environment outside of history. Indeed, Ward's fiction carefully traces a genealogy from chattel slavery's ensnarement of Black people in the plantation regime to the environmental crises of the twenty-first century, where the afterlives of slavery linger in the organized abandonment of African American communities. Even as planetary climate crisis and universalizing concepts such as the Anthropocene augur humankind's vulnerability, that vulnerability fractures along the fault lines of race, gender, sexuality, dis/ability, region, class, and myriad other subject positions. As educator and activist Hop Hopkins succinctly explains, "You can't have climate change without sacrifice zones, you can't have sacrifice zones without disposable people, and you can't have disposable people without racism."[6] What constitutes environments worth saving, and who is deemed worthy of protection, are deeply shaped by systems of power and privilege. From this perspective, this chapter's discussion of ecocriticism and the body in American literature will be especially attentive to embodied difference within the broader articulation of environmental thought in the contemporary literary and critical imaginations.

To remix Ward's phrase slightly, bodies tell ecological stories. To read and interpret the ecological body in literature is to participate in the broader methodology of ecocriticism, a mode of analysis that studies the relationship between the physical environment and cultural forms. Cohering as a subfield in the 1990s, ecocriticism marries textual analysis with a diverse range of interpretive approaches and makes kin with disciplines spanning the earth sciences, science and technology studies, urban studies, Indigenous studies, multispecies ethnography, sociology, feminist and disability studies, queer studies, and more. As such, ecocriticism works "at the crossroads of cultural formations and material worlds."[7] Ecocritics increasingly recognize the human as co-constituted by more-than-human agencies, embedded in complex networks that span the scales of the cellular and the planetary. In *Bodily Natures: Science, Environment, and the Material Self* (2010), Stacy Alaimo explains that the transit across human bodies and nonhuman nature demands diverse and complex modes of analysis that "travel through the entangled territories of material and discursive, natural and cultural, biological and textual."[8] This recognition also necessitates "transit across traditional disciplinary boundaries."[9] As a methodology invested in both cultural production and the natural sciences, ecocriticism offers a way to critically "read" scientific discourse, on the one hand, and to situate cultural analysis alongside scientific data, on the other. At its core, it recognizes that environmental problems – from climate crisis, ocean acidification, species loss, and deforestation, to racialized geographies and disabling environments – cannot be addressed by science alone. Rather, these problems require alternative ways of making information meaningful – ways that literature and criticism are especially attuned to.

Since the popular coinage of "the Anthropocene" by chemist Paul Crutzen in 2000, the concept remains a prominent analytic for literary studies, as the hazardscapes of global risk society constitute the material worlds that much literature and ecocriticism traverse. Yet I take a cue from Stephanie LeMenager and qualify this abstracting concept by bringing it down in scale. The "everyday Anthropocene,"[10] she explains, offers a quotidian and embodied vantage point that invites ecocritics to consider how environmental artists and writers represent "getting by, living alongside the world, living through it."[11] The "everyday Anthropocene" thus locates the body as a key site of ecocritical inquiry.

Ecocritics recover the body from within the forces of exclusion and toxicity, and recenter the everyday knowledges that challenge, resist, and remake unjust environmental relations. This discussion focuses on three concerns that inform approaches to the body in ecocriticism and the broader environmental humanities: the entanglement of human and other-than-human nature; the capacity of the "othered" body to enable productive counter-readings; and the accumulation of toxicity as an embodied way of knowing neoliberal globalization. These environmental epistemologies crisscross and overlap, much like the ecological, political, and social forces they trace. Thus, the sections in this chapter do not constitute discrete themes or approaches, but rather interconnected ways of knowing what it means to be an ecological subject in the uneven material worlds of the twenty-first century. The discourses assembled here invite ways of reading not only as methods of diagnosing the "slow violence"[12] of neoliberal globalization, but also as means of imagining more just and sustainable environmental futures.

## Worldly Entanglements

In his 1991 treatise *We Have Never Been Modern*, Bruno Latour contends that "the ozone hole is too social and too narrated to be truly natural."[13] Four years later, Kate Soper remarked that "it is not language that has a hole in its ozone layer."[14] This exchange testifies to one of the underlying tensions in ecocriticism, emerging with particular force in discussions of the body at the intersections of social constructivism and positivism. To what extent do we understand the body as a discursive field, and to what extent do we recognize it as a material assemblage? Where do these epistemologies of the body meet and diverge? Greg Garrard, for example, cautions that ecocritics must "keep one eye on the ways in which 'nature' is always in some ways culturally constructed, and the other on the fact that nature really exists."[15] Ecocritics are thus presented with a knotty problem: How do we acknowledge that the very idea of "nature" is discursive, while at the same time recognize that the more-than-human world teems beyond the boundaries of discourse? How we answer these questions has important implications for the ways we interpret literature. The natural world may be interpreted, for example, as metaphor or symptom of broader social systems. Thus, in Ward's *Salvage the Bones*, the Batiste family's rural land – over-mined for clay and strewn with stripped cars, feral chickens, and discarded items – powerfully registers the systemic exploitation and abandonment of Black communities. Reading the Batistes' home from this perspective illuminates how experiences of race, class, and disposability manifest in the environment. An ecocritical approach that centers the materiality of the nonhuman world might in turn emphasize the moments when the natural world punches through the discursive. As the family seeks refuge indoors from the storm, Esch describes the flood growing in the yard: "It moves under the broken tree like a creeping animal, a wide-nosed snake. Its head disappears under the house where we stand ... and that great tail stretches out behind it into the woods ... The wind ripples the water and it is coming for us."[16] Katrina, personified as a woman, "made things happen that had never happened before."[17] In these examples, Ward's prose invests the nonhuman world with its own powerful agency, necessitating a critical shift from reading the environment as a reflection of discursive power relations to recognizing the natural world as unpredictable, inscrutable, and agentive.

The influential concept of naturecultures, introduced by Donna Haraway, offers a way of understanding these worldly entanglements and the mutual embeddedness of human culture and more-than-human materialities.[18] Kindred approaches across disciplines further embody the material turn in the environmental humanities and point to the ethical dimensions of corporeal feminist ecocriticism. If early US-based ecocriticism, with its investment in male Anglo-American perspectives and the idea of wilderness as a salve for the wounds of modernity, reifies the illusory boundary between the human ("culture") and the other-than-human ("nature"), corporeal ecocriticism collapses these boundaries and rebuilds from the wreckage. Traversing urban centers, industrialized spaces, borderlands, toxic bodies and ecosystems, and transnational sites of industry while attending to the inextricable links between environment, power, and justice, twenty-first-century ecocriticism engages an expansive archive of environmental texts and subjects informed by critical race and postcolonial studies, feminism, and queer studies, among other critical traditions.

Increasingly, as the term naturecultures suggests, scholars have responded to the discursive–materialist debate by advancing ecocritical theories that refuse the division of nature and culture descended from the Enlightenment tradition.[19] In doing so, ecocritics also dethrone the Western human subject, who has historically claimed a position of superiority over all other human and more-than-human life. The logic of boundaries thus gives way to entanglement and assemblage. Contemporary ecological subjects must recognize their embeddedness in the material worlds that humanism has traditionally sought mastery over. Simultaneously, we must grapple with the interdisciplinary travels this perspective compels, for it is no longer tenable to "take refuge in a vision of science as an objective, separate sphere of knowledge-making."[20] Rather than dispensing with Western science altogether, Heather Houser investigates the integration of "positivism with ways of knowing rooted in the body and emotion"[21] to articulate a theory of "entangled epistemologies" that emerges across a range of recent environmental culture, from climate visualizations and natural-history aesthetics to novels and film. In ways such as these, contemporary ecocritics not only expand the archive of environmental texts; they also herald a broader landscape of interpretive strategies attentive to both dominant and devalued forms of knowledge production.

One such approach is embodied by feminist new-materialism, which shrugs off "objective" ways of knowing the environment in favor of situated, embodied, and sensory forms of knowing. This critical approach champions a multispecies environmental-justice ethic that refuses the hierarchies of domination implicit in Western attitudes toward nonhuman nature. A feminist new-materialist critic, for example, may forego canonical American "nature writing" – with its investment in crossing rather than collapsing nature/culture boundaries – and instead engage texts that challenge binary thinking about the natural world. Alaimo's theory of transcorporeality names the material movements across human and nonhuman bodies and considers the political and ethical possibilities emerging from the "literal contact zone between human corporeality and more-than-human nature."[22] In particular, she focuses on the intersecting phenomena of environmental justice and environmental health, where "the often unpredictable and always interconnected actions"[23] of systems, toxins, and bodies play out. An analysis of Percival Everett's postmodern environmental-justice mystery *Watershed* (1996), for example, reveals the increasingly hazy boundaries between activist and scientist, as embodied knowledges of the environment collide with the "perceived objectivity"[24] of science. The novel's protagonist Robert Hawks, a Black hydrologist, ultimately becomes an advocate for Native American sovereignty amid ongoing reflections on the embodied realities of racialization and environmental injustice in the US settler state. Here, the ecocritic's investment in uncovering the interactions of material environments, bodies, and power reflects the recognition of worldly entanglement.

Unpredictability and interconnection, two conceptual linchpins of recent ecocriticism, ultimately require epistemological humility on the part of the critic (and the human), who must embrace the discomfiting immersion in material worlds that erode familiar modes of understanding. Trans-corporeal critiques of objectivity and distance build on earlier ecofeminist work that interrogates the standpoint of mastery implicit in binaries, from man/woman and self/other to nature/culture and body/environment. In the late 1970s and 1980s, ecofeminist critics in the United States theorized the domination of the nonhuman world as a form of patriarchal subjugation. In her canonical 1980 study *The Death of Nature: Women, Ecology and the Scientific Revolution*, Carolyn Merchant implicates the development of the modern sciences in the objectification and "feminization" of the nonhuman world through the mutual subjugation of women and environment.[25] A shift during the Scientific Revolution from ideologies of nature as "nurturing mother" to nature as an unruly force underwrites the central premise of modernity: power over nature.

The ecofeminist tradition importantly decouples the category of woman from biological essentialism by emphasizing gender as a discursive construct. Yet at the same time, this critical move to disaggregate "woman" from biological essentialism necessitates the maintenance of a clear boundary between nature and culture. This boundary inadvertently reifies the authority of each category, posing a challenge to a trans-corporeal ecocriticism premised on the entanglements of the biological and the discursive. Instead of doubling down on binaries, scholars such as Alaimo advocate for the transformation of dualisms (nature/culture, body/mind, subject/object) by "endow[ing] them with flesh."[26] To grapple with the material-discursive natures of the environment and the self is to transform dualistic epistemologies into dynamic and embodied ways of knowing. This framework offers a vital methodology for reading American literature – one that decenters the authority of liberal humanism, with its investment in individual agency, and instead recognizes the intersecting forces of history, environment, and discourse.

Relatedly, trans-corporeality invites engagement with the discourse of race, since one of the sites through which race materializes is the uneven exposure to hazards borne by Black, Indigenous, and people of color communities. There has long been critical consensus about the social rather than biological origins of race as a modern category of difference; indeed, social deconstruction works precisely by redirecting attention from material bodies toward their discursive construction to dismantle essentialist claims about the "natural" basis of race. This social-constructionist tradition remains invaluable in disrupting the reification of white supremacy. At the same time, environmental justice necessitates a focus on the bodies of racialized people, since it is at these sites that toxic flows materialize and create the conditions of possibility for health or sickness. In considering how this extends to the study of literature, Julie Sze notes the value of fiction's signal language of subjectivity – visual images and metaphor – for representing the bodily assaults of environmental injustice in ways that transcend a "strictly documentary account of the contemporary world" (163).[27] An ecocritical emphasis on embodiment can trace the roots and routes of toxicity and map the local onto the global, bridging vast scales, from the cellular to the planetary. Doing so reveals broad networks of bodily and environmental plunder that would otherwise be invisible. For these reasons, ecocriticism advances methods of reading the environment, the body, and the literary text that foreground embodied and everyday ways of knowing.

## Disabling Environmentalisms

Ecocriticism is increasingly invested in tracing how systems of power, from white supremacy to heteropatriarchy and ableism, invest different bodies and environments with vastly different meanings, rights, and privileges. Some people's bodies and communities are deemed worthy of protection and environmental access, while others are erased, silenced, and displaced. Geographer Carolyn Finney begins *Black Faces, White Spaces: Reimagining the Relationship of African Americans to the Great Outdoors* (2014) by reminding readers of the whiteness of mainstream environmentalism, noting that whiteness "becomes the way of understanding our environment"[28] in the United States. Through analyses of popular films, advertisements, and environmental discourse, she demonstrates how the Euro-American emphasis on conservation, preservation, and outdoor recreation ignores African Americans' environmental knowledge while also failing to consider Black communities' differential access, needs, history, and privilege.[29] Similarly invested in critiquing the making and unmaking of environmental subjects, Sarah Jaquette Ray introduces the concept of environmental otherness in her 2013 study *The Ecological Other: Environmental Exclusion in American Culture.* Advocating for a more inclusive environmentalism, she examines how marginalized communities reimagine mainstream environmentalism and its foundational codes, terms, and narratives. Reading alongside the "ecological other" reveals how the discourse of the "healthy" and "whole" body is weaponized against specific groups, including disabled people, Indigenous communities, and immigrants to maintain the hierarchies of domination embedded in mainstream environmentalism.[30]

One of the tenets of ecocriticism is the constant transit between the human body and other-than-human natures, and disability scholarship has a longstanding kinship with this perspective. Disability studies has long rejected medical and liberal models of the bounded human body in favor of understanding the bodymind[31] in a network of material worlds. Rosemarie Garland-Thomson succinctly explains that "changes that occur when body encounters world are what we call disability,"[32] while Alison Kafer advocates for a "cripped environmentalism" that embraces how "the experience of illness and disability presents alternative ways of understanding ourselves in relation to the environment."[33] Mainstream environmentalism can itself be seen as a "disabling set of practices and beliefs"[34] for many individuals and communities, and "ecological otherness" locates the physical body as a primary site through which the dominant culture casts specific communities as "threats to nature" or otherwise unworthy of environmental protection. Mining an archive of "green" cultural discourses, Ray reads the body as a "metonym for contemporary environmental values,"[35] while turning to the literature and activism of marginalized communities to read the body as a site of resistance and negotiation. In doing so, she reveals how the binary rhetorics of purity and pollution are yoked together. Referring to her approach as corporeal ecology, Ray demonstrates how the affect of environmental disgust determines which bodies are "good" for nature and which are harmful, unnatural, and thus targets for removal.

"Ecological otherness" offers a way of reading the flipside of the empowered ecological subject in literature, whose green consumer choices and environmental privilege signal their virtue. In order to critically examine the figure of the ecological other alongside the mainstream US environmental movement, Ray focuses on three contemporary case studies, beginning with the emphasis on "risk" in outdoor adventure culture. Here, she analyzes advertisements and other outdoor-recreation media alongside contemporary environmental psychology to reread the iconic American ideal of the fit, self-sufficient body against the disabled person assumed to be the very embodiment of environmental crisis. Throughout American history, the figure of the disabled body has served as the "quintessential symbol of humanity's alienation from nature,"[36] implicated in various forms of othering within the mainstream environmental movement. Yet environmentalism's others "are not silent about their exclusion."[37] Ray's analysis of Sherman Alexie's short fiction and Leslie Marmon Silko's novel *Almanac of the Dead* (1991), which reckons with the legacies of uranium mining, illuminates the foundational role of the body in many Native American criticisms of mainstream environmentalism and its investment in colonial-capitalism. Through a concluding study of immigrant bodies along the Mexico-Arizona border, where the Organ Pipe Cactus National Monument is a site of contestation between the people of the Tohono O'odham Indian Reservation on one side and the Barry Goldwater Military Range on the other, Ray argues that contemporary environmentalist discourse indicts certain racialized bodies for "pollut[ing] the national body politic" and fomenting national "insecurity."[38] In this way, ecocriticism's attention to the overlapping rhetorics of pollution and racialized otherness offers a much-needed invitation to reread the canon of American literature, in which the imagination of "pristine" wilderness remains a central theme. Works ranging from *The Adventures of Huckleberry Finn* and Willa Cather's Great Plains novels to contemporary environmental fictions frequently idealize the untouched wilderness as an escape from increasingly globalized, industrialized, and racially diverse worlds. Reading works such as these through the lens of ecological otherness unsettles the fantasy of purity that has been weaponized against marginalized peoples.

Critical attention to the figure of the disabled body reveals how ideologies of environmental purity have tended to hinge on the idea of the "whole" and "healthy" body, while toxicity is registered through deviations from wholeness and health. An eco-disability approach thus critiques the medical model that casts disability as individual, problematic, and in need of repair. From this perspective, Ray's work takes up where Alaimo's leaves off by implicating ecocriticism's failure to trouble the correlation between the healthy body and the healthy environment. By leaving this correlation largely intact, critics run the risk of reifying the ableist value of a whole, healthy body while rehearsing long-running anxieties about "disfigurement as nature gone wrong."[39]

Ecological otherness reveals how environmentalism's assumed critique of the status quo in many ways reinforces dominant social hierarchies. As an embodied epistemology, or way of knowing and experiencing the world, "ecological otherness" offers a way to read the literature and activism of marginalized communities against the exclusionary discourses of mainstream environmentalism and its expression in the canon of American environmental literature. It provides a valuable framework for dispensing with facile assumptions about "health" that inform both contemporary restoration ecologies and the medical model's curative politics. Confronting the injustices that render certain environments disabling must not come at the expense of disabled people. Eli Clare points toward an environmental-justice ethic when he asks: "How do we witness, name, and resist the injustices that reshape and damage all kinds of bodies – plant and animal, organic and inorganic, nonhuman and human? And alongside our resistance, how do we make peace with the reshaped and damaged bodies themselves, cultivate love and respect for them?"[40] In order to bring the concerns of environmental-justice movements into conversation with those of literary scholars, ecocritics must engage ways of reading the ecological body in literature that do not stigmatize the disabled body. In a disability-informed ecocritical approach, the disabled body does not serve as a passive register of environmental harm but as a vibrant way of interpreting and reimagining the entanglements of bodies, power, and ecosystems. Such an eco-crip theory[41] can be extended to literature in the environmental justice tradition, such as Indra Sinha's narrative of the Bhopal chemical disaster, *Animal's People* (2007), and Helena Maria Viramontes' narrative of Mexican-American farm workers in California, *Under the Feet of Jesus* (1995). A disability-informed ecocritical lens also extends to modern classics such as David Foster Wallace's *Infinite Jest* (1996) and Don DeLillo's *White Noise* (1985). The protagonist of DeLillo's novel, for example, learns of his exposure to a substance known as Nyodene D. after a nearby airborne toxic event and is warned that the substance will stay in his body for thirty years. In tandem with his preexisting fear of death, his capacity to sense in minute detail the environment around him (the titular "white noise") heightens, illuminating the alternative ways of sensing, orienting, and knowing the world that are embodied by characters with environmental sickness or disability. The next section will delve further into the figure of the toxic body in the ecocritical tradition, extending the discussion of personhood, embodiment, and ecological otherness to consider ways of reading race alongside disability.

## Toxicity

Scholars generally trace the emergence of the modern environmental movement in the United States to the mid-twentieth century, when a dizzying array of postwar petrochemical byproducts, plastics, and other synthetics found their way into American homes. In 1962, eight years before the establishment of the Environmental Protection Agency (EPA), marine biologist Rachel Carson published a book about the proliferation of synthetic pesticide use in US agriculture. *Silent Spring* was at once an investigation into the bodily harms caused by widespread chemical use and an indictment of the chemical industry's misinformation campaigns. Written for a popular audience, the book met with public acclaim alongside criticism from corporations including DuPont and Monsanto, while precipitating a nation-wide ban on the insecticide dichlorodiphenyltrichloroethane (DDT) and increasing awareness of how invisible everyday chemicals find their way into our homes and bodies. *Silent Spring* thus marked a turning point in the popular imagination, as environmentalism expanded its purview to encompass the permeable human body. One of the most persistent and formative figures in ecocriticism, the porous and vulnerable human body, emerges across a broad archive of American cultural texts, including novels by Silko, Richard Powers, and Attica Locke, and popular films such as Todd Haynes's *Safe* (1995) and *Dark Waters* (2019), and Steven Soderbergh's *Erin Brockovich* (2000). In Heather Houser's analysis of late twentieth-century environmental fiction, narratives of "ecosickness" reveal the "conceptual dissolutions of the body–environment boundary" and a capacity to shift "environmental perception and politics."[42]

*Silent Spring*, though a work of nonfiction, begins by entangling science and fiction. It opens with a short piece titled "A Fable for Tomorrow" in which Carson paints the portrait of an idyllic all-American town suddenly afflicted by a "strange blight" of white powder that sows sickness across the land.[43] "The people," she concludes, "had done it themselves."[44] Thus, as Greg Garrard notes of this preface, the modern environmental movement begins with the literary genres of the apocalypse and the pastoral, signaling its kinship with narrative and storytelling.[45] In many ways, Carson's evocative fable folds her book-length argument into a two-page story that warns of widespread disease and death, urging readers to wake up to the invisible dangers of pesticides. Yet it also evinces the universalizing and moralizing language of environmental catastrophe that flattens the bad actors into a single undifferentiated mass: The people had done it to themselves. Throughout this section, we will tug at the threads of this statement to reveal the uneven distributions of agency and privilege experienced by different groups in relation to toxicity.

How do the embodiments of race, disability, and toxicity intersect in an age of neoliberal globalization and compounding environmental risk? Interdisciplinary scholar Mel Y. Chen's *Animacies: Biopolitics, Racial Mattering, and Queer Affect* (2012) is one influential response to this question. Their study travels through cognitive linguistics, queer animality, popular film and media, and the social lives of heavy metals, illuminating the "marriage of bodies and chemicals"[46] in the twenty-first century and bringing together theories of racialization, queerness, biopolitics, and toxicity to examine the discursive boundaries of "life" and "death." Chen's study considers environmental "wrongness" and "unnaturalness," extending Ray's theorization about disability and environment to matter "that is considered insensate, immobile, deathly, or otherwise 'wrong.'"[47] Doing so reveals how these categories in fact "animate" cultural life in significant ways. From this perspective, Chen's discussion pushes at the seams of both bodies and discourse, troubling the foundational ideas of life, death, and the liminal spaces in-between. Applying this theorization to the analysis of literature reframes agency in important ways that work against the binary of active-human/passive-environment. We can thus read the nuclear waste that recurs in Silko's fiction, including *Ceremony* (1977) and *Almanac of the Dead* (1991), as an agentive force whose simultaneous liveliness and unnaturalness establish what Jessica Hurley calls the "conditions of possibility" for both the narratives themselves and for the radical resistance of the Laguna Pueblo people, whose land has been expropriated by the nuclear-industrial complex.[48]

In the political economies of life and death, the fragile boundary between animate and inanimate is ruthlessly policed and reproduced. Chen defines animacy as "a specific kind of affective and material construct"[49] that is deeply shaped by sexuality and race and invested in certain types of matter and "mattering," from the heavy metals and chemicals that populate our environments to the people deemed "toxic" to dominant culture. Chen does not seek to simply reinvest inanimate matter with life, for to do so would be to reify the binary of life/death. Rather, they strive "to remap live and dead zones away from those very terms"[50] and toward the dynamic and liminal site where liveliness and deathliness are negotiated. Animacy thus theorizes contemporary anxieties around "the production of humanness"[51] by attending to the ways in which binaries (life/death, subject/object, environment/culture, human/animal) shape understandings of human life, agency, and kinship. Indeed, as lead is "animated" by its perceived threat to human bodies and the US body politic, it simultaneously "deterritorializes," erasing the spatial and conceptual boundaries between here and there, inside and outside.[52] In this way, animacy constitutes a "queering" of normative categories of life and death, sex, intimacy, nationalism, and imperialism. As a theory that fundamentally destabilizes fantasies of containment, animacy offers an interpretive analytic that necessitates reading literature against the grain of liberal humanism and its investment in the autonomous human subject.

Bringing together theorizations of worldly entanglement, embodied otherness, and toxicity allows ecocritics to attend to the distributive injustices of the Anthropocene as they become legible in literature and culture. In an era where petrochemical by-products, heavy metals, and other hazardous substances constitute the material of everyday life, how can we think with and through these forms? In response to this question, Chen investigates what "enlivened toxins like transnational lead, their effectivity and affectivity in young white bodies, and their displacement of deathly black and contagious Asian bodies"[53] could teach us as neoliberal subjects. Identifying lead toxicity in particular as an "animated, active, and peculiarly queer agent"[54] through an analysis of the 2007 panic about lead paint, Chen articulates the normative, racialized, and gendered ways that liveliness and deathliness are mediated in political and public discourse. They assemble an archive of mainstream news media from the early aughts to demonstrate how lead paint in a range of imported children's toys became "animated and racialized as Chinese,"[55] while the victims of the lead paint were construed primarily as white Americans. Chen reproduces a widely circulated advertisement for an at-home lead-testing kit called Abotex Lead Inspector that shows a smiling white baby with its bare arm resting on a stuffed toy flower bearing a smiling face. This domestic scene reifies the parental fantasy that a toy "must be a familiar and safe substitute for a 'person,'"[56] further underscoring the insidious and animate threat posed by lead matter in the toy. A subsequent analysis of NPR's coverage of lead poisoning among African American communities reveals how commonplace descriptors such as "puzzling" deny a long history (and knowledge) of the metal's overrepresentation in Black neighborhoods. Through examples such as these, Chen simultaneously demonstrates the racialization of lead toxicity as "Chinese" and the discursive deflection of the targets of lead poisoning away from domestic concerns about the exposure of urban Black and low-income children.

Examining literature, popular media, and cultural discourse through the framework of animacy allows us to critically read "dead" materials – lead, uranium, pesticides – and to grapple with their reanimation through the biopolitics of race. In ways that echo the agency of nuclear waste in Silko's fiction, lead achieves "its own animacy as an agent of harm"[57] in American culture precisely because of its threat to normative and racialized bodies. The multitude of contact zones between lead and human bodies through mining, the workplace, toys, recycling, and transnational distribution ultimately reflects the expansive landscape of global capital's toxic bodies. As an ecocritical intervention, animacy heralds a way of reading, interpreting, and reimagining the biopolitical life of neoliberal modernity through the "stuff" of the everyday, while unsettling the normative codes through which different ecological bodies come to matter.

## Conclusion

Returning to Jesmyn Ward's *Salvage the Bones*, we find an opportunity to reflect on the worldly entanglements, disabling environments, and racialized biopolitics of the "everyday Anthropocene." The morning after Hurricane Katrina makes landfall in the coastal community of Bois Sauvage, the Batiste family huddles together in the attic of their home watching the churning floodwater slowly recede. "We were a pile of wet, cold branches, human debris in the middle of all the rest of it," fifteen-year-old Esch reflects.[58] The young protagonist invokes the stark collapse of boundaries between the human and the nonhuman incited by the storm. Yet the phrase "human debris" signals the biopolitics of Katrina's violence: "Debris" is a discursive category, much like "waste" or "weeds," defined by its excess and unwantedness. Esch's categorization of her family as "human debris" following a description of them as nonhuman debris brings into sharp relief the making and unmaking of the human subject performed by the ongoing violence of white supremacy, poverty, ableism, and other interlocking systems of oppression.

The intersecting realities of anti-Black violence, environmental racism, and public health crises in the twenty-first century underscore the challenges and potentials of ecological embodiment for critics, writers, artists, and activists who continue the work of building more just and equitable environmental futures. This chapter has considered how ecocriticism comes to know the interconnections between the human and more-than-human world, and how environmental literature and culture bring these affinities into affective presence. From the human's entanglement with other-than-human materiality to confrontations with the whiteness and ableism of mainstream US environmentalism, and finally to the recognition of toxicity as a racialized and queered embodiment of neoliberal life, the critical landscape outlined here reflects approaches to reading the ecological body in American literature that simultaneously diagnose and imagine otherwise. In different ways, these approaches advocate for the critical embrace of vulnerability as a way of thinking with and responding to environmental injustices. The overlapping critical discussions presented here testify to the importance of staying with the trouble, to borrow a phrase from Haraway, and to staying with the fraughtness of the ecological body on the page, in the world, and everywhere in between.

## NOTES

1 Jesmyn Ward, *Salvage the Bones* (New York: Bloomsbury, 2011), 83.
2 Ibid., 97.
3 Ibid., 217.
4 Ibid., 45.
5 Christopher Lloyd, "Creaturely, Throwaway Life after Hurricane Katrina: Salvage the Bones and Beasts of the Southern Wild," *South: A Scholarly Journal* 48, no. 2 (Spring 2016): 246–264, 246.

6 Hop Hopkins, "Racism Is Killing the Planet," *Sierra: The National Magazine of the Sierra Club*, June 8, 2020, www.sierraclub.org/sierra/racism-killing-planet.

7 Stacy Alaimo, *Bodily Natures: Science, Environment, and the Material Self* (Bloomington: Indiana University Press, 2010), 8.

8 Ibid., 3.

9 Ibid., 11.

10 Stephanie LeMenager, "Climate Change and the Struggle for Genre," in *Anthropocene Reading: Literary History in Geologic Times*, ed. Tobias Menely and Jesse Oak Taylor (University Park: Pennsylvania State University Press, 2017), 220–238, 221.

11 Ibid., 221.

12 Rob Nixon, *Slow Violence and the Environmentalism of the Poor* (Cambridge, MA: Harvard University Press, 2011). Although Nixon's work focuses on global Anglophone rather than US-based literature, "slow violence" remains a ubiquitous analytic in contemporary American ecocriticism and itself points to the limiting frame of the nation-state for apprehending environmental crises.

13 Bruno Latour, *We Have Never Been Modern* (Cambridge, MA: Harvard University Press, 1993), 6.

14 Kate Soper, *What Is Nature?: Culture, Politics, and the Non-Human* (Hoboken, NJ: John Wiley & Sons, 1995), 151.

15 Greg Garrard, *Ecocriticism* (New York: Routledge, 2012), 10.

16 Ward, *Salvage the Bones*, 227.

17 Ibid., 248.

18 Donna Haraway, *The Companion Species Manifesto: Dogs, People, and Significant Otherness* (Chicago: University of Chicago Press, 2003). Additionally, see Anna Tsing, *The Mushroom at the End of the World: On the Possibility of Life in Capitalist Ruins* (Princeton, NJ: Princeton University Press, 2015), and Eben Kirskey, ed., *The Multispecies Salon* (Durham, NC: Duke University Press, 2014).

19 For recent examples, see Stacy Alaimo, *Exposed: Environmental Politics and Pleasures in Posthuman Times* (Minneapolis: University of Minnesota Press, 2016); Donna Haraway, *Staying with the Trouble: Making Kin in the Chthulucene* (Durham, NC: Duke University Press, 2016); Melody Jue, *Wild Blue Media* (Durham, NC: Duke University Press, 2020); and Sami Schalk, *Bodyminds Reimagined: (Dis)ability, Race, and Gender in Black Women's Speculative Fiction* (Durham, NC: Duke University Press, 2018).

20 Alaimo, *Bodily Natures*, 65.

21 Heather Houser, *Infowhelm: Environmental Art and Literature in an Age of Data* (New York: Columbia University Press, 2020), 1.

22 Alaimo, *Bodily Natures*, 2.

23 Ibid., 3.

24 Ibid., 64.

25 Carolyn Merchant, *The Death of Nature: Women, Ecology and the Scientific Revolution* (New York: Harper & Row, 1980), 2.

26 Alaimo, *Bodily Natures*, 5.

27 Julie Sze, "From Environmental Literature to the Literature of Environmental Justice," in *The Environmental Justice Reader: Politics, Poetics & Pedagogy*, ed. Joni Adamson, Mei Mei Evans, and Rachel Stein (Tucson: University of Arizona Press, 2002), 163–180, 163.

28 Carolyn Finney, *Black Faces, White Spaces: Reimagining the Relationship of African Americans to the Great Outdoors* (Chapel Hill: University of North Carolina Press, 2014), 3.

29 Ibid., 4.

30 Sarah Jaquette Ray, *The Ecological Other: Environmental Exclusion in American Culture* (Tucson: University of Arizona Press, 2013).

31 This key term in disability studies is a rejoinder to the Western severing of body and mind, and instead acknowledges the integration of embodiment, affect, and cognition. For an important study on Blackness and bodyminds, see Schalk, *Bodyminds Reimagined.*

32 Rosemarie Garland-Thomson, "Disability and Representation," *PMLA* 120, no. 2 (March 2005): 522–527, 524.

33 Alison Kafer, "Bodies of Nature: The Environmental Politics of Disability," in *Disability Studies and the Environmental Humanities*, ed. Sarah Jaquette Ray and Jay Sibara (Lincoln: University of Nebraska Press, 2017), 201–241, 204.

34 Ray, *The Ecological Other*, 10.

35 Ibid., 6.

36 Ibid.

37 Ibid., 180.

38 Ibid., 33.

39 Ibid., 8.

40 Eli Clare, "Notes on Natural Worlds, Disabled Bodies, and a Politics of Cure," in *Disability Studies and the Environmental Humanities*, ed. Sarah Jaquette Ray and Jay Sibara (Lincoln: University of Nebraska Press, 2017), 242–265, 252.

41 Ray and Sibara, *Disability Studies and the Environmental Humanities.*

42 Heather Houser, *Ecosickness in Contemporary U.S. Fiction: Environment and Affect* (New York: Columbia University Press, 2014), 3.

43 Rachel Carson, *Silent Spring* (New York: Houghton Mifflin, 1962), 2.

44 Ibid., 3.

45 Garrard, *Ecocriticism*, 2.

46 Mel Chen, *Animacies: Biopolitics, Racial Mattering, and Queer Affect* (Durham, NC: Duke University Press, 2012), 1.

47 Ibid., 2.

48 Jessica Hurley, *Infrastructures of Apocalypse: American Literature and the Nuclear Complex* (Minneapolis: University of Minnesota Press, 2020), 187.

49 Chen, *Animacies*, 5.

50 Ibid., 11.

51 Ibid., 3.

52 Ibid., 167.

53 Ibid., 7.

54 Ibid., 10.

55 This was certainly not the first nor the most recent example of members of the US public and government blaming China for global public health crises. Indeed, as a recent example, there are stark resonances with the Trump administration's targeting of China in the COVID-19 pandemic.

56 Chen, *Animacies*, 161.

57 Ibid., 187.

58 Ward, *Salvage the Bones*, 237.

# FURTHER READING

Abitz, Dan. "Beauty and Blindness: Navigating the Techno-Body in Henry James's 'Glasses," *The Henry James Review* 37, no. 3 (2016): 284–291.

Ablow, Rachel, ed. *The Feeling of Reading: Affective Experience and Victorian Literature*. Ann Arbor: University of Michigan Press, 2010.

Achenbaum, W. Andrew. "A History of Ageism Since 1969." *Generations: Journal of the American Society on Aging* 39, no. 3 (2015): 10–16.

Alger, William Rounseville. *Life of Edwin Forrest: The American Tragedian*. New York: Arno Press, 1977.

Antebi, Susan, and Beth E. Jörgensen. *Libre Acceso: Latin American Literature and Film through Disability Studies*. Albany: State University of New York Press, 2016.

Armengol, Josep M. "Gendering the Great Depression: Rethinking the Male Body in 1930s American Culture and Literature." *Journal of Gender Studies* 23, no. 1 (2014): 59–69.

Armstrong, John. "Gothic Matters of De-Composition: The Pastoral Dead in Contemporary American Fiction." *Text Matters: A Journal of Literature, Theory and Culture* 6, no. 1 (2016): 127–143.

Armstrong, Rhonda Jenkins. "Rewriting the Corpse in Suzan-Lori Parks's Getting Mother's Body." *Southern Quarterly* 53, no. 1 (2015): 41–56.

Auyong, Elaine. *When Fiction Feels Real: Representation and the Reading Mind*. New York: Oxford University Press, 2018.

Baiada, Christa. "Loving the Unlovable Body in Yamanaka's *Saturday Night at the Pahala Theatre*." *Asian American Literature: Discourse & Pedagogies* 7 (2016): 39–53.

Bares, Annie. "'Each Unbearable Day': Narrative Ruthlessness and Environmental and Reproductive Injustice in Jesmyn Ward's *Salvage the Bones*." *MELUS* 44, no. 3 (2019): 21–40.

Bennett, Michael, and Vanessa D. Dickerson. *Recovering the Black Female Body: Self-Representations by African American Women*. New Brunswick, NJ: Rutgers University Press, 2001.

Bieger, Laura. "'Freedom, Equality, Beauty for Everyone' – Notes on Fantasizing the Modern Body." *Amerikastudien/American Studies* 57, no. 4 (2012): 663–688.

Bladow, Kyle, and Jennifer Ladino, eds. *Affective Ecocriticism: Emotion, Embodiment, Environment*. Lincoln: University of Nebraska Press, 2018.

Blevins, Jennifer Renee. "'I Ain't You': Fat and the Female Body in Flannery O'Connor." *Tulsa Studies in Women's Literature* 39, no. 1 (2020): 61–83.

Boonin-Vail, Eli. "'The Body of the Nation': Ta-Nehisi Coates' Black Panther and the Black Literary Tradition." *Inks: The Journal of the Comics Studies Society* 4, no. 2 (2020): 135–155.

Bouson, J. Brooks. *Embodied Shame: Uncovering Female Shame in Contemporary Women's Writings*. Albany: State University of New York Press, 2009.

Bracken, Rachel Conrad. "Influenza and Embodied Sociality in Early Twentieth-Century American Literature." *American Literary History* 32, no. 3 (2020): 507–534.

Brown, Caroline A. *The Black Female Body in American Literature and Art: Performing Identity*. New York: Routledge, 2012.

Burcon, Sarah Himsel. *Fabricating the Body: Effects of Obligation and Exchange in Contemporary Discourse*. Newcastle upon Tyne: Cambridge Scholars Publishing, 2014.

Butler, Judith. *Bodies That Matter: On the Discursive Limits of Sex*. London; New York: Routledge, 1993.

Castro Borrego, Silvia del Pilar. *The Search for Wholeness and Diaspora Literacy in Contemporary African American Literature*. Newcastle upon Tyne: Cambridge Scholars Publishing, 2011.

Chen, Fu-jen. "The National Body: Gender, Race, and Disability in John Okada's *No-No Boy*." *ARIEL: A Review of International English Literature* 50, no. 4 (2019): 25–50.

Chu, Seo-Young. *Do Metaphors Dream of Literal Sleep? A Science-Fictional Theory of Representation*. Cambridge: Harvard University Press, 2010.

Cohen, William A. *Embodied: Victorian Literature and the Senses*. Minneapolis: University of Minnesota Press, 2009.

Colbert, Soyica Diggs. *The African American Theatrical Body: Reception, Performance, and the Stage*. Cambridge: Cambridge University Press, 2011.

Crane, Jacob. "'Razed to the Knees': The Anti-Heroic Body in James McCune Smith's 'The Heads of Colored People.'" *African American Review* 51, no. 1 (2018): 7–21.

Dames, Nicholas. *The Physiology of the Novel: Reading, Neural Science, and the Form of Victorian Fiction*. New York: Oxford University Press, 2007.

DeCoste, Marcel. "This Is My Body: The Saving Knowledge of Suffering Flesh in Flannery O'Connor's *Wise Blood*." *Religion and Literature* 49, no. 2 (2017): 69–91.

Dery, Mark. "Black to the Future: Interviews with Samuel R. Delany, Greg Tate, and Tricia Rose." In *Flame Wars: The Discourse of Cyberculture*, ed. Mark Dery 179–222. Durham, NC: Duke University Press, 1994.

Devereux, Cecily, and Marcelle Kosman. "The Automated Body [Special Issue]." *English Studies in Canada* 42, no. 1–2 (2016): 1–20.

Diamond, Elin. *Unmasking Mimesis: Essays on Feminism and Theater*. New York: Routledge, 1997.

Dillon, Grace L., Michael Levy, and John Rieder, eds. "Indigenous Futurism." *Extrapolation* 57 (Spring-Summer 2016): 1–2.

Dujaković, Stela. "Masculinity beyond Repair: Aging, Pathology, and the Male Body in Jonathan Franzen's *The Corrections*." *Anafora* 6, no. 2 (2019): 469–491.

Etter, William M. *The Good Body: Normalizing Visions in Nineteenth-Century American Literature and Culture*. Newcastle upon Tyne: Cambridge Scholars Publishing, 2010.

Farrell, Molly. *Counting Bodies: Population in Colonial American Writing*. New York: Oxford University Press, 2016.

Fear-Segal, Jacqueline, and Rebecca Tillett. *Indigenous Bodies: Reviewing, Relocating, Reclaiming*. Albany: State University of New York Press, 2013.

Field, Hannah. *Playing with the Book: Victorian Movable Picture Books and the Child Reader*. Minneapolis: University of Minnesota Press, 2019.

Franzino, Jean. "'Harmonies of Form and Color': Race and the Prosthetic Body in Civil War America." *Literature and Medicine* 38, no. 1 (2020): 51–87.

Fusco, Serena. *Incorporations of Chineseness: Hybridity, Bodies, and Chinese American Literature*. Newcastle upon Tyne: Cambridge Scholars Publishing, 2016.

Ghosh, Pradip, and Madhusmita Pati. "Writing the Body: Self, Illness, and Experience in AIDS/Gay Life Writing." *Ravenshaw Journal of Literary and Cultural Studies* 8 (2018): 21–31.

Giroux, Henry. "Reading Hurricane Katrina: Race, Class, and the Biopolitics of Disposability." *College Literature* 33, no. 3 (Summer 2006): 171–196.

Griffiths, Jennifer L. *Traumatic Possessions: The Body and Memory in African American Women's Writing and Performance*. Charlottesville: University of Virginia Press, 2009.

Harper, Mihaela P. "Fabric Frontiers: Thread, Cloth, Body, Self in Latina Literature and Film." *Hispanic Review* 81, no. 2 (2013): 165–180.

Harrison, Summer. "Environmental Justice Storytelling: Sentiment, Knowledge, and the Body in Ruth Ozeki's *My Year of Meats*." *Isle: Interdisciplinary Studies in Literature and Environment* 24, no. 3 (2017): 457–476.

Henderson, Carol E. *Scarring the Black Body: Race and Representation in African American Literature*. Columbia: University of Missouri Press, 2002.

Henneberg, Sylvia. "Fat Liberation in the First World: Lucille Clifton and the New Body." *Women's Studies: An Interdisciplinary Journal* 47, no. 1–4 (2018): 60–79.

Horowitz, Sara R. "Mediating Judaism: Mind, Body, Spirit, and Contemporary North American Jewish Fiction." *AJS Review* 30, no. 2 (2006): 231–253.

Hurley, Jessica. *Infrastructures of Apocalypse: American Literature and the Nuclear Complex*. Minneapolis: University of Minnesota Press, 2020.

Jackson, Zakiyyah Iman. *Becoming Human: Matter and Meaning in an Antiblack World*. New York: New York University Press, 2020.

Jeffery, Scott. *The Posthuman Body in Superhero Comics: Human, Superhuman, Transhuman, Post/Human*. New York: Palgrave Macmillan, 2016.

Johns, Adrian. The book is a monograph, so I struck the citation to just a chapter title. *The Nature of the Book: Print and Knowledge in the Making*, 380–443. Chicago: University of Chicago Press, 1998.

Karno, Valerie. "Legal Hunger: Law, Narrative, and Orality in Leslie Marmon Silko's *Storyteller* and *Almanac of the Dead*." *College Literature* 28, no. 1 (2001): 29–45.

Keeling, Kara. *Queer Times, Black Futures*. New York: New York University Press, 2019.

Kimak, Izabella. *Bicultural Bodies: A Study of South Asian American Women's Literature*. New York: Peter Lang, 2013.

Kruger, Loren. *The National Stage: Theatre and Cultural Legitimation in England, France, and America*. Chicago: University of Chicago Press, 1992.

Kupetz, Joshua. "Disability Ecology and the Rematerialization of Literary Disability Studies." In *The Matter of Disability: Materiality, Biopolitics, Crip Affect*, edited by David T. Mitchell, Susan Antebi, and Sharon L. Snyder. Ann Arbor: Michigan University Press, 2019.

Lam, C. Christina. "Flipping the Script: Memory, Body, and Belonging in Dahlma Llanos-Figueroa's *Daughters of the Stone*." *Afro-Latina/o Literature and Performance* 7 (2017): 1–9.

Lavender, Isiah, III. *Race in American Science Fiction*. Bloomington: Indiana University Press, 2011.

Lee, Yoon Sun. "Racialized Bodies and Asian American Literature." *American Literary History* 30, no. 1 (2018): 166–176.

Lelekis, Debbie. *American Literature, Lynching, and the Spectator in the Crowd: Spectacular Violence*. Lanham, MD: Lexington Books, 2015.

LeMenager, Stephanie. *Living Oil: Petroleum Culture in the American Century*. New York: Oxford University Press, 2013.

Lima, Lázaro. *The Latino Body: Crisis Identities in American Literary and Cultural Memory*. New York: New York University Press, 2007.

Luckhurst, Roger. "Iraq War Body Counts: Reportage, Photography, and Fiction." *MFS: Modern Fiction Studies* 63, no. 2 (2017): 355–372.

Madsen, Deborah L. *Beyond the Borders: American Literature and Post-Colonial Theory*. London: Pluto Press, 2003.

Malcolmson, Cristina. "'The Fairest Lady': Gender and Race in William Byrd's 'Account of a Negro-Boy that Is Dappel'd in Several Places of His Body with White Spots (1697)." *Journal for Early Modern Cultural Studies* 18, no. 1 (2018): 159–179.

Malinowska, Agnes. "Charlotte Perkins Gilman's Fungal Female Animal: Evolution, Efficiency, and the Reproductive Body." *Modernism/Modernity* 26, no. 2 (2019): 267–288.

Mann, Anika. *Reading Contagion: The Hazards of Reading in the Age of Print*. Charlottesville: University of Virginia Press, 2018.

McAllister, Marvin. *"White People Do Not Know How to Behave at Entertainments Designed for Ladies and Gentlemen of Colour": William Brown's African and American Theater*. Chapel Hill: University of North Carolina Press, 2003.

McLaughlin, Thomas. *Reading and the Body: The Physical Practice of Reading*. New York: Palgrave, 2015.

Merrydew, Aimee. "Reflecting (on) the Body: Trans Self-Representation and Resistance in the Poetry of Ely Shipley." *Comparative American Studies: An International Journal* 17, no. 1 (2020): 58–72.

Mielke, Laura. "Performance, Theatricality, and Early American Drama." In *A Companion to American Literature, Volume 1*, edited by Susan Belasco, Theresa Strouth Gaul, Linck Johnson, and Michael Soto, 428–444. New York: Wiley-Blackwell, 2020.

Miles, Caroline S. "Representing and Self-Mutilating the Laboring Male Body: Re-Examining Rebecca Harding Davis's 'Life in the Iron Mills.'" *ATQ (The American Transcendental Quarterly)* 18, no. 2 (2004): 89–104.

Millar, Susanna. *Reading by Touch.* New York: Routledge, 1997.

Miller, Meredith. "Tuberculosis and Visionary Sensibility: The Consumptive Body as Masculine Dissent in George Eliot and Henry James." In *The Victorian Male Body,* edited by Joanne Ella Parsons and Ruth Heholt. Edinburgh: Edinburgh University Press, 2018.

Mintz, Susannah B. *Unruly Bodies: Life Writing by Women with Disabilities.* Chapel Hill: The University of North Carolina Press, 2007.

Morrison, Toni. *Playing in the Dark: Whiteness in the Literary Imagination.* New York: Vintage Books, 1993.

Mukattash, Eman. "The Democratic Vistas of the Body: Re-Reading the Body in Herman Melville's *Typee.*" *Journal of Language, Literature & Culture* 62, no. 3 (2015): 157–175.

Murdoch, James. *The Stage, or, Recollections of Actors and Acting from an Experience of Fifty Years; A Series of Dramatic Sketches. 1880.* Philadelphia: J. M. Stoddart and Company, 1969.

Murison, Justine S. *The Politics of Anxiety in Nineteenth-Century American Literature.* Cambridge: Cambridge University Press, 2011.

Niebylski, Dianna C. *Humoring Resistance: Laughter and the Excessive Body in Latin American Women's Fiction.* Albany: State University of New York Press, 2004.

Okajima, Kei. "Bodily 'Touch' and Racial Formation in Milton Murayama's *All I Asking for Is My Body.*" *The Explicator* 71, no. 3 (2013): 173–176.

Parkin-Gounelas, Ruth. "Poetry, Automaticity and the Animal Body: Jacques Derrida with Emily Dickinson." *Textual Practice* 32, no. 5 (2018): 841–858.

Patterson, Mark R. *Authority, Autonomy, and Representation in American Literature, 1776–1865.* Princeton, NJ: Princeton University Press, 2014.

Peers, Laura. *Playing Ourselves: Interpreting Native Histories at Historic Reconstructions.* Lanham, MD: Rowman & Littlefield Publishers, 2007.

Price, Leah. *How to Do Things with Books in Victorian Britain.* Princeton, NJ: Princeton University Press, 2013.

Prieto, René. *Body of Writing: Figuring Desire in Spanish American Literature.* Durham, NC: Duke University Press, 2000.

Putzi, Jennifer. *Identifying Marks: Race, Gender, and the Marked Body in Nineteenth-Century America.* Athens: University of Georgia Press, 2006.

Quinn, Roseanne Giannini. "'The Willingness to Speak': Diane di Prima and Italian American Feminist Body Politics." *MELUS* 28, no. 3 (2003): 175–193.

Radway, Janice. "Reading Is Not Eating: Mass-Produced Literature and the Theoretical, Methodological, and Political Consequences of a Metaphor." *Book Research Quarterly* 2 (1986): 7–29.

Ray, Sarah Jaquette. *The Ecological Other: Environmental Exclusion in American Culture.* Tucson: University of Arizona Press, 2013.

Ray, Sarah Jaquette, and Jay Sibara, eds. *Disability Studies and the Environmental Humanities.* Lincoln: University of Nebraska Press, 2020.

Rivera, Lysa. "Future Histories and Cyborg Labor: Reading Borderlands Science Fiction after NAFTA." *Science Fiction Studies* 39, no. 3 (2012): 415–436.

Roh, David S., Betsy Huang, and Greta A. Niu. *Techno-Orientalism: Imagining Asia in Speculative Fiction, History, and Media.* New Brunswick, NJ: Rutgers University Press, 2015.

Russell, Emily. *Reading Embodied Citizenship: Disability, Narrative, and the Body Politic.* New Brunswick, NJ: Rutgers University Press, 2011.

Schnur, Kate. "'I Found Another to Admire': The Thing of the Female Body in William Carlos Williams' Medical Narratives." *William Carlos Williams Review* 33, no. 1–2 (2016): 172–188.

Seltzer, Mark. *Bodies and Machines.* New York: Routledge, 1992.

Seymour, Nicole. *Strange Natures: Futurity, Empathy, and the Queer Ecological Imagination.* Champaign: University of Illinois Press, 2013.

Shaheen, Aaron. *Androgynous Democracy: Modern American Literature and the Dual-Sexed Body Politic.* Knoxville: University of Tennessee Press, 2010.

Sibara, Jennifer Barager. "Disease, Disability, and the Alien Body in the Literature of Sui Sin Far." *MELUS* 39, no. 1 (2014): 56–81.

Sierra, Erick. "Visioning the Body Mosaic: Enchanted Transracial Selfhood in Postsecular American Literature." *European Journal of American Studies* 10, no. 2 (2015): 1–17.

Silverman, Gillian. *Bodies and Books: Reading and the Fantasy of Communion in Nineteenth-Century America.* Philadelphia: University of Pennsylvania Press, 2012.

Simonson, Mary. *Body Knowledge: Performance, Intermediality, and American Entertainment at the Turn of the Twentieth Century.* New York: Oxford University Press, 2013.

Sinno, Nadine. "'Dammit, Jim, I'm a Muslim Woman, Not a Klingon!': Mediating the Imigrant Body in Mohja Kahf's Poetry." *MELUS* 42, no. 1 (2017): 116–138.

Sohn, Stephen Hong, ed. "Alien/Asian." *MELUS* 33, no. 4 (Winter 2008): 5–22.

Sorisio, Carolyn. *Fleshing Out America: Race, Gender, and the Politics of the Body in American Literature, 1833–1879.* Athens: University of Georgia Press, 2002.

States, Bert O. *Great Reckonings in Little Rooms: On the Phenomenology of Theater.* Berkeley: University of California Press, 1985.

Stewart, Garrett, *Reading Voices: Literature and the Phonotext.* Berkeley: University of California Press, 1990.

Stilley, Harriet Poppy. "'White Pussy Is Nothin but Trouble': Hypermasculine Hysteria and the Displacement of the Feminine Body in Cormac McCarthy's *Child of God*." *The Cormac McCarthy Journal* 14, no. 1 (2016): 96–116.

Stokes, Michael Dale. "The Future Is Scar-y: The Connective Tissue of Emotion, Body, & Identity." *MOSF Journal of Science Fiction* 3, no. 2 (2019): 51–63.

Sullivan, Mecca Jamilah. "'Put My Thang Down, Flip It and Reverse It': Black Women's Interstitial Languages of Body and Desire." *American Literary History* 29, no. 4 (2017): 704–725.

Thompson, Carlyle Van. *Eating the Black Body: Miscegenation as Sexual Consumption in African American Literature and Culture.* New York: Peter Lang, 2006.

Tompkins, Kyla Wazana. *Racial Indigestion: Eating Bodies in the 19th Century.* New York: New York University Press, 2012.

Tsing, Anna Lowenhaupt, Heather Anne Swanson, Elaine Gan, and Nils Bubandt, eds. *Arts of Living on a Damaged Planet: Ghosts and Monsters of the Anthropocene*. Minneapolis: University of Minnesota Press, 2017.

Tuana, Nancy. "Viscous Porosity: Witnessing Katrina." In *Material Feminisms*, edited by Stacy Alaimo and Susan J. Hekman, 188–213. Bloomington: Indiana University Press, 2008.

Vester, Katharina. "'Reduce Your Appearance Instantly!' Representations of the Female Body in the Comic Books for Women and Girls." *Forum for Inter-American Research* 10, no. 2 (2017): 47–65.

Villalobos, Jonathan. "Sexual Assault and the Rape of Nature in *Child of God* and *Deliverance*." In *Ecocriticism and the Future of Southern Studies*, edited by Zackary Vernon. Baton Rouge: LSU Press, 2019.

Ward, Robert. "'[A] Great Body Sleeping and Stirring': Representations of the Bread-Line in American Left Writing of the 1930s." *EAPSU Online: A Journal of Critical and Creative Work* 2 (2005): 12–21.

Wilmer, S. E., ed. *Native American Performance and Representation*. Tucson: University of Arizona Press, 2009.

Womack, Ytasha L. *Afrofuturism: The World of Black Sci-Fi and Fantasy Culture*. Chicago: Lawrence Hill Books, 2013.

Zamora, Maria C. *Nation, Race & History in Asian American Literature: Remembering the Body*. New York: Peter Lang, 2008.

Zhu, Ying, and Nhu Le Quynh. "Body, Time, and Space: Poetry as Choreography in Southeast Asian American Literature." *Dance Chronicle* 39, no. 1 (2016): 77–95.

# Cambridge Companions To ...

## AUTHORS

*Edward Albee* edited by Stephen J. Bottoms

*Margaret Atwood* edited by Coral Ann Howells (second edition)

*W. H. Auden* edited by Stan Smith

*Jane Austen* edited by Edward Copeland and Juliet McMaster (second edition)

*Balzac* edited by Owen Heathcote and Andrew Watts

*Beckett* edited by John Pilling

*Bede* edited by Scott DeGregorio

*Aphra Behn* edited by Derek Hughes and Janet Todd

*Saul Bellow* edited by Victoria Aarons

*Walter Benjamin* edited by David S. Ferris

*William Blake* edited by Morris Eaves

*James Baldwin* edited by Michele Elam

*Boccaccio* edited by Guyda Armstrong, Rhiannon Daniels, and Stephen J. Milner

*Jorge Luis Borges* edited by Edwin Williamson

*Brecht* edited by Peter Thomson and Glendyr Sacks (second edition)

*The Brontës* edited by Heather Glen

*Bunyan* edited by Anne Dunan-Page

*Frances Burney* edited by Peter Sabor

*Byron* edited by Drummond Bone

*Albert Camus* edited by Edward J. Hughes

*Willa Cather* edited by Marilee Lindemann

*Catullus* edited by Ian Du Quesnay and Tony Woodman

*Cervantes* edited by Anthony J. Cascardi

*Chaucer* edited by Piero Boitani and Jill Mann (second edition)

*Chekhov* edited by Vera Gottlieb and Paul Allain

*Kate Chopin* edited by Janet Beer

*Caryl Churchill* edited by Elaine Aston and Elin Diamond

*Cicero* edited by Catherine Steel

*J. M. Coetzee* edited by Jarad Zimbler

*Coleridge* edited by Lucy Newlyn

*Wilkie Collins* edited by Jenny Bourne Taylor

*Joseph Conrad* edited by J. H. Stape

*H. D.* edited by Nephie J. Christodoulides and Polina Mackay

*Dante* edited by Rachel Jacoff (second edition)

*Daniel Defoe* edited by John Richetti

*Don DeLillo* edited by John N. Duvall

*Charles Dickens* edited by John O. Jordan

*Emily Dickinson* edited by Wendy Martin

*John Donne* edited by Achsah Guibbory

*Dostoevskii* edited by W. J. Leatherbarrow

*Theodore Dreiser* edited by Leonard Cassuto and Claire Virginia Eby

*John Dryden* edited by Steven N. Zwicker

*W. E. B. Du Bois* edited by Shamoon Zamir

*George Eliot* edited by George Levine and Nancy Henry (second edition)

*T. S. Eliot* edited by A. David Moody

*Ralph Ellison* edited by Ross Posnock

*Ralph Waldo Emerson* edited by Joel Porte and Saundra Morris

*William Faulkner* edited by Philip M. Weinstein

*Henry Fielding* edited by Claude Rawson

*F. Scott Fitzgerald* edited by Ruth Prigozy

*Flaubert* edited by Timothy Unwin

*E. M. Forster* edited by David Bradshaw

*Benjamin Franklin* edited by Carla Mulford

*Brian Friel* edited by Anthony Roche

*Robert Frost* edited by Robert Faggen

*Gabriel García Márquez* edited by Philip Swanson

*Elizabeth Gaskell* edited by Jill L. Matus

## TOPICS

CPSIA information can be obtained
at www.ICGtesting.com
Printed in the USA
BVHW041807210622
640313BV00001B/5